Our Intimate

Relationships

Our Intimate Relationships

—MARRIAGE AND THE FAMILY—

Ollie Pocs
Illinois State University

1817

HARPER & ROW, PUBLISHERS, New York
Cambridge, Philadelphia, San Francisco,
London, Mexico City, São Paulo, Singapore, Sydney

This book is dedicated
to my parents and the past;
to my spouse and the present;
to my sons, their wives, and the future;
and
to my students—past, present, and future.

A list of text and illustration credits can be found on pp. 481–483, which are hereby made part of this copyright page.

Sponsoring Editor: Alan McClare
Project Editor: Carla Samodulski
Text Design: Laura Ferguson
Cover Design: Lucy Krikorian
Cover Illustration: Ben Shahn, *Spring*, 1947, 17" × 30," tempera on Masonite, courtesy of Albright-Knox Art Gallery, Buffalo, New York, Room of Contemporary Art Fund, 1948.
Text Art: Fineline Illustrations, Inc.
Photo Research: Mira Schachne
Production Manager: Jeanie Berke
Production Assistant: Paula Roppolo
Compositor: ComCom Division of Haddon Craftsmen, Inc.
Printer and Binder: R. R. Donnelley & Sons Company
Cover Printer: Lehigh Press

Our Intimate Relationships: Marriage and the Family

Copyright © 1989 by Harper & Row, Publishers, Inc.

Library of Congress Cataloging-in-Publication Data

Pocs, Ollie.
    Our intimate relationships: marriage and the family/Ollie Pocs.
        p. cm.
    Bibliography: p.
    Includes indexes.
    ISBN 0-06-045351-6
    1. Marriage. 2. Family.   I. Title
HQ728.P56   1989
306.8—dc19   88-29764
                        CIP

88 89 90 91 9 8 7 6 5 4 3 2 1

Brief Contents

Detailed Contents

Preface

This text is for undergraduate introductory courses offered in a variety of departments. The basic goal of the text is to answer questions that are or will be important to the student from a sound academic perspective and in a straightforward fashion. The approach is one of realistic optimism; that is, the text shows a positive concern for the value and significance of our intimate relations, yet presents a realistic look at the problems and concerns contained within these relationships.

I have covered the major contemporary issues by incorporating the latest research findings. While eclectic in approach, the text demonstrates a recognition of how basic social structures relate to practical concerns in a variety of life-styles and during the different stages of life. The book's process format covers the establishment and maintenance of marriage, the expansion into a family, and the reorganization and termination of relationships. The institutions of marriage and the family are seen as changing and adjusting to the ever-changing world. They are also seen as having a future.

The 16 chapters are relatively self-contained to provide flexibility for instructors. Their length should enable students to maintain their interest and concentration as well as to gain a sense of accomplishment at the end of the topic. The Perspective section at the end of each chapter provides supplementary material that increases understanding of and lends perspective to the major concepts or topics just covered by examining a relevant topic of interest. While the book primarily emphasizes sociology and social psychology, I have carefully avoided the common jargon terms of these fields and included the necessary special or technical terms in the glossary.

At the conclusion of each chapter is a list of questions for thought and discussion. If you and your students have become involved in the material presented in the chapter, you could spend hours thinking about and discussing the topics covered and the various options presented. The object is for students to make choices based on knowledge and reality, instead of myths and fantasy. This should get them closer to their desired life goals and life-styles and thus increase their satisfaction with and happiness in intimate relationships.

A book such as this cannot be produced by one individual. The author wishes to thank the many people involved in its "birth." Special appreciation goes to Robert H. Walsh for the initiative he provided in getting this project started and for his continued support, to Karen Ament for her writing skills, and to the numerous students and secretaries for their many and varied contributions. Thanks also go to the publishing house of Harper & Row, especially to the sponsoring editor, Alan McClare, the project editor, Carla Samodulski, and all the other staff people involved in this project. I especially want to thank the reviewers for their thoughtful comments:

Darla Botkin, University of Kentucky
Mark Eckel, McHenry County College
Peter Chroman, College of San Mateo
Janice Stroud, Sandhills Center
Constance Shehan, University of Florida
Gregory E. Kennedy, Central Missouri State University
Anne E. Imamura, University of Maryland
Charles Petranek, University of Southern Indiana
Sharon K. Houseknecht, Ohio State University

Thank you all, your efforts are appreciated.

Ollie Pocs

PART 1

Background

What Are Marriage and Family?

INTRODUCTION

Marriage, sex, family—intimate and exciting relationships covering significant periods of your life. Each individual has different perceptions about them based on experiences with parents, peers, and others. And each has unique expectations from marriage, sex, and family life. Some people believe that after finding the right mate, one will live happily ever after. Others, less idealistic, believe that if things don't work out in a first marriage, one can always look for a more suitable partner and try again.

I have enjoyed writing this book, although the joy was tempered with occasional frustration when the words didn't fall neatly into place. Such frustration is likely to be a part of your life, too. But persistence and know-how can lead to success in life as well as in writing, and I hope that this book will help you to achieve your personal goals.

ABOUT THE BOOK: PLAN AND PURPOSE

As its title implies, the emphasis of this book is on intimate relationships. It examines the establishment, maintenance, expansion, and reorganization or termination of these ties. We begin where you probably are now—at the dating stage—and then go on through the typical patterns for our society to where your parents are at present. Finally, we trace your course on to your grandparents' stage. It is a route that most of us travel, although no two people do it in exactly the same way.

The purposes of this book are (1) to help you make observations about the relationships around you, (2) to raise valid questions about human relationships throughout the life cycle, and (3) to present evidence and ideas that will help you work out answers to the questions you will face. It is hoped that you will find realistic optimism about marriage, family, sex, and intimate relationships in these pages.

This book is not a how-to book, because probably no one person can hope to have all the answers. But you *can* find in it lots of information that may help you arrive at the best answer among several choices—best for you, in your situation, at this particular time in your life.

In reality you cannot teach people anything, but you can help them find things out for themselves.

Give me a fish, and I eat for a day; teach me to fish, and I eat for a lifetime.

You must realize that there are a number of topics, points, and statistics that are "shortchanged" in this book or not included at all. Whole volumes have been written on some topics that we have omitted here or covered in only a page or two. Depending on the orientation of your instructor, some topics may be added to the text or expanded upon while others are deemphasized or eliminated. You can read the latter on your own while paying special attention to material presented by your teacher.

TO YOU, THE STUDENT

In this book you, the reader, are addressed more directly than usual, and the assumption is that you are about twenty years of age, single, dating, partying—and also serious about education and your future. Very likely, you will marry within the next five years.

Over the past semesters, I have been asking college students what they would want in a marriage-and-family textbook, and these preferences have been taken into account in the writing of this book. We hope that you will find it interesting and that it will give you things to think about, to discuss both in and out of class, and to apply in your life.

WHY STUDY MARRIAGE AND FAMILY?

Most people grow up in families. Why do we need a course about them? First of all, the problems in male/female relationships before marriage, the high divorce rate, the number of people who are in unhappy relationships, plus the abuse of children and spouses all attest to the problems in marriage and family life. Any one person's experience of these situations may not suffice to solve them. Indeed, most of us probably know more about the moon or biology than we do about human relationships.

Second, you are already or soon will be participating in various types of male/female relationships—whether you are now single, married, divorced, widowed, living with someone, dating around, or between relationships. This book will help you to make informed decisions about the many important questions that arise. It will make you a better consumer in the marriage-and-family market.

What kinds of problems does the book cover? It tackles such questions as: How do I meet and get along with someone of the opposite sex? Should I live with someone? Will I marry? Whom will I marry and when? Will I be a parent? As I grow older, what will change in my relationships with my parental family, my spouse, and my children? Remember that this book cannot give you specific answers, but it may give you a broader perspective than one based on your experience alone.

Why study marriage and family? I grew up in one.	Are marriage and family for everyone?	I know what I'm like, but how do I find out about others?	Everyone knows what love is.
How do I know if someone wants to date me?	Will people be able to tell if she had sex?	How will our relationship change after marriage?	What makes for a happy marriage?
What problems? Love conquers all, doesn't it?	Do different men make love the same way? Do different women?	How safe are the various methods of birth control?	How does having children change your relationship?
How can there be such a thing as no-fault divorce?	At what age do people stop having sex?	Is homosexuality natural?	Where is our society going with marriage and family?

FEATURES OF THE BOOK

The material in this book is presented through text, graphs, and tables in a clear, readable fashion with as little academic or sociological jargon as possible. However, just as the term "force" has a special meaning in physics, we use some terms ("monogamy" and "polygamy," for instance) that are not often heard in everyday talk. These key terms are defined in a glossary at the back of the book. Note that there are also subject and author indexes as well as a complete bibliography, including all items referenced throughout the text.

In the belief that men and women should have equal rights and opportunities, an effort has been made to avoid sexism in content and language. However, there are occasions when women (and sometimes men) are discriminated against, have fewer options, or are treated in a stereotyped fashion. The reality is that women do not earn as much as men, mothers are still expected to care for children, girls are socialized differently from boys. That reality is reflected in this book.

Information on very current topics and problems has been included. Sometimes the topic is so new that no really good data have yet appeared in the professional journals. In these cases, the best material available has been used, even if it is from small samples or from the popular press.

A special feature of the book is the "Perspective" section at the end of each chapter. This chapter's Perspective is a look at some common opinions on marriage and family. In other chapters, additional viewpoints, highlights, or key examples are offered, giving *perspective* to the subject.

THE INSTITUTIONS OF MARRIAGE AND FAMILY

VARIOUS WAYS OF LOOKING AT MARRIAGE

Almost everyone grows up in a family, and about 90 percent eventually marry. For most people, no other single day has the emotional impact of the wedding day—not even college graduation. If you had to define marriage, you could probably do so in a minute or two. You could also define other important concepts like love and family. But if you compared your definitions with those of your classmates, you would find that your ideas differed. Similarly, if we look at various textbook definitions of love and marriage, we find many ideas. Consider just a few definitions of marriage:

> That act by which a man and woman unite for life, with the intent to discharge toward society and one another those duties which result from the relation of husband and wife. The act of union having been once accomplished, the word comes afterward to denote the relation itself. (Schouler, 1882, p. 19)

> A socially legitimate sexual union, begun with a public announcement, undertaken with some idea of permanence, and assuming a more or less explicit contract that spells out reciprocal rights and obligations between spouses and any children they may have. (Stephens, 1963, p. 5)

> The legal status, condition, or relation of one man and one woman united in law for life, or until divorced, for the discharge to each other and the community of the duties legally incumbent on those whose association is founded on the distinction of sex. (Black, 1979, p. 876)

> A socially acceptable union of individuals in husband and wife roles with the key function of legitimation of parenthood. (Reiss, 1980, p. 50)

The key points these definitions have in common are (1) people, (2) social and sexual relations, and (3) a socially sanctioned relationship.

In the United States, marriage is a legal contract between two people, with the state as a third party. Married people must be of a certain minimum age (this varies by state) and of different sexes. They must be able to give legal consent (that is, they must not be insane, mentally incompetent, minors, etc.). They must not be closely related. They must be single. Marriage partners must have sexual intercourse to consummate their marriage. If they do not, the marriage can be annulled legally. Both partners must voluntarily consent to the marriage, and husband and wife are expected to live together.

What is acceptable as marriage to some people may be quite different from what is acceptable to most people. For example, some people accept commuter

For the rest of their married life, this couple's way will never again be this smooth, straight, and level.

marriages, marriages between homosexual partners, or polygamy (the marriage of more than two people). Furthermore, as we shall see in Chapter 2, people from other cultures introduce even greater differences. Considering the differences of opinion, is there a broadly acceptable definition of marriage in the United States? We propose the following: Marriage is a socially sanctioned union of one man and one woman who are expected to play the roles of husband and wife.

What Is Family?

If you were asked to define the term "family," your answer would probably be influenced by the type or types of family structures in which you have lived. Since we come from a variety of different backgrounds, it is difficult to arrive at a uniform definition of family. The resolution to this problem is simply to realize that there is no one form of family structure but a variety of different structures.

Many of us grew up in a family structure consisting of a mother, father, and

It is said that a family that plays together stays together.

child or children. This structure, called a *nuclear family,* is found in most parts of the world. Sometimes the nuclear family is embedded in a larger structure called the *augmented family,* that includes both relatives and nonrelatives in the same household. When a nuclear family loses a parent through death or divorce, the resulting structure is called an *attenuated family.* Other single-parent families may result from a decision not to marry or from single-person adoptions. When two single parents marry, the new family is called a *blended family.* The nuclear family has been—and may continue to be—the ideal in our society, but less than one-third of families in the 1980s are of this type.

In his classic definition, George Murdock (1949) maintains that the four essential functions of the nuclear family are economic cooperation, sexual relations, reproduction, and socialization of children. Although the nuclear family usually provides these functions, other family structures can provide them too. A two-parent family has the advantage of either two income producers or an income producer and a homemaker. However, those of us who have lived in a one-parent household know that such a family can function successfully. There is no one structure that is right, normal, and natural.

MARRIAGE, FAMILY, AND CHANGE

As are most aspects of our lives, marriage and family, as institutions, are changing rapidly today (see Box 1.1). Experts through the years have been concerned about family stability. Over seventy-five years ago Thwing and Thwing (1913) noted that the divorce rate was increasing faster than the population rate. "The bonds of marriage are legally severed to an extent which awakens grave apprehension for the perpetuity of important social institutions. . . . We are fast coming to have the state of matrimony only in name" (pp. 187, 198). Some years later Watson (1927) predicted, "In fifty years, unless there is some change, the tribal custom of marriage will no longer exist" (p. 1). Burgess and Wallin (1953) warned that because of the complexity of the American society, the rapidity of

---

BOX 1.1   IF A MILLION YEARS* OF HUMAN HISTORY
WERE COMPRESSED INTO THE LIFETIME
OF ONE 70-YEAR-OLD MAN†

1,000,000 years of history	Compressed into one 70-year lifetime.
1,000,000 years ago	*Pithecanthropus erectus* is born.
500,000 years ago	He spends half his lifetime learning to make and use crude stone axes and knives.
50,000 years ago	And most of the next half in improving them.
40,000 years ago	Three years ago he began to use bone and horn tools.
10,000 years ago	Nine months ago the last ice age ended, and he left his cave dwellings.
7,000 years ago	Six or eight months ago he began to make pottery, weave cloth, grow crops, and domesticate animals.
5,000 years ago	About three months ago, he began to cast and use metals and built the Pyramids.
3,000 years ago	Ten weeks ago he invented the spoked wheel and began making glass.
2,000 years ago	Seven weeks ago, Christ was born.
700 years ago	Two weeks ago man finished the Crusades.
200 years ago	Five days ago he crossed the Delaware with Washington.
65 years ago	Yesterday he invented the airplane.
30–35 years ago	This morning he fought World War II.
7–11 years ago	This afternoon he landed on the moon.
In the year 2,000 A.D.	Tonight he will celebrate the arrival of the twenty-first century!

*Or several million years, according to some anthropologists.

†This example, which compresses all of human history into one person's lifetime, illustrates the tremendous increase in the speed of change. This 70-year-old person would have left the cave at age 69, heard about the airplane being invented yesterday, and today, after lunch, would watch the landing on the moon on television. Many people are still alive today who were born before automobiles were available or TV was invented. (Adapted from Horton & Hunt, 1964, p. 56.)

change, and the lack of training for married life, young people must be quite competent and above all adaptable to make their marriages successful. What can we conclude from these opinions? One safe conclusion is that the intimate relations in marriage and family life have gone through changes in the past, are changing today, and will continue to change in the future. Another safe conclusion is that change in these familiar institutions tends to alarm people. Consider the following questions: (1) What changes are occurring in today's society? (2) What effects do these changes have on marriage and family? Let's examine a few key changes and the reactions to them.

First, in the last several decades there has been a significant increase in options for both women and men in regard to marriage, parenting, birth planning, cohabiting, and male/female equality. Most college students see these increased options as positive. However, some people have interpreted the changes as detrimental to traditional views of marriage and family institutions. They list increases in premarital sex, abortion, illegitimacy, and divorce as being destructive to what marriage and family should be. They would understand the viewpoint behind the old Chinese curse that says "May you live in a period of rapid social change."

Second, the increasing participation in the labor force of wives and mothers is viewed by some people as positive. Others, who hold the traditional belief that woman's place is in the home, see working wives and mothers as a detriment to family life. Increased labor force participation by women has been made possible by such things as industrialization, lower birthrates, a shorter period of childbearing, and generally smaller families and households (Giele, 1979).

Third, people today can expect to live longer and therefore to be married longer than their ancestors were. In 1900, the average woman lived about 48 years; the average man about 46. A woman born in 1960 has a life expectancy of 73 years; a man, 67 years (*World Almanac*, 1984, p. 910). If we assume that a couple marries when they are both 20, their marriage, if not ended by divorce, may last about fifty years. On the other hand, if two people born in 1900 married at age 20, their marriage might have lasted about twenty-five years.

Fourth, in the past, marriages were more likely to end when one of the partners died; today, more are dissolved by divorce. Last, if the trends stay stable, the woman married in 1990 will have to be concerned with ten or more years of widowhood. Most husbands are not only older than their wives at the time of marriage but also have a shorter life expectancy.

MARRIAGE AND FAMILY TODAY—HOW HEALTHY ARE THEY?

For the past several decades, some commentators have been saying that marriage and the family are deathly ill. Others believe that, all things considered, they are quite healthy.

The decade of 1965–1975 was a period of significant social unrest in the United States. Social issues such as American participation in the Vietnam War, the civil rights movement, the women's movement, and the greater freedom of college students were on center stage. It was a time of questioning the way social institutions, including the family, operated. Some maintained that marriage was an unhealthy institution. *Marriage Is Hell* (Perutz, 1972) said it was even worse than that. Other writers called marriage "a wretched institution" (Cadwallader, 1966) and "obsolete" (Roy & Roy, 1975).

The complaints against marriage and the family break down into the following three general categories:

1. *The nuclear family structure is inadequate for the functions expected of it.* This complaint may come from the unrealistic and idealistic demands placed on the couple relationship. Husbands and wives are asked to be total partners in economics, emotions, and sexuality. They must give each other total satisfaction. These are enormous demands to put on any relationship. Couples with expectations as high as these are likely to be disappointed. It is more sensible, some critics argue, for marriage partners to turn to people outside the marriage for the satisfaction of some of their needs (O'Neill & O'Neill, 1973). Margaret Mead, the well-known anthropologist, often suggested that members of nuclear families engage in more extended family and community relationships.

The author's belief is that the nuclear family is not as isolated as one might at first think. We actually have a modified extended-family system. In other words, many families are nuclear in structure but extended in sentiment and communication.

2. *The family has abdicated its responsibility to other societal structures and forces.* The family was once an integrated economic production unit. When most families engaged in farming, as they did until the twentieth century, the activities of economic production were shared by family members. Some of them planted and harvested while others worked the raw goods into finished products for family use or for sale. Today, most family members go to separate places to do their daily work—parents to different workplaces, children to school. Jobs today are not passed on from parent to child but are learned in schools or through apprenticeships.

Families today continue to teach values. Children learn about right and wrong, about what is acceptable and unacceptable within the family. School, religion, scouting, other public and private organizations, and the mass media increasingly contribute to the socialization process. Recreational activities outside the home have become widely utilized.

3. *Women are unequal members of marriages and families.* In the workplace, women are paid about one-third less, on the average, than are men. In the home, women receive no pay, no social security, no seniority, and no vacations. Noted sociologist Jessie Bernard (1982) says that women give up more and get less in marriage than do men; she talks not about *the* marriage but about the *husband's* marriage and the *wife's* marriage. Women who are wives and mothers and who also hold outside jobs—as 59 percent of such women do—are shown to do much more housework and child care than do men who are married and working (Smith, 1979). Many commentators note that women today often hold the equivalent of two full-time jobs—mother/homemaker plus an outside occupation. There is also a wide disparity of household income between families headed by men versus those headed by women. For example, the average income of families

headed by a single woman is only $11,789 (*Information Please Almanac,* 1986, p. 749).

On the other hand, some observers examining marriage and the family have given them a clean bill of health, cautioning, however, that preventive medicine is always in order. These observers point out that couples can learn to be more realistic in their expectations of what marriage can and cannot do for them. They note that most married people are satisfied with their marriages. Indeed, the Gallup Polling Organization conducted a series of public opinion surveys in early 1980s that showed "a ringing endorsement" of the importance of family in the American value system; a nationwide cross section of Americans polled also shows that almost 90 percent of those surveyed were highly satisfied with their marriages (Gallup, 1982). Another indication of positive attitudes toward marriage is that over 90 percent of Americans marry. In one study of unmarried college students, 96 percent felt they could develop a good marriage (Whitehurst, 1977). Our high divorce rate does not indicate a dissatisfaction with marriage as an institution but only with particular marriages.

As *Roots,* the highly successful television series, showed, millions of Americans are keenly interested in family history and kinship ties. We maintain that part of the attack on the nuclear family grows out of a myth that in a more desirable bygone era, people lived more happily in extended families. Yet many authors have clearly shown that we have always been a nation of individualists with emphasis on nuclear families (Furstenberg, 1966; Gordon, 1978). Stereotypes of the past can give us a false picture.

> Like most stereotypes, that of the classical family of Western nostalgia leads us astray. When we penetrate the confusing mists of recent history we find few examples of this "classical" family. Grandma's farm was not economically self-sufficient. Few families stayed together as large aggregations of kinfolk. Most houses were small, not large. We now *see* more large old houses than small ones; they survived longer because they were likely to have been better constructed. The one-room cabins rotted away. True enough, divorce was rare, but we have no evidence that families were generally happy. Indeed, we find, as in so many other pictures of the glowing past, that in each past generation people write of a period *still* more remote, *their* grandparents' generation, when things really were much better.
>
> If, then, the stereotype of the United States and Western family is partially incorrect, we may suppose stereotypes of other past family systems to be similarly in error. (Goode, 1970, p. 7)

Almost everyone, it seems, has a dream of the good old days. The dream sustains us and keeps alive our ideals. However, we live with the less-than-perfect reality. What are we to conclude, realistically, about the health of marriage and the family? The author tends to agree with this opinion:

> All things considered, many sociologists have come to the conclusion that, despite the existence of certain points of strain, the American family of today has not only adapted quite satisfactorily to changing economic and social conditions, but has attained a level of democratic operation and personal happiness superior to that of most other societies. (Kephart, 1981, p. 14)

Some Cautions About Research in This Field

To Whom Does Most of the Research and Description Apply?

This book is based on the best available evidence to support the points presented. Sometimes evidence from professional journals, such as the *Journal of Marriage and the Family* or *Family Relations,* is cited. Sometimes books reporting on research studies are used. In addition material from popular magazines such as *Psychology Today, Ms.,* and *Working Mother* is included. In general, material from scholarly journals is likely to be more valid, reliable, and precise than material from popular sources. It has been approved by an editor and is critically read by at least two scholars knowledgeable in the area. The research for major books is often supported by grants from the federal government or private foundations. Researchers compete for these funds; panels of professionals decide which research should be funded and which rejected.

Social scientists have more information about some segments of the population than others. For instance, college students are the most accessible population to researchers. Students given the choice of writing a term paper or filling out a questionnaire almost always choose the questionnaire. Therefore, more is known about college students than other categories of people. Unfortunately, this limits research to mostly middle-class, white, young adults. We know that there are significant differences between those young people who are in college and those who are not (Yankelovich, 1974), let alone the other segments of society.

Similarly, we know about premarital sex from college students, but we know very little about marital sex. Married people are harder for social scientists to reach or to investigate. Married life is considered more personal and private. As you read this book, you will note that there is a great deal of research evidence but little opinion on some topics and, on others, relatively little evidence but more opinion.

Research Concerns

Research Differences: Physical and Social Sciences Sociology can be just as scientific as the natural sciences—such as chemistry, physics, and biology—because they all use the *scientific method* of research. However, there are three crucial differences between research in the physical sciences and research in the social or behavioral sciences. First, measurements of key variables are often, necessarily, less precise in the social sciences. For example, most of you have been in love. How do you define and measure love? Are you more in love today than yesterday? Than a year ago? If so, how much more? Unfortunately, some of the things that we are really interested in, such as love, marital happiness, and successful marriage, are particularly difficult to measure. In contrast, chemists can measure the weight of a material very precisely, and physicists know that matter behaves according to universal laws.

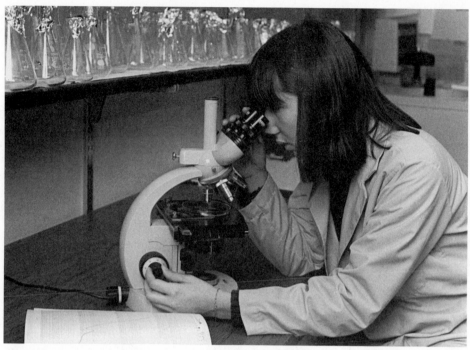

Much marriage and family research does not lend itself to test tubes and microscopes.

A second problem in social science research is data gathering. A chemist can observe a compound directly, but in many cases a social scientist must ask people to report on their behavior. There is very little actual observation of how married people behave. There is, instead, reported behavior ("self-reports") plus studies of attitudes people have about their marriages and families. To get information, researchers need people's cooperation. Yet because family research involves people's intimate lives, some of them may refuse to cooperate. Lack of cooperation results in a biased sample. For example, to study the sexual attitudes and behavior of teenagers, Sorenson (1973) had to obtain parental permission. Some refused. Do you think those students whose parents would not allow them to be studied are different from those whose parents would? No one knows for sure, but chances are the participants were different from those barred from study.

A third problem in social science research is control of variables. For example, in order to demonstrate Boyle's law of gasses, a chemist can vary the temperature and pressure in a beaker to see the effects on the solution inside. However, a family researcher who suggests that there is a difference in commitment between married students and those who live together can hardly make those living together marry to see how marriage might change their relationship. Similarly, researchers could study the effect of a lack of early childhood socialization on infants by rearing one child with virtually no social interaction and another in a loving family. However, this type of experiment would be unethical, so even though the research design can, theoretically, be as solid in the social sciences as it can in chemistry, such a research design cannot be implemented because it would put the welfare of human beings at risk.

Sources of Data   Data for family study come from the U.S. Census Bureau, *survey research*, occasional *experimental research*, and *clinical studies*. The best kind of sample is a *random sample*, one in which every unit and every combination of units has an equal chance of being included. We want samples to be representative of the population being studied. For instance, if a fourth of the students on your campus are in the fraternity-sorority system, you would want a sample of your school that showed that kind of Greek-independent distribution. A good random sample of your campus can tell us about your campus but not necessarily about college students in general. For example, would you expect the same attitudes from students at New York University as from those at Iowa Wesleyan?

Clinics are another large source of data, but again cases researched may not represent a random sample of their group. Thus, if a psychiatrist reports, from office records, on problems of prostitutes, those statistics and conclusions would apply only to patients—people who have sought treatment for some problem— and probably would *not* apply to the general population of prostitutes. After all, why would a happy hooker go to a psychiatrist? By reporting only on those with problems, clinicians can inadvertently give the impression that they are reporting on the mainstream of that group.

These examples illustrate the fact that there are situations in the social and behavorial sciences that create research difficulties different from those found in other sciences. Whenever research subjects are people, cooperation is essential. The more personal or intimate the topic, the less the probable extent of cooperation. However, researchers are making progress as they improve their research techniques.

Interpretation of Data   A value judgment is a belief as to what is desirable, right, or wrong. People naturally interpret facts on the basis of their own values, and researchers are no exception. Researchers try to be objective in interpreting data. However, past experience indicates that they are more likely to accept findings that support their points of view and to find fault with those that disagree. This problem is potentially greater in the study of marriage and the family because the subject matter is especially value-laden. For example, U.S. Census Bureau data show that the divorce rate more than doubled between 1965 and 1982. Some people interpret this fact as a sign that the institution of marriage is faltering, while others see it as a sign that many people are finding their way out of bad relationships.

Here is another example. It is a fact that an increasing percentage of married women in their twenties are postponing motherhood. Whether these women are called childless or child-free indicates a value judgment about the simple fact that they do not have children. "Childless" has a negative connotation, while "child-free" is more positive. It is important to examine all statements to see if they represent an objective presentation of facts or if they are value judgments.

Other problems may arise in comparing differences between two samples. Suppose a scientist finds an apparent difference in attitude between two samples of married couples living in different cities. She concludes that the difference is based on the area of the country in which they live. Has she been careful that the groups are not different in other ways—say, income, background, religion, number of children, and so on—which may be reasons for the apparent attitudinal difference? Has she used the same instrument and measurement scale for each group? Has she conducted her research in the same time period? After all, times change. For instance, a classic study of blue-collar marriage by Komarovsky (1967) found that working-class wives accepted the term "housewifery." It is questionable that the same attitude would be found today in the same community.

What Science Cannot Do   The scientific method is very useful in determining what is actually happening—whether, for example, the divorce rate is going

Dr. Alfred Kinsey spent a lot of time and care conducting interviews for his two books on human sexual behavior.

up or leveling off or what the course of the birthrate may be—but it is less accurate in telling us *why* something happened or what is *going to* happen. There are some things that science simply cannot determine. Science cannot say what is good or bad, right or wrong. Science cannot answer theological or philosophical questions such as: Is there life after death? What is real? Who am I? Is there heaven and hell? In some areas, researchers can give trends or figure the probabilities of certain results. Thus, the probability is that the average college junior will live for 55 more years, that a teenage marriage will more likely end in divorce than one between partners in their late twenties, and that teens will be more likely to have automobile accidents than those over age 25. However, science cannot tell us which one of you will fit which specific case.

FAMILY THEORY

THE UTILITY OF THEORY

When we think of theory, we think of two separate but related concepts: substantive theory and conceptual frameworks. *Substantive theory* is an interrelated set of propositions or statements that attempt to explain a given phenomenon. Substantive theory has a logical organization: a major premise, a minor premise, and a conclusion. For example, a classic study at Harvard (Bales & Slater, 1955) concerning the way small groups of students solved problems in a laboratory setting revealed that each group developed an instrumental leader and an expressive leader. Research by Zelditch (1955) found that in most families around the world, the male was more likely to be the instrumental leader and the female the expressive leader. Here is what the process looks like in logical sequence:

> Small groups differentiate the roles of instrumental and expressive leader (found true in the lab).
> The family is a small group (commonsense observation).
> If the family is a small group, then it should differentiate the roles of instrumental and expressive leader (logical conclusion).
> The family does differentiate the roles of instrumental and expressive leader (found from Zelditch's cross-cultural research).

This example of substantive theory shows how knowledge grew from the facts learned in a small-group laboratory setting to a statement generally true for families across the world.

While a substantive theory is rather specific, a *conceptual* framework (or theoretical orientation or perspective) is a more general approach to understanding human behavior. The conceptual framework guides the researcher to look for certain concepts and to ignore others. The view of the family will differ according to the assumptions of different conceptual frameworks, but all frameworks guide research and help give a consistent frame of reference, so that seemingly unrelated findings can be integrated into a meaningful whole.

SOME THEORETICAL APPROACHES

Family theory has developed rapidly in the last couple of decades. The three approaches that are having a major impact in the family field, according to Holman and Burr (1984), are *interactionist theory, exchange theory,* and *systems theory.* These authors also recognize that other well-known approaches, such as *conflict theory* and *developmental theory,* play more minor roles. While there are many other important theoretical approaches, we will limit our discussion to these five.

The Interactionist Approach This approach has been in extensive use for several decades. It is based on the fact that people interact with each other through verbal and nonverbal symbols. Asking someone for a date is an example of verbal communication; eye contact is an example of nonverbal communication. Our self-concept is enhanced if someone with whom we have had eye contact accepts our invitation for a date, and it is diminished if we are rejected.

The self and roles of persons within the family group are key concepts in interactionism. Consider the situation of a father who is laid off his job. An interactionist is concerned with the father's self-concept and his status as head provider for the family. Also, if the mother now has to work outside the home, does her job increase her status within the family? Her self-concept? Do the interaction patterns in the family change along with the roles?

Question: What has changed, the situation or the concepts?

I used to think that I was poor. Then I was told that I wasn't poor, I was NEEDY. They then told me it was self-defeating to think of myself as needy, because I was DEPRIVED. Then I was told that deprived gave me a bad image, I was UNDERPRIVILEGED. Then they told me that underprivileged was overused, that I was DISADVANTAGED. I still don't have a dollar, but I have a GREAT vocabulary. (Anonymous)

The Exchange Approach Human interaction requires an exchange. If you don't believe it, just try to play catch with someone who won't throw the ball back to you! Children who have not learned to play with others do not participate in the give and take of exchange. Female/male interaction in marriage and family requires exchange. An excellent summary of the exchange approach is this:

The underlying assumption of exchange theory is that human behavior is determined on the basis of rewards and costs. Individuals will voluntarily engage in behavior only as long as the rewards for the behavior are greater than the costs involved. If an individual or group obtains a net reward (total reward minus costs) from the behavior, it will continue. When a net reward is no longer realized, the behavior will cease. (Eshleman & Clarke, 1978, pp. 12–13)

It is clear that reciprocity, as noted by Scanzoni (1972) in his book *Sexual Bargaining,* is a key concept in exchange theory. Let us look at the relationship in our previous example from the exchange perspective. After the father is laid off, the mother secures a part-time job to help pay the bills. Since the mother has added work from outside the home to the work she was doing inside, she expects the father to reciprocate by doing more cleaning and laundry. If the father fails to do this, the mother could complain that there is not enough exchange or reciprocity in their relationship.

The Systems Approach   "Systems theory comes closest to the language of computer analysis when it is applied to family communication. There are communication linkages that involve feedback, and feedback maintains family homeostasis or order, as the family members react to each other's communication" (Adams, B. N., 1980, p. 113).

From a systems approach, we note that the newly employed mother in our example may have to explain the homemaking tasks that she wants her husband to perform. The changes in time and investment of effort will have to be agreed upon if the family is to continue functioning well enough. Various roles and priorities will have to be reordered, desired changes communicated, and new responsibilities accepted.

The Conflict Approach   The basic concepts of the conflict approach are competition, conflict, and consensus. Some authors see power, with the accompanying interactions, as the main concept in explaining the various researchable manifestations of overt conflict.

As long as marriage and family are viewed as process, we can expect perpetual give and take among the people involved. Some of these interactions are likely to include conflict. Conflicts need to be resolved so that consensus about future directions is achieved. Ideally, each conflict should lead to increased cooperation for common goals and a consensus on what those goals should be.

In our example of the newly employed wife and laid-off husband, a power shift is to be expected. Perhaps the wife will demand more input in spending decisions. Maybe the husband will resent his loss of status as a breadwinner. They can expect a certain amount of conflict until the restructuring of family roles, even if temporary, has been agreed upon. Conflict in marriages and families has been typically found to involve confrontations about rules, roles, and status privileges (Sprey, 1979).

The Developmental Approach   This approach is based primarily on family life-cycle or life-span issues. Most of the literature using this approach has deemphasized the family process and emphasized individual changes over the life span (Holman & Burr, 1984). Some authors have investigated variations in marital satisfactions over the life cycle. The life-cycle stages typically include establishing marital and family relationships, childbearing and rearing, and aging. Different tasks are appropriate for different stages, and a failure to accomplish a task at one stage may negatively affect behavior in a later stage. For example, parents must help their young children develop responsibility for their own safety. The more responsibility the children learn, the more freedom their parents and teachers will allow them.

The adult couple must also continue to develop individually and together. A couple who had a good relationship at the honeymoon stage may find that the stresses and strains of the young-parent stage hamper their relationship. In her book *Family Careers,* Aldous (1978) emphasizes that the developmental approach, in contrast to others, "includes a systematic analysis of the changes that the members of a family can expect throughout its existence," and that "the content and timing of past events in individual and family histories affects present interaction patterns among the family's members" (p. 5).

To elaborate on our previous example, suppose the mother suggests that the father take a basic business course in adult education and open an electronics repair shop so he will not be dependent on his factory job. The father does not do so and is rehired. A few years later he is again laid off temporarily. The relationships he now has with his family are a result not simply of his present situation but also of his earlier refusal to reduce his dependence on the factory.

From this short introduction to five theoretical approaches, you should be able to see that (1) they do guide us in selecting a focus on situations we wish to learn about and (2) the same problem can be usefully examined from a number of different approaches.

SUMMARY

- Studying marriage and the family can help you to understand relations around you, to raise valid questions, and to make intelligent decisions about your own life.

- Defining marriage and the family is not a simple task, especially when cross-cultural variations and individual conceptions are considered.

- In our society, marriage is defined as a socially sanctioned union of one man and one woman who are expected to play the roles of husband and wife.

- "Family" is defined as any one of a variety of structures such as the nuclear family, extended family, augmented family, attenuated family, or blended family.

- Marriage and family institutions are in a constant state of adjustment and change. A significant change has been the opening of more options and alternatives in man-woman and parent-child relations.

- Marriage and family institutions are seen as both healthy and popular, although some problems continue and some new ones have been added.

- The best available thought and research are provided in a wide variety of resources. However, in some areas there is little solid research. Reasons include less precision in measurement, difficulties with data gathering, control of variables, and interpretation of data.

- Theory is useful in family studies. Five common conceptual frameworks are the interactionist, exchange, systems, conflict, and developmental approaches.

PERSPECTIVE: SOCIETAL VALUES ABOUT MARRIAGE AND FAMILY

Below are some generalizations about societal expectations regarding marriage and the family. These value statements do not necessarily represent actual behavior or even reality but rather common traditional opinions about cultural values and ideals. You are likely to agree with some and disagree with others. As you read, try to evaluate and critique the statements and to look for changes and directional trends. You might ask yourself whether your judgments are based on ideals or reality, emotions or facts, personal preferences, or other reasons.

1. Youthful qualities are the most desirable.

"Young" is a key word in our society. Our culture stresses the new or youthful in life-style, clothing, cars, music, and general outlook on life. Young people are expected to be innocent, energetic, enthusiastic, and desirous of change, which is perceived as progressive. These same qualities are believed to be characteristic of the United States as a nation and typical of Americans as people. In contrast to many other societies, Americans pay less attention to the elderly or to the wisdom of the past.

The psychological development of self in childhood depends primarily on parents. In adolescence, however, the peer group becomes very influential in how youths feel about themselves, the kinds of values they hold, the activities they engage in, and the types of relationships they form. Society promotes youth, for example, by electing young, attractive, unmarried women to be queens of cherry blossom or homecoming festivals.

2. Prior to marriage, one should date a number of people.

In colonial America, there was little casual dating. A young man and woman who began seeing each other were expected to carry a short courtship onward quickly to marriage. Today dating has become quite informal and many students refer to it simply as "going out." To many young people, the number of dating partners is a symbol of popularity. Parents are supportive of this pattern because they expect that dating a number of people will minimize the chances of a premature involvement and increase their child's chances for a happy marriage.

3. Romantic love is the reason for marrying and staying married.

Our society stresses love as the basis for marriage and, in contrast to some other societies, looks upon arranged marriages or marriages for family or personal gain with disapproval. The vast majority of adults, when asked why they got married, will answer that they were in love, and many would respond similarly when asked why they stayed married.

Americans esteem love in songs, poetry, movies, magazines, and Valentine's Day cards. Informal research over the past two decades has shown that at any one time over half of U.S. college students are in love. There is societal support for this since such love experiences are seen as helping an individual to grow toward a lifelong partnership.

4. Sex should be reserved for marriage.

While youthful activities such as dating and falling in love are societally pre-scribed and acceptable, premarital sex is not. It is especially condemned by traditional religious groups and by parents of teens. For college students, who tend to marry in their mid-twenties, it means that for about ten years society will let them hold hands at the movies and kiss goodnight but not to express their sexuality fully. To do that, one is expected to marry.

Yet other messages come through as well. In advertising, for example, cars are shown with pretty women or handsome men behind the wheels, often suggesting that the auto is far more than merely a means of transportation and that it is important to own the right one. Advertisements for toothpaste and mouthwash promise to make you more desirable, and it is implied that the "right" clothes will do the same. The unmarried are expected to see references to sex displayed all around them yet to remain celibate.

5. The marital relationship should fulfill all the couple's needs.

In the view of society, the married couple should be able to satisfy all their own and each other's needs "as long as the two shall live." This includes emotional, physical, and sexual needs as well as all interpersonal needs. Faithfulness should naturally follow, since all the needs are mutually met within the mar-riage. This high expectation remains even though society does not provide information or require education and preparation for this complex lifelong task. The legal requirements for marriage in most states amount to less than those for obtaining a driver's license. Society does make an implied promise of rewards that can be expected only through the marriage relationship. One of these is the pleasure of marital sex.

6. *Marital sex is good and good for marriage.*

According to society, what was bad until the wedding night suddenly becomes good, even beneficial, to the maintenance of the marital relationship. One reason is that since society cannot perpetuate itself without new members, sex for procreation is a necessity. However, there has recently been less cultural emphasis on procreational sex and more acceptance of recreational sex for the good of the marriage.

While marital sex is good, it should be enjoyed in a normal way, for the right reasons, and in moderation. While coital frequency is expected to be high among newlyweds, it is expected to play a less significant role in maintaining a happy relationship with the arrival of children and advancing age. The absence of the natural result of marital sex (children), variance in sexual practices, or placing too high a value on sexual activity is expected to lead to marital unhappiness and even failure.

7. *Marital conflict is bad but will pass with time and communication.*

In the past, marital conflict was not expected to surface publicly and there were few provisions for dealing with it. Today conflict is still viewed as undesirable and a threat to social stability. The most common reason for an unhappy marriage is seen as a poor choice of mate. Individuals who matured in dating, fell in love, and abstained from premarital sex should live happily ever after. It is not part of the cultural perception that a couple that were in love prior to marriage and now express this love in marital intimacy need to fight about money, sex, children, or anything else.

If conflicts occur, they will pass if the partners are patient and/or make efforts to communicate. While reluctantly admitting that individuals and families are likely to experience various crises as they pass through their life stages, it is expected that problems will fade and disappear in the context of a strong family. When special crises threaten individual families, it is expected that the informal support system and neighbors will help out. If the problem is severe, then the more formal system of government and private agencies is expected to provide support.

8. *Children are good for marriage and should be reared in their own world.*

The expectation persists that children can stabilize a marriage and may even save a shaky one. After all, one basis for the acceptance and high value of marital sex is its natural role in procreation. Marriages without children are sometimes looked upon as undesirable failures. More recent expectations include the idea that the couple should plan when and how many children they will have. The basic prescription is that they should have no more children than they can support financially, physically, and emotionally. Since children are good for a marriage, they should have a chance for a good life.

The cultural theme is that children should have a period of time in which to enjoy childhood, protected from the problems of the adult world. They are expected to mature slowly and to spend their first decade or so free to play and indulge themselves. Only occasionally are they expected to perform some small tasks. This, it is felt, will help them to enter adolescence with a sense of psychological security.

Various laws restrict adolescents from participating fully in the adult world, and parents are generally expected to maintain effective control over their children. In some cases parents can be held legally responsible and liable for the misbehavior of their offspring. The parents' responsibility continues as their adolescent children gradually become more independent. Yet by the time they leave the home and family more or less permanently, young adults are expected to have learned the proper values and behavior patterns.

9. *Marriage should be permanent, but in case of great unhappiness, divorce is sanctioned.*

A basic cultural value is that people should get married on the basis of love and live happily ever after in a monogamous relationship. Society has come to realize, however, that some marriages will not achieve these high expectations. In exceptional cases, therefore, the breakup of marriages and families has been sanctioned as an alternative preferable to constant fighting, unhappiness, and possible violence. Breakup is perceived as a necessary escape valve in situations where, otherwise, the consequences might be even more detrimental to the well-being of the family and to society.

10. *A strong family system is important to our future.*

Society expects everyone to get married—it is seen as the only normal way for adults to live. It is supposed to provide greater fulfillment and more content-ment than other life-styles. The young are expected to marry as soon as they have finished their education or are self-supporting.

Being a never-married adult does not fit the cultural prescription. If one's single status is a matter of choice, it is likely to arouse suspicion about one's character. Even those who have failed at marriage are expected to try it again. So are widows and widowers—unless they are considered too old to need sexual or romantic love.

Our values consider a strong family system a basic, important institution for individual and social well-being. It is generally believed that strong families are necessary for a strong society. Anything that threatens the family system threatens society's strength and health. Yet society does not expend much time, effort, or money on ensuring a strong family system.

QUESTIONS FOR THOUGHT AND DISCUSSION

1. What are *your* reasons for studying marriage and the family? How are they similar to or different from the reasons given in the book? Just how important is studying marriage and the family to you?

2. Think about what marriage means to you and come up with your own definition. What is the most important aspect of marriage to you? How do you think your view of marriage differs from that of your parents? Your friends? If possible, compare your definition with those of your classmates and discuss differences.

3. Think back to the various types of family structures that were described in this chapter. Which best describes your family? How important do you feel the family structure is to the success or failure of a family unit? Explain.

4. What are some of the most important changes that have taken place in the area of marriage and the family? How have these changes affected people's attitudes toward marriage and the family and its place in our society? Which of the four discussed changes affecting marriage and the family has influenced your own family? Explain.

5. Some social scientists feel that marriage and the family are in serious trouble. Others feel that they are doing fairly well, considering the circumstance of society today. What do you think? Is the nuclear family ideal in your opinion? Why or why not?

6. Obviously, Watson's prediction in 1927 did not materialize. Make your own prediction about marriage for 50 years from now. On what basis did you make your prediction?

7. Explain and expand on Bernard's definition of marriage. Why did she put it the way she did?

8. What could be meant by "preventative medicine" for marriage?

9. How would you go about developing a good marriage relationship based on the evidence in Chapter 1?

10. Often, the type of family that we grow up in colors our view of the world in general, and specifically our view of marriage and the family. Think about the type of family in which you were raised and how it has affected your view of

marriage and family relationships (i.e., is it positive or negative, conservative or liberal?).

11. What are some of the problems with social science data? How does research in the social sciences compare with research in the natural sciences? How accurate can we say social science research is?

12. The ability to define variables clearly enough that they can be measured is called *operationalizing*. How might you operationalize marriage if you were a social scientist?

13. Consider the situation below from two of the five theoretical approaches discussed in the chapter. How would each explain the situation?

Mary and John are married and live with their two teenage sons. John's father died several years ago, and his mother, who is 78, has been doing well living on her own until recently, when she has been forgetting things—such as food cooking on the stove. Mary and John both agree that she must come live with them. John's mother refuses; she doesn't want to "be a burden." John is against placing her in a nursing home. Mary has just returned to school and plans to graduate with an MBA in May. John owns his own appliance business, which keeps him very busy. John's mother's move into their home would mean that the boys would again have to share a room, and this distresses them. The family considers hiring a caretaker for John's mom during the day, but this would put a strain on the family budget, especially the boys' plans for college.

14. Think about the generalizations of societal expectations regarding marriage and the family. Do they seem accurate and realistic to you? Do you agree with them? Are they appropriate for life in society today? Why or why not?

Historical and Cross=Cultural Insights

Historical Perspectives

Variations in Marriage Forms and Family Structures

Historical Roots of Present Relationships

Cross-Cultural Insights

What Are Some Messages for Us Today?

   Box 2.1 The Creation of Woman—Sanskrit (Hindu)

   Box 2.2 The Creation of Woman—The Bible

   Box 2.3 Eskimo Wife Lending

Summary

Perspective: Universalities

HISTORICAL PERSPECTIVES

Suppose you had just been elected to the U.S. House of Representatives and were assigned to the Subcommittee on Marriage and Family. The following presentation has been made to your committee and you've been asked to evaluate it for your fellow representatives.

Ladies and gentlemen, I am here to tell you that our institutions of marriage and family are falling apart, and something must be done about it. What has happened to marriage? The divorce rate has doubled since 1965. Nobody cares if this causes social disorganization; people only care about themselves. Look at the evidence: there is an increase in people living by themselves. More and more college students, our future leaders, are living in sin rather than in monogomous marriage—the form preferred all around the world.

Why is marriage in trouble? Because we no longer have strong families. We need a return to the strong extended family that has recently been torn apart. Today young people marry and move away from parents and relatives rather than stay home, as in the old days. This results in a lack of advice from older relatives to the new couples. Our selfish nuclear family system shows a lack of respect and concern for the elderly. Where are the big houses of yesteryear, where there was room for Grandma and Uncle George?

In addition to the problems of the family, nobody cares about children. The birthrate has been going down since 1958. Family size is only about half what it was when this country began. All women care about anymore are careers, materialism, and consumerism. This is proven by the fact that about half of all women and, even worse, more and more mothers are employed.

Ladies and gentlemen, I hope your committee will come up with a proper bill to strengthen marriage and family life in America. Thank you.

HAS THE PAST PASSED OR IS IT TODAY'S ROOTS?

Much of what we expect from family life bears the stamp of an earlier time. —JOHN DEMOS

Those who do not remember the past are condemned to repeat it.
—GEORGE SANTAYANA

The presentation to the committee reflects a typical contemporary viewpoint; it is based on a comparison between the present and the past. To understand our present traditions and behavior properly and to plan for the future, we must have some understanding of the past. For example, our social life is often linked to the past, especially in family traditions. Your family may recognize certain traditions with regard to celebrations, gift giving, decorations, and holiday foods.

Today some of our traditions seem unusual and even nonsensical, but in historical context they made sense. Thus, our nine-month school year may be inefficient today due to high winter fuel costs and the expense of buildings standing empty in summer, but this school year was clearly useful a hundred years ago, when young people had to help out on the farm during the summer months. The traditions of the old country and the realities of the colonial era combined to share our American way of life. Unfortunately, our view of the past is often based on incorrect information, which can only lead to incorrect judgments about the present and future.

The Value of the Historical Viewpoint

With this in mind, let us analyze the presentation given to the House Subcommittee on Marriage and the Family. First, the speaker says we need to return to the strong extended family. Much of that argument rests on the validity of the statement that there has been a change from a "strong extended family" to a "selfish nuclear family." In truth, the extended family was never the dominant family type in the United States (Demos, 1970); the nuclear family has always been the dominant form. As far back as colonial times, most young couples did not move in with their parents unless, as occasionally happened, there was a housing shortage or the couple could not afford a home of their own. Therefore, the presenter's argument is based on a false view of the past.

Second, the argument that divorce causes social disorganization is false. Divorce may cause personal disorganization, but less than 10 percent of U.S. adults live in a divorced status at any one time. This small number does not cause social disorganization. Although it is true that some college students cohabit, most will eventually marry. Contrary to the presentation, a higher percentage of the U.S. population was married in 1989 than in 1900.

Third, the birthrate has declined since 1958, but many will contend that people today are concerned about a higher quality of life for fewer children rather than uninterested in parenthood. Fourth, when we look at cross-cultural information, we find that monogamous marriage (one man to one woman) is dominant, but polygyny (one man to several women) is the preferred form. Finally, the role of U.S. women in the family and in the labor force has changed as we have moved from an agrarian to an urban/industrial society. Present evidence shows that if women are able to obtain adequate child care in a day-care center or with relatives, there is no basic difference in the development of children whose mothers work as opposed to those whose mothers stay home.

Overall, the presentation does contain several correct statements, such as that the divorce rate has doubled since 1965, more college students are cohabiting, more women are working outside the home, and the birthrate has decreased since 1958. These correct statements give the presentation a ring of truth. However, the package of correct and incorrect statements presents a misleading case. The cause-and-effect interpretation is especially open to question. Courses in logic teach us to avoid *post hoc, ergo propter hoc* thinking, or assuming that simply because event B happened after event A, event B was *caused by* event A.

In summary, when you encounter an opinion about marriage and family, make sure that the argument contains facts, not false opinions, and that the conclusions are logical. Strong views are often based on only limited knowledge.

VARIATIONS IN MARRIAGE FORMS AND FAMILY STRUCTURES

Let us look at the wide variety of forms and structures—past and present—that have been reflected in marriages and families around the world. As you study these, keep in mind three questions: (1) Which of these forms or structures have existed and/or exist in the U.S. today? (2) Which is currently the dominant form or structure in our society? and (3) What trends or directions of change, if any, are occurring today?

Mate-Selection Regulations:

Exogamy—a requirement to marry outside one's own group of close relatives
Endogamy—a requirement to marry within a certain group or groups

As to the exogamy requirement, some societies define "close" as first or second cousins, while others consider anyone within particular side of the family or within the entire tribe as "close." The exogamy requirement is believed to be associated with the incest taboo. The endogamy requirement relates to such variables as race, religion, and nationality. Sometimes these regulations are simply folkways, and sometimes they have become law. For example, most U.S. states do not permit first-cousin marriages (i.e., exogamy), and informal pressures suggest that you marry within your own race (i.e., endogamy).

Forms of Marriage Based on the Number of People United:

Monogamy—marriage of one man to one woman
Polygamy—marriage of one woman to several men or one man to several women
Polygyny—marriage of one man to several women
Polyandry—marriage of one woman to several men
Group Marriage—marriage of several women to several men

Of these forms, only monogamy and polygyny have been known to exist with any great frequency. Our society expects monogamy to last for a lifetime, although recently considerable attention has been focused on serial monogamy—a series of monogamous marriages in one individual's lifetime. However, most Americans marry only once.

Where polygyny is practiced, it is associated with the husband's high economic standing or power. The best-known historical example of polygyny in our society is the Church of the Latter Day Saints (Mormons). Cross-culturally, the two commonly identified forms of polygyny are the sororate (marriage of a man to his wife's sister or sisters, usually after the wife has died or proved sterile) and the levirate (marrying the widow of one's brother, as required by ancient Hebrew law).

Polyandry has existed as an institutional form of marriage; however, it is quite rare. It appears to be related to two factors: general sexual freedom, as in the case of Marquesans, or hard living conditions, as in Tibet or among the Toda of India. Tibet's rigors gave rise to fraternal polyandry—whereby the younger brothers are considered married to the older brother's wife (Stephens, 1963). Group marriage has never existed as a dominant form in any society. It offers few if any advantages over the other forms of marriage and would be difficult to institutionalize and systematize. In the United States, group marriage existed during the late 1800s in the Oneida Community (New York State), and it is now found in some utopian communes.

Kinship Reckoning or Descent Tracing:

Unilineal (Unilateral)—reckoning kin only in wife/mother or only in husband/father lineage

Matrilineal—tracing kin along wife/mother lineage

Patrilineal—tracing kin along husband/father lineage

Bilineal (Bilateral)—reckoning kin in both wife/mother and husband/father lineage

Our society recognizes kin or blood relatives in both lineages. We also recognize other relatives on legal or religious grounds. The term "patrilineal" is often confused with "patrinomial," taking the male's/father's last name. In our society, the father's surname traditionally becomes that of the children.

Classification by Place of Residence:

Matrilocal—residing with the parents of the wife

Patrilocal—residing with the parents of the husband

Neolocal—residing in a new or independent residence

When our country was primarily agricultural, young couples sometimes had a patrilocal residence, especially if the husband expected to take over the family farm. Now most young couples establish an independent residence upon marriage. However, student couples sometimes reside with one set of parents during the summer, particularly for the sake of nearby employment.

Classification by Formal Authority, Dominance, or Power:

Matriarchy—a family with a dominant wife/mother

Patriarchy—a family with a dominant husband/father
Egalitarian—a family with equal dominance between husband and wife

Historically, patriarchal families have been common in numerous societies, including our own. The degree of patriarchal power has varied from the almost absolute authority of the *paterfamilias* in the classical Roman family to the relatively nominal power of the father in many present-day U.S. families. The historical trend in America has been away from patriarchal families toward an egalitarian family system. Individual variations, however, continue to exist.

Types of Family Structures:

Nuclear (Conjugal, Immediate)—family consisting of a mother, father, and children
Extended (Consanguine)—family consisting of a mother, father, children, and other relatives

The nuclear family is the most common in the United States. However, many families may become extended families for limited periods of time.

The *U.S. Census User's Guide* (1980) is a primary source regarding living arrangements as well as other basic information about families. The census defines a family as two or more persons living in the same household who are related by blood, marriage, or adoption. A household is defined as a group of related or unrelated individuals who share living quarters. Thus, two sisters, a single parent with an adopted child, or a family of three generations living together would each be classified as both a family and a household. Four unrelated people sharing living quarters or a cohabiting couple would be classified as a household but not a family.

Using the newly introduced terminology, we could describe our marriage and family system as primarily:

Exogamous and endogamous in regard to mate selection
Monogamous based on the number of people married at any one time
Bilineal in regard to kinship
Neolocal by place of residence
Egalitarian according to placement of formal authority
Nuclear in structure

Of course, you can find many exceptions to these generalizations. For more classifications and examples, refer to Murdock (1949) or Stephens (1963). You may wish to discuss this subject in class.

HISTORICAL ROOTS OF PRESENT RELATIONSHIPS

A current topic of interest is the role of women. Both men and women are asking questions such as: Should a woman work outside the home or concentrate on being a homemaker? Should a woman be a mother or be child-free? Should a woman relate to men as an equal or in a supporting role? People are also evaluating different types of male/female relationships—marriage in a traditional sense, egalitarian marriage, marriage contracts, commuter marriages, living together, and creative singlehood.

Let us look at some practices of the past that have influenced the present. Remember, though:

> It should be understood by now that we do not expect to find a direct line of evolution through which the family has come to its present state in our own or any other culture. Neither are we looking for data to support the belief that ours is the most satisfactory form this institution has ever assumed. (Queen, Habenstein, and Quadagno, 1985, p. 12)

Males, Females, and Their Relationships

Many of us use a religious belief system to justify our beliefs about the relationships of men and women. Compare the two versions of the creation myth as it concerns women presented in Boxes 2.1 and 2.2. What messages does each of these myths give us about female/male relations? How are the stories similar? How do they differ? Why are males given priority, by a male deity, over women?

Queen, Habenstein, and Quadagno (1985) suggest that "Perhaps the priority of man in both the Sanskrit and Hebrew accounts reflects male dominance in India and Arabia at the time these stories were composed" (p. 12). In any event, it is clear that these long-ago stories have remained with us and still influence many people regarding the roles of the sexes.

In prehistoric times there was often more equality between males and females because they shared in the provision of food. Men gained status as successful hunters, women as gatherers of roots and berries. Note—as we look at female/male relationships throughout history—how closely woman's status correlates with her role as economic provider for the family.

The classical Hebrew society was the first to have some direct influence on today's male-female relations. The Hebrews had a patriarchal family system. Both monogamy and polygyny were practiced. A woman was considered important in her place, which was that of wife and mother of several children.

Classical Greek society was similar: The basic function of Greek wives was to provide children for their husbands. Aristotle made the Greek viewpoint clear when he said that the male is by nature superior and the female inferior; the one rules and the other is ruled.

Early Roman life too (about 700 to 200 B.C.) was characterized by a very strong patriarchal system. The power of the husband is reflected in this quote by the influential Roman Cato in 195 B.C.:

> Suffer women once to arrive at an equality with you, and they will from that moment become your superiors. . . . The husband is the judge of his wife, if she has committed a fault, he punishes her; if she has drunk wine, he condemns her; if she has been guilty of adultery, he kills her. . . . If you were to catch your wife in adultery, you would kill her with impunity without trial; but if she were to catch you, she would not dare to lay a finger upon you, and indeed she has no right.

BOX 2.1   THE CREATION OF WOMAN—SANSKRIT (HINDU)

In the beginning, when Twashtri came to the creation of woman, he found that he had exhausted his materials in the making of man, and that no solid elements were left. In this dilemma, after profound meditation, he did as follows. He took the rotundity of the moon, and the curves of creepers, and the clinging of tendrils, and the trembling of grass, and the slenderness of the reed, and the bloom of flowers, and the lightness of leaves, and the tapering of the elephant's trunk, and the glances of deer, and the clustering of rows of bees, and the joyous gaiety of sunbeams, and the weeping of clouds, and the fickleness of the winds, and the timidity of the hare, and the vanity of the peacock, and the softness of the parrot's bosom, and the hardness of adamant, and the sweetness of honey, and the cruelty of the tiger, and the warm glow of fire, and the coldness of snow, and the chattering of jays, and the cooing of the kokila, and the hypocrisy of the crane, and the fidelity of the chakrawaka, and compounding all these together, he made woman, and gave her to man. But after one week, man came to him, and said: Lord, this creature that you have given me makes my life miserable. She chatters incessantly, and teases me beyond endurance, never leaving me alone: and she requires incessant attention, and takes all my time up, and cries about nothing, and is always idle; and so I have come to give her back again, as I cannot live with her. So Twashtri said: Very well: and he took her back. Then after another week, man came again to him, and said: Lord, I find that my life is very lonely since I gave you back that creature. I remember how she used to dance and sing to me, and look at me out of the corner of her eye, and play with me and cling to me; and her laughter was music, and she was beautiful to look at, and soft to touch, so give her back to me again. So Twashtri said: Very well: and gave her back again. Then after only three days, man came back to him again, and said: Lord, I know not how it is; but after all, I have come to the conclusion that she is more of a trouble than a pleasure to me so please take her back again. But Twashtri said: Out with you! Be off! I will have no more of this. You must manage how you can. Then man said: But I cannot live with her. And Twashtri replied: Neither could you live without her. And he turned his back on man, and went on with his work. Then man said: What is to be done? for I cannot live either with her or without her.

SOURCE: Bain (translator), 1899, pp. 13–15.

Even though there was little equality in Roman marriage, upper-class women were held in high esteem. There was strong emphasis on marriage and remarriage. As in Hebrew and Greek societies, there was little room for unattached persons. The higher-class Roman woman was in charge of the household and she enjoyed a relatively good life, but she was not a citizen with voting rights. Between the second century B.C. and the fall of the Roman Empire, men were often away at war, so the women achieved independence and engaged in business. Slaves captured in war were brought home to work on farms and estates. Family relations deteriorated and marriage lost much of its meaning.

The early Christians, partly in revolt against the corrupt morals and deteriora-

BOX 2.2   THE CREATION OF WOMAN—THE BIBLE

And the Lord God said, "It is not good that man should be alone; I will make him a help meet for him. And out of the ground the Lord God formed every beast of the field, and every fowl of the air; and brought them unto Adam to see what he would call them: and whatsoever Adam called every living creature, that was the name thereof. And Adam gave names to all cattle, and to the fowl of the air, and to every beast of the field; but for Adam there was not found a help meet for him. And the Lord God caused a deep sleep to fall upon Adam, and he slept; and he took one of his ribs, and closed up the flesh instead thereof; and the rib, which the Lord God had taken from man, made he a woman, and brought her unto man. And Adam said, "This is now bone of my bones, and flesh of my flesh: she shall be called Woman, because she was taken out of Man." Therefore shall a man leave his father and his mother, and shall cleave unto his wife: and they shall be one flesh.

SOURCE: Genesis 2:18–24.

tion of the family in latter-day Rome, returned in many respects to the old Hebrew ways. The status of women, however, greatly declined under Christianity. Both women and men were thought to have souls and were therefore equal in the sight of God, but women were also seen as descendants of the temptress Eve and were therefore put under strong controls.

Although Christianity was seen as antifeminist (Bullough, 1974) and responsible for lowering the status of women, it did institute some changes in marriage which can be seen to this day. Polygyny, which had been allowed by the Hebrews, was replaced with monogamy. Sex was restricted to marriage. Concubinage (a mistress of sorts living with a man and his wife or wives) was abolished. Prostitution was formally forbidden. Divorce was allowed in the early days of Christianity. But when marriage became a sacrament, divorce was forbidden. Later, priests were prohibited from marrying and had to remain celibate.

The Anglo-Saxon family in medieval England was patriarchal, but this was a much weaker patriarchy than that exemplified by classic Greek and Roman families. It was legal for a man to beat his wife, although wife beating was relatively infrequent. The household was a major form of social structure, and marriage was very much an economic arrangement made by parents or guardians. The development of family estates was important, so the primogeniture system (whereby the oldest son inherited all of the land) was used to keep an estate undivided and in the family.

Twelfth-century chivalry and courtly love raised the status of those women who belonged to the nobility. They were put on pedestals and poems and songs were composed for them. However, women in general were still seen as descendants of Eve and potentially evil. The Renaissance was essentially an urban movement, and city women who stayed at home lost power compared to the rural women who worked in the fields. It was only among the urban elite that there was any gain for women.

Marriage was highly valued among the American colonists; women were often seen as partners in marriage because they contributed to the work and management of their households. Rich widows were especially valued, since they had both experience and inheritance. Ben Franklin supposedly noted that rich widows were the only second-hand goods that sold at first-class prices. This comment illustrates that marriage was often more an economic affair than a romantic one. Divorce was rare. In fact, there was no legal provision for it in most of the colonies.

America has always had a spirit of independence; therefore both courtship and family have been less structured here than they were in Europe. This was especially true on the frontier. Although arranged marriages were not as common as they had been in England, economic considerations were important and young men were expected to obtain permission from a young lady's father or guardian to court and marry her. Even though women were valued in colonial days, they were not considered the intellectual or moral equals of men. Women in the colonies were not supposed to meddle in men's affairs. They could not vote or hold property except under certain conditions. One colonial governor felt that the insanity of a particular woman was due to her habit of spending a great deal of time in reading and writing.

Nineteenth-century America witnessed the influence of the Victorian era. With an increase of urbanization and industrialization, men and women were not as likely to work side by side as they had been in the colonial period. Upper-class women were set apart and protected from harsh realities. While some people may have considered this an improvement in the women's status, their influence was actually reduced because they were less in touch with the lives and interests of men. They were expected to remain in the home and to fulfill only the roles of ladies and mothers. The Victorian woman was expected to live for and through her husband and children, having little to do with the world beyond her family circle.

In the first half of the twentieth century, the role of woman remained that of helpmate. In times of necessity, as during an economic depression or war, women might serve in the labor force temporarily. However, they were expected to remember that their place was primarily in the home.

In the "Fabulous Fifties," when many of your parents were dating, sex roles were quite clear: The male was expected to be the task or instrumental leader in the family and the female the expressive or emotional leader. Family focus was a major concern. Targ (1979), in an analysis of attitudes toward the family since World War II, maintains that the 1950s were marked by social stability and a return to normalcy following the disruptions of World War II. Women who had worked during the war were now expected to return to the roles of housewife and mother.

The rush to the suburbs in the 1950s also influenced the family. The father's workday became longer because of his commute to the city, so the suburban mother became Supermom as, in addition to running the house, she transported children to their activities and her husband to and from the commuter station. The middle-class suburban mother's life was truly based on home and family. Obtaining material goods and living in suburbia became young people's goals. Couples who were married in the mid-1950s averaged the youngest marriage age ever.

Now sex roles are in transition; women in their early twenties are postponing marriage, and marriage is seen more as an emotional than an economic arrangement.

PARENT/CHILD RELATIONSHIPS

In Hebrew society, as in other agrarian societies, young couples were expected to have large families. This fit the Old Testament command to increase and multiply. The role of children was to be subject to their parents—to "honor thy father and mother." Parents had almost unlimited authority; they were even allowed to sell children into slavery. Discipline was strict, as illustrated by Proverbs 13:24: "He that spareth his rod hateth his son." Nonetheless, Nass and McDonald (1982) note that "the early Christians placed a high value on each human life. As a result, they strongly opposed the severe treatment of children that characterized the earlier societies.... Abortion, infanticide, child selling, and sentencing children to death were all condemned" (p. 22).

Although we know relatively little about parent-child relations during Greek and Roman times, children appear to have been harshly treated. Especially in Sparta, weak or sickly infants, girls in particular, were often left in the mountains to die. This practice shows the absolute life-and-death authority parents had over children.

From the first few centuries after Christ until colonial days, children continued to be subject to strict parental authority. At various times and places, children were sold. Parents in the Middle Ages were strict disciplinarians who expected respect and obedience. They beat their children when they felt it necessary. Yet this harsh physical discipline did not mean a lack of concern (Queen et al., 1985). Colonial American children were strictly disciplined and were expected to work as soon as they were able. Children were treated as small adults and were dressed in smaller versions of adult clothing. Among Puritan families especially, there was a feeling that children were born selfish and corrupt because of original sin, and that they had to be broken in spirit and taught to obey both God and parents. Religious training and discipline was a grim and serious business; children "were to be seen and not heard."

In the 1800s, the Victorian era not only changed the role of women but also created a role for children. The emergence of compulsory education delayed the entrance of the child into the labor force (Gordon, 1972). It also removed the child from some job socialization by the father and allowed children to interact with others of their own age. American parents became quite permissive, by European standards, and the Victorian debate between permissive and restrictive child rearing is still going on today.

The twentieth century has seen a lengthening of the childhood period, since young people today rarely hold regular jobs before they reach their teen years. As the country became more urbanized and industrialized, there was more need for education and less need for manual labor. Those who did not enter the work force until after college added several years of economic dependence. The influx of youth to high schools and colleges allowed the adolescent subculture to develop. This is a significant change from colonial days, when people aged 16 to 21 were part of the adult labor force.

During the 1950s, large families, affluence, and a child-centered life-style were

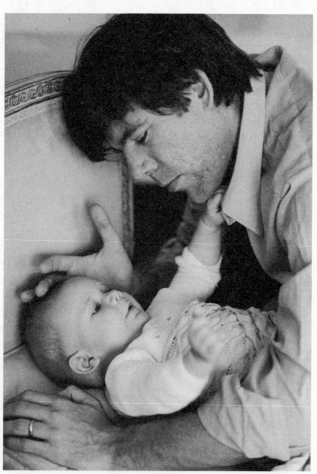

Throughout time and in most cultures, fathers have given special attention to their firstborns, especially sons.

typical. The permissive approach to child rearing was led by Benjamin Spock in his best-selling *Pocket Book of Baby and Child Care* (1951). Discipline was often left to schoolteachers. One comedian has pointed out that "Dads of the past were known as strict disciplinarians. What happened to slow them down? The electric razor took away the razor strop, gas furnaces took away the woodshed, tax worries took away dad's hair and hairbrush. So, the answer is easy—Dad ran out of weapons."

Mothers were usually home to care for their children; only about a quarter of the mothers with school-age children worked outside the home in 1950, compared with over half today. The 1960s saw many parents and children at odds over the new life-styles and the protest movements of the time—although recent research has shown that these differences have often been perceived as greater than they really were.

The parents of the 1970s and 1980s seem to be more interested in small families than their parents were. Young couples often delay starting a family and limit their family's size so as to be able to buy high-priced consumer goods. The cost of living, increases in college and career education among women, and other economic concerns appear to be factors that will influence age at marriage, age at birth of first child, and eventual family size among those reaching adulthood in the final decade of this century.

RELATIONS WITH KIN

Throughout history, there has been an emphasis on large families. In 1790 the United States was 95 percent rural, so large families were desirable to work the land. And, as is often the case in rural societies, the family was more familial than spousal; that is, there was more emphasis on the needs of the whole family than on those of the individual couple.

Even though the typical family structure was nuclear, kin were important, and most people lived in the same communities as their relatives. Marriage for the good of the family was considered an important way to increase human resources. Colonial wives had a great number of children, since often only five of ten would live to maturity. The importance of building families in colonial America is illustrated by the fact that "Hartford taxed single men 20 shillings a week" for living alone and "Connecticut ordered that no young man could live alone without the consent of the town" (Queen et al., 1985, p. 196). The expectation was that every single person, male or female, would live with family members.

An important point to remember about families in early America is that they were major agencies of community order. The key functions of religion, economics, government, and education were performed in, or at least learned in, the family to a much greater extent in colonial days than they are today. Often various kin were involved in these functions.

America's westward movement tended to decrease the interaction of kin in the community as the younger people moved away, although those who moved away tended to support each other. The westward movement often meant that young people had to build a family name on their own, and accomplishment became the key to status. However, resources brought along from a wealthy family were certainly not a handicap.

Leaping ahead historically, we find that people in the 1950s considered family a high priority. The peak year for the birthrate, the bulge of the baby boom, was right around 1960 (Kent, 1984). However, the rush to the suburbs and single-family houses of the 1950s led some sociologists to question the amount of neighboring and kin visiting left. Research by Greer (1956) and others shows that there was more visiting, especially kin visiting, than many once believed. The same holds true for the 1970s and 1980s. The author agrees with the conclusion of Gordon (1972), who maintains that "The number of kin with whom families interact and, more importantly, live, has not changed significantly" (p. 20).

From colonial times to the present, we have seen four basic changes in household composition. First, the percentage of families with live-in servants has drastically declined. Second, the percentage of households containing boarders or lodgers has also declined (Gordon, 1978). Third, in addition to changes in household composition, there has been a long-term decline in household size (Kent, 1984). Finally, there has been a dramatic increase in single-person households, because many young, unmarried persons and elderly widowed people are living alone.

While there may be a decrease in overall kin participation in family life, there are two areas in which relatives may well increase their contributions. Parents may be an important source of gifts or loans to their married offspring, especially when grandchildren appear. Also, with ever-increasing numbers of two-income families, grandparents can serve a vital function as baby-care specialists.

LOVE AND SEX

While romantic love as we know it did not appear until the twelfth century, sex has, of course, always been with us. Hebrew and Greek societies had a double standard regarding sexuality. Hebrew men could have several wives and concubines, but women could be stoned to death for adultery. In Greece, males enjoyed wide sexual freedom. They were permitted and, in fact, expected to have heterosexual relations with concubines, prostitutes, and courtesans (hetaerae) as well as homosexual relationships with comrades, mentors, or protégés. Greek women, on the other hand, remained quietly behind the scenes, with the exception of those few who became hetaerae or priestesses. They had no social status, received no education, and were little more than chattel. In the early years before the Punic Wars, Roman society was more sexually conservative than Greek or Hebrew Society; Romans did not allow polygyny and frowned upon relations with concubines. After the Punic Wars, the period of so-called Roman decadence began. The importance of marriage, family, and children declined, and sexual freedom became the pattern. "By the fourth century A.D., divorce and marital disruption had reached the stage of public scandal, and both premarital and extramarital sex relations had become sources of official embarrassment" (Kephart, 1981, p. 55).

The early Christians felt that the second coming of Christ would occur within their lifetimes, so they were not concerned with marriage and family. Probably as a reaction to the sexual excesses of the Romans, Christianity repressed sexuality. Polygyny, abortion, infanticide, and adultery were forbidden and the double standard was formally but not in actual practice replaced with repression for everyone. Virginity and celibacy were preached and preferred, even within marriage. Sex within marriage was seen as an evil that was necessary for reproduction. The Catholic Church adopted a philosophical approach called dualism, whereby the nature of man was seen as consisting of a pure spirit and a sinful body. The sins of the flesh were to be renounced.

Beginning in the twelfth century, troubadors and knights idealized aristocratic ladies. Men would travel to other castles to express their love to someone else's lady. For their courtly behavior they might be rewarded with a ribbon, a scarf—or other favors—from the lady.

Consider this curious case brought before Queen Eleanor of England's court:

> A gentleman was deeply smitten with a lady who had given her affections to another. She, however, was so favourable to him, that she promised if ever a time should arrive when she should be deprived of her first lover, she would then give ear to his prayers and adopt him as the successor. A little time afterwards the lady and her first lover married. The gentleman immediately, pleading a decision of the Countess of Champagne's, demanded the love of the newly-married lady, for in that decision it was solemnly laid down that real love cannot exist between married people. The lady, however, resisted his application, declaring that she had not lost the love of her lover by marrying him. After careful deliberation of the court, Queen Eleanor pronounced the decision as follows:
>
> "We are not inclined to controvert the decision of the Countess of Champagne, to the effect that true love cannot exist between married people. This, a solemn and deliberate decree of the afore-mentioned court, ought to hold good. Accordingly we order that the lady grant to her imploring lover the favours which he so earnestly entreats, and which she so faithfully has promised. . . ." (Bernard, Buchanan & Smith, 1959, pp. 149–150)

By the sixteenth century, the prevailing mode of romantic love had resulted in adulterous situations that were disruptive to the social system (Reiss, 1980). In the seventeenth century, romantic love was transferred from extramarital to premarital relationships. The middle class learned to value love and soon carried it over into marriage—thus contradicting the view that love could not exist in marriage. By 1900, many young people in some parts of Europe and in the United States were looking upon love as the basis for marriage.

The Puritans held that sexual behavior was a necessary good within marriage for procreation (Queen et al., 1985). They were very much against nonmarital sex or any public displays of affection. Adultery could be punished by death, although this was extremely rare. Branding with the letter "A" or, more commonly, public whippings were the punishments for adultery or fornication (Scott & Wishy, 1982). Carson (1966) uncovered a case in which a man was caught having sexual relations with a cow. The man was executed—and so was the cow! One sea captain, who had just returned from a three-year voyage, was seen kissing his wife on their front porch. For this unseemly behavior on the Sabbath, the captain was put in the public stocks. Hoult, Henze, and Hudson (1978) contend that "it is latter-day Calvinism that, to a large degree, accounts for the sexual hang-ups and guilt feelings afflicting so many Americans" (p. 35).

To understand the Puritan view of sexuality, it is important to distinguish between normatively approved behavior and actual behavior. Sometimes the two are very similar: Murder, for example, is normatively condemned and most people do not actually commit murder. On the other hand, since 1980 the national speed limit has been 55 miles per hour, or 65 on some rural highways, and most people violate this norm.

With this distinction in mind, you might ask, "How pure were the Puritans?" While nonmarital sex was condemned, there were many instances of it. According to Calhoun (1945), about one-third of the couples married in Grotton Church, Middlesex County, Massachusetts, between 1761 and 1775 confessed to fornication. Considering the harsh penalties involved, it is clear that many Puritans desired and obtained sexual pleasure. With so many breaking the normative code, there was a gradual lessening of the penalties, although the code itself still stood.

Premarital sex in colonial America should be seen in relation to the system of courtship. There was no getting together at the local bar for young unmarried persons. There was not even much dating. Instead, there was serious courtship. Mate selection, mainly a matter concerning the family, was based heavily on economics. The industry of the husband and the homemaking skills of the wife were important for the family's survival.

In the Victorian days of the 1880s, a sexual double standard and strict sex-role segregation were the order of the day. With women expected to be pure and passionless, there was a rapid growth in houses of prostitution. However, recent historical research (Smith, 1978) has shown a considerable increase in premarital sexual activity in the last few decades of the nineteenth century. It seems that once again actual behavior differed from the moral norms.

By the 1930s, romantic love had become an important reason for marriage. In the thirties and forties, couples married at earlier and earlier ages.

Others were interested in participating in sex, but the social climate and opportunity structure were limiting. In the 1940s, there were few cars and few women attended college. By the 1950s, more women were going to college, but there were no coed dorms and males were allowed only in the lounges of the women's dorms. College women had to be in their dorm rooms by a certain time—for example,

10 P.M. during the week and midnight on weekends. Undergraduates were not allowed to live in off-campus apartments.

The 1960s saw a revolution in campus rules, as the doctrine of *in loco parentis* ("in place of parents") was replaced with due process for students. Along with other freedoms came a major increase in sexual activity among college students, especially women. The so-called sexual revolution of the 1960s was really an accelerated phase in a long-term evolutionary path of increased sexual permissiveness (Walsh, 1978).

Today, love is still the main reason for marriage, and premarital sex is approved by the majority of college students. Students and others in their twenties have more personal freedom than ever before.

CROSS-CULTURAL INSIGHTS

THE VALUE OF CROSS-CULTURAL RESEARCH

The preceding pages show that what is appropriate in one culture may be inappropriate in another, even in the complex area of marriage and family. Several reasons explaining the need for cross-cultural information have been suggested: (1) it gives us knowledge of the range of possibilities by showing how people do things in other lands, (2) it tells us something about which ways of doing things are relatively common and which are relatively unique, and (3) it lets us know how we as Americans compare with the rest of the world (Stephens, 1963).

Sociologists call people who consider other cultures inferior or unnatural ethnocentric. Just as it is helpful to have an objective view of yourself by putting yourself in the place of others, it is helpful to be emotionally detached and rational—to objectively view the society in which you live. The philosopher Spinoza has said, "I have made a ceaseless effort, not to ridicule, not to bewail, nor to scorn human actions, but to understand them."

SOME CROSS-CULTURAL EXAMPLES: DIFFERENT WAYS OF LOOKING AT THE SAME OLD THING

Just as it is interesting and helpful to understand the history of American male-female, parent-child, and kinship relationships—as well as love and sex—it is good to look at these relationships in other societies. The following examples are not necessarily right or wrong but simply other ways to do the same old thing.

Overall, the trend in female-male relationships has been toward more equality. For example, women in Sweden are treated more equally in employment. They are provided with such benefits as flextime, government-supported day-care centers, and a six-month leave of absence with 90 percent pay after the birth of a child. On the other hand, in some parts of the world a woman has to wear a veil over her face and walk three steps behind her husband.

In the United States, people are free to marry whom they choose. In other parts of the world, such as rural India, some marriages are arranged by parents. Legally, marriage in the United States must be between one man and one woman, while Murdock (1949) has shown that over 80 percent of all societies allow polygyny and that strict monogamy is the rule in less than 20 percent of all societies.

All societies recognize that spouses may have difficulties in marriage and most allow divorce. However, some (such as Ireland and the African Zulu nation) do not allow divorce at all. Divorce in some countries is a long legal battle, but an American Zuñi Indian wife can end her marriage simply by putting her husband's belongings outside the teepee.

Worldwide, parent-child relationships have often shifted between permissiveness and strict control. Anthropologist Margaret Mead (1950) has shown that in the Arapesh society of New Guinea, parents do everything they can to make childhood an easy and happy time. Some adult is consistently available to hold and to comfort the small child, since it is considered a tragedy for a child to cry.

In societies other than our own, marriage and family mean different things, and families are arranged in other ways that are different from ours.

In contrast to this permissive approach, the Mundugumor children of New Guinea are given only minimal care. Parents do not feel comfortable with their children and children are reared to feel uncomfortable in the presence of their relatives. Within the Mundugumor family, there is hostility between a father and his sons and between brothers.

In many societies, children may be exchanged among relatives if there are child-parent conflicts. The Trobriand Islanders have a matrilineal society in which the male child is not socialized by his biological father but rather by his mother's brother. While the father does not socialize his own son, he is responsible for socializing his sister's son (Malinowski, 1929).

The Israeli kibbutz sometimes still features a combination of parent and non-parent child rearing, where all children are brought up in a communal nursery, but they have the opportunity to eat the communal evening meal with their parents and to spend the Sabbath with them. Child psychologist A. S. Makarenko concentrates on development of character in the Soviet Union. A major goal of child rearing there, according to him, is to develop loyalty to the state (Makarenko, 1967).

Family forms vary across the world; so do kin relations. At one extreme, the classic Chinese extended family subordinates the couple to the family. This family ideally consists of three or more generations living in the same house with thirty or more members. Queen et al. (1985) note that these families emphasize family pride and the father-son relationship. Notice how different this is from the Mundugumors, where there is hostility among family members and brothers and sisters belong to different lineages. The only kind of close contact Mundugumors allow between brothers is public abuse and fighting (Mead, 1950).

Love and sexual activity do not appear at random but are tied to the cultural beliefs and behavior of various groups. The story of Eskimo hospitality (Box 2.3) is one example of an approach different from that in the rest of the United States. In the Trobriand Islands, premarital intercourse is the expected behavior. When a boy reaches puberty, he may take a young girl to a bachelor house he and several other boys share to engage in sexual relations. Even though there is open acceptance of premarital sex, adultery on the part of women is condemned.

In general, Polynesian societies are sexually liberal and active. Mangaia youngsters compete for sexual partners; masturbation is accepted and sometimes occurs in public. By marriage age, a virgin is extremely rare. Evidence from Marshall (1971) shows that the average 18-year-old male has orgasm 21 times a week.

In contrast to this high level of sexual permissiveness and activity, a New Guinea tribe called the Dani practically ignores sex. Intercourse does not occur until two or more years after marriage, and a couple may not have sexual relations for as many as five years following the birth of a child.

It is hoped that these various examples of relationships and views of love and sex—combined with the historical review—make it clear that there is great diversity in how people and families can and do function. Ours is simply one alternative—sometimes better, sometimes worse—but now we know something about how we fit into the spectrum of possibilities.

BOX 2.3   ESKIMO WIFE LENDING

"You said the fellow you killed provoked you?"

"So it was."

"He insulted Asiak?" [an Eskimo wife]

"Terribly."

"Presumably he was killed as you tried to defend her from his advances?"

Ernenek (her husband) and Asiak looked at each other and burst out laughing.

"It wasn't so at all," Asiak said at last.

"Here's how it was," said Ernenek. "He kept snubbing all our offers although he was our guest. He scorned even the oldest meat we had."

"You see, Ernenek, many of us white men are not fond of old meat."

"But the worms were fresh!" said Asiak.

"It happens, Asiak, that we are used to foods of a quite different kind."

"So we noticed," Ernenek went on, "and that's why, hoping to offer him at last a thing he might relish, somebody proposed him Asiak to laugh (have sexual intercourse) with."

"Let a woman explain," Asiak broke in. "A woman washed her hair to make it smooth, rubbed tallow into it, greased her face with blubber, and scraped herself clean with a knife, to be polite."

"Yes," cried Ernenek, rising. "She had purposely groomed herself! And what did the white man do? He turned his back to her! That was too much! Should a man let his wife be so insulted? So somebody grabbed the scoundrel by his miserable little shoulders and beat him a few times against the wall—not in order to kill him, just wanting to crack his head a little. It was unfortunate it cracked a lot!"

"Ernenek has done the same to other men," Asiak put in helpfully, "But it was always the wall that went to pieces first."

The white man winced. "Our judges would show no understanding for such an explanation. Offering your wife to other men!"

"Why not? The men like it and Asiak says it's good for her. It makes her eyes sparkle and her cheeks glow."

"Don't you people borrow other men's wives?" Asiak inquired.

"Never mind that! It isn't fitting, that's all."

"Refusing isn't fitting for a man!" Ernenek said indignantly. "Anybody would much rather lend out his wife than something else. Lend out your sled and you'll get it back cracked, lend out your saw and some teeth will be missing, lend out your dogs and they'll come home crawling, tired—but no matter how often you lend out your wife, she'll always stay like new."

SOURCE: Ruesch, 1950, pp. 103–105.

WHAT ARE SOME MESSAGES FOR US TODAY?

IS THERE A BEST FORM OF MARRIAGE AND FAMILY?

In general, there is probably no one form of either marriage or family that is best. As we have seen, different forms have worked in different times and places. Goode (1970), in *World Revolution and Family Patterns,* maintains that the world is moving toward some version of the nuclear family. In the United States, there are still many versions of the nuclear family. Thus, many people will opt for a dual-career family. Others will decide to have the husband work full-time while the wife takes care of the home and looks after the children. Most couples will want to be biological parents, while others will adopt children or have none. You may be aware of successful examples of each of these types of families.

IS MARRIAGE AND FAMILY FOR ALL?

In our society, the answer is generally yes. A historical review shows virtually no place for single adults in most societies. Before the industrial revolution, societies needed high birthrates to overcome the high rate of death. Marriage was and is used as a means of social control, and sex is regulated in various ways, often through marriage. The laws and customs of most societies favor the married couple by giving their children legitimate status, the right of inheritance, and other privileges.

If a society does not manage to perpetuate itself through an adequate birthrate, it will eventually die off. For example, in the United States, a religious group known as the Shakers reached their peak level of membership about the time of the Civil War. The Shaker religion forbade sexual relations; therefore its members had no natural replacements. By the late 1800s, many Shaker communities were folding; by 1925, most of the remaining groups had dissolved. By 1950, only a scattered few were left (Kephart, 1982).

Over 90 percent of the present population of the United States will eventually be married. Our society is not well suited for people who are single after age 30. Friends and relatives with good intentions try to match single adults, and some employers still consider married personnel more stable. Yet there have been changes in our sexual and social views that make it less unpleasant to be single in the 1980s. Thus, more open attitudes toward living together and nonmarital sex, "soup for one" (food sold in single portions), and condominiums for singles all make a useful and creative single life-style possible.

On a personal level, should one marry or remain single? The answer to this question, of course, depends on the values of the individual. Can people expect to marry and live happily ever after? The evidence says no: Nearly half of all marriages end in divorce; some of those that last are unhappy. However, consider these qualifications: First, there are very few two-person relationships that have a better success rate than marriage. New business partnerships have a high breakup rate, even though they do not contend with the wide range of emotions and interactions of the marital relationship. Second, many people (probably the majority) are as happy in their marital relationships as in any others that they have, and some are extremely happy in their marriages. Finally, although some people are unhappy in one marriage, they can hope to find happiness in another.

SUMMARY

- An understanding of the history of male/female, parent/child, and kin relationships—as well as love and sex—helps us to understand our present culture.

- Marriage forms and family structures in the United States can be classified as both exogamous and endogamous, monogamous, bilineal, neolocal, egalitarian, and nuclear.

- History shows that (1) male/female relationships have a long tradition of male dominance, with a recent trend toward equity; (2) parent/child relationships have followed a long evolutionary path from absolute parental authority and early employment to childhood freedom and expanded education to the development of an adolescent subculture; (3) kinship relations have been important throughout American history and have changed little; and (4) while sex has always been with us, romantic love as we know it today is only a couple of centuries old.

- Cross-cultural information provides us with a range of possibilities of doing things, tells us about the common and unique behaviors, and lets us compare our ways with those of the rest of the world.

- There is no such thing as one best form of marriage or family. What is appropriate in one time and place may not be appropriate in another.

- Considerable pressure for both marriage and parenthood still exists in our society, although both have become more optional.

- Choice of life-style is an important individual decision for Americans today.

PERSPECTIVE: UNIVERSALITIES

The complex combination of geography, climate, political and economic systems, individual characteristics and abilities combines with social and cultural traditions, beliefs, and behaviors to allow a vast variety in the ways humans interact with each other. Some of the forms of interaction are common to all people and some vary from one group of people to another.

As we all proceed through the life cycle, society imposes certain rites of passage to mark changes in our status. Think of the important rites of passage in your life. When you were born, perhaps your family celebrated by having a baby shower or a family gathering, or perhaps cigars were passed out to the men. Your baptism and confirmation or bar mitzvah marked your membership in your church or synagogue. You might think of a first date, your first formal dance, your graduation from grade school or high school, the day you got your driver's license, or the first time you were old enough to vote as events marking your passage from one life stage to the next. The change from the single to the married state is marked by a wedding ceremony. Even the final stage, death, is marked by a ceremony of some type—a funeral, visitation, wake, or burial. Different societies, of course, have different ceremonies to mark these rites of passage.

Some aspects of marriage and family have been found to be universal, that is, pertaining to all people everywhere. Stephens (1963) calls these aspects "cross-cultural regularities."

Note the following universalities:

1. Some kind of family group exists. The nuclear family is found in almost all societies, although it may be part of a larger polygamous family structure.
2. The family, in whatever form, socializes the young children.
3. Men and women cooperate economically for the good of the family.
4. Families tend to have a power structure and division of labor based on sex and age.
5. Men usually have more power and privileges than women.
6. The influence of the mother on the children is usually greater than that of the father.
7. Sexual activity is regulated. Society says who can do what with whom and under what circumstances.

So, although the rites of passage concerning marriage and family may differ from one ethnic group or tribe to another, there are a number of common aspects. These common aspects allow scholars to find and analyze the structural and functional similarities in the world's cultures and the various systems of exchange in intimate human relationships.

QUESTIONS FOR THOUGHT AND DISCUSSION

1. Think about what you know about the past in marriage and family life in America. Where did you get most of your information? Were some of the "commonsense" fallacies things you thought were true? Why do you think the past is often described as better than it actually was?

2. What are the most frequent forms of marriage cross-culturally? What are some practical reasons why these are the most common? Which form do you think is best for our society and why? Is there one form that appeals to you personally more than any other? Explain.

3. Though the specific forms of marriage and family and the role of women have changed throughout history, there are some similarities among the different cultures and time periods. What are the similarities? What are the differences? What do these similarities and differences say about the importance of economics in marriage and family?

4. How did the rise of Christianity change the status of women and children in the family? Were these changes for the better or for the worse, in your opinion? Explain.

5. How did changes from an agrarian or agricultural society to a more industrial, education-oriented society affect the status of the family and its members?

6. How does being an economic provider affect the status of a woman in today's family?

7. How has the status of single people changed since colonial times? What were society's concerns about singles in colonial times? How important was the family?

8. What are some of the most basic changes that have taken place in household composition since colonial times?

9. What has been the role of sex in marriage throughout history? How has the sexual double standard affected attitudes and behaviors at different points in history? In your opinion, does the sexual double standard still exist? Think of an example and explain it.

10. What has been the role of love in marriage throughout history? How does economic necessity affect the role of love and the type of marriage that takes place?

PART 2

Establishing

Relationships

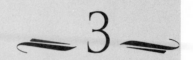

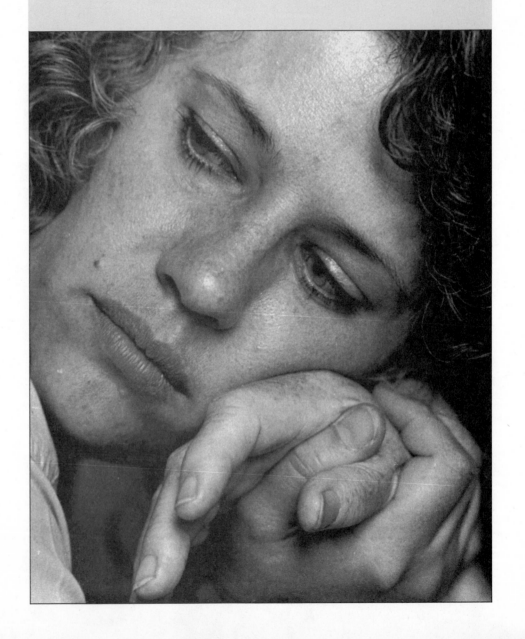

Understanding Yourself, Relating to Others

WHO AM I?

Dating, marriage, and other types of interpersonal relationships—from intimate love relationships to impersonal business deals—are all influenced by an understanding of oneself and others. To secure and maintain meaningful relationships with others, you must first have a comfortable relationship with yourself.

To understand yourself more thoroughly, try the following experiment. Please do it, because it is very important for your understanding of this chapter and yourself. First, take a sheet of lined paper and number the lines from 1 to 20. Now, in six minutes, please answer, with a word or phrase after each number, the following question about yourself: "Who am I?" Start.

Your self-concept becomes apparent in the series of statements you make about yourself (Kuhn & McPartland, 1954). The test you have just taken is called the Twenty Statements Test (TST), which reveals what you think about yourself.

Let us examine the actual responses of a student and a businessperson to the TST.

Sue	*John*
1. a student	1. John _____
2. a woman	2. a successful businessman
3. Sue _____	3. a hard worker
4. A Delta	4. the director of 20 people
5. Jim's girl	5. a member of the Chamber of Commerce
6. a member of student government	6. a diabetic
7. a sociology major	7. director of the park board
8. a Methodist	8. a husband
9. talkative	9. a father
10. a fun person	10. a Methodist
11. a redhead	11. a good dancer
12. from Toledo	12. a golfer
13. old-fashioned	13. a friend
14. tall	14. like to travel
15. fast-food junkie	15. interested in cars
16. good typist	16. a gardener

17. part-time employee
18. afraid of the water
19. partygoer
20. Joan's best friend

17. overweight
18. family man
19. midwesterner
20. good dresser

When experts examine the TST, they look for several clues. The items listed first are assumed to be more important or salient to the self-concept. Our example shows that John's identity is closely related to his occupation, while Sue's is closely related to college. Notice that items relating to family and religion were important enough to come to John's mind, but they are not first on his list. Look at the statements on your list. Do you have your name or gender near the top? This is a common response. Do your priorities include relationships with a partner, your parents, siblings, or close friends?

The self-test you just took is not conclusive. If you were to take the TST in a religion class, you might find that religion would have higher saliency. If you were to take it with your boyfriend or girlfriend next to you, you might put that person's name near the top of your list. The TST is just one of several methods used to investigate the self-concept.

Various factors—self-concept, self-actualization, defense mechanisms, and the ability to communicate—all influence your relationships with others. An understanding of these factors won't keep your relationships problem-free, but it can help you to develop and maintain them. Although social scientists still have a lot to learn about human relationships, we do know that humans are both complex and unique. Therefore, what will work for one person or relationship may not work for another. All of us are a complex blend of heredity, the values of family and close friends, societal status and role prescriptions, and overall cultural values. (Remember the cultural value statements from Chapter 1?) In addition, each of us is unique because of our combination of these factors.

IMPORTANCE OF THE SELF-CONCEPT

WHAT IS THE SELF?

Before discussing self-concept any further, let us define it precisely. The *self-concept* is the sum of thoughts, feelings, and ideas that people have about themselves in reference to themselves as objects. By looking at himself or herself as an object, a person "can perceive, define, and evaluate other things" (Kotarba & Fontana, 1984, p. 25). The content of the self includes a person's social identity, dispositions, and physical characteristics.

If you look at John's TST, you will find that he lists several references to his social identity—"director," "member," "father." Sue also lists items describing her disposition—"talkative" and "fun person." They both mention physical characteristics—"redhead" and "diabetic." Does your TST include all three aspects of the self-concept? The content of your self-concept has a regulatory effect on your behavior. For instance, for Sue and John, certain behavior would not be consistent with their Methodist identity.

While the self-concept comprises what we think of ourselves, *self-esteem* is the positive or negative value we put on our self-concept. "While both [self-concept and self-esteem] include one's idea of self, esteem has a valuative component which is not included in self-concept measures" (Juhasz, 1985). Family experience, performance feedback, and social comparison are all sources of self-esteem (Michener, DeLamater, & Schwartz, 1986).

Notice that John did not say simply that he was a dancer but that he was a good dancer. It is important for our relationships with others and for our social maturation that we have a positive self-concept.

THE NEED TO KNOW WHO WE ARE

Every person needs an identity. The set of answers to the question "Who am I?" is one way to determine *your* identity (Vander-Zanden, 1984). A sense of identity serves as a social anchor. Imagine how lost you would feel if the phrases on your TST, which make up your identity, suddenly ceased to have meaning for you. To have amnesia and not know your name, your address, your occupation, your religion, your friends' names, and so on would be a major loss. It has been said that you can tell how important something is in your life by seeing if you can do without it.

Although an extreme loss of the self-concept such as that from amnesia is rare, other changes in our lives can make a change in our identity and our self-concept necessary. Research by Masuda and Holmes (1967) on social adjustment to stressful events shows that the three most stressful events for a married person all relate to marriage. These events include the death of a spouse, divorce, and separation. All these events remove from a person's life not only someone who has been important in establishing and maintaining that person's identity but also a basic set of relationships.

THE NEED FOR SOCIAL ANCHORS FOR THE SELF

In *The Transparent Self*, Jourard (1971) maintains that "life begins to lose meaning most rapidly when he [one] becomes estranged from his [one's] fellows" (p. ix). This statement fits research showing that people find it important to be part of a group. Indeed, most of us see the hermit as a sad and lonely figure. The importance of being anchored within the social group was demonstrated by the famous sociologist Emile Durkheim, who found that the suicide rate among people who were anchored or socially integrated within their communities was lower than that among people who did not have strong ties to others.

If you think about social anchors that help a person maintain a stable self-concept over a long period of time, you will find that the role of friend or spouse is a key one. This social anchor is important in many ways. For one thing, it provides important feedback about who we are from those who **are especially** close to us—our significant others.

THE NEED TO KNOW OURSELVES TO RELATE TO OTHERS

According to Samuel Johnson, "No man can completely know another, but by knowing himself, which is the utmost in human wisdom." Harry Stack Sullivan (1953) has also noted that, peculiarly, one can find in others only that which is already within oneself. George Mead (1934) contends that the self develops in the process of social interaction. These notable people are telling us that a vital interaction exists between the self and others. Further, to know and understand others, we must first understand ourselves; and to understand the emotions of others, we must first experience those emotions ourselves, making them a part of the self. Thus, to really love another, we must first like ourselves. Liking ourselves does not mean adoring ourselves in a vain, narcissistic way but rather feeling that "I'm O.K." and accepting ourselves.

If you have a strong sense of self or identity—if you feel comfortable about yourself—then you can be trusting and open in interpersonal relationships. The following example helps to show the importance of self-esteem in interpersonal relations:

Two 20-year-old women were both of about average height and both about thirty pounds overweight. Nan believed she had a weight problem and felt very negative about herself. Georgia knew she would be healthier if she lost some weight, but she generally felt good about herself. She dressed attractively, was good-natured, and was a knowledgeable conversationalist. While Nan rarely had a date, Georgia led an active social life. Why did Georgia relate so well to others? Part of the reason is that she had a good self-concept that allowed her to be outgoing and friendly rather than defensive.

DEVELOPMENT OF THE SOCIAL SELF

All of us seem to be willing to change humanity (i.e., others), but not ourselves.

There's an old Chinese proverb that says: "Lord, the world is so bad. Make it better—beginning with me."

There's only one corner of the universe you can be certain of improving, and that's your own self.

We have seen what the self-concept is; now let's ask how it develops. How do you change from an ego-centered infant, concerned only with being fed, dry, and comfortable, to an adult who is concerned about starving people on another continent or worried about preserving the environment for future generations? The self develops in dialogue, in social relationships—in short, in a social context.

STAGES OF SELF-DEVELOPMENT

George Herbert Mead (1934) says that the self develops in social interaction. He outlines three stages: a play stage, a game stage, and a stage of the generalized other. In the play stage, a child starts to develop a social conscience and begins to be able to take on the role of another. As children learn to do this, they begin to be able to imagine how the other might feel and to reflect on themselves. This reflexive character of the self allows one person to identify with another and is a first step toward *empathy*, which plays an important role in mature relationships. After the play stage, the child enters the game stage and learns to take the roles of many others. This role-playing activity expands the self-concept and prepares the child for adult interaction and adult games. In the third stage of self-development, the individual learns to relate to the community or group and to its values. Mead calls this the stage of the *generalized other*, in which the individual internalizes the community's values.

Mead also maintains that the regulation of behavior is accomplished by an internal conversation between one phase of the self, which he calls the *I*, and another, called the *me*. The "I" is the unique, individualistic, innovative part of the self while the "me" represents the societal values that have been accepted and internalized. For example, a while ago, there was a fad of "streaking" (running nude) across college campuses. The "I" might say, "That would be fun to do," while the "me" might say, "That might be fun, but I could lose my music scholarship if I got caught." The "I" might point out that you are a senior and will therefore probably graduate before the scholarship could be withdrawn. The "me" could counter that you would embarrass your mother if someone took your picture while you were streaking. Thus, the "I" speaks primarily for the individual's desires, while the "me" speaks for the societal values that the individual has internalized. Both aspects are important. The "I" makes us each unique and provides diversity in personal relationships. The "me" makes it possible for us to cooperate so we can live together in families, neighborhoods, and nations.

It is also important to understand that the self is never entirely complete; it is always changing. It has a core of identities that remain quite constant; other aspects of the self, however, change with time and place.

Let's look back at Sue, who took the TST. She may always be a Methodist, talkative, and a fun person. However, many of the aspects of herself that she considered important when she took the test—such as student, member of student government, partygoer, and others—may change as she matures. She may break up with Jim or marry him. Either change will alter her view of herself.

Understanding this changeability is very important for your future relationships because the selves that you and your partner have today will be different ten years from now. What now makes you two compatible may not do so later on. This helps explain why people who seemed so right for each other at marriage find themselves divorced several years later—they are no longer the same people (or selves)!

SELF WITHIN SOCIETY

According to Charles Horton Cooley (1902), we develop our self-concept by seeing ourselves as others see us. To Cooley, the reaction of other people is our social mirror or "looking glass." First, we imagine how we appear to the other person; second, we imagine how the other person judges our appearance; and third, as a result, we respond—by feeling proud or mortified.

When you create the self, you are importing society into yourself (Hewitt, 1984). First, before you act, you imagine others' responses to you. Second, you are restricted in your alternatives by what you perceive to be acceptable. Third, in judging yourself, you assume the roles of those around you. Fourth, you try to behave in a way that will preserve, protect, and defend your position in society. Fifth, you incorporate or adopt as your own the moral standards of society.

We are constantly guessing—sometimes incorrectly—how we appear to others, and these images help to shape us and our behavior. However, we do not make changes for just anyone—only for those who are *significant others*. A significant

Who am I? Where am I going? Where do I belong? What's likely to happen to me? How . . . ?

other (such as a teacher) may be significant in only some areas of our lives or in most areas (a spouse or parent, for example).

Students enter college after about eighteen years of socialization in the home and family. College is a time of testing the self-concept and of using peers as well as parents as social mirrors. It is a period of relative freedom from many adult controls and also a time to sort out the parts of the past to be kept, modified, or discarded and to find the way the lessons of the present and the past will be combined to prepare for the future. Thus, during the college years, people commonly test and change their self-concepts in preparation for the intimate relationships of the future. Remember, as we said earlier, the self is never complete but is always in a process of growth and change. Knowing this can help you to make adjustments as your relationships change.

FACTORS THAT INFLUENCE THE SELF

Having seen what the self is and how it develops, let's briefly examine three factors that influence our self-concepts: biology and heredity, status and role, and culture.

BIOLOGY AND HEREDITY

Some of us are tall, others short. Some of us are overweight, others underweight. We differ in mental and physical abilities. Many of these differences are due to heredity, and these factors affect our self-concepts.

The hereditary factors we possess make us unique. Only identical twins, who grow from the same single fertilized egg (zygote), have the same genetic structure; all others start with a different inheritance. We are not born fully human; we inherit many potential traits that can develop only in response to the environment. Therefore, social interaction is an important part of the self-development process.

With rare exceptions, biology has already begun to influence our sexual selves at birth. That is, there are already significant biological differences between the sexes in infancy. But overlapping in behavior is also extensive. Human adaptability is so great that both sexes are capable of exhibiting most forms of human behavior. There may be only a few behaviors that can be viewed as solely within the province of one sex. After all, as Doyle (1985) emphasizes, each of us has only one sex chromosome but more than forty make us human beings.

STATUS AND ROLE

Even though biology plays a part in our identities, the human environment is largely cultural, and cultural factors greatly influence human behavior (Hewitt, 1984). Within our culture, we all have status and roles. A *status* is a position in

I wonder what others think of me. How do they perceive me? Are they OK? Will they think I'm OK?

a social setting. We often hold several positions or statuses at the same time; for instance, you may be a student, employee, girlfriend, and roommate. Some statutes are *ascribed.* You may be black, or female, or a farmer's son. These positions are given to us at birth; we have no control over them, but they do affect our self-concepts. Some of our statuses are *achieved;* we earn the position of college graduate or spouse. If we are successful in the status we achieve, we usually have high self-esteem.

In turn, each status has a *role,* or a set of behavioral expectations. A student is expected to attend class, read books, and take tests. Therefore, in the role of a student, you are expected to engage in these activities. Some roles are very tightly defined, while others allow a great deal of flexibility. The role played by a military officer is well defined, while there is great flexibility in the way the parental role is played.

Roles also vary in importance.

> The ascribed statuses of female and male and their accompanying roles are to many people the most important social structures that each of us must contend with. These specific social structures literally give definition to each person's daily life. (Doyle, 1985, p. 87)

The *sex role* is seen as the core of one's identity and of importance to knowing one's total self. Recent concern with sex roles has emphasized their inhibiting effect on self-development and self-concept.

Females especially have been restricted by their ascribed status and sex roles. In the areas of economics and politics, sex roles may restrict opportunities to choose an occupation and to succeed in it. Most top positions in government and business are held by men. Although about half of the population is female, there has never been a woman president or vice president of the United States.

Socialization of females into typical girls' activities, as opposed to boys' activities, has an influence on the personality traits women are likely to adopt. The 1970s and 1980s have seen major changes in women's roles. Female college graduates are achieving a more equal place in the political and occupational world of work than was possible in the past. Relationships between women and men can be expected to change as women achieve greater equality in relationships with spouses or partners. The ability of both men and women to develop self-concepts strong enough to deal with changing individual and couple roles is important for the long-term maintenance of relationships.

CULTURE

"Who am I?" is clear in a society with distinct rites of passage and little social change. Much of the world, however, is now a mass society characterized by rapid social change ("future shock"). Many of us live in a society that stresses formal secondary relationships, a detailed contract instead of a handshake, and a desire to own and consume things. Mass society and communications from computer to computer can make life impersonal if we let it.

Mass society can have two basic influences on the self. First, because of the pervasive impersonality of this society, people can readily evade open relationships involving trust. Fear that others might take advantage of us if we reveal too much of ourselves can lead us to become guarded not only in business but also in intimate relationships.

Second, people tend to distrust the larger culture, seeking greater self-fulfillment and ego reinforcement within the family circle. In our society of nuclear families and couple-oriented marriages, the desire for self-affirmation from primary relationships can put a very heavy emotional load on the marriage and the family. It may well be that our high divorce rate is partly due to unrealistic expectations for self-fulfillment placed on the couple relationship.

We are unique individuals because the self is a product of both heredity and environment. We do not develop a self in isolation but only in interaction with other people. This development of self is also affected by our biological givens, such as being male or female; by the statutes we achieve as well as those ascribed to us; and by our overall culture, with its discontinuities, rapid change, and impersonality.

WALKING THE TIGHTROPE TO MATURITY

You are only young once, but you can stay immature indefinitely.
—THOMAS LaMANCE

Age alone does not determine a person's maturity. You may know some people who are quite mature, socially and emotionally, at age 16, and some who lack maturity at ages 26 or 56. An all-around maturity calls for effort, knowledge, and insight in developing the self and relating to others.

PRIMARY NEEDS AND SELF-ACTUALIZATION

If you don't know what you want, you can never go get it.

Consider the turtle—it doesn't make any progress unless it sticks its neck out.

I wondered why somebody didn't do something; then I realized that I was somebody. . . .

The famous Swiss psychologist Jean Piaget (1952) sees adaptation as the key to human development, while the Danish philosopher Kierkegaard (1941) suggests that we work toward becoming the self that we truly are. Abraham H. Maslow (1970) talks about the process of becoming a self-actualized person, maintaining that, as humans, we have certain basic needs that must be fulfilled before we can fully develop our potential. Maslow lists five such needs: (1) physiological needs (air, water, etc.); (2) safety needs (security, protection); (3) belongings and love needs; (4) esteem needs; and (5) self-actualization. The highest need is for self-actualization, "man's desire for self-fulfillment, namely, the tendency for him to become actualized in what he is potentially. . . . to become everything that one is capable of becoming" (p. 46). Maslow points out that we must achieve the lower-level needs before we can fulfill ourselves (become self-actualizing). Thus, before we can gain a favorable self-concept or self-esteem, we need to feel loved and to have a feeling of belonging. All should be able to climb the ladder of needs to self-actualization. However, some people get stuck on one level and never get off. For example, a business executive may use big profits as her sole source of self-esteem and quit at this level. A student may make getting on the honor roll an end in itself and not care if he actually learns the material.

We know that divorce rates are highest among the poor. We also know that those who achieve levels 3, 4, and 5 in Maslow's hierarchy should have strong self-concepts and be able to form intimate relationships. Could these two statements be related? It just might be that many of the poor have to be so concerned with the basic physiological and safety needs (levels 1 and 2) that they do not have the opportunity to develop the love, esteem, and self-actualization levels that Maslow has described. Jourard (1958) expresses a similar view. He suggests that the person with a healthy personality "can take himself more or less for granted and devote his energies and thoughts to socially meaningful interests and problems beyond security, or lovability, or status" (p. 21). While there are many factors involved in divorce, it is possible that that the kind of self one brings to a marriage may be one of these factors.

EMOTIONAL MATURITY AND THE NEED FOR BALANCE

*If you are not big enough to accept criticism, you are too small to
be praised.* —EDITH DURHAM

Try to see yourself as others see you, but don't let it make you mad.

The dictionary defines a mature individual as one who "is brought by natural means to a condition of full growth and development; fitted by growth and development for any function, action, or state appropriate to its kind; full-grown, ripe."

A peach may become mature or ripe, and it may become overmature or rotten. You can easily tell by biting into it. However, when we talk about humans, maturity is a goal that is only approximated. Maturity is a process, not a state of being. "Thus development is a lifelong process of becoming—a process that profoundly affects our thoughts, emotions, and behavior" (Coleman & Glaros, 1983, p. 81).

At what age should you be allowed to vote? To drink? To marry? To engage in certain adult behavior? In some societies there are rites of passage that clearly define maturity by allowing and expecting certain behavior of those who have gone through the rites, while those who have not are restricted. In a sense, passing a driving test is a rite of passage in the American teenage subculture. Being able to drive provides such advantages as more mobility, greater freedom, the chance to date, and prestige. But what about voting, drinking, and engaging in sexual relations with a consenting partner? At what age is one mature enough to do these things? Are there tests to take in these areas? By the definitions we have given, some people are relatively mature at age 16 while others remain immature at age 46.

During late adolescence, one should establish an independent identity in an adult manner. By college age, young adults should have a strong enough self-concept that they can accept themselves in an independent role and yet maintain relationships with their parents and significant others. In establishing an independent identity, young adults have two key decisions to make: what career, if any, to follow, and whom, if anyone, to marry. These decisions clearly identify one as being independent of the parental home and on the road to maturity. You can appreciate how important it is to enter either a career or a marriage with a strong self-concept.

In fulfilling the developmental tasks of young adulthood, it is essential to strike a balance between various factors (see Figure 3.1). Each person and each couple must work out for their situation and to their satisfaction what that balance should be. For instance, consider these balance decisions:

Set a high, challenging goal	or	Set a goal low enough so you won't become frustrated
Look out for yourself	or	Care for other people
Be dependable and solid	or	Be spontaneous and innovative
Cooperate with others	or	Compete with others
Maintain your principles	or	Be flexible so as to adapt to change

As a college student, you have more freedom—and more responsibilities—than you had in high school. For example, you no longer have study hall or parents to tell you when to study. Have you learned how to manage your time successfully? Time management is one of the key differences between those who accomplish much and those who accomplish little. If you look at the leaders in government, industry, and labor, you will find that they give enormous amounts of time to their jobs. If they do their jobs well and sustain successful intimate relationships, they have learned how to manage time. We maintain that time management is a sign of maturity, but there must be a balance between planned uses of time and the flexibility to alter a schedule when necessary.

Intimate relationships, such as marriage, present a paradox. On the one hand, intimate relationships offer the possibility of sharing and growing together in a mutually reinforcing condition where one can be free and open. On the other hand, even in marriage people need to have their space.

Thus, emotional maturity requires that we feel comfortable about ourselves, which, in turn, enables us to relate to others so they feel good about themselves. If we are successful in this, we will often find that others will reciprocate, and that makes us feel good. Mature individuals will develop the self in interaction with others, but they will also use some moments of privacy to contemplate who they are and where they are going. The mature person will learn from the past and prepare for the future but live in the present.

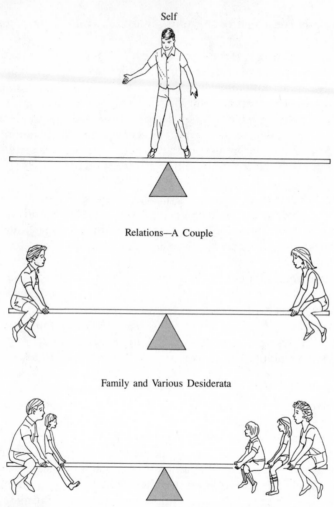

Self

Relations—A Couple

Family and Various Desiderata

FIGURE 3.1   LIFE IS LIKE A SEESAW: IT ALWAYS REQUIRES BALANCING.

DEFENSE MECHANISMS AND THE SELF

A defense mechanism is a distortion of reality that serves the purpose of protecting the self against anxiety or frustration. Used in moderation, defense mechanisms can be helpful. However, used excessively, they can cause problems both for the self and for relationships with others.

Since our self-concept is important to us, most of us tend to become defensive when our self-esteem is threatened. Sometimes, when people disagree with our behavior, they seem to be attacking us. Thus, if you have a disorderly room and your mother says, "You are messy," you may react defensively. If your mother says, "Your room is messy," you may not feel as threatened.

Psychologists and social psychologists have identified over two dozen defense mechanisms. We all use them occasionally. Let us illustrate a few. *Rationalization* is a common defense whereby we explain away our mistakes or inadequacies in a false but apparently reasonable manner. For instance, you may say you failed a test because the instructor is biased against people of your race, sex, or ethnic group. Even if the instructor actually is biased, that may not be the reason you failed the exam. However, it is easier on your self-concept to blame the instructor rather than yourself for the failure. Some teachers may rationalize their poor teaching by saying that their students are not very able or not really trying.

We can protect ourselves by *filtering* what is allowed into awareness. Filtering can be done on both a conscious and an unconscious level. A person may choose to interact only with those who flatter her and tell her what she wants to hear, whether it is true or not. Unfortunately, in choosing significant others primarily because they accept or cater to her, this person risks being cut off from new ideas and new opportunities for change and challenge. Another way you can protect yourself by filtering is by selective perception. A person who is deeply in love may notice all the positive characteristics of the partner and block out all the bad habits, attitudes, and other negative characteristics. One can also take neutral or ambiguous information and interpret it in a positive way so as to maintain self-esteem. This kind of self-delusion can greatly hamper self-analysis and growth.

In *displacement,* we vent our anger about our own failure on someone or something else. If you fail to keep the car properly tuned and then find it won't start, you may kick it and blame the manufacturer for producing a poor product. This displacement can be more troublesome in interpersonal relations, as when you blame your spouse for "buying the damn car in the first place."

In *compensation,* we make up for an inadequacy in one area by being exceptional in another area. Thus, if a husband has difficulty expressing his feelings to his wife, he may offer her gifts instead—for example, by constantly making things for her in his shop. By giving her handcrafted bookcases, stereo speaker cabinets, or whatever, he shows love—and he may also win praise for his craftsmanship. The problem, of course, is that he has not tried to improve his ability to express himself in words.

Finally, there is *fantasy*—mental activity that focuses on the false or imaginary. For example, a person may become a superb lover in fantasy. The danger here is that he or she will try to deal with problems only in the imaginary world and not in the real one. On the other hand, a certain amount of fantasy is beneficial, for it allows people to explore safely in dreams or imagination what they might later try in real life.

If defense mechanisms become a person's only or habitual way of dealing with problems, they can be very destructive. On the other hand, the reason everyone uses them is that they provide short-term satisfaction. The important thing to remember is that when defense mechanisms prevent someone from coming to grips with a problem, they themselves can become a major problem to that person and to his or her relationships.

DEALING WITH DEPRESSION, GUILT, AND REJECTION

If you insist on being blue, make it a light blue.

Even if a pessimist is proved right in the end, an optimist will have a lot more fun on the trip.

The best way to cheer yourself is to try to cheer somebody else up.
—MARK TWAIN

Nothing can bring you peace but yourself.
—RALPH WALDO EMERSON

None of us is perfect, and therefore we sometimes make errors, feel guilt or rejection, and become depressed. Dealing with these problems is ironically both very simple and very complex. As with physical illness, for long-lasting or serious problems, you should seek professional help. This help might be found at a student counseling center, a local mental health association, or a local family service agency. In some cases, depression may be due to a physical problem. You should check to see that a real or imagined health problem is not becoming an emotional crutch that restricts you and your ability to relate to others.

How do you perceive your ongoing communication with others? What can you do to improve your relationships?

In general, we should attack depression in the same manner we attack other problems: find the cause and try to cure it. This action may require a good dose of honest self-appraisal. Are we using defense mechanisms because of rejection or guilt? Are we using alcohol or drugs as an escape? Are we feeling sorry for ourselves in an attempt to gain attention?

There are several simple ways to deal with depression. First, don't just sit there, do something! Activity—whether it is playing cards or tennis, working in the garden or the shop—can help get your mind off your minor problems and make you feel good about what you accomplish. Choose an activity that requires concentration; you will know if you lose too many hands of cards or if too many tennis balls go past you. Jogging allows us to think and have privacy, so—while it is useful in other respects—it is not as helpful for depression.

Be willing to realize that nobody, not even you, is perfect. This really sounds simple-minded. Of course, we know that no one is perfect. However, as counselors and therapists know only too well, there is a difference between what we know on an intellectual level and what we accept on an emotional level. Often a feeling of rejection or failure, especially in intimate relations, is due to our having unrealistic or unattainable goals. Without using this as an excuse for mediocrity, setting realistic goals, and then working to achieve them, can save us from guilt, rejection, and depression.

Acting happy can also help. If we interact with others in an upbeat manner, they are likely to reciprocate similarly. Research has shown that behavior often shapes and alters attitudes and feelings; thus, acting happy can make us feel happier.

In dealing with rejection, it is important to find out what is being rejected. Is it your total self, or is it some of your ideas and behaviors? Many times people are not rejecting us but only a specific attitude or behavior.

In conclusion, many problems can be resolved by being active, setting realistic goals, and thinking positively. As mature people, we must learn to deal with criticism, guilt, rejection, and depression. If you find you cannot handle your emotional problems with these simple techniques, however, seek professional help. A counselor or therapist may be able to help you sort through your feelings.

THE SELF IN RELATIONSHIPS: THE WHEEL THEORY

Worry is like a rocking chair; it gives you something to do, but doesn't get you anywhere.

No one has the power to make you feel inferior unless you consent.

How do you interact with others? In other words, how much of yourself do you—or should you—reveal in interaction with others? It is clear that we reveal more of our real selves in an intimate relationship, such as marriage, than in a secondary relationship, such as dealing with the cashier at the campus bookstore. A model of the basic process of developing primary social relationships, the wheel theory, has been developed by Reiss (1980). According to this model, the development of intimate relationships occurs in four stages: (1) rapport, (2) self-revelation, (3) mutual dependency, and (4) intimacy need fulfillment.

When we see someone we want to get to know, we arrange to meet that person and try to develop *rapport*—a harmonious relationship, a feeling of mutual ease, and mutual confidence. Although any two people can develop rapport, it arises more easily between people who can readily communicate with one another. Generally, this communication is helped by a sense of similarity between the people and by strong self-concepts.

Next, we move to the *self-revelation* or self-disclosure stage. The self that we have developed, and sometimes worked hard to protect, now opens up to another person. You notice that a person does not usually reveal his or her true self to others until rapport has been established. In initial interaction, people tend to put their best foot forward. Later, after they feel comfortable, they reveal more of their true selves. As Brehm (1985) explains:

> One way to view self-disclosure is as an interconnected, reciprocal process: you tell me something about yourself, and I'll tell you something about me. Indeed, there is considerable evidence that self-disclosure often is reciprocal. People who are told highly intimate things by another person tend to respond by telling highly intimate things about themselves.

In a study of undergraduate students, Hatch and Leighton (1986) found that women disclosed more about themselves and revealed more of their strengths than did men. Both men and women tended to reveal more to a same-sex friend than to anyone else. Some of you have had a close roommate or friend since entering college. Think back to how you reacted to that person in the first few encounters. Do you react differently to him or her now?

Immediate reciprocal self-disclosure may be crucial when we are trying to get close to someone; it helps a relationship grow. In an established relationship, where trust has been developed, empathy and expressions of support may replace self-disclosure. However, we must not be trapped into shielding ourselves from others when we want to develop primary or intimate relationships. Reciprocal self-disclosure, along with giving and receiving empathy and support, are key elements in establishing true intimacy.

The third spoke in the wheel model is *mutual dependency*. Reiss maintains that we build habits of interdependency with the people who make us feel comfortable. Consider your roommate again. Have you developed the habit of depending on him or her? Some students have learned to depend on their roommates to serve as alarm clocks. "Make sure I get up tomorrow morning because I have a test in my 8 o'clock." Sometimes a person may become too dependent on a partner, so that there is not enough space for independence and personal growth. Thus, as we noted earlier, a balance between independence and dependence must be maintained.

The final stage in the wheel model is called *intimacy need fulfillment.* Here, the person with whom you feel comfortable, and whom you trust and depend on, fulfills your basic emotional needs. In intimate relationships, these needs would include someone to confide in, to love, to love you in return, to share sexual relations with, and to give you basic emotional support.

IMPROVING RELATIONSHIPS

When people are wrapped up in themselves, they make pretty small packages.

Bores are people who talk about themselves when you want to talk about yourself.

Always remember there are two types of people in this world; those who come into a room and say, "Well, here I am!" and those who come in and say, "Ah, there you are!"

The self can never reach its full potential outside of relationships with others. Therefore, we need to develop goals not only for ourselves, but also for our relationships. Psychologists call the process of complimenting others "stroking"; they note that we all want positive strokes. In productive relationships, there is reciprocal stroking, and all involved feel better about themselves.

WHAT IS INVOLVED?

Regardless of what we want from relationships, we eventually need to communicate our needs to others. In his book *Becoming Partners* (1972), Carl Rogers contends that to achieve permanence and enrichment in a relationship, "we each commit ourselves to working together on the changing process of our present relationship, because that relationship is currently enriching our love and our life and we wish it to grow" (p. 201). The key words in this quote are "working" and "together." Whether the relationship is with someone you love or with someone you must deal with on the job, changing and improving relationships requires work and cooperation. If only one partner voluntarily commits to improving the relationship, chances are it cannot be done. The person who is not interested will either not work hard enough or will sabotage the other's efforts.

In trying to improve relationships, it is important that you do not dump your problems on your partner. As we have mentioned in discussing the self, you must first be happy with yourself, then you can relate to others. For example, if two lonely people marry, they cannot expect their marriage to cure their loneliness. If the individuals don't change, even though they are together physically, they will still be two lonely people in a lonely relationship.

Rogers (1972) has provided guidelines for successful relationships. We should (1) focus on the nature of our commitment—on what is happening between us rather than on the "oughts" we have learned; (2) try to keep in touch with our inner self; (3) develop "role transcendence," which involves overcoming the societal role prescriptions in order to create roles acceptable to us; and (4) keep the channels of communication open.

COMMUNICATION

Communication can certainly improve relationships and provide the feedback necessary for growth. Communication, usually defined as any transfer of information from one person to another, is important because it is impossible for us not to communicate. Even the child or lover who refuses to talk is communicating. As long as someone is there to receive the message, communication exists. Both verbal and nonverbal behavior are important components of communication.

Verbal Communication   A phone call or a personal conversation is what we usually think of when we hear the word "communication." Written communication has an instant-replay quality, which may improve its accuracy. If you write a letter, you have time to proofread, edit, and reconsider what you have written; the recipient can reread it several times to make sure he or she understands. However, in verbal communication, it is more difficult to think on your feet and edit your thoughts before they become words. Therefore, none of us is perfect, and we can all easily say something the wrong way, say something that is misinterpreted, or simply say something we should not. To improve communication, we should learn to express exactly what we mean; also, we should monitor others' reactions to what we say to see if the message we send is the message someone else receives. We should also clarify or restate the comments of others to be sure we understand what they meant. Someone has summarized these difficulties by noting that: "I know you believe that you understand what you think I said but I'm not sure you realize that what you heard is not what I meant."

As we develop more rapport with others, we naturally improve our communication techniques. We should also learn when not to use verbal communication. Sometimes a friend or spouse simply wants to be listened to, to be held, or just not to be alone as he or she works out a problem. Thus, you both can be in the same room or on the same couch and still have privacy if your partner understands that your "Do Not Disturb" sign is up. As an example, there is the story of the farmer who would roll up one pant leg if he did not want to be disturbed. If he came to the door with both pant legs in the normal position, his wife would talk to him. If one was rolled up, she would leave him alone.

We must also remember that while self-disclosure is necessary for a complete relationship, one does not have to tell one's entire life history to a new partner. There are times when disclosure is needed and appropriate, and there are times when the partner is not ready for self-disclosure and heavy conversation. Bienvenu (1970) found, from a marital communication inventory, that the factor which best discriminated between happy and unhappy couples was "Does your spouse have a tendency to say things which would be better left unsaid?" Those who answered yes were more likely to be unhappy than those who answered no. Again, we see the need to achieve that delicate balance between too much and too little communication. The answer, of course, is to say what needs to be said and not to say what does not need to be said. Unfortunately, it is difficult to distinguish between the two.

"Most verbal behavior has both a *content* (or informational) component and an *affective* (or emotional) one" (Hendrick & Hendrick, 1983, p. 197), and men, especially, have trouble with the latter. In many cases it is not that people are unwilling to interact or afraid of verbal interaction, they are simply inept. It is not always easy to match both components.

Nonverbal Communication Communication that does not depend on words is important; it includes posture, gestures, facial expressions, inflection and tone of voice, and other actions. A gift of a single red rose, for example, says a great deal. So does clenching your teeth and turning your head.

As message senders and receivers, we need to be aware of our nonverbal as well as our verbal messages (Brehm, 1985). You may say that you would like to go to a movie with your partner, but your tone of voice and the way you drag yourself around may indicate otherwise. Little children might thank Grandmother for the new shirt and socks, but their facial expressions may reveal the feeling that "I'd rather have a new toy."

The fact that we cannot *not* communicate is especially true regarding body language. In fact, body language probably communicates emotions more forcefully than verbal language. We constantly send nonverbal messages, and sometimes we don't realize the messages our posture, style of dress, facial expressions, and so on are sending. Others act on the basis of these nonverbal messages, which can cause us problems if others perceive messages we don't realize we are sending. Uplifted eyebrows, a smile, a shrug of the shoulders, and general posture all serve as signals to others of what we are feeling. The famous sociologist W. I. Thomas has said that if a situation is defined as real, it is real in its consequences. Thus, whether or not we intend to send a certain message, others will react to what they perceive our message to be.

It may be that those in other cultures are more aware of body language than we are in the United States. It is certainly true that other cultures have more physical contact, such as kissing and hugging. According to a study by Jourard and Rubin (1968), the average Paris couple came into physical contact 110 times an hour while conversing. Couples in San Juan, Puerto Rico, caressed, tickled, and touched 180 times during the same time span. However, couples in America touched only once or twice and London couples never touched at all. Which of these couples are most like you?

Active Listening   One way to get the proper feedback to improve communication is to listen attentively. Imagine that a wife is balancing the bank statement. Her husband returns from the market with an expensive steak. The wife says, "We have to do something about our spending." The husband replies, "Why blame me? You're the one who likes rib-eye steak." Here, the wife has made a global statement about finances without any explanation. The husband feels threatened and becomes defensive. By being specific, the wife could have better communicated her thoughts about their budget. In turn, by listening actively, the husband could have moved the conversation along in a meaningful way. He might have said, "Why don't we sit down after supper and talk about our budget?" He would then be giving himself a chance to see if his wife was really upset about the steak or was making a general statement about their finances. By specifying a time and method to finish the conversation he would allow them to discuss the situation calmly, without feeling threatened.

Improving Communication   Better communication means better relationships. However, we must not assume that improved communication is in itself a cure-all for relationship problems. Unfortunately, there are a number of things which are destructive to good communication in intimate relationships. First, social or background variables may serve as barriers to communication (Bernard, 1972). These variables include age differences, differences in experience, and socioeconomic factors such as social class, education, and religion. Cultural stereotypes and societal norms may also increase communication difficulties. For example, blue-collar workers may be intimidated by professionals and not be able to express themselves. A group of nurses using a lot of medical jargon in a conversation might unconsciously exclude a friend who works in an office.

Second, numerous individual differences and preferences in communication styles confuse conversations. One important style that leads to improved communication is "I" language, or speaking for the self. "I" language means that people communicate not only their views but also their feelings, and that they do so as directly and honestly as possible. With "I" language, one takes ownership of and responsibility for one's thoughts and feelings.

Taking full responsibility for one's feelings has been emphasized by many authors. Grando and Ginsberg (1976) say, "An example of not taking responsibility for one's feeling is 'You're no good. And you don't care how you make me feel.' While an example of owning one's feelings is 'I'm very hurt by what you did, and I'm so angry that I want to hurt you too' " (p. 467). Can you see the difference in sound and in emotional response between these two examples?

Good communication in intimate relationships has been found to be associated with deliberate and frequent efforts to converse. Factors that improve the effectiveness of communication include the way anger is handled in disagreements,

---

BOX 3.1   A CREDO FOR RELATIONSHIPS

You and I are in a relationship which I value and want to keep. Yet each of us is a separate person with unique needs and the right to try to meet those needs. I will try to be genuinely accepting of your behavior when you are trying to meet your needs and when you are having problems meeting your needs.

When you share your problems, I will try to listen acceptingly and understandingly in a way that will facilitate your finding your own solutions rather than depending upon mine. When you have a problem because my behavior is interfering with your meeting your needs, I encourage you to tell me openly and honestly how you are feeling. At those times, I will listen and then try to modify my behavior.

However, when your behavior interferes with my meeting my own needs, thus causing me to feel unaccepting of you, I will tell you as openly and honestly as I can exactly how I am feeling, trusting that you respect my needs enough to listen and then to try to modify your behavior.

At those times when we cannot modify our behavior to meet the needs of the other, thus finding that we have a conflict of needs in our relationship, let us commit ourselves to resolve each such conflict without ever resorting to the use of either my power or yours to win at the expense of the other losing. I respect your needs, but I must also respect my own. Consequently let us strive always to search for a solution to our inevitable conflicts that will be acceptable to both of us. In this way, your needs will be met, but so will mine—no one will lose, both will win.

As a result, you can continue to develop as a person through meeting your needs, but so can I. Our relationship can always be a healthy one because it will be mutually satisfying. Thus, we can each become what we are capable of being. We can continue to relate to each other in mutual respect and love, in friendship and in peace.

SOURCE: Adapted from Gordon, 1970.

---

the tone of voice used in discussion, attempts to understand the other, and good listening habits. Nagging, conversational discourtesies, and uncommunicativeness are factors that contribute to poor communication (Bienvenu, 1970). In attempting to improve a relationship, you will find it useful to start with some issues of immediate concern. Make sure you are specific enough to stay on the topic; avoid making global statements about the other person or resorting to ego attacks. Just because something in the self or in the relationship is in need of change does not mean that the whole person or relationship has to be discarded for something new or different. End each communication session on a positive note. Discuss each other's strengths and the potential for continued growth and development. If something does not work out right, no one individual is to blame, since both partners are responsible for the accuracy of the messages exchanged.

These are only a few points in the complicated process of interpersonal communication. Learning to communicate is a lifelong process and should not be oversimplified. Perhaps it is remarkable that communication works at all, considering the many obstacles. Its importance for intimate relationships, however, cannot be overemphasized. In his book *Personal Adjustments*, Jourard (1958) delineates the characteristics of a healthy relationship. The participants know each other as distinct individuals, like more traits in each other than they dislike, feel concern for one another's happiness and growth, impose reasonable demands on each other, and can communicate effectively, making themselves known and understood. Communication is necessary to initiate and maintain any relationship, and good communication is crucial for a healthy and satisfying intimate relationship.

SUMMARY

- You must have a good understanding of yourself before you can have mature relationships with others.

- The self-concept is the sum of thoughts, feelings, and ideas that we have about ourselves.

- Every person tries to form an identity, and loss of identity leads to anxiety.

- The most stressful events for married people have been found to be related to their marriage.

- Humans find it important to be part of group life. Our significant others are a key in maintaining a stable self-concept.

- The social self is shaped through several stages as we develop communication and interaction skills. This never-ending process is influenced by the social mirror of others, especially our significant others.

- Three basic factors influence the self and its development: biology and heredity; status and roles; and culture.

- Sex role is of crucial importance in self-development and self-concept.

- The concept of self-actualization involves the human desire for personal fulfillment—the need to become everything that one is capable of being.

- In growing toward emotional maturity, there is a need for a balance between individual and social components. We need intimate relationships as well as some privacy and personal space.

- The use of various psychological defense mechanisms to protect the self is helpful, but their excessive use can hinder real growth.

- Emotionally mature people have enough self-esteem to handle occasional depression and rejection.

- The wheel theory illustrates the formation of relationships starting with establishing rapport and moving toward self-revelation, mutual dependency, and eventual intimacy and need fulfillment.

- To improve their relationships, people need to work together.

- Good verbal and nonverbal communication are important in maintaining and improving relationships.

- Improving communication is a key to improving relationships, although communication is in itself not a cure-all for relationship problems.

PERSPECTIVE: THE "OLD" AND THE "NEW" GOLDEN RULE

The Golden Rule with which you are familiar says, "Do unto others as you would have them do unto you." Good thought, right? Then why is a new Golden Rule being proposed? Well, read the new one carefully: *"Do unto others as they would like to have done unto them."*

What is the difference between these two? Note that in the original version you were imposing your desires, preferences, and values on the other. Is treating others as you want to be treated the same as treating them the way they want to be treated?

The famous German poet Goethe once stated, "Treat people as if they were what they ought to be and you help them to become what they are capable of being." At first, this seems like a fine suggestion—to hold others to high standards. But who decides what people ought to be? Do you decide that your child or spouse should be a doctor or a home economist or a sociologist, or do you let him or her decide? If you have true empathy for a partner, or if you and he have communicated about what he wants to be and is capable of being, then you can try to aid him to reach that goal.

It has been said that true love is primarily giving, not receiving. Our love for the other should not be like a garage sale where we sell what is of little use to us. Rather, it is important to communicate and to find out what the other wants. To give to the other person what he or she desires calls for empathy on our part. Thus, the corollary to the new Golden Rule regarding love is to give what is of value to the receiver and not necessarily what you think the receiver should value.

Writing about sex, Penney (1985) states, "The precondition for great sex is certainly equality but, paradoxically, the underlying sexual principle to be learned is the opposite of the Golden Rule: *DON'T do* unto each other as you would have him/her do unto you" (p. 38). Although Penney was speaking specifically about sex, you may find her words applicable in many other areas of your life. Perhaps the idea presented in the new Golden Rule will offer some perspective on the improvement of your own relationships.

QUESTIONS FOR THOUGHT AND DISCUSSION

1. When you did the TST, did it reveal anything about yourself that surprised you? How would it be different if you did it five years ago? How about five years from now? Why is your self-concept important in maintaining relationships with others? How does self-esteem affect these relationships?

2. How does having a positive self-concept or high self-worth affect your relationships with others? Think about your own interactions. Are they different at those times when you feel good about yourself as opposed to times when your self-image is less positive? Try to explain any differences that you note.

3. What are the "I" and the "me," and how do they affect the decision-making process? Which part of the self do you feel should have more input in making decisions? Which part has more influence on you? Why?

4. What are some of the effects of our mass society on the individual and on marriage and the family? Do you feel any of these forces in your life? How can people best deal with these changes?

5. What is self-actualization as Maslow describes it? Why does he say that we must meet other needs before we can satisfy our need for self-actualization? Do you feel that you have reached self-actualization? Using the information provided in this chapter, explain why you feel you have or have not reached self-actualization?

6. What are defense mechanisms? Under what conditions are they used positively or negatively? How often do you use them? What are some types of defense mechanisms and how is each used?

7. What are some ways to deal with depression? If you envision trying one next time you are feeling depressed, which one do you think would work best for your personality and life-style?

8. What are the four stages of Reiss's wheel theory? Is it legitimate in your opinion? How does each stage bring us closer to the other person and to intimacy? What are some differences between males and females in these stages?

9. We all want to improve our relationships. The chapter states that improving communication is a key to improving relationships. Think of an example

when social or background variables might serve as barriers to communication.

10. Speaking for the self and being responsible for one's own feelings is a way to improve communication. Make a statement in "I" language, then change it to an example of not "owning" one's feeling.

11. What is your favorite part of "A Credo for Relationships"? Why?

12. How does the new Golden Rule coincide with the information in the chapter about understanding ourselves and others?

Love

Have you ever felt that you were in love? How did you know? Was it because you experienced shortness of breath, a palpitating heart, sweaty palms, or a ringing sensation in your ears when you were with the right person? Or did you find love a little more rational and comfortable? Few people, even those who have studied love, can agree on a proper definition of it. Yet many people believe they have been in love and believe love should be the main reason for marrying. The late Abraham Stone, an eminent marriage counselor, said that most people, even those who are happily married, don't know what love is. "So many husbands are like the man who said he 'loves oranges.' If an orange could answer back, it would say, 'What do you mean you love me? All you really want to do is squeeze me, take the best out of me, and then throw me away!' "

What Love Is and Is Not

Love is like lightning—you may not know what it is, but you do know when it hits you! When Tevye, in *Fiddler on the Roof,* suddenly wants to know if his wife of 25 years loves him and finds that she does, he realizes that the words may not mean as much as their past experiences, yet he says, "It's nice to know." Perhaps it is more important to experience love than to define it. Nevertheless, the study of love and its variants can lead to a better understanding of love and problems in loving.

Definitions and Descriptions

The word "love" is often used instead of "like" or "enjoy." "I love to play tennis." "He loves cherry pie." Love is often confused with sexual or emotional desire. "I love you" may mean "I desire you physically." "Love" is also used to convey pride in or admiration of someone or something, such as "I love my country." Because of our confused actions concerning love and the limitations of our language (which has only one word for love), the definition of love can vary a great deal. Anyone could write a definition of love and find someone to agree with it.

Even when you narrow "love" to mean deep emotional feelings for another person, the definition varies. The Greeks, for instance, distinguished three basic types of love: (1) *eros*, or physical love; (2) *agape*, or spiritual love; and (3) *philos*, or brotherly love. You know from experience that the love you felt for a junior high teacher or a rock star is different from that which you felt the first time you went steady. Your love for your parents is not the same as that for your spouse or children.

There is even a doubt as to whether scientists should try to define and study love. When sociologist Nelson Foote (1953) published a short paper entitled "Love," most of the comments from other scholars were cynical, joking, or sentimental. Few took him seriously. Some scientists are concerned about value judgments tending to bias research on love. Morton Hunt (1959) says, "Most of the learned people who write about love seem to equip themselves in advance with a special theory; with this as a kind of butterfly net, they then sally forth and attempt to capture cases to prove or exemplify their point" (p. 8).

Other scholars are simply wary of research in such a basic and personal area as love. A panelist at an American Psychological Association symposium several years ago declared: "The scientist, in even attempting to interject love into a laboratory situation, is by the very nature of the proposition dehumanizing the state we call love" (Rubin, 1982, p. 34). By contrast, Masters and Johnson have been criticized for being too mechanical in their research and ignoring love. However, many others support research in the area of human love. Perhaps the eminent scholar Abraham H. Maslow, said it best: "We *must* study love; we must be able to teach it, to understand it, to predict it, or else the world is lost to hostility and to suspicion" (Rubin, 1982, p. 34).

So what is love? Freud saw love as "aim-inhibited sex." Waller (1938) also felt that "the idealization of romantic love is founded upon a temporary blocking or frustration of sexual impulses" (p. 123).

Many researchers now believe that love is a relationship of exchange in which the lovers help to fulfill each other's needs. In the love relationship, people exchange affection and seek to help each other to the point at which, according to some writers, the needs of the other become as important as the lover's own needs, and satisfying those needs gives the lover great satisfaction. The emotions experienced in fulfilling each other's needs are intense and help strengthen the attachment. Lederer and Jackson (1981) quote the late psychiatrist Harry Stack Sullivan as having said, "When the satisfaction or the security of another person becomes as significant as is one's own satisfaction or security, then the state of love exists" (p. 55).

Jorgensen (1986) reports that 1300 undergraduate students were asked to list "essential ingredients of love as a basis for marriage." They listed 21 different ingredients. Although "caring and concern for the other" was listed by 40 percent, "no single item was mentioned by at least one-half (50 percent) of those responding" (p. 65). Apparently young people who date don't agree on a definition of love any more than scientists do.

TYPES OF LOVE

Love between a woman and a man falls into three basic categories: infatuation, romantic love, and mature love. It will also become quite obvious that there is considerable overlap among these categories.

Infatuation   Have you ever been infatuated with someone—maybe a TV personality, a campus celebrity, a political or sports figure? Infatuation is characterized by an unrealistic idealization of the loved one and is quite common among teenagers and preteens. It usually begins with physical attraction. One teen described love as "a sort of hot, choking sensation you feel when you see or think about a certain person—usually someone very good-looking." You may not know anything about the person. Maybe you have never even met.

Interestingly, people often see their past relationships as infatuations and their current one as love. "Notice that whenever individuals speak of their infatuations, it is nearly always in the past tense. . . . What apparently happens is that when love affairs terminate, especially those of relatively short duration, they tend to become viewed in retrospect as infatuations" (Kephart, 1981, p. 262). One reason

The young can always find a time and place for expressing or "impressing" their love symbols.

for describing a past love as merely an infatuation may be to rationalize that a current love is the only genuine love the person has ever experienced. This is particularly true if the current relationship is serious or leading to marriage.

In class discussions, students have asserted that they were in love in high school. Now, however, they are glad that those relationships have ended, even though breaking up was painful. They also say that their high school relationships were not really love, even though they perceived them as such at the time. Students generally believe that the experience of love has made them happier.

Romantic Love   Romance means adventure or excitement. Rubin (1973) found romantic love to consist of three things: (1) affiliation and a need for the loved one; (2) a predisposition to help the lover; and (3) absorption in the relationship to the exclusion of others. Other components of romantic love which Kephart (1981) found include a strong emotional attachment to someone of the other sex, a tendency to idealize this person, and a marked physical attraction which is fulfilled through touch. Unfortunately, if lovers idealize one another, they are unlikely to develop a realistic view of their situation. Later, as they learn to know each other better, they may become disillusioned with their relationship.

Davis (1985) identifies two categories unique to love: (1) the passion cluster, which includes fascination, exclusiveness, and sexual desire; and (2) the caring cluster, which includes giving the utmost and being a champion advocate for the partner.

Mature Love   While infatuation and/or romantic love may be described as "falling for" someone, mature love is "standing with" someone. Stability is an important element of mature love. "Companionate love," as Brehm (1985) calls it, "rests on a more certain, less fragile attachment to the partner: respect, admiration, and trust are all major aspects" (p. 93). Others have found similar elements to be basic to mature love: a mutual sense of personal worth and respect, empathy, care, and commitment. Mature love is evolutionary and takes time to develop, since it is a trustful love, one that seeks the welfare of the loved one. Mature love is a reasoned, reasonable, and pleasant way of life, with the relationship reaching a basic plane on which it rests except for occasional highs and lows.

Mature lovers are actively concerned about one another's well-being; they are responsive to each other's needs, respect the individuality of the other, and know the other well enough to sense problems or needs before they are mentioned. Mature love tends to be more selfless and to involve a relationship of giving. In romantic love or infatuation, on the other hand, the lover may chiefly seek to gain something—attention, admiration, and so on—from the partner. Mature love is not possessive. "I love you" does not mean "I want to possess you" or "I desire you." Instead, the lovers try to help each other and their relationship to grow, not to exploit each other.

Yet, as Forisha (1978) points out, "In most marriages love, as a vital, caring feeling, diminishes over time" (p. 207). Part of the change in feeling may simply mark the transition from romantic love to mature love. In fact, Forisha notes that a failure to go beyond romantic love to a more mature love is a major factor in marital failure. Many couples find that the excitement of frenzied romantic love turns into a relationship of affection and companionship. The lovers become friends who rely on each other for emotional support, intimacy, sexual fulfillment, and more. While mature love may not burn as hot or as bright as the flame of infatuation or romantic love, it burns more steadily and for a longer period of time. "The fundamental problem we all face in living satisfying lives is to achieve a balance between the two types of loving. Passionate love is excitement and adventure. . . . Companionate love thrives on a sense of security and well-being" (Schulz & Rodgers, 1985, pp. 128–129).

> *How do I love thee? Let me count the ways.*
> *I love thee to the depth and breadth and height*
> *My soul can reach, when feeling out of sight*
> *For the ends of Being and ideal Grace.*
> *I love thee to the level of every day's*
> *Most quiet need, by sun and candlelight.*
> *I love thee freely, as men strive for Right;*
> *I love thee purely, as they turn from Praise.*
> *I love thee with a love I seemed to lose*
> *With my lost saints,—I love thee with the breath,*
> *Smiles, tears, of all my life!—and, if God choose,*
> *I shall but love thee better after death.*
>
> —Elizabeth Barrett Browning

TYPES OF LOVERS

Just as there are several different types of love, there are also different types of lovers. In an extensive questionnaire study, Lee (1977) identified six basic types of lovers: erotic, ludic, storgic, manic, agapic, and pragmatic.

1. *Erotic.* The erotic lover is the romantic who searches for an ideal mate and believes that there can be only one true love for him or her. This type of lover falls in love and identifies closely with the loved one, wanting to know all about that person. The erotic lover remembers birthdays and anniversaries and the likes and dislikes of the loved one. Sexual involvement usually comes early. Once in love, the erotic lover is usually monogamous, although sometimes taking part in a series of exclusive erotic relationships. When erotic lovers break up, they do not do so gently.

2. *Ludic.* The ludic lover is playful and enjoys taking part in several relationships at once, desiring little dependency or commitment from the partner or partners. In fact, any indication of dependency can drive the ludic lover away. The ludic lover generally has a good self-concept and enjoys being around secure individuals. Since the ludic lover enjoys variety without commitment, this type of lover never reveals many personal feelings and prefers partners who also refrain from deep intimacy. Love with the ludic lover is usually fun while it lasts.

3. *Storgic.* Storgic lovers are usually affectionate companions who realize gradually that they are in love. They believe in the permanence of the relationship and treat their lovers as irreplaceable friends. Storgic lovers know each other well and prefer to discuss everything together. They rely on the security of the relationship, trust one another, and do not seek other lovers. Sex comes late to storgic lovers, but they appreciate it when it does finally occur. If their relationship should end, storgic lovers would probably continue to be friends.

4. *Manic.* Manic lovers are generally highly dependent and extremely jealous. They often become so obsessed with the loved one that they cannot sleep or work. The manic lover experiences great depths and peaks in love and resists separation from the loved one. Usually manic lovers have poor self-concepts and low self-esteem, which make them unattractive to others and very dependent on the relationship. When the relationship ends, the manic lover cannot stop wondering what went wrong.

5. *Agapic.* The agapic lover is the least possessive and the most forgiving of all the six types. Extremely patient and easy to get along with, the agapic lover will accept almost any behavior in the loved one. Agapic lovers do not fall in love but always make their love available to the extent that the loved one needs or desires it. Some researchers believe that the agapic lover in the extreme may be a masochist, always supportive of the loved one no matter what. When relationships end, agapic lovers are generally willing to allow their lovers to leave for their own good.

6. *Pragmatic.* Pragmatic lovers are practical people who approach the search for love like a search for the best car value. The pragmatic lover totals up the assets of the loved one, even examining potential in-laws, and attempts to make the best bargain available. Pragmatic lovers never care for someone unworthy of their love. As long as the relationship continues to live up to the original terms, the pragmatic lover will continue to love; but if the partner should not live up to expectations, the pragmatic lover feels justified in seeking someone else.

Note that these six types of lovers are ideal, generalized types. Rarely would anyone fit neatly into just one of these categories; most people are mixtures of several. In fact, "a person's preferred love style may change over a lifetime or even during the course of a given love relationship" (Hendrick & Hendrick, 1983, p. 119).

LOVE IN OUR SOCIETY

It is reported that after a visit to the United States, the French writer DeSales stated that America appears to be the only country in the world where love is a national problem. In our society, songs moan about love; movies, TV programs, and books explore love; advertisers sell love; and advice columnists offer counsel to lovers. Americans, like Romeo, seem to be in love with love.

Often our culture guides our emotions, compelling us to come up with the right emotion for the occasion—to feel happy at weddings and sad at funerals—no matter what our actual feelings may be. Teenagers are socialized into falling in love; their parents and peers pressure them to date and view with suspicion those who do not date. A teenage boy who isn't attracted to girls and does not date may find his masculinity questioned. The girl who is not asked out could be considered unattractive and unpopular.

> *True love is like a ghost: everybody talks about it but few have seen it.*

> *No matter how lovesick you may be, don't take the first pill that comes along.*

> *Life is one darn thing after another and love is two fool things after each other.*

> *It might be a mistake to fall in love with a dimple and marry the entire person.*

> *Love is blind: that's why you see so many spectacles in the university quad in the spring.*

> *All the world may not love a lover, but all the world watches one.*

The cultural ideal for love has a strong romantic element. Chastity is valued and premarital sex is discouraged, but romantic love is encouraged. Similarly, many people think that sexual intercourse should never occur without love. Therefore, some people say or believe they are in love when they are actually feeling only physical desire.

Society has a stake in love because love often leads to marriage, which, in turn, leads to the birth of a new generation and the perpetuation of the human race. Since our society links love and marriage, people are often pressured to love others of their own age, social status, and racial, religious, and ethnic background. Yet linking romantic love with marriage has had its own problems. Forisha (1978) quotes Arthur Schlesinger, Jr., as having said, "The American experience in love has not yet proved itself. The national attempt to unite passion and marriage led many Americans into hypocrisy in the nineteenth century and into hysteria in the twentieth" (p. 207).

DEVELOPMENT AND FUNCTIONS OF LOVE

How did you come to love? Did you fall into it? Jump into it? Or consciously decide to love? Does love develop instantly like a Polaroid picture or does it happen more slowly? Some people jump into love because they feel the need to be in love with someone constantly, while others systematically seek love because finding someone who really cares about them reaffirms their self-worth in an otherwise impersonal world.

How fast a love relationship develops presents a paradox. On the one hand, lovers are pressured to declare their love and commitment in order to gain the rewards of intimacy. On the other hand, they don't want the relationship to develop faster than they can handle. In this bargaining stage of the relationship, the lovers need to maintain a delicate balance between these conflicting pressures so neither partner feels exploited.

THE DEVELOPMENT OF LOVE

Love is first learned from parents. Parents who have strong self-concepts and who love their children and each other make good role models for the learning of love. On the other hand, some parents set a bad example by not caring for each other or their children. Still others smother their children with so much "love" that the children have no room to explore their own personalities, to develop strong self-concepts, to experience occasional rejection, or to learn to compromise.

Love, like maturation, is a process. Love begins with two people who feel comfortable with one another and results in a new interdependent relationship. It begins with knowing yourself and developing a good self-concept. Self-love is not narcissistic or exclusive of others but allows you to develop self-acceptance and to learn to accept and to appreciate others. If you are comfortable about yourself, you can become more honest with others. Self-confidence can minimize the necessity to falsify yourself in order to gain acceptance. By putting others first, you make yourself more attractive.

As love progresses, it must adapt to the changing needs of the individuals. The movement from being in love to loving is difficult and comes through work and increasing openness. Many people believe that developing love needs a firm basis in friendship, particularly as the relationship develops into mature love. Since liking, according to the O'Neills (1972), is more rational than romantic love and is based on respect for the other person, it offers a firmer basis for mature love. When lovers interact with equal give and take, they can become dependent on each other yet still retain their own autonomy. They can respect each other's desires, life-styles, and goals as individuals and still be a couple with common bonds and goals.

> But let there be spaces in your togetherness,
> And let the winds of heaven dance between you.
> Love one another, but make not a bond of love:
> Let it rather be a moving sea between the shores of your souls.
> Fill each other's cup but drink not from one cup.
> Give one another of your bread but eat not from the same loaf.
> Sing and dance together and be joyous, but let each one of you be alone,
> Even as the strings of a lute are alone though they quiver with the same
>   music.
>
> —Kahlil Gibran

True intimacy in love develops when the individuals exchange freely, loving with a high degree of honesty that is not possible in other relationships. Windemiller (1976) says, "Practically, love is seen as the working out of difficulties in the areas of parenting, showing affection, adjustment of sexual needs, and the balance of power or decision making" (p. 289).

THE FUNCTIONS OF LOVE

In addition to serving society by leading to marriage and procreation, love serves a variety of personal needs. "People enter into romantic relationships primarily out of a variety of near-universal needs—intimacy, closeness, sexual gratification, a family—and out of more narrow and idiosyncratic ones, such as status, recognition and validation" (Lynch & Blinder, 1983, p. 91).

You feel important when someone cares for you. Love helps you to develop an

Touch is the most valued expression of positive emotions for women—men need to be reminded of this.

independent identity. Love can bolster your self-confidence, making you feel valued and valuable. Love also helps people avoid loneliness. It offers them companionship, security, and a feeling of togetherness. Unfortunately, some people stay in relationships only because they are afraid of being alone.

Love may also help you to feel revitalized, since the knowledge that you love and are loved gives you a sense of joy and well-being. The physical sensations of love are exhilarating, and romantic love, with its accompanying idealization of your lover, can make you feel admired. Love can lead to selflessness as you seek to be giving to your partner. People in one study who were in love and who had recently been reminded of their partners even perceived strangers to be more attractive than did those who were not in love (Benassi, 1985). This finding seems to suggest that your whole outlook on life may be more positive when you are in love. It has been said that those who love deeply never grow old; they may die in old age, but they die feeling young.

Occasionally, however, love brings some negative results, such as the loss of time for other people, an unwanted dependence on a lover, or a loss of independence. People who find that love limits them as individuals or who withdraw from other aspects of their lives may want to consider their reasons for loving.

LOVE AND PASSION

When you feel the physical changes associated with love—increased heartbeat, heavy breathing, raised blood pressure, and so on—are you really reacting to love? Interestingly, researchers have found that the physical changes people experience when they are in love are very similar to those that go with other emotions such as anger, fear, and hate. In fact, some researchers have demonstrated that the physical effects actually precede the emotion. That is, you may experience sweaty palms on a date and decide that your physical reaction is love. However, you may have sweaty palms again when you interview for a job; then you would interpret your reaction as nervousness or fear.

Similarly, adding other emotional stimuli has been demonstrated to increase passion. Walster (1974) writes, "Loneliness, deprivation, frustration, hatred, and insecurity may in fact supplement a person's romantic experience" (p. 286). She suggests that anything that arouses emotion can increase passion. Thus, fear often causes an increase in passion. Dutton and Aron (1974) demonstrated the effects of fear on passion in a classic experiment. They had two groups of men walk across two different bridges. One bridge was a high, shaky walkway above a canyon, the other a low, solid structure. Each subject was approached by an attractive woman. The men on the more dangerous-looking bridge showed more romantic and sexual interest in the woman than did those on the apparently safer one.

According to Meer (1985), people experience loneliness in many different ways and under many different conditions. He quotes psychologist Jeffrey Young, who differentiates among three types of loneliness: (1) transient loneliness, a very temporary condition that lasts only a few minutes or a few hours and is probably not serious; (2) situational loneliness, caused by a specific event such as a divorce, the death of a loved one, or a geographic move, which can last up to a year; and (3) chronic loneliness, which affects people who generally have difficulty making social contact and achieving intimacy. Loneliness is considered chronic when it lasts more than two years.

People turn to others to overcome loneliness and are satisfied when their desires and needs for social intimacy and attachment are matched by the quality and quantity of their attachments. Therefore, one person could be lonely with many friends while another was content with only a few.

We gain different benefits from our various social contacts—families, friends, teachers, and co-workers. Specifically, we look to spouses or romantic partners for safety and security. "The situational lonely said that they gradually made friends to overcome their loneliness, but the chronically lonely felt that, although they may have made friends, the only thing that could halt their lonely feelings was finding a romantic partner, something they didn't seem able to do" (Meer, 1985, p. 32).

People who like themselves, who enjoy spending time in their own company, are hardly ever lonely. If you find yourself interesting and lovable, others are likely to see you that way too. If you find yourself unlovable, others may also see you that way. For the most part, people accept your evaluation of yourself. Therefore a healthy, positive self-image is likely to lead to warm, pleasant relationships and put a stop to loneliness and a view of the world as a cold, unfriendly place.

Furthermore, the fear of rejection can act as a strong stimulus to passion. Walster (1980) writes, "Socrates, Ovid, Terence, the Kamma Sutra and 'Dear Abby' are all in agreement about one thing: the person whose affection is easily won will inspire less passion than the person whose affection is hard to win" (p. 30). Rejection will often encourage someone to try even harder to win the desired individual, although continual rejection will probably eventually cool the ardor.

That is why playing hard to get is often more appealing and stirs more attention than being easy. Sexual frustration and anxiety, which often accompany love, may also feed the emotions. Therefore, even though positive reinforcement can help love develop, occasional negative reinforcement may also arouse passion— up to a point. Parents who oppose their teenager's choice of dates or decision to go steady may only fuel the romantic feelings, since opposition merely increases frustration. This reaction is called the "Romeo and Juliet effect."

LOVE AND SEX

Society says that sex without love is not proper, so people who experience sexual desire may convince themselves they are in love to justify their sexual feelings or activities. This linkage of love and sex in popular culture is so strong that a teenage boy who feels sexually attracted to his girlfriend is likely to tell her that he loves her. He may really mean simply that he desires her, not that he loves her. He temporarily deludes even himself into believing that he loves her in order to justify his feelings and his sexual advances. To him, the love is real. His girlfriend, in turn, may convince herself that he really loves her, even though some doubts may remain, since his love makes their sexual relations more acceptable to her.

This is by no means a new or recent phenomenon. Hunt (1959) cites a story from the third century A.D. according to which Hypatia, a philosophy lecturer at the Alexandrian Museum, attracted many students for both her brilliance and her beauty. "As lovely as she was, Hypatia chose to remain a virgin, and when one student professed his passionate love for her, she hoisted her dress to the waist and contemptuously said, 'This, young man, is what you are in love with, and not anything beautiful' " (p. 102).

If people could learn to recognize the difference between love and sexual desire, hypocrisy might decrease and they might feel more able to admit when they are feeling sexual desire rather than love. "When a feeling for another person is more sexual than emotional, people are likely to mask their true feelings of sexual attraction by convincing themselves that their emotion is 'pure' and thus, love" (McCary, 1980, p. 149).

On the other hand, love can sometimes exist without a sexual basis. Friendship is one example. Strong friendships between people of the same sex have been discouraged or looked on with suspicion by our society, which tends to see such close, loving relationships as homosexual in nature. "The overemphasis in our society on the sexual overtones to any relationship and the prejudicial attitudes that many people have about homosexuality cause our society to look askance at a relationship between people of the same sex, even though the notion that love cannot exist apart from sex (or sex apart from love) is nonsensical" (McCary, 1980, p. 149).

It is important to realize that love between parents and children, between children, or between adults may have large erotic components but is not rooted primarily in sexual dynamics or hormonal drives. Although love and sex can be separated, they often go together for both homo- and heterosexual people. Symonds (1974) notes this intertwining of love and sex. He suggests that "physiologically, love and sex have much in common. They both represent the operation of the parasympathetic nervous system" (p. 129). It is our society's cultural values that have been instrumental in the attempt to separate the two into almost dichotomous categories. The present "permissiveness with affection" standard, however, tends to reunite love and sexualities.

MALE/FEMALE DIFFERENCES

As mentioned before, different subcultures within our society have differing perceptions of love. One marked division is between women and men. Traditionally, women have been thought to be more romantic than men, but research in the last few decades seems to indicate otherwise. English writer Dorothy Sayers has reportedly pointed out that the sentiment, "Man's love is of man's life a thing apart; 'tis woman's whole existence" is, in fact, a piece of male wishful thinking, which can only be made to come true by depriving the life of the leisured woman of every other practical and intellectual interest.

Recent studies have shown that women tend to be more practical about love than men. For one thing, women are socialized into desiring marriage and are generally interested in love at an earlier age than men. Secondly, "marriage may have a more powerful effect on a woman's life than on a man's and, there-fore, elicit more careful premarital behavior. Even today, a married woman's socioeconomic status is often determined by her husband's status" (Brehm, 1985, p. 104).

Men, besides being more romantic than women, also tend to fall in love or become attracted to women more quickly, while women take time to decide. Once women do decide, however, they tend to feel love more intensely. "She chooses and commits herself more slowly than the male but, once in love, she engages more extravagantly in the euphoric and idealizational dimensions of loving" (Kanin, Davidson, & Scheck, 1970 p. 70). Hendrick and Hendrick (1986) con-ducted a study of over 800 students using a scale based on the six types of lovers described by Lee (1977). They found that "Males were significantly more ludic than females. Females were significantly more storgic, pragmatic, and manic than males. Males and females did not differ on Eros and Agape" (p. 397). Kando (1978) also found that upper-class students were less romantic than lower-class students, while Knox and Sporakowski (1968) found that engaged couples were less romantic than nonengaged ones and that older students were less romantic than younger ones.

Women also tend to tie sex and love more closely together than do men and generally will have sexual relations only when they feel they are in love. Fengler (1974) also found that as a relationship progressed, romanticism increased for men and decreased for women. Women are also more likely to end a relationship than men are, while men feel more grief when the relationship ends (Skolnick, 1978). Differences in levels of liking for the partner have been observed in men and women who are in love. Rubin (1973) found that both had about the same levels of love in the relationship, but that the women had significantly higher liking scores for their partners than their partners did for them.

Overall then, research indicates that men are more romantic, fall in love more quickly but less intensely, do not have as high levels of liking for their partners, and do not tie love and sex together as closely as women do. Conversely, women tend to be more pragmatic about love, since it can lead to mate selection and marriage, which still plays an important role in their lives.

LOVE'S PROMISES AND PITFALLS

When two people are under the influence of the most violent, most insane, most delusive, and most transient of all passions, they are required to swear that they will remain in that excited, abnormal, and exhausted condition continuously until death do them part. —GEORGE BERNARD SHAW

That which is love should be held in an open hand, not in a closed fist.

LOVING AND BEING LOVABLE

The three words "I love you" probably have more influence than any others in our lives. What makes someone lovable or a good lover? Someone who showers you with affection and gifts or someone who loves quietly but deeply, making sacrifices for you? What other criteria come to your mind? Rubin and McNeil (1981) found that the more couples report being in love with each other, the more they actually gaze into each other's eyes. Perhaps eye contact is a sign of deep love.

Love, particularly mature love, is a process of exchange that involves sexual attraction, companionship, caring, and confirmation. Love helps to fulfill per-

To the frequent surprise of the young, wrinkles and gray hair do not mean the end of love or the need for its expression.

sonal needs, and the process of exchange allows the lovers to help meet each other's needs. A good relationship of exchange contains both unconditional and conditional love. The ideal of unconditional love allows love to grow by inviting intimacy and security, while conditional love allows partners to offer constructive criticism that can help them to make necessary adjustments over time.

People tend to fall in love with those who can help meet their needs, whatever their needs may be. Lovers must be able to adapt to each other's needs because their own needs, their partner's needs, and their relationship as well will change over time. The parent-child relationship provides a good example of changing needs. Parents exercise greater control over their children when they are infants than when they are teenagers. The infant needs constant attention, while the teenager needs more freedom to develop the independence necessary for adult life. Often, to meet the needs of others, individuals must subordinate their own needs.

Is it possible to love more than one person at the same time? Certainly, you say. I love my parents. I love my friends. I love all humanity. *And* I love my boyfriend or girlfriend. These are all different types of love. Is it possible to be *romantically* in love with two people at the same time? Some studies have found that college students report having loved more than one person at a time. On the other hand, Sorenson (1973) found that only about half of the teenagers in his sample believed that it was possible to love two people at the same time. Although people may have had more than one love at a time, they are usually forced to choose. For one thing, bigamy is illegal in our society, so one cannot be married to two spouses at once. Secondly, most partners, if they are serious about their relationship, will demand exclusivity or break up.

This discussion, then, leads us to the question: Is loving only one person enough to fulfill all your emotional needs? The traditional American ideal says that all one's needs are to be fulfilled by a single partner in a lifelong monogamous marriage. For decades, scientists have questioned whether this is possible. Strauss (1947) found that in a study of nearly four hundred engaged and newly married persons, less than 20 percent had their needs extremely well satisfied by their mates. Today, this old idea of love is not only being questioned but occasionally replaced by a new version of love that allows for some need satisfaction outside the marital relationship. In fact, a whole book on this idea has been written by the O'Neills (1972). However, an open marriage is not for most people, and they may find divorce rather than love and happiness.

LOVE AND MARRIAGE

> *There are two objects in marriage—love or money. If you marry for love, you will certainly have some very happy days, and probably many uneasy ones; if for money, you will have no happy days and probably no uneasy ones.*
>
> —LORD CHESTERFIELD

Especially today, love is the foremost reason given for marriage.

In a classic study done almost half a century ago, Burgess and Wallin (1953) found that only slightly over 10 percent of nearly a thousand young engaged people thought it acceptable for people in America to marry even though they were not in love. That figure has not changed much today, as the vast majority of Americans still consider love as the basis for marriage and often see romantic love as leading to marriage. While you—and almost everyone else—may consider love a positive emotion, think about the reverse. Is love really a good basis for marriage? Does love help or hinder marriage?

Marriage, despite what you might think, is not based solely on love. Family and societal pressures lead people to choose mates with similar backgrounds. In fact, the more similarities partners share—such as age, religion, socioeconomic class, education, and cultural background in general—the more likely they are to have a lasting marriage.

In addition, romantic love is not the only type of love that exists between married people. Other types generally develop to take the place of declining romantic love. Examples include friendship and companionship. Because romantic love usually declines early in marriage, to marry solely on the basis of romantic love is illogical. In fact, it can be dangerous, because when two lovers stop idealizing their partners and see each other more as they really are, love may die and the relationship may end. However, Spanier (1972) believes that, in general terms, "romanticism does not appear to be harmful to marriage relationships in particular or the family system in general, and is therefore not generally dysfunctional in our society" (p. 481). Kephart (1981) suggests that most of us show few ill effects from romantic love and that our system of mate selection through romantic love would have to be shown to be more ineffective than it seems to be before we abandon it. Note that both authors only conclude that romantic love is not negative, not that it is positive.

Several studies of romance in marriage find that romantic love apparently never entirely leaves a marriage. Although it diminishes during the early years, it returns later. Knox (1970) found that high school seniors and those who had been married for over twenty years both had a more romantic view of love than those who had been married less than five years. Based on his research, Knox came to the conclusion that apparently high school students still had not given up their romantic view of love, and the older couples had romantic ideals as a result of their long-term investment in their marriages. Those who had been married a short time were more realistic, perhaps because of the problems inherent in new marriages (money troubles, childbearing and rearing, and other matters).

WHEN LOVE ENDS

Love is not static but always subject to change. In some ways love is like a roller coaster going up and down, and at some point some people may want to get off.

Love ends for many reasons. Sometimes couples have differing views of what love entails. For example, one partner may favor a more open relationship than the other would prefer. One person may think that love involves close sharing, while the partner may want more privacy and independence. Someone who has not learned love in childhood through the experience of parental love may not be able to sustain a relationship. Treating a partner as an object can lead to the end of love. A wife may tire of being shown off as a prized possession or treated as a neglected piece of property. A husband may come to feel he is nothing but a meal ticket, a valued source of money.

Sex roles also cause problems in love, forcing people to play roles rather than to be themselves. For instance, if a man thinks he must be silent to be masculine, he may be restricting his freedom of expression. A woman who resorts to emotional displays may curtail her chance for meaningful dialogue with her mate. Power struggles also tear some relationships apart, since some people like to use love in a manipulative way in order to gain power, granting love or withholding it as a way of controlling the partner.

BOX 4.1   HOW DO YOU TREAT THE ONE YOU LOVE?

A husband who treats his wife as if she were a servant quite possibly grew up in a traditional patriarchal family. In such cases, the husband has no appropriate model for his relationship with his wife, only that of the superior male–inferior female. Clark Vincent (1973) has observed that it is sometimes useful for the husband to compare his treatment of his wife to his treatment of his dog. This comparison can be disturbing, as the following list shows:

His Dog	*His Wife*
He rubs and scratches her when, where, and how she likes most to be rubbed and scratched.	He may caress her when, where, and how *he* thinks she should be caressed.
His greeting to her reflects enthusiasm.	His greeting to her may reflect fatigue.
He brags about her to his friends.	He may complain about her to his friends.
He feeds her when *she* is hungry.	*She* feeds him when *he* is hungry.
He gives her the freedom to be whatever kind of dog she is.	He may insist that she be the kind of wife *he* thinks she should be.
He immediately rewards her for performing very simple tricks.	He may take for granted very complicated tasks she performs for his benefit.
He accepts the fact that she is too tired to frolic or play.	He may criticize her for being too tired for sex.
He greets her more enthusiastically than he greets other dogs.	He may greet her less enthusiastically than he greets other women.

SOURCE: Vincent, 1973, pp. 107–108.

How do people end a relationship? They can see each other less frequently, allowing the love to fade away, or they can end it abruptly.

In a recent study of nearly four hundred students who said they had terminated at least one personal relationship with someone of the opposite sex, "nearly 90 percent chose to tell their partner the real reason for wanting to break up, compared with about 10 percent who concealed the real reason with a cover story" (Knox, 1985, p. 132). The most frequent truthful reason for breaking up was "the perception that they had different values and goals, and that the relationship wasn't going anywhere" (p. 131). Those who made up a cover story said they didn't want to hurt their partners. They cited "a deficit in the partner, such as a lousy kisser, ugly, no ambition" (p. 131), or the fact that they wanted to be involved with someone else as the main reason for ending their relationship.

Perhaps love can be considered a paradox. It is talked about frequently but is hard to define. Love can be categorized, but any love relationship may overlap the divisions. Lovers, too, can be categorized, but rarely does one lover exactly fit into a single type. People love for a variety of reasons—some good, some bad. Finally, of course, love causes great happiness at times and extreme pain at other times. The only aspect of love that is relatively certain is that it is likely to be a part of our lives and a factor in human relationships for a good long time.

SUMMARY

- Love is hard to define, yet most people believe that they have been in love.

- Love can be considered a relationship of exchange in which the lovers help to fulfill each other's needs.

- The three categories of love are infatuation, romantic love, and mature love.

- Lovers can be categorized as erotic, ludic, storgic, manic, agapic, and pragmatic. Usually people are a combination of two or more types or change from one type to another.

- Love is heavily promoted in our society, which sometimes pressures people into loving.

- Love is a process. It is learned from parents. Ideally it begins with a good self-concept and progresses to self-revelation, mutual dependency, and fulfillment of needs for intimacy.

- Love serves a variety of personal needs, including helping you to develop an independent identity, to feel good about yourself, and to experience exhilaration.

- Passion has been closely linked to other emotions and may not be solely a result of love.

- People may convince themselves they are in love when they actually are experiencing sexual desire. Conversely, love can exist without sex.

- Men tend to be more romantic, to fall in love more quickly but less intensely, and to separate love from sex more than do women. Women are more pragmatic about love and report liking their partners more than men do.

- What makes someone lovable varies with the perceiver.

- Researchers question whether marriage partners can fulfill all each other's needs.

- A stable marriage is based on more than romantic love.

- Because love is a constantly changing process, some people may want to end their love relationships. Breaking up can occur at any stage of a relationship.

- Although love is hard to define and to discuss, it is a definite and important aspect of human life.

➤ PERSPECTIVE: JEALOUSY

Jealousy, like love, is difficult to define. Knox (1984) defines jealousy as "a set of emotions that occurs when one person perceives the love relationship he or she has is being threatened. The specific feelings are those of fear of loss or abandonment, anxiety, pain, anger, vulnerability, and hopelessness" (p. 275). Jealousy can occur in any type of relationship, including friendship, and is difficult to conceal.

Like love, jealousy takes various forms. Mazur (1973) describes six types of jealousy: envy, possessiveness, exclusion, competition, egotism, and fear.

1. "Envy-jealousy" is closely related to the level of self-esteem; it occurs when an individual feels that the partner is better and that this superiority threatens the relationship. This type of jealousy often results in wishful thinking about self, self-pity, or depression.
2. "Possessive-jealousy" develops out of a sense of ownership and a lack of acknowledgment that the partner has a separate identity. Often the person who exhibits possessive jealousy seeks power over the partner.
3. "Exclusion-jealousy" stems from feelings of exclusion or neglect and may arise because of time the partner spends in pursuing a career, hobby, or friendships with other people.
4. "Competition-jealousy" is again related to self-esteem and perceived inadequacies. Often one partner's accomplishments pose a threat to the self-concept of the other, arousing feelings of inadequacy and uneasiness.
5. "Egotism-jealousy" is closely related to roles and occurs when one partner fails to let the other express individuality but expects that person to fulfill a traditional role.
6. "Fear-jealousy" occurs when the relationship is perceived as being threatened—when one partner is afraid of being rejected and fears that

the other partner has little commitment to the relationship. This type of jealousy results from personal insecurity and is accompanied by severe anxiety.

Jealousy is not inborn but is learned through the process of socialization. Research has found that the degree of jealousy depends on the methods of the society. Some societies—such as the Eskimo, the Marquesas Islanders, and the Toda of southern India—emphasize sharing, not possessiveness, and are characterized by little jealousy. In contrast, ours is a possessive society that produces a great deal of jealousy. Our society fosters competitiveness; it stresses individual ownership of private property and the possession not only of material goods but even people. American children raised in this environment by the typical two-parent family—in comparison to children raised in a non-possessive, polygamous family system—will be possessive of "my toys" and "my mommy."

Our society also puts a great deal of emphasis on the couple or two-person relationship as opposed to the extended family relationship. This stress on the dyad emphasizes the dependence of one partner on the other and increases the likelihood of jealousy. A group of three or more can lose one member and still remain a group, but a dyadic relationship ends when one partner leaves. Thus, dyads are particularly vulnerable to destruction by jealousy. It may well be that the high value we put on the couple relationship sometimes leads to jealousy, which in turn can destroy the relationship.

Brehm (1985) says that jealousy is caused by three different feelings:

1. When someone feels that the love relationship is threatened by the partner's interest in another person or thing. "If you believe that your partner is only involved with you, and not interested in anyone or anything else, you cannot be jealous. . . . You will not be jealous as long as it is clear to you that you are considerably more important to your partner than these other interests" (p. 260).
2. Jealousy seems to be based on insecurity, either in the relationship itself or in one's ability to cope with a change in the relationship. Those who feel inadequate or who are heavily dependent on the relationship are more vulnerable to jealousy.
3. Jealousy is fostered by the desire for sexual exclusivity, which is prevalent in our society.

"There are many gradations of jealousy," says Katchadourian (1985). "At one end, there is the perfectly understandable self-interest in preserving one's stake in a valuable relationship. . . . At the extreme, there is pathologic jealousy, where intense suspiciousness without good reason makes the person highly intolerant of any friendly interaction or attention involving his or her partner" (p. 315).

As is love, jealousy is also experienced and expressed in different ways by men and women. Clanton and Smith (1977) report that men are more jealous of their partners' sexual activity and women of their partners' emotional involvement with another. Men tend to deny their feelings of jealousy but express jealousy in rage or violence, while women are quicker to admit feeling jealous and react by being depressed. Men are more apt to blame their partners and compete with their rivals. Women tend to blame themselves and cling to their partners.

Dating women were found to be more jealous than men in situations where the partner spent time on a hobby or with family members but not in other situations (Hansen, 1985). Also, people oriented to traditional sex roles were more jealous than any other group. Most of the subjects in the study said they expected their partners to give up close personal friendships with people of the opposite sex and expected sexual exclusiveness early in their relationship.

One recent study found few differences in the jealousy experienced by men and women. Those who reported the most jealousy also reported three basic personality characteristics: having low self-esteem, seeing themselves as different from what they would like to be, and placing a high value on visible achievements (Salovey & Rodin, 1985). These researchers also found people especially likely to experience jealousy in the area of their biggest desires. For example, someone who values wealth might be jealous of a wealthy rival. One who values beauty may be jealous of an attractive rival.

Is jealousy good for a relationship? It depends. "Occasional mild feelings of jealousy are normal for people in love. It can even be argued that such feelings are adaptive in that they provide motivation to please one's partner. Stronger feelings of jealousy, however, can be destructive of relationships and in extreme cases, may lead to physical violence" (Kilmann, 1984, p. 339). While jealously may initially seem a sign of great love, the actions of a jealous partner may become so restrictive over time that the relationship will end. For instance, a more deeply involved lover may become jealous and demand an exclusive commitment from his or her partner. Then the less involved partner may react by withdrawing from the relationship.

To overcome jealousy, it is important to start with self-examination and then move on to the relationship problems. Hatfield and Walster (1981) suggest three steps: (1) Try to understand your feelings and pinpoint exactly what is making you jealous, (2) try to put your feelings in perspective—decide if you are being overly sensitive or if there really is a problem in your relationship; and (3) talk with your partner and try to achieve a balance between security and freedom in your relationship.

What is the future of jealousy? Is it here to stay? Noted sociologist Jessie Bernard (1971) thinks jealousy is likely to decline. "With respect to the incidence in our society, marital jealousy is declining as our conception of the nature of the marital bond itself is changing" (p. 200). She further suggests, "If monogamous marriage as we have known it in the past is in a process of change, there may be less and less need for jealousy to buttress it, and less and less socialization of human beings to experience it or move to control it" (p. 209). Pines and Aronson (1983) tend to disagree. They think, perhaps as Freud suggested, "that jealousy is universal and inevitable because it originates very early in life in relation to rivalry for the exclusive love of the mother. It is felt again whenever the fear of losing the object of our love is aroused" (p. 127).

They note the possibilities that people may learn to cope with jealousy so as to avoid jealous relationships, to develop better self-concepts, and to trust each other more. Only time will tell which opinion is correct.

Jealousy has many aspects. It can be considered a positive or negative feeling. It takes many forms and comes in many degrees. Although it seems to be a learned behavior, men and women seem to experience it in different ways. There are a number of ways to deal with jealousy, yet researchers cannot conclude that it will ever be eradicated.

QUESTIONS FOR THOUGHT AND DISCUSSION

1. Why is it so difficult to study and define love? Come up with what you consider to be a good definition of love.

2. What are the three types of love covered in the chapter? What are the similarities and differences among them? How do they correspond to the different types of lovers?

3. Why is love so important in our society? What place does love have in society? How is its place different today as opposed to the past?

4. How is love a process? How are maturation and self-love important in this process? Give some thought to how you fall in love. Explain.

5. How is loneliness defined? What are different types of loneliness? How do expectations affect loneliness?

6. Think about the song sung by Whitney Houston, "The Greatest Love of All." Does the chapter agree with this song? How?

7. Are lonely people different in any way from those who are not lonely?

8. Our society dictates that love and sex go together. Do you think that they should? Why or why not?

9. Are men or women, in general, more romantic? Who falls in love more quickly? More intensely? What types of love are men more susceptible to? Women?

10. What effect does the progression of a relationship have on romantic love? On pragmatic love? Are there any differences between men and women in the way they progress in romantic love?

11. What are some common reasons people give for terminating a relationship? Have you personally experienced such a situation?

12. Have you ever been jealous? Do some of the suggestions for overcoming jealousy seem plausible? What can you do to overcome jealousy in your relationships?

Dating and Marrying

FROM COURTSHIP TO GETTING TOGETHER

Since the beginning of time, unmarried men and women have had personal, one-to-one interactions with each other. They always have and probably always will. In America the term for this interaction has changed from "courting" to "dating" to simply "getting together."

Courtship, which existed in America from colonial days until the early 1900s, is parentally approved interaction between a man and a woman with a view to eventual marriage. A family member would introduce a gentleman to a young lady. The gentleman was then expected to ask permission to escort the young lady to chaperoned social events. If he saw her more than a few times, it was assumed that he hoped soon to marry her. Courting was serious business and was as much a concern of the church, the community, and the families as the couple.

Dating came into existence around the time of World War I and the Roaring Twenties. Dating is a prearranged couple activity aimed primarily at socializing and recreation. Dating is formal in that the couple prearranges the time and place, but it involves less parental control than courting. While dating was the formal way young men and women socialized until several decades ago, people used some less formal methods too. For instance, in the 1950s, a group of girls might have met a group of boys at a movie or gathered at a beach or park. A "Coke date" might have occurred, for example, when a couple happened to meet at the library and he suggested they go to the student union for a soda.

Getting together is the best term for today's casual system of socializing between young men and women. This system, which emerged in the 1970s, tends to be informal, lacking in commitment, and not heavily couple-oriented. People often go to parties in groups or wander in alone. Some may pair off for the evening, others may establish no couple relationships at all. Spontaneity is a key factor in getting together.

WHY THE CHANGES?

Three factors were primarily instrumental in the change from a courtship to a dating system. First, the development of technology after the industrial revolution created a demand for educated people. Second, the emergence of the coeducational school system gave young people a chance to meet in places other than home or church. Third, the advent of the automobile reduced the social controls of the family and allowed young people more privacy. In addition, thousands of soldiers who fought in World War I learned about romance, love, and sex during their tours of duty overseas. They were no longer satisfied with letting their parents choose their mates. During this same period, Margaret Sanger pioneered birth control and Freud made sex a scientifically respectable topic.

In the last generation, attitudes have changed the dating system to one of simply getting together. One reason is that many young people dislike the game playing involved in formal dating. It is easier simply to go out than to make specific plans. Second, getting together involves less risk to the ego. You don't have to risk feeling lonely if no one calls or feeling rejected if someone should turn you down for a date. Finally, society now places fewer restrictions on women. They are freer to choose where they will go, with whom, and what they will do. A woman may suggest a date to a man and even invite him to her home.

Even considering all these important changes, perhaps dating has not changed as drastically as you might think. For instance, while courting was very formal, a gentleman in 1890 could call on a young lady and casually sit and talk with her in the parlor. And while we think of simply getting together today, people often make elaborate preparations to go to a formal dance or plan weeks ahead to attend a rock concert.

Whatever type of dating people do, Henslin (1980) says, "In our society everyone is expected to date. For many, dating must seem like a game of bingo; if you keep playing long enough your number is bound to come up. For others, it must be like Dorothy's 'Yellow Brick Road'; just keep following it, for the rainbow is out there somewhere" (p. 129).

Is Dating Important?

You bet it is! Dating is important because it performs vital functions for society, the family, and the individual. According to Kelley (1979), "The heterosexual dyad is probably the single most important type of personal relationship in the life of the individual and in the history of society. It occasions the greatest satisfactions and also the greatest disappointments" (p. 2).

For society and the family, dating is the first step toward marriage and procreation. For the individual, dating is important because of the role it plays in interpersonal relationships. On a date, a person learns to communicate with another and to relate to another's feelings. These skills carry over into other personal relationships as well as business encounters. Dating is also important simply because it is a major investment of time. Many hours of a student's week are often spent in getting together and partying. If you start to date in your teens and don't get married until your twenties, you will have spent a decade—more than 10 percent of your life—dating. In fact, the length of time you spend dating your future spouse may affect your happiness later. A 1985 study revealed that long periods of dating seemed to be associated with subsequent marital happiness. The researchers suggest that longer dating time allows partners to screen out incompatible partners and to learn about their daily conflicts before they marry (Grover, Russell, Schumm, & Paff-Bergen, 1985).

CHARACTERISTICS OF THE DATING SYSTEM

Suppose one day, as you are walking across campus, a spaceship lands on the quad. A Martian, here to gather information about earth, asks you to characterize our dating system. What could you say? Consider these aspects: our dating system is elaborate, flexible, pluralistic, competitive, progressive, participant-run, and has a double standard.

ELABORATE

One reason our system is elaborate is that the people who date range so widely in age. Dating generally begins in the early teens. In a comprehensive study of an entire high school, Hollingshead (1975) noted that between the ages of 14 and 16, "the associational pattern changes from an almost exclusive interaction with members of their own sex to a mixed associational pattern similar to that found in adult life" (p. 167). Today, dating probably starts even earlier for most people.

Why do teens date? A 1981 study found that sexual development did not influence dating behavior in youths aged 12 to 17. Rather "social pressures, based on behavior considered typical and appropriate at various ages, determines the onset of dating in adolescents" (Dornbusch, Carlsmith, Gross, Martin, Jennings, Rosenberg, & Duke, 1981, p. 179).

Dating may continue throughout life. Someone may date a long time before marrying or never marry at all. Others may return to dating after being divorced or widowed. Quite a few single people over 65 not only date but are sexually involved with someone. In fact, older daters experience the same "sweaty-palm syndrome" when they fall in love and feel the same about romance as younger daters do (Bulcroft & O'Conner-Roden, 1986).

The many ways people get together also help make the system elaborate. High school and college students may find their dating activities centered on concerts, dances, sporting events, and other school-sponsored activities. Dating for older people usually takes place in commercial establishments. Singles bars and apartment complexes are popular with many people in their twenties, while older singles find less frantic places for their dates.

FLEXIBLE

Americans are free to choose how frequently they will date, how exclusively they will date, and even whether or not they will date. Some individuals may go out only rarely throughout high school, then get a job, meet someone, quickly fall in love, and get married. Another person might date many people and go out frequently in high school and college before living with someone or getting married. Because people are free to vary the dating script, many variations exist simultaneously.

PLURALISTIC

In contrast to societies with caste systems or monarchies, the pluralistic nature of our dating system allows anyone to compete, legally, with anyone else for a date or a mate. Considerable socializing across such traditional boundaries as religion, social class, ethnicity, and race adds to the pluralism of the system. As people move from simply going out to going steady, engagement, or living together, however, the influence of families and tradition becomes more restrictive.

COMPETITIVE

The competitive nature of our society is reflected in our dating system. People vie for a top-paying job, the best school, the number-one team—and the most popular date. The dating system becomes a marketplace where people barter for the best possible prize.

Generally, the upper-class man has an advantage because he is willing to date women of his own class and the middle class and sometimes especially attractive women of the lower class. Women of the upper class, however, show some reluctance to date men belonging to lower classes.

The majority of students date people within a year or two of their own age. Specifically, men tend not to date older women and women tend not to date younger men (see Table 5.1). If a man and woman are approximately the same age and equally attractive, the man has the competitive edge, since he can date younger women. The woman, as she ages, has to compete with younger and younger women because most of the men her age or older are now married.

PROGRESSIVE

The dating system involves the participant's progressive commitment. Although there are other alternatives, the typical dating sequence consists of four major stages: (1) initial dating, (2) dating steadily, (3) exclusive dating, and (4) being engaged. Generally, as one proceeds through the stages, deeper and more permanent emotional and sexual commitments are likely. However, our system's flexibility allows one to exit at any stage and to start new.

TABLE 5.1 Age of Dating Partner

	For Women	For Men
Younger	10%	37%
Same	36%	43%
Older	52%	15%

SOURCE: DeLamater and MacCorquodale, 1979, p. 150.

Initial dating refers to both the very first date of one's life and the first date with a specific person. It includes group dates, blind dates, and playing the field. In initial dating, one goes out with many different people with little or no commitment to the relationship.

When people are *dating steadily,* they go out primarily with just one person but still maintain the freedom to date others. This affords the couple some security in the relationship: they can count on having a regular date and develop a degree of closeness. On the other hand, they are also protected against getting too deeply involved before they are ready. Quite frequently, a college student will go steady with someone back home while maintaining the freedom to date others at college.

Exclusive dating, or being "engaged to be engaged," includes going steady, being pinned or lavaliered, or exchanging a promise ring. Most college students today have gone steady at least once and find steady relationships important.

Exclusive relationships offer advantages to people who are not ready for engagement but who want a steady relationship. These relationships can function as preparation for marriage, giving people practice in building and maintaining a relationship over a period of time. They involve less exploitation, posing, and game playing than the more casual dating situations. Once the steady relationship is established, the partners may feel secure enough to be themselves. Some people gain prestige from exclusive relationships, particularly if they are going with someone who "counts."

Exclusive relationships also have some disadvantages. They keep people from learning to interact with many different types of personalities. Exclusive dating can push some people into making a greater commitment to a relationship than they want to make. Particularly in high school, students may be rushed into making decisions about premarital sex, engagement, or marriage before they are ready to make them.

Engagement, or a commitment to marry, is the most formal and public stage. It involves not only the individuals concerned but their families as well. Once the engagement is announced, the families view the relationship as serious and the fiancées as potential relatives.

To test the progression in couples' love relationships, King and Christensen (1983) devised a Relationship Events Scale consisting of 19 items ranging from "My partner has called me an affectionate name" to "We have spent a whole day together" to "We are engaged" (p. 674). The test showed that couples followed an ordered progression in their relationships as marked by these events. The study also showed that couples who had progressed further in the scale were more apt to stay together.

PARTICIPANT-RUN

Sociologist Ira Reiss (1980) calls our dating system an "autonomous participant-run" system; that is, young people are relatively free to go out with whomever they please and do what they want to do. Parents exert little direct power over dating. The freedom increases as teens grow older and move away from home.

DOUBLE STANDARD

The double standard of our society is reflected in the dating system. It traditionally gives more advantages to the male than to the female. First, women tend to lose their "market value" earlier than do men. Society generally views the older woman with graying hair and sagging skin as unattractive, while the male with silver hair and wrinkles is seen as more distinguished.

Second, because of the traditional differences in expectations for men and women, until recently, men have had greater freedom in fulfilling their sexual desires. Women who lost their virginity before marriage also lost their good reputation, while men were expected to gain sexual knowledge before marriage.

Third, males and females are still brought up in different subcultures and, as a result, have different views of dating. A recent study (Nevid, 1984) found that "males placed relatively greater emphasis than females on the physical characteristics of their prospective romantic partners. Females more strongly emphasized the personal qualities of their prospective partners than did males. However, both sexes more heavily weighed various personal qualities than physical characteristics in the context of romantic choice in a meaningful relationship" (p. 401).

FUNCTIONS OF DATING

Some 50 years ago, Waller (1938) found four basic functions of dating: recreation, socialization, status, and mate selection. While numerous other functions have since been added to this basic list, Waller's conceptualization, with minor changes, is still very applicable today.

RECREATION

The recreation function of dating includes fun, entertainment, thrills, companionship, fulfillment of leisure time, and sexual activity. Often dating is simply a way to enjoy yourself. You are more apt to go to a movie, a ballgame, a festival, a concert, or a dance with a date. Other times dating offers companionship—someone to talk with at dinner or to share your good news. Dating offers a pleasant way to spend your leisure time and may provide the excitement of being with someone special, going new places, or meeting new people.

SOCIALIZATION

The socialization function of dating includes developing interpersonal skills, exploring one's own personality, preparing for adult roles, and developing social and personal competence. For people who do not have siblings of the opposite sex, dating provides a perspective on the subculture of the opposite sex and moves them from association with same-sex peers to association with both same- and opposite-sex peers. In a study of dating patterns at Harvard University (Vreeland, 1972), men stated that finding a friend of the other sex that they could talk with was a primary reason for dating. The development of interpersonal skills and personality exploration can be achieved in same-sex company, but dating helps to prepare individuals for adult life and to gain skills in relating to the opposite sex.

STATUS

The status function of dating includes gaining prestige, asserting popularity, enhancing the ego, gaining peer-group acceptance, and acquiring power. Students tell us that there is both prestige and ego-enhancement in being seen with the right person. Indeed, men feel that their status with peers is increased by being seen with an attractive or popular woman. While a man tends to gain prestige by talking about the physical characteristics of his date, a woman tends to brag about the car her date drives or where he takes her. For high school students, the status gained among same-sex peers for having a date with a desirable person may be more important than the date itself.

While the admiration of peers is one source of ego-enhancement, the private response of your date can be another. When you receive comments such as "Gee, you're a good dancer," "You look great tonight," and "I like being with you," you feel good about yourself.

MATE SELECTION

Finally, dating provides an opportunity to meet people of the opposite sex with the possibility of finding someone you may eventually marry. This may be done on a conscious level, or you may find yourself quite unexpectedly looking at your date as a possible spouse, not merely a companion for Saturday night's party.

INITIATION OF RELATIONSHIPS

What happens when you go to your first class or party at college? How do you choose someone to talk with? Why do you ignore someone else? What is the first thing you notice about someone on the other side of the room? What attracts you to that person?

Generally, men are more concerned with a woman's physical appearance. Two recent studies found this to be true. One found that women initially choose men with higher status and physical attractiveness while men select women mainly for their physical attractiveness (Green, Buchanan, & Heuer, 1984). The other concluded that "in general, men were more concerned with physical characteristics, while women stressed psychological factors" (Deaux & Hanna, 1984, p. 363).

However, women are concerned about looks in date selection too. A clever study by Walster, Aronson, Abrahams, and Rottman (1966) supported this idea. Based on a previous analysis of their personality, intelligence, and appearance, over seven hundred students were paired off for a dance by a computer. At the

On their way. . . . Dating or just getting together . . .

dance, at intermission time, the students were briefly questioned about their dates. The major finding was that both men and women said physical attractiveness was the main quality they liked in their partner. The Walster et al. research also indicated that students seek the best-looking partners, not those who are similar to themselves in attractiveness.

Since the dating system reflects our societal values, it is not surprising that good looks are valued in dating. The findings about the importance of physical attractiveness clearly relate to the status function of dating. After all, your friends can quickly and easily see if your date is good looking. It takes them longer to appreciate his or her personality characteristics.

If looks are so important in attraction between men and women, how do people who are, as one author put it, "less than lovely" get into relationships? Fortunately, (1) looks are not the only factor in attraction, (2) someone who is unattractive to many may be very attractive to some, and (3) while some people may not be described as beautiful or handsome, they may have sex appeal. Belkin and Goodman (1980) maintain that a "sexual stimulus value" is "the total effect of one person on another" (p. 113).

The components of Belkin and Goodman's sexual stimulus values are self-confidence, power, public recognition, demonstration of interest in others, and gentleness. You may list other values. The point is that personal characteristics other than physical ones contribute to a person's ability to be attractive to others.

In discussing what college students value in a date, one study found that of 18 qualities, chastity was ranked seventeenth by men and eighteenth by women, which suggests that in the dating scene today, chastity is not as important as it once was (Hudson & Hoyt, 1978). Another found that "the ten characteristics most valued in a mate are [that he or she be a] good companion, considerate, honest, affectionate, dependable, intelligent, kind, understanding, interesting to talk to, and loyal" (Buss & Barnes, 1986, p. 562).

Some people also find others attractive because they share the same religious or political beliefs, hobbies, or interests. Sometimes a person's material possessions—an expensive car, fashionable clothes, spending money, and so on—can make him or her more attractive. One study showed that people are often attracted to dates who have the characteristics they wish they themselves possessed (Mathes & Moore, 1985).

BREAKING UP

Breaking up can occur at any stage in the dating process, whether the couple has had only a few dates or is engaged. For several reasons, nonmarital breakups are not considered as serious as those that occur after marriage. First, no legal problems are involved. Second, dating relationships do not have the same strong family and societal support as do marriages. Families expect teenage relationships to end and do not see such events as personal failures. Third, people who end a relationship in high school or college will find a larger field of accessible dates than will those who break up later in life. Even though dating breakups are considered less serious, they can be very traumatic for those involved.

Why do couples break up? If you've ever been in a relationship that ended, you can probably think of reasons why. Did you drop the other person, or were you dropped? Problems with your partner's family could have ended the relationship. Hill, Rubin, and Peplau (1976) studied college upperclassmen in the Boston area. Two years later almost half of the over two hundred couples in the study had broken up, after an average length of 1½ years together. Boredom with the relationship was a number-one factor reported by both men and women, but differences in interests, desire to be independent, differences in backgrounds, and conflicting sexual attitudes also contributed to the breakups. An interest in someone else was reported by 40 percent of the women and 30 percent of the men.

Which has caused more breakups, love or sex? Hill et al. (1976) found that living together or having sexual intercourse were "totally unrelated to breaking up" (p. 152). Specifically, they found that a nearly equal percentage of both the couples that did and those that did not engage in sexual intercourse subsequently broke up. Couples who did stay together, when compared to those that broke up, were more likely to report being in love, dating exclusively, and considering marriage. Apparently, emotional commitment has more effect on maintaining a relationship than does intimate physical behavior.

The same research showed that breakups are more likely to occur in college during hectic times, such as at the start or finish of a semester or during summer school. Such times of stress—with exams, moving, and other pressures—can put either partner in a bad mood. The beginning of a new semester also brings with it the possibility of competition from new acquaintances, while summer vacation may allow a weak relationship to die.

As long as the dating system allows experimentation, exploration of new relationships, and easy movement into and out of the dating system, breakups will remain an integral part of the participant-run system of dating. Although breakups may cause short-term disappointments, the testing period of participating in a variety of relationships helps prepare people for eventual long-term pairing.

CONCERNS WITH DATING TODAY

People find many advantages in dating—fun, companionship, prestige, security, personality growth, and eventual mate selection. However, dating has possible problem areas that can range from a specific concern about one date—the drunk, the bore, the one who is sexually aggressive—to more complex problems. Let's consider some problematic aspects of dating today.

BARGAINING

Since the dating system is so competitive, it is not surprising that a certain amount of bargaining occurs. Individuals who have the most to offer—looks, personality, or some other valued asset—are in the best bargaining position for securing a desirable date.

Bargaining is considered satisfactory when the people involved believe that they are engaging in reciprocal exchange—that is, trading things of equal value. If both are satisfied that the trade is equal, then both are happy. However, if dating partners make promises they don't intend to keep, or if they misrepresent themselves, then they are exploiting each other. For example, if a man promises he will marry a woman if she becomes sexually involved with him but secretly has no intention of keeping his promise, he is using fraud for his personal gain. Similarly, if a woman tells a man she is an account executive when she is really a receptionist, she is misrepresenting herself to gain his companionship. Some people might suggest that no bargaining should exist in intimate relationships, but this ideal is unrealistic and does not fit in with other elements of our competitive society.

THE PRINCIPLE OF LEAST INTEREST

Often, the principle of least interest can lead to exploitation. If one person has less interest in maintaining a relationship than the other, the person who cares the least may exploit the one who cares the most. Typically in our society the woman cares more about the dating relationship and is more likely to get hurt as a consequence. The classic analysis of this inequality appears in a study by Skipper and Nass (1966) of female student nurses in a Chicago area hospital. These student nurses often dated male medical students or interns, hoping for a desirable marriage. The interns, on the other hand, dated for a good time or for sex. Do you think the nurses were exploiting the interns? Do you think the interns were exploiting the nurses? Was their bargaining equal?

Despite recent changes in roles for men and women, this system of bargaining still exists. One way to study this phenomenon is to review the personal columns in newspapers. Those who advertise in lonely hearts columns indeed consider physical characteristics to be important, according to one study. Tall male and lightweight female advertisers received more responses than did others. Red or salt-and-pepper haired advertisers received more responses than did blondes or brunettes (Lynn & Shurgot, 1984). Men and women who advertised in the personal column of one metropolitan newspaper disclosed information about themselves at an equal rate. Both sexes stipulated physical attractiveness, athleticism, and the desire for companionship equally often. However, women more frequently mentioned the need for financial security in potential marriage partners (Sitton & Rippee, 1986).

POSING AND GAME PLAYING

People have complained that the traditional dating system encourages too much posing or game playing. To appear as attractive as possible, a short man might wear elevator shoes or a bald man might invest in a toupee. On the other hand, some people have pretended to be less than what they are in order to keep from intimidating their partner. Women in particular have pretended to be less intelligent or skillful in order to remain attractive to men.

In her classic study, Komarovsky (1946) found that college women had to deal with two contradictory role models. The traditional role prescribed that the woman be less dominant and aggressive but more emotional and sympathetic than the man. The modern role expected women to be somewhat competitive with men. Specifically, women were told by their fathers to get good grades in school (the modern role) but not to show up the men (the traditional role). As a result, women often pretended to be dumb in order to flatter the man's ego and to keep from losing him.

This situation has changed little. Discussions with students indicate that some women students still occasionally play dumb in dating situations. Pretending to be inferior seems to them to be one way of increasing their chances of being liked by a date. One student noted that her boyfriend becomes upset if she beats him at tennis. Perhaps this concept is consistent with the belief that a subordinate should never show up a superior. How often does a colonel beat the general at golf or a junior executive beat his boss at bridge? If society, however incorrectly, perceives the male as superior to the female, one can hardly blame women for sometimes pretending to be inferior in order to initiate or maintain a relationship.

Game playing includes limited self-disclosure on initial dates. Both men and women try to protect their egos by simply not revealing too much about themselves until they get to know their partners better.

Brehm (1985) notes that as partners find superficial communication enjoyable, they can increase their intimacy by increasing the breadth of their conversations (adding more topics of discussion) and by increasing the depth of their conversations (talking about more personally meaningful topics).

SEX

Some young people are rushed into making decisions about sexual activity before they are really ready to do so, particularly when one partner wants to engage in sexual intercourse when the other is reluctant. If the boy is more interested in sex than the girl (which has traditionally been the case), then the conflicts caused by this disagreement can create problems in the relationship, particularly if he persuades her to have sexual intercourse when she does not want to do so. Although women have greater sexual freedom today than in the past, they still have to worry more about their reputations and to bear most of the blame if they become pregnant. Interestingly, college students who feel guilty about sexual intercourse are less likely to use contraception than are those who do not feel guilty (Berger, Jacques, Bender, Gold, & Andres, 1985). Thus, those women who need to be talked into having sex are those who are most likely to feel guilty and also to become pregnant.

CHANGING SOCIAL NORMS

People who are going out in the 1980s find that the norms, or guidelines for expected behavior, are in a flux. The dating scene is less formal, more flexible, and more egalitarian. Sexual morality exhibits this flexibility, and people who are dating have more freedom from parental or societal controls than ever before. However, many young people are finding that with increased freedom and new opportunities come new responsibilities. College students must decide their own morals and limitations rather than relying on parental or school rules. For example, a college student who finds her date to be a bore must make up an excuse to go home early or tell him she is not enjoying his company. She cannot use a dorm curfew as a reason to end a date. A man who does not want to have sex with his date must let her know how he feels. He cannot rely on dorm policy to restrict her from accompanying him to his room.

Because more women are pursuing careers, they are not so anxious to find a husband by the time they graduate from high school or college. They know they have the option of staying single and working. Today's greater equality between the sexes is apparent in dating too. For instance, a woman may initiate a date with a man, although most still prefer that the man take the lead in the early stages of a relationship. One woman notes that she feels comfortable in "making herself available" so the man can start up a conversation and ask her out. She also notes, however, that if she were to ask him out, he might think her too aggressive and be intimidated by her.

Dating partners also have to consider whether or not they should pay their own way on a date. Should she occasionally pick up the whole tab? Should she offer to drive? Should he offer to cook dinner for her? Should she invite him to her apartment? Feminists initiate and share expenses more often than do nonfeminists. However, even nonfeminist, traditional women are venturing into these roles (Korman, 1983).

Perhaps the more casual system of going out and the greater equality between women and men has changed some of the customs of dating. The large number of college students who participate in exclusive relationships, however, suggests that commitment is still an important part of dating. Spending at least part of the dating years in committed relationships allows people to gain experience in the process of give and take. Those who do not gain any experience in exclusive relationships may have problems in learning the compromises necessary in marriage.

MATE SELECTION

Dating sometimes leads to marriage. You may select your date for the prom next month extra carefully because you expect it to be the social highlight of the semester and you want to be sure of having a good time. The evening is important to you. Your choice of a marriage partner, with whom you intend to spend the rest of your life, is infinitely more crucial to your happiness.

FILTERING PROCESS

Have you ever stopped to think about how you actually select a marriage partner? It may seem that you date those who are attractive to you and eventually find yourself in love and ready to marry. Scientists have taken a closer, more systematic look at how you really select your particular mate from a field of almost 5 billion people. The selection occurs through a filtering process. First, you must exclude several large groups of people:

1. Those of your own sex. This eliminates about half the world's population.
2. Those you will never meet. "Propinquity" refers to geographic nearness. Although you are technically free to choose a mate from anywhere in the world, you will not meet most of the world's people and hence will not have the chance to fall in love with them. Chances are you will not only marry someone from the United States but, in fact, someone from your own hometown or campus. As Kephart (1981) notes, "When all is said and done, the 'one and only' may have a better than 50-50 chance of living within walking distance" (p. 241).
3. Those you cannot legally marry. The law forbids you to marry a close relative, a person below a certain age, one who is already married, and so on.
4. Those who will not have you. Even among those you know well and are

not excluded by law, there are possible mates who are simply not interested in you. They may not find you attractive or may be interested in someone else.

In addition to the possible mates that are automatically ruled out for you, you will probably choose to eliminate others from your field of eligibles. The practice of marrying outside your own group is called *exogamy*. The practice of marrying within your own group is called *endogamy*. Consider these social units:

1. *Race.* Interracial marriages in the United States are still rare. For example, only one out of every thousand marriages are between a black and a white spouse. In 1974, the "survival rate" over a ten-year period of marriages between two whites was about 90 percent; between two blacks, about 75 percent; between a white husband and a black wife, only about 50 percent (Heer, 1974). Today, with the increasing break-up rates, all categories are likely to be significantly lower. Apparently stress due to lack of acceptance by the community is harmful to mixed-race relationships.

2. *Religion.* Most students today are not terribly concerned about the religious background of their dates, and marriages of mixed religious background have increased in the past decades. However, some students still worry about their family's reaction to their marrying someone of a different faith. The level of stability in marriage, measured by the divorce rate, indicates that marriages between Jews have the lowest divorce rate (considerably less than 10 percent). Marriages between Catholics have the next lowest rate (about 10 percent), while the highest rate (about 33 percent) was found in marriages in which the wife was Protestant and the husband did not belong to any of the three major religious groups (Bumpass & Sweet, 1972). In the eighties, a high degree of religious homogamy is being reported; however, much of it is due to the fact that often one partner switches religious affiliation during engagement or at the time of marriage to agree with the spouse's (Glenn, 1982).

3. *Age.* How old would you like your prospective mate to be? Most people marry someone about the same age as they are, especially in their first marriage. Twenty-year-old college women tell us that they would be interested in marrying a handsome and wealthy man of age 25, perhaps 30, but not 35. However, 25- to 30-year-old women express interest in the 35-year-old or older male. As people get older, they enlarge the acceptable age range for a potential spouse.

Bytheway (1981) found that those who have been married before are more likely to become involved with someone less close in age than are those who have never been married. The average age for first marriage is 24 for men and 22 for women (National Center for Health Statistics, 1984). College-educated men marry almost a year later than the average man, and college-educated women marry slightly over two years later than the average woman.

4. *Social class and education.* Despite the fairytales in which a prince or a princess marries a peasant, most people actually marry within their social class. This may be partly due to choice, but it also relates to the fact that people in the same social class have more opportunity to meet and date. The term *mésalliance*

refers to marriages between people of different social classes; *hypergamy* means marrying upward and *hypogamy* marrying downward. Research has shown that women, especially those who are attractive or have more education, tend more toward hypergamy than hypogamy.

What other factors do you consider important in the selection of a potential spouse? Perhaps there are aspects of a person that you consider without realizing it. For example, people who share the same reaction to humorous stimuli are more disposed to marry than those who don't. "Shared humor probably reflects similar values, similar needs (aggressive, sexual, etc.), resulting in consensual validation with an intimate other on how one perceives the world" (Murstein & Brust, 1985, p. 639). You may find some other factors even more important in your mate-selection process. What are some of these?

FAMILY INFLUENCE VS. LOVE

Your family will have an influence on whom you marry. Most families will try to exert some control over the process of mate selection. Thus, while you might consider love and the personal qualities of your partner far more important than his or her background, your parents might be weighing social status, family background, wealth, and other aspects of your potential mate more heavily. They might point out their concerns or otherwise try to control your love relationships.

After marriage, both your family and your spouse's family will have an influence on your lives. When you marry your partner, you marry into a whole new family with its own customs and traditions. These traditions may be religious, ethnic, or regional. Some habits are unique to the individual family. For instance, if you marry into a family in which the members seem to be constantly hugging and kissing one another and you were brought up in a family where touching was not a common pattern, you may find get-togethers difficult. On the other hand, interaction with your partner's family might be helpful. One student said he enjoyed going to his girlfriend's home. Her parents were pleasant and got along well. He found her family a refreshing change from his constantly bickering household. Whatever your reaction to your partner's family, you must remember that they have had an influence on your partner for all his or her life and will continue to have an effect on your relationship.

THEORIES OF MATE SELECTION

A number of researchers have proposed various theories explaining the factors that influence mate selection. Generally, these theories incorporate the idea that "humans seek rewards and avoid costs to achieve the most profitable or least unprofitable outcome" (Nye, 1980, p. 480).

The Winch (1971) theory of complementary needs, for example, says that individuals marry those who can provide them with maximum need gratification.

Further, the needs of one partner tend to complement the needs of the other. The classic example of this theory is a dominant man who marries a submissive woman or a domineering woman who marries a man who needs to be dominated. Although little empirical evidence has been found to support this theory, most of us can think of couples who seem to fit this model.

Kerckhoff and Davis's (1962) filter theory adds social and cultural homogamy and value consensus to Winch's idea of need complementarity. They found that when couples had all three components, they could move toward a more permanent commitment in their relationship.

The exchange theory sees mate selection as a business transaction. Simply put, it states that if your profits or benefits from a relationship exceed your losses, you will stay in the relationship. If a relationship changes and you perceive that you have a net loss, you may want to get out of the relationship. If an alternative relationship promises a greater net profit than the one you are in, you may "sell" the old relationship and "buy into" the new one. Farber (1964) calls this movement in and out of the marital marketplace "permanent availability." A person may at any time leave a relationship for one that appears more rewarding. McCall (1966) says, "Courtship teaches the individual how to bargain—how to form, maintain, and leave relationships. The emphasis in modern life is on keeping up one's bargaining skills, for one never entirely leaves the market" (p. 197).

Murstein's (1970) stimulus-value-role theory emphasizes your free choice in selecting a mate. Everyone, according to the SVR theory, has both open and closed fields of eligibles from which to choose. In an open field, the male and female do not know each other but are free to relate to each other with no roles assigned. An example would be meeting someone on a plane, at a football game or party, or in a large class at the beginning of the semester. In an open field, physical appearance provides much of the stimulus.

In a closed field, you relate to others in assigned roles—as nurse-patient, teacher-student, or perhaps co-workers. In a closed field, you have more opportunity to learn about the other person and to decide if you want to get to know him or her better. Physical appearance is not as big a factor in a closed field. As one student who worked in a fast-food restaurant remarked, "Jodi was only average looking, but as time went by, I noticed how much fun she was and how helpful she was to the new people. I'm sure glad I asked her out."

In the second (value) stage, the partners learn about each other through self-disclosure. They can find out what they have in common and what they disagree on. If they find that they are compatible, they may move on to the next stage.

Finally, in the role stage, the partners see how they each operate in their roles as husband and wife. They must decide if their role expectations are compatible. Is one partner going to have a job and the other work in the home? Will they have children? Who will do what household chores? Who will make the decisions? Researchers have found that when a couple agree on marital roles, the chances of marital satisfaction are increased. For example, in a study of married couples, those who thought they were in agreement with their spouses about their roles and those who perceived their spouses as fulfilling their agreed-upon roles reported more marital happiness than those who did not (Bahr, Chappell, & Leigh, 1983).

Nye (1980) proposes a general theory called "choice and exchange," which incorporates the other isolated theories. Humans, he says, seek the most profitable long- and short-term outcomes. People tend to seek relationships that provide them with social approval, autonomy, predictability, a mate with similar beliefs and values, conformity to norms, and money. Therefore, they make choices and exchanges based on these sources of rewards.

While theories are interesting, necessary for research, and revealing as to the way people select a marriage partner, they are not rules to follow in deciding your personal future.

CONSIDERATIONS FOR MARRIAGE

How should you decide whether to marry, when to marry, or whom to marry? Is love enough to make a good marriage? No, but it helps. Actually, although love is listed as a number-one reason for marrying, marriage sometimes results from being in the right relationship at the right time and place. For instance, a couple

When couples start looking at wedding rings, the wedding can't be too far off.

graduating from college is more likely to marry than one dating in junior high school simply because they are a more appropriate age for marriage. European social critic Denis DeRougemont (1959) said that love alone is a poor basis for marriage. "We are in the act of trying out—and failing miserably at it—one of the most pathological experiments that a civilized society has ever imagined, namely, the basing of marriage, which is lasting, upon romance, which is a passing fancy" (p. 452).

SOME REASONS NOT TO MARRY

People find many reasons to marry. Many of them are not the right ones. Here are a few, and you can add others:

> Everyone else is getting married.
> My parents want me to get married.
> My friends really like my partner.
> I am getting old and may never find anyone else.
> I am lonely.
> I don't want to live with my parents anymore.
> I am pregnant.

Most of these reasons are perceived pressures from family, friends, a personal situation, or society in general. Trying to cure a problem through marriage usually only creates more problems.

BEING READY FOR MARRIAGE

If you are thinking of marrying, you might ask a few questions about yourself and your relationship. Have you had enough dating experience to know what types of couple relationships are possible? Does each of you really know how to communicate your feelings? Are you both committed to the relationship? Have you practiced fighting fair when you disagree?

Age can be an important factor in the success of your marriage. Numerous studies have found an inverse relationship between the age at marriage and the probability of divorce. For instance, in a study of women who had been or were currently married, "the youngest brides (married before age 17) averaged fewest surviving marriages at each year since marriage. Intactness was highest for women married at ages 22 through 29, and declined again thereafter" (Carlson & Stinson, 1982, p. 261).

However, many people now marry before they reach this preferable age. Teenage marriage partners often lack social and/or psychological maturity as well as the education, training, and experience needed to get a good job.

Marriage partners need to be compatible. Do you have common interests? Do you agree philosophically? Do you have similar religious, economic, and political views? Do you agree on the amount of time that should be spent participating in religious activities, in social activity, or even with each other? If one partner wants to party every weekend and the other prefers to stay home and read a book, problems can ensue. If your partner is an early riser and you like to stay up and sleep late the next morning, you may need to compromise. Can you both at least agree to disagree and be accepting and happy with that arrangement?

You should consider financial matters before marriage. First, can you afford to get married? Second, do you agree on the way your budget should be handled? Expecting to live on a starting salary the way your parents live today, after many years of marriage, is unrealistic and can cause disappointment and strife.

> To Have and Too Old
>
> *The bride, white of hair, is stooped over her cane,*
> *Her faltering footsteps need guiding,*
> *While down the church aisle, with a wan, toothless smile,*
> *The groom in a wheel chair comes riding.*
>
> *And who is this elderly couple, you ask?*
> *You'll find, when you've closely explored it,*
> *That here is that rare, most conservative pair,*
> *Who waited till they could afford it.*
>
> Armour, 1954, p. 5

The last stage of the premarital relationship is a good time for continued testing and discussing. During the engagement period, you can examine your relationship and make plans for the future. You can also gain feedback from friends and relatives who now know that you intend to marry. Although breaking an engagement is often difficult for both parties, it is usually less difficult than breaking up a marriage by divorce. Most couples who are realistic about their relationship test it before becoming formally engaged, but engagement offers a last chance to make certain that both partners truly want to get married. While many engaged couples consider their engagement a time to plan their wedding ceremony rather than the rest of their lives, the latter is far more important. Research shows that those who believed planning their marriage was more important later report better marital adjustment than those who concentrated on their wedding.

THE WEDDING

The wedding ceremony itself serves several functions. It is a rite of passage marking the change from single to a married status. It establishes a legal framework for a new family. It also makes public your commitment to each other and establishes you as a couple in the eyes of the community.

The wedding should help to bring together the families. However, Firth, Hubert, and Forge (1970) found that almost 10 percent of the parents in their study were not invited to the wedding or refused to come because of differences between the parents and children. Working out differences prior to the wedding is important, since marriages that have family support are more likely to last.

There are many details to consider before the wedding—including how large the wedding should be, how much you should spend, where to have it, when to have it, what type of service to have. The wedding ceremony can be a time of fun and festivity, and it is an important social event for the couple, their families, and their friends. Even more important, it is the beginning of a life together for you and your spouse.

SUMMARY

- Social interaction between men and women has changed from a formal courtship system to dating to the informal system of getting together and going out.

- Our dating system can be characterized as elaborate, flexible, pluralistic, competitive, progressive, participant-run, and having a double standard.

- The dating system functions to benefit the individual, the family, and society.

- The main functions of dating include recreation, socialization, status or prestige, and mate selection.

- Male-female relationships generally progress from initial attraction through the stages of initial dating, going steady, exclusive dating, and engagement.

- Breakups, for a variety of reasons, can and do occur at any stage.

- Some general areas of concern in dating relationships include bargaining, exploitation, the principle of least interest, posing, and sex.

- Recent changes in societal norms have given dating individuals greater freedom as well as created certain difficulties.

- Dating, in whatever form, will continue for the foreseeable future as long as it continues to benefit the individual, the family, and society.

- People select a mate through a filtering process in which some potential mates are eliminated for them and they eliminate others by choice. Race, religion, age, and social class are considerations for mate selection.

- Families often influence a person's choice of spouse.

- Some of the theories of mate selection suggested by researchers include the Winch theory of complementary needs, Kerchoff and Davis's filter theory, the exchange theory, Murstein's stimulus-value-role theory, and Nye's choice and exchange theory.

- There are many poor reasons to marry, and you should never feel pressured into marriage.

- Couples contemplating marriage should consider many aspects of their own personalities and their relationship before making the final decision.

- The wedding ceremony marks the rite of passage from the single to the married stage of life.

PERSPECTIVE: COHABITATION

In the early 1980s, over 1.8 million unmarried American couples were living together. That is more than three times as many as lived together in 1970 and represents about 4 percent of all U.S. couples (Spanier, 1983). Who are the people who cohabit? Why do they live together rather than marry? Is cohabiting beneficial? What are its problems?

While several definitions of cohabitation have been suggested, Macklin (1983) offers this widely accepted definition: "sharing a bedroom and/or bed for four or more nights a week for three or more consecutive months with someone of the opposite sex to whom one is not married" (p. 265). The majority of cohabitants are college students, and their number is rising. Some cohabitants are middle-aged and elderly, although the proportion of senior citizens living together is decreasing compared to young adult cohabitants (Spanier, 1983).

Although research has been limited to date, scientists have found cohabitants surprisingly similar to couples who do not live together. "Most researchers have been more impressed by the similarities than by the differences between cohabitants and non-cohabitants" (Macklin, 1983, p. 270). The differences that do exist suggest that people who cohabit are less religious and generally have more liberal attitudes. Student cohabitants are more likely to be liberal arts students than business majors. According to Macklin (1983), cohabitants are *"not* more likely to come from unhappy or divorced homes, do not have lower academic averages, and are not significantly less likely to want eventually to marry" (p. 270).

Why do couples choose to live together? There are a variety of reasons, including economics, convenience, rebellion, and simply because they dislike the idea of marriage. Elderly individuals often cohabit to save money, because retirement and social security benefits often penalize married couples by giving them less combined income than what they could receive as singles. Many researchers believe that cohabitation is a form of courtship. Most women do not consider cohabitation a permanent life-style but rather a step toward marriage (Tanfer, 1987). People who cohabit generally plan to marry later, although not necessarily each other, and cohabiting couples are no less likely to marry or more likely to break up than noncohabiting couples (Risman, Hill, Rubin, & Peplau, 1981). In the United States, cohabitation unions that do not end in marriage last an average of 18 months.

Cohabiting couples report that they decided gradually, in a low-key fashion, to live together. They say they discussed few plans for the future, obligations, or other key issues before moving in together (Kotkin, 1985). Those who had cohabited and later married, however, say that the decision to marry was not as casual as the one to cohabit; marriage involved more trust, security, and commitment. Most cohabiting couples married when they had jobs and felt settled. Those living together and not planning to marry cite ease of dissolution, personal autonomy, and being treated as individuals rather than as a couple as reasons for living together. "While cohabitation is merely a relationship, marriage is an institution as well" (Kotkin, 1985, p. 158).

Cohabiting couples apparently enjoy their life-style. They report a greater satisfaction in their relationships than noncohabiting couples. Cohabiting men report a higher satisfaction in sexual intercourse than noncohabiting men, while the women in each situation report the same degree of satisfaction. What about after they marry? Bentler and Newcomb (1978) found no significant difference in the divorce rate between couples who had lived together before marriage and those who had not. DeMaris and Leslie (1984) found, however, that married couples who had previously lived together reported a lower quality of communication and less marital satisfaction than married couples who had not.

What are the problems of cohabiting? Some are similar to those of married people. Couples may have trouble deciding who should do what chores, how their joint incomes should be handled, and how to deal with sexual problems. It seems, however, that while cohabitors are more liberal in their view of sex, they are very traditional in their views of the division of labor, and the woman often finds herself doing more of the housework.

Despite their prevalence among college students, "cohabitational relationships are not only less regulated than marital ones, but also less honored and respected" (Kotkin, 1985, p. 157). Parents especially disapprove. Consequently, many cohabiting students, particularly coeds, live with their partners but also maintain—and pay for—a dorm room so that their parents will think they are living with a same-sex roommate.

Another problem for cohabitors is nomenclature. What do you call your partner—friend, lover, or roommate? There are as yet no specific titles such as husband and wife. Similarly, there are no names for other aspects of the relationship. Married people can refer to their wedding, honeymoon, spouse, and marriage, but there are no corresponding words for those living together.

Legalities pose other problems. Although it is rarely prosecuted (and perhaps cannot be under the Constitution), cohabitation is still illegal in about 20 states (Lavori, 1976). Also, since cohabiting partners are not legal dependents or spouses, they may not qualify for insurance benefits, inheritance, visiting rights in a hospital, and other privileges granted to a marriage partner.

Other legal problems can occur when cohabiting couples break up. Courts in about fifteen states have already heard palimony suits, in which one partner has to pay the other when their relationship ends. Mark Golden, a lawyer in the case brought against the actor Lee Marvin by his former live-in lover, commented, "It's ironic that those people who probably wanted to avoid the financial responsibilities of marriage are actually facing greater complications than people who do marry" (Macovsky, 1983, p. 226).

Breaking up is an emotional time. Frederick G. Humphrey, president of the

American Association of Marriage and Family Counselors, says, "Unmarried couples may want the pseudo-intellectual belief that they are free to leave, but when they split up, the emotional pain and trauma is often virtually identical to married couples getting a divorce" (Schwartz, 1977, p. 49).

How does cohabitation affect a subsequent marriage? Recent research in Canada shows that premarital cohabitation appears to be positively associated with marital stability (White, 1987). On the other hand, a U.S. study of newly-weds and couples married for four years shows that those who cohabited prior to marriage were no more well adjusted to marriage than their counterparts.

The long-term effects of living together cannot yet be accurately evaluated, since cohabitation is such a recent development. Whether it reduces the marriage or divorce rates, makes couples happier or unhappier, or makes them better or worse marriage partners is not yet known. Whatever the effects, however, cohabitation will definitely remain a part of the dating system for the foreseeable future.

QUESTIONS FOR THOUGHT AND DISCUSSION

1. What three factors were instrumental in the change from a courtship to a dating system? Why have attitudes changed from dating toward "getting to-gether" in recent years? Is this a change for the better, in your opinion? Why or why not?

2. What are some of the functions that dating serves for society? Why are these important?

3. How do you feel about computer dating services?

4. What are some aspects or characteristics of our dating system?

5. What are the four major stages of the typical dating sequence? How do they illustrate the progression of a relationship?

6. What is the double standard? What are some of its characteristics? How has it changed in the past few decades? Do you feel that it still exists? If so, give some examples.

7. How do men and women differ in the way that they gain status from a dating partner?

8. What are important factors that affect the initiation of relationships? How do men and women differ in the importance that each of these factors has for them? What is usually the most important factor for both sexes?

9. According to the text, how important is physical attractiveness in the initiation of relationships? In the maintenance of relationships? How important is it for you?

10. What tends to be more important in determining a breakup of a relationship: the amount of physical intimacy or the amount of emotional intimacy? Explain.

11. What are some common causes of breakups? What are some common times? What are some explanations for these trends?

12. What is the "principle of least interest"? How does it affect relationship maintenance and interaction? How does it affect bargaining?

13. How does the filtering process of mate selection work? How does it affect whom you meet and date?

14. What are some of the theories of mate selection? How are they similar? How are they different?

15. How do you feel about cohabitation? Is it a good or bad idea for couples?

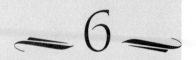

Premarital Sexuality: Attitudes and Behaviors

Since all of you have had premarital sex, this chapter should be of special interest. That's right—all of you have had premarital sex.

The reason everyone is included is because the definitions of premarital sex differ greatly. Consider "What is sex?" You may automatically think of sex as sexual intercourse, but the activities included under the heading of sex range from holding hands and kissing to petting, masturbation, coitus, and even erotic dreams and fantasy.

Sexual behavior has to be considered in biological, sociological, psychological, and ethical dimensions. Humans are sexual beings; unlike other animals, their sexuality is not closely related to the fertility cycle. What is sexual for you depends on the society in which you grew up and on your unique experiences. Revealing clothing, tight jeans, or pictures of nudes may be erotic to you but have no effect on someone else. To one individual, sex is a deeply personal experience; to another, it is a recreational activity; and to still others, it signifies power or surrender.

Experiments with monkeys illustrate the importance of social learning and its effect on sexual behavior (Harlow, 1962). It was found that monkeys raised in isolation were unable to mate, but that monkeys that were raised with others, even other young monkeys, had developed skills in social interaction that enabled them to mate. If sexual learning is necessary for monkeys, it is even more necessary for humans, with their more complicated feelings, values, and multitude of behavioral options.

Although biology gives us our sex drive, cultural conditioning tells us where, when, and how it should be satisfied. Most of us have seen dogs copulating in daylight on a college campus or in a schoolyard, but—while we may be equally interested in sex—we have been conditioned to believe that the campus quad at high noon is not the appropriate time and place for sexual intercourse. Our feelings of propriety are cultural, not biological. Our sexual practices are embedded in a mass of social and cultural standards, rules, norms, and taboos.

If "sexuality" is difficult to define, so is "premarital." Some people prefer to avoid the latter term because it implies that marriage will eventually follow. Some authors use "premarital" in connection with an unmarried couple whose relationship is marriage-oriented and "nonmarital" to refer to a situation where marriage is not a factor. For our discussion, we will follow Libby and Carlson's (1978) lead:

"The term 'premarital' is used here to include sexual behavior before marriage. No assumption is made that marriage will occur or that all premarital sexual behavior is marriage-oriented" (p. 164).

SEXUAL REVOLUTION OR EVOLUTION?

> *Bumper sticker: Remember when the air was clean and sex was dirty?*

For the past two decades or so, the popular press has been discussing a supposed sexual revolution, which, they say, has radically and recently changed sexual behavior in our society. Has there really been a revolution in sexual attitudes and behaviors?

MEDIA, ATTITUDES, AND BEHAVIOR

In his article "Adolescents and Sex," James Elias (1980) notes that discussion about a sexual revolution usually occurs on three levels. First, the media have seen an increase both in number of articles and other materials concerning sexuality and in the types of candid and sexually explicit material available. Second, on the attitudinal level, frankness and openness in the discussion of sexuality has increased. Many of your parents' generation engaged in premarital sex but did not openly discuss sexuality. Today's adolescents may talk more about it than they do it. One study, for example, found that neither male nor female students reported being very active sexually, but both perceived more active sexual behavior among their peers (Rubinson, Ory, & Marmata, 1981). Another reported that their subjects were much more likely to favor premarital sex than to have actually engaged in the activity (Lawrance, Rubinson, & O'Rourke, 1984).

Elias sees a revolution both in the media and in attitudes toward sexuality. However, on the third level—actual sexual behavior—he does not see a revolution. He states, "Kinsey reported a 20 to 25 percent nonvirginity rate for college females. A more recent study at the Institute for Sex Research shows that this rate has risen to 33 percent. This increase has occurred over a twenty-five-year period and certainly cannot be called 'revolutionary'" (p. 141). Other researchers found college students "no more likely to favor premarital sexual intercourse in 1982 than they were ten years before" (Lawrance et al., 1984, p. 24).

A WORD ABOUT NUMBERS

Most students do not like to memorize numbers and percentages. "How well do we have to know all these stats?" they ask.

This chapter contains a particularly large number of percentages because of the various studies and trends. Notice that most of the percentages have been rounded off to the closest target number—for example, 53 percent to one-half, 64 percent to two-thirds. If you need the exact figures, consult the proper reference.

Remember, too, that it is hard to compare statistics from different studies because of the different ways the studies were conducted, the different questions asked, the different kinds of samples used, and so on. For example, in comparing sexual behavior rates, one study is from a community in Michigan, another from one in Colorado, and a third is a national sample. Even the questions asked were not identical. Therefore, exact percentages would have little meaning. An understanding of the general trends and approximate figures is much more meaningful.

Also, Kinsey's data for the 1950s showed that about 60 percent of college-educated females were nonvirgin at the time of their marriage (Kinsey, Pomeroy, Martin, and Gebhard, 1953); 1980s figures range from three-fourths to 90 percent. Darling, Kallen, and Van Dusen (1984) reviewed 35 studies conducted between 1903 and 1980 concerning premarital coitus. They found two major trends: (1) a major increase in the proportion of young people reporting having had intercourse and (2) a more rapid increase in the proportion of women reporting coitus than the proportion of men. Before 1970, twice as many college men reported intercourse; today the proportions of men and women are nearly equal.

In truth, the United States has had a long-term sexual evolution in attitudes and behavior. Perhaps the perceived revolution is more in the number of people, especially women, who admit to having had premarital sex than in the increase in sexual activity per se.

VARIOUS POPULATIONS

Many statistics and studies pertain to college student groups simply because college students are easily accessible for research. Recent studies have turned to other populations as well. How do the various groups compare?

Teenagers   There appear to be two key points about sex among high school students. First, it appears that a higher percentage of teenagers are engaging in coitus than in the past. Second, teenagers are engaging in intercourse at earlier ages. Hass (1979) found that over 80 percent of the teenage boys questioned in his survey thought it was okay for a boy his age to have sexual intercourse with a girl. Similarly, over half of the girls aged 15 to 16 and nearly two-thirds of the girls aged 17 to 18 thought it okay for a girl her age to have intercourse with a boy. About 70 percent of the younger girls and 60 percent of the boys said they had had intercourse; approximately half of the older teens said they had. Nearly 10 percent of the girls and nearly 20 percent of the boys aged 15 to 16 said they had had their first sexual experience by age 13.

One survey of teenage girls aged 15 to 19 revealed some interesting information (Zelnik, Kantner, & Ford, 1981). The average age for first coitus was found to be

A young couple off to the woods to commune with nature for the weekend.

about 16. The girls' partners averaged 2½ to 3 years older. Three-fourths of the respondents said their first coitus took place in a home—their partner's, theirs, or a friend's. Those who had had more than one partner varied according to how long the girl had been sexually active. About 10 percent of those who had been active for less than a year had more than one partner, while 80 percent of those who had been active for four or more years reported more than one partner. The girls reported having intercourse approximately 2½ times per month.

Interestingly, U.S. teens today are more preoccupied with sex than teens in other countries. In a 1986 survey, virtually all of the American teenagers cited premarital relations as one of the three most important issues facing today's youth. Only about 30 percent of those in other countries ranked it among the top six problems. However, when asked to name three things that would bring them happiness, teens all over the world replied "love" (*U.S. News & World Report,* 1986). So while American teens are engaging in premarital sex at a greater and greater rate, they also consider it a problem. Perhaps, as one punster suggested, "Sex is a two-way treat."

College Students   The trends in premarital sexual attitudes and behavior are similar for college-age youth. One longitudinal study found an increase in the overall prevalence of premarital sexual behavior, especially intercourse; an increase in the number of partners among experienced people; a decrease in the average age of first coitus; and a trend toward more liberal attitudes about premarital sex (Clayton & Bokemeier, 1980).

While numerous studies show an overall increase in the percentage of students who have engaged in sexual intercourse, the major increases in sexual experience are among women. Jessor and Jessor (1975) and Walsh, Ferrell, and Tolone (1976) show that both men and women became more permissive in sexual attitudes and behavior as they moved from freshman to senior year. Another study shows that the percentage of women in college who have had premarital sexual experience has gone from approximately 20 percent in the late 1960s to 80 percent by the mid-1970s; it dropped to 50 percent in the early 1980s (Clatworthy, 1985).

Men continue to report a higher incidence of sexual behavior than do women, about twice as high, according to Lawrance et al. (1984). The highest rate of intercourse for males (about 90 percent) was found in several sex-role classes at an Illinois university (Jesser, 1978), while the highest intercourse rate for women (nearly 90 percent) was found among college seniors in Colorado (Jessor & Jessor, 1975). Two studies—Jessor and Jessor (1975) in Colorado and Miller (1976) at Stanford in California—found women to be more sexually active than men.

Nonstudents   Very little sex research has been done on young adults who are not in college. DeLamater and MacCorquodale (1979) conducted a unique study of a large population of college students and nonstudents in Madison, Wisconsin (see Table 6.1). First, they found little difference between the two groups. Second, the data show what may be a trend toward less difference between male and female behavior. Finally, note that a majority of both students and nonstudents had participated in the sexual behavior listed. However, the statistics do not show promiscuity. Most people want most of their sexual activity to occur in situations of love or affection. Most report few coital partners.

Adults   Studies of adult populations show findings similar to those based on student surveys. They indicate more permissive sexual attitudes and behavior but little promiscuity.

Bell and Balter (1975) found that about two-thirds of over two thousand married women nationwide reported premarital coitus. Levin and Levin (1975), in a *Redbook* magazine questionnaire of over a hundred thousand women, found that two-thirds of those married before the mid-1960s were sexually experienced at the time of marriage and that, by the mid-1970s, about 90 percent of them were experienced at the time of marriage. One advantage of doing studies with married respondents, rather than mostly single college populations, is that the serious relationship and engagement periods are included in the married samples. These studies can be more accurate because they include the respondents' entire premarital experience.

TABLE 6.1 Sexual Behavior Among Students and Nonstudents

Behavior	Male				Female			
	Student		Nonstudent		Student		Nonstudent	
	%*	Age†	%	Age	%	Age	%	Age
Necking	97	14.2	98	13.9	99	14.8	99	14.9
French kissing	93	15.3	95	15.1	95	15.8	95	16.0
Breast fondling	92	15.8	92	15.5	93	16.6	93	16.6
Male fondling of female genitals	86	16.6	87	16.3	82	17.2	86	17.5
Female fondling of male genitals	82	16.8	84	16.7	78	17.4	81	17.8
Genital apposition	77	17.1	81	16.8	72	17.6	78	17.9
Intercourse	75	17.5	79	17.2	60	17.9	72	18.3
Male oral contact with female genitals	60	18.2	68	17.7	59	18.1	67	18.6
Female oral contact with male genitals	61	18.1	70	17.8	54	18.1	63	18.8

SOURCE: DeLamater and MacCorquodale, 1979, p. 59.
*Percent of entire sample.
†Age of first intercourse of those who engaged in the behavior.

REASONS FOR CHANGING SEXUAL ATTITUDES AND BEHAVIORS

The changing social context of sexual attitudes and practices, which has become more open and liberal, has been a part of the accelerated sexual evolution which, according to many scholars, reached peaks in the 1920s, when sexual activity became more acceptable. It peaked again in the 1960s, when society reduced its restrictions, especially on youth, and allowed for a more widespread acceptance of varied sexual behaviors, such as oral-genital sex.

Darling, Kallen, and Van Dusen (1984) summarize three general eras characterized by different sexual standards:

1. The double standard, which allowed sexual behavior for men but not for women. This era lasted until the late 1940s or early 1950s.
2. The era of "permissiveness with affection," as coined by Reiss (1967),

which permitted sex between partners in a love relationship that was expected to lead to marriage. This era lasted until approximately 1970.

3. The current era, in which intercourse is considered natural even without the expectation of marriage.

MOVEMENTS

Recent increases in premarital sexual behavior have taken place in a social context, as part of various social movements. The women's movement, for example, has given women more opportunity to meet men in the workplace and on campus. Women can opt to stay single. It is acceptable for women to be aware of their own sexuality. They may now initiate relationships and sexual behavior. With new birth-control methods, they can feel free to engage in sex without the fear of pregnancy.

Media now explore a variety of sexual behaviors. Talk shows address problems ranging from venereal disease and teenage prostitution to rape and child abuse. *Playboy* now shows the entire nude female body, and *Playgirl* came along to join its counterpart on the newsstands, although it had a rather short life.

The youth movement of the 1960s emphasized rights and autonomy for minors and succeeded in removing students at least partially from parental control as well as from that of college administrations. Youth questioned adult values, including sexual values, and shifted their emphasis from traditional institutions to situational ethics. With more freedom, youth now have more opportunities for sexual activity. Even the trend to marry later gives youth more premarital years and thus increases their chances of engaging in premarital sex.

RELIGION

Religion has been a key definer of morality and values for centuries and has had a great influence on sexuality. Religious organizations in general have historically restricted and/or repressed sexuality. Numerous studies have shown a negative relationship between religiousness and premarital sexual permissiveness for both men and women. My own research in the 1970s shows that student piety and church attendance decline over the college years, while sexual permissiveness increases. While this is only a correlation, not necessarily a causal relationship, I have found fewer students mentioning religion as a major referent of their sexual values. The approximately 10 percent who still see religion as a major source of values have remained sexually conservative. However, in 1984, Sack, Keller, and Hinkle (1984) compared students' sexual behavior with several factors and found no association between it and their religiousness. An increase of scientific knowledge and publication about sexual behavior by such key figures as Kinsey, Masters and Johnson, and others has given rise to alternative sources of information about sexual matters.

Now the acceleration seems to have reached a plateau, and several scholars agree that the 1980s is a time of consolidation. The eighties could be called a time of "cooling out" and stabilization of attitudes. Dryfoos (1985) notes, "The proportion of teenagers who are sexually active has plateaued" (p. 1). A possible reason for this stabilization is that "events external to the campus, such as the new evangelical religion, the pro- and anti-abortion movements and the new conservatism may have affected student attitudes and behavior" (Robinson & Jedlicka, 1982, p. 237). The recent AIDS scare may also have influenced this "cooling out" period by causing young people to take their sexual participation more seriously and thoughtfully.

FACTORS RELATED TO SEX ATTITUDES AND BEHAVIORS

Sex takes the least amount of time, but causes the most amount of trouble.

Our fifth-grade science class has proved sex doesn't exist. They put a bird and a bee in a cage. Nothing happened.

In fact, the more things are forbidden, the more popular they become. —MARK TWAIN

Your decision to engage in sex or not to is, of course, your personal choice. "Will I or won't I?" "Should I or shouldn't I?" No one else makes the decision for you. However, even though the final choice is yours, you are influenced by a number of factors—some of them in your environment, others within you.

SOCIETAL VALUES

Societal values are really a paradox for young people. On the one hand, society promotes premarital sex by allowing young people freedom to date and to form relationships, by displaying sexual activities through the media and advertising, by supporting love, and by encouraging youth to develop independence. On the other hand, it upholds the ideal of virginity until marriage.

Sometimes adolescents and young adults find that even their parents hold paradoxical views. Although there is some evidence showing that a majority of adults approve of premarital intercourse, they do not approve of it for their own children. Youth, therefore, often find that their parents have a double standard on sexual behavior—one for young people in general and a more restrictive one for their own children.

YOURSELF

Who you are influences your decisions about sex. For instance, almost all research has found differences between men and women regarding sexual activity in such areas as age at first intercourse, frequency of intercourse, percentage

Touching another's being can be done with words or with hands, feet, faces, and eyes.

of nonvirgins, importance of commitment or love, and others. Men are generally more liberal than women in sexual behaviors. However, the picture may be changing. According to Darling et al. (1984), the proportion of young women reporting coital involvement now is nearly equal to that among men.

Racial differences, which may actually be attributed to social class differences, also affect sexual behavior. According to a study of teenage girls, blacks are more likely to have premarital sex (although the relative difference is narrowing), to begin at an earlier age, but also to have fewer partners and to engage in sex less often than white girls (Zelnik et al., 1981). Mahoney (1983) notes, "These differences can be understood only by understanding differences in sexuality in the black and white segments of American society and the factors that shape these differences" (p. 213).

The amount of education a person has also seems to correlate with premarital intercourse. Those with less education experience their first coitus at an earlier age, but college-educated people eventually have more frequent and varied premarital sexual experiences as well as more partners than do people without college.

As you might expect, people become more conservative about sexual behavior as they age. People who were young adults in the 1960s, during a period of accelerated evolution in sexual behavior, probably once had liberal sexual attitudes. However, as they have grown older, they have become more conservative. Also, once they become parents, their sexual attitudes also become more conservative, not because of advancing age itself but because the parental role makes them responsible for their offspring.

Guilt may affect decisions about premarital sex. People who have higher levels of guilt about sexual behavior are less likely to be sexually experienced than those who feel less guilty. Sometimes sexual guilt occurs only in specific situations. For example, some people believe it is okay to have sex if the partner is loved. When such a person then has casual sex, guilt feelings may follow. Sack et al. (1984) found that sexual guilt had a slight negative effect on men's premarital coitus and an even higher influence on women's behavior.

Many studies have shown that religion is negatively correlated with sexual permissiveness; that is, people with conventional religious beliefs are likely to have conservative sexual standards. Surprisingly, Sack et al. (1984) recently found that male students with conventional religious attitudes tended to have sexually active friends who significantly influenced them to be sexually active. Conventional religiousness did not seem to affect women's behavior. Many people who feel guilty over their sexual behavior change their standards to reduce their guilt rather than change their behavior. As they continue the behavior, especially if it is pleasurable, they find reasons to justify sexual permissiveness.

Sex drive and opportunity also affect these decisions. The higher a person's sex drive, the more likely he or she is to engage in premarital sex. Those with more opportunities, likewise, are more apt to participate. Generally, more attractive persons have more opportunities for sexual activity and therefore have more sexual activity and more partners.

Christopher and Cate (1984) distinguish four factors underlying the decision to have intercourse: positive affect/communication, obligation/pressure, arousal/receptivity, and circumstantial. They also found that women considered positive affect/communication a little more important than did men, while men considered obligation/pressure slightly more important. People with more sexual experience saw arousal/receptivity as more important than those with less experience.

Based on all these personal characteristics and the way they relate to sexual experience, who on your campus is most likely to be a virgin? You might draw this portrait: a white freshman woman who attends church regularly, feels guilty about all sexual activity, and has a low sex drive.

CHARACTERISTICS OF THE RELATIONSHIP

Generally, the more committed the partners are to their relationship, the more likely they are to engage in coitus. Women particularly are more likely to engage in intercourse if they believe they are in love than if they are not. Simon, Berger, and Gagnon (1972) found that slightly over 10 percent of the male respondents to one study were planning to marry the woman with whom they had their first experience of intercourse, while practically two-thirds of the women were planning to marry the man with whom they first engaged in intercourse.

The closer the relationship is to marriage or the longer it lasts, the more likely it is to lead to intercourse. Although a person may be able to stay "on the verge" for a few months, it is more difficult to abstain for a year. Eventually, the "urge to merge" will probably win out. Spanier (1975) says that people who date frequently are more likely to engage in sexual activity because they have the opportunity, desire, and pressure to increase intimacy. Sexual behavior tends to follow a progression from kissing to petting—light to heavy—and then to intercourse or oral sex. Spanier notes that current relationships or situations are more influential on present behavior than past socializing experiences and that being in love or having a partner with whom one can share sexual relations are major reasons for premarital sexual behavior.

In a study of students spanning their college careers, Walsh (1978) found that students who changed from nonpermissive to permissive sexual attitudes mentioned the current situation—being in love or in a stable relationship—as the reason they changed their standards. As one woman senior said, "When I was a freshman, sex was an abstract thing; now that I'm in love it is a reality."

One aspect may be the individuals' attitudes toward sex. In the beginning stages of dating, partners often differed in their opinions about sex, but as their relationships developed and as they grew older, they became more compatible in sexual desires and behavior (McCabe & Collins, 1984).

INFLUENCE OF OTHERS

Since we are all social animals, we are influenced by others. And just as we have trouble finding anchors in times of change, our significant others may also be somewhat confused about what is now appropriate regarding sexual attitudes and behavior. Indeed, a *Time* magazine poll (1977) conducted by the Yankelovich organization found that almost two-thirds of a national sample felt it more difficult today than in the past to know what is right and wrong regarding sexual behavior.

Parents, of course, influence their children's sexual behavior, but not in completely predictable ways. Researchers have found that adolescents with lenient parents tended to have more permissive attitudes and the greatest amount of experience with sexual intercourse, while those who thought their parents were moderately strict had the least permissive attitudes and experience with intercourse. Those who saw their parents as being very strict and having many rules rated intermediate in their sexual attitudes and behaviors (Miller, McCoy, Olson, & Wallace, 1986).

Young people are more likely to follow the example of their less conservative peers than the advice of their parents or religious teaching. Shah and Zelnik

(1981) questioned young women about the influences of their parents and peers on several aspects of their lives. They found that parents were a major influence in college, career, and money matters, but most of the women's opinions on premarital sex more closely resembled those of their peers. Those who were more influenced by their friends reported more sexual experiences than those more influenced by their parents. Sack et al. (1984) found that men's sexual behavior, too, was influenced by their friends, but in a slightly different way. They found that the greatest influence on a man's premarital sexual behavior is "the number of close male friends he believes have had premarital intercourse." However, "the degree of approval from close friends for engaging in intercourse was not influential" (p. 178). The women in their study, on the other hand, said they place more value on their friends' opinions of them. Women with higher levels of guilt tend to have fewer sexually active friends and expect less approval from those friends for permissive behavior; this, in turn, limits their sexual activity.

PRESENT SEXUAL STANDARDS

> *Americans are firmly of two minds about it all, simultaneously hardheaded and idealistic, uncouth and tender, libidinous and puritanical; they believe implicitly in every tenet of romantic love, and yet they know perfectly well that things don't really work that way.*   —MORTON HUNT

> *Sex isn't the best thing in the world, or the worst thing in the world—but there's nothing else quite like it.*   —W. C. FIELDS

> *While experience may be the best teacher, only fools refuse to learn by any other means.*   —BENJAMIN FRANKLIN

We all operate in some sort of compromise between our personal desires and the norms of our society. Sexual matters are no exception. Ira Reiss (1960), a leading scholar in sexual norms or standards, points out that we do not have a single standard for sexual behavior but rather four separate standards:

1. Abstinence, where premarital intercourse is wrong for both males and females, regardless of circumstances.
2. Permissiveness with affection, which allows premarital intercourse for both men and women when they are involved in a stable, affectionate relationship.
3. Permissiveness without affection, where premarital intercourse is acceptable for both men and women, regardless of the amount of affection or stability in the relationship.

4. The double standard, which finds premarital intercourse acceptable for men but not for women.

Isadore Rubin (1965) classifies sexual standards into six categories:

1. Traditional repressive asceticism prohibits premarital intercourse under any circumstances, links marital intercourse with procreation, allows no deviation from heterosexual norms, and does not see sex as fun.
2. Enlightened asceticism believes in discipline as a guard against self-indulgence in sexual matters, emphasizes the maintenance of social control, and prohibits premarital intercourse.
3. Humanistic liberalism allows greater flexibility in sexual matters and is similar to Reiss's permissiveness-with-affection category. It states that decisions about sexual matters should be based on possible consequences to the individuals and the relationship.
4. Humanistic radicalism advocates sexual freedom with no moral prescriptions and views sex as a natural act.
5. Fun morality advocates premarital sex, views sex as fun, and encourages people to have as much fun as they wish in order to be well-adjusted individuals.
6. Sexual anarchy advocates the abolition of all controls over sexuality and notions of sexual immorality. Everything is acceptable as long as no one is injured.

While these categories can divide people into groups on the basis of their attitudes, they say little about what the population as a whole believes or does.

WHAT IS REALLY HAPPENING?

Due to the changes brought about by the sexual revolution, fewer people accept abstinence as a sexual standard. Several authors indicate that permissiveness with affection is becoming the most widely accepted sexual standard. There is also an increase in what Jurich and Jurich (1974) call the "nonexploitative permissiveness without affection standard." Under these norms, people must use a higher level of moral reasoning, taking into account the desires of the partner and the appropriateness of sexual behavior in each situation.

The level of affection necessary to justify sexual involvement has declined over the past several decades. Bell and Coughey (1980) studied college women in Philadelphia and found increases in the percentage of nonvirgins and a change in the social circumstances under which they engaged in sexual intercourse. While about one-third of the engaged women participated in sexual intercourse in 1958, about half of those simply in a dating relationship did so in 1978. Evidence from DeLamater and MacCorquodale (1979) suggests that now simply liking someone and wanting physical satisfaction is sufficient grounds for intercourse.

Looks like a mutual decision has been made.

Conversely, although young people are more involved with sexual activity than in years past, most view it in a context of affection, love, and relationship. Conley and O'Rourke (1973) found that "the youth of today are more concerned with honest, viable, meaningful relationships as justification for premarital sexual intercourse and that the majority have not opened themselves up to casual sex" (p. 289). A follow-up to this study ten years later reported few changes. "In general, young people tend to be more knowledgeable and accepting of alternative lifestyles, but they desire to continue the institution of marriage and family" (Lawrance et al., 1984).

Young people tend to have few partners and to have relatively stable relationships. Finger (1975) found that over a 30-year period at one college, the "number of partners has tended to decline over the decades" (p. 308). About one-third of the Wisconsin students in DeLamater and MacCorquodale's (1979) study had been in their relationships for over one year. Two-thirds of the men and about nine-tenths of the women described their first intercourse as occurring in a context of love or affection. Most had had relatively few partners.

A study of teen girls found that over half reported they had been going steady with their first sex partner and another fourth said they were dating their partner when they engaged in sex the first time (Zelnik & Shah, 1983). Thus, while participation in premarital sex has increased overall, the relationships that include it are generally ones of affection and stability. Most young people are not really promiscuous.

THE DOUBLE STANDARD

A double standard is a type of discrimination in which one person or category of persons is judged on or held to a different standard than another. The traditional double standard for sexual behavior in our society has held that all women must be virgins until marriage, but men are allowed "to sow their wild oats"—that is, to engage in sex at will. The classic study of the double standard by Reiss (1960) discusses sex that is body-centered, with an emphasis on it as a physical outlet, and sex that is person-centered, in which a person cares as much about the partner as the sexual activity. Reiss suggests that in person-centered sex, men are less likely to exploit women because they care about their partners as individuals.

Most researchers have found that the traditional double standard has been declining and that person-centered sexual activity has become a more popular standard. Two studies done in the 1970s (Jessor & Jessor, 1975; Miller, 1976) found women more sexually experienced than men, although this finding is not indicative of an overall trend. Men and women disagree somewhat on their attitudes. Jessor and Jessor (1975) found that almost two-thirds of the men and slightly less than half of the women agreed that it was acceptable "for two young people who are not married to engage in sexual intercourse if they both want to when they hardly know each other and have no special feelings for each other" (p. 483).

Men still generally initiate dates, make the arrangements, pay the bills—and initiate sex. Women may fear that if they suggest sex, they will appear too pushy or will frighten a partner away. Burstein (1975) found that two-thirds of the college women in her study reported they did not feel comfortable letting their partners know what turned them on or in initiating sexual behavior themselves. Jesser (1978) notes that college men are not likely to be turned off by a woman's interest; they find it flattering and a boost to their ego. However, about one-third of the college women thought the men would be turned off by their aggressive behavior.

Women are generally the limiters of sexual activity, probably because they have more to lose than men. First, they must consider their reputations. College women who did not limit their sexual behavior to relationships involving a strong degree of affection were considered bad, immoral, and irresponsible by both male and female peers (Janda, O'Grady, & Barnhart, 1981). "In short," says Mahoney (1983), "the sexually liberal female today is viewed in much the same light as she was 30 years ago. Cultural traditions do not rapidly change regardless of behavior" (p. 210). More importantly, women also face the problem of possible pregnancy and the accompanying decision of either having an illegitimate child or an abortion. Finally, women are also more stigmatized if they contract venereal disease.

Lawrance et al. (1984) found that the double standard still persists in that men are more likely than women to favor premarital sexual intercourse and that women tended to want more commitment from a partner before engaging in sex.

Robinson and Jedlicka (1982) have found a new twist to the double standard. They discovered an increase in both men and women subjects who agreed that premarital coitus for both sexes is immoral and sinful. They predict "the beginning of a new form of double standard in which men expect stricter morality of women and women expect stricter morality of men. . . . More women are now expecting apparently better behavior from males than from themselves. In short, these women reject a masculine definition of right and wrong" (p. 240). Therefore, it appears that even with the trend toward liberalism in sexual attitudes and behaviors and equal rights for women, the sexual double standard is quite persistent in our society.

SOCIAL AND SEXUAL SCRIPTS

Sexuality is learned behavior, and the process of socialization teaches us our sex roles. The term "roles" suggests that we view life as a play with a script, characters, plot, and roles. According to Clayton and Bokemeier (1980), sexual scripts identify who, what, when, where, and why sexual behavior is appropriate. For example, behavior between a male gynecologist and a female patient in the doctor's office will be interpreted one way (nonsexual), but behavior between the same gynecologist and his girlfriend on a water bed will be interpreted in another way (sexual). Sexual scripts consider such factors as gender, religion, social class, race, privacy, type of relationship, and reason for involvement. The script will often differ from one culture or even subculture to another.

How we act, talk, and dress is part of the script. Women particularly have to walk a fine line in their behavior. They want to appear attractive and alluring to men yet not seem "easy," so that they are exploited. Do clothes such as T-shirts, tight jeans, and short skirts signify that a woman is being fashionable or available? A woman may be confused as to what to wear; a man may be confused in interpreting the signals he receives.

Sexual situations contain much nonverbal communication, including gazes, touches, and movements. Imagine you have met someone at a party and afterward go to his or her apartment. The two of you are alone and the bedroom door is open. What sexual message would you get if the bedroom were quite ordinary? What if it contained a water bed, indirect lighting, mirrors on the ceiling, and a video cassette player? Jesser (1978) found that the most popular signal for wanting sex was touching, which included kissing, while the second most popular signal was letting one's hands wander. The third most frequently used method, among both men and women, was to ask directly. Jesser also noted "a higher proportion of females reported the use of eye contact, changes of appearance or clothing, and change of tone of voice" (p. 123). Awareness of what constitutes a sexual signal is a learned part of socialization and is written into sexual scripts.

Some Noncoital Sexual Behavior

Sex, including premarital sex, can include activity other than intercourse, such as masturbation, petting, oral-genital sex, fantasies, nocturnal orgasms, and more.

Masturbation

Knox (1984) defines masturbation as "stimulating one's own body with the goal of experiencing pleasurable sexual sensations" (p. 147). Our society has long been fearful that masturbation may produce a sexual desire which, in turn, will lead to intercourse. In at least some religions, it has been considered self-abuse, and young people have been warned that masturbating can cause them to go blind or to give birth to idiot children. One argument against it is that it does not involve love, so it is a selfish act, but as comedian Woody Allen retorted, "Don't knock masturbation. It's having sex with someone I deeply love."

In truth, masturbation does not result in any harmful physical effects. "Masturbation can be part of a healthy sexual experience. Medical authorities today view masturbation as harmless, noting that there is no evidence to support any claims of physical damage resulting from masturbation. From a psychological point of view, masturbation is a normal, universally practiced activity of childhood and adolescence. Many view masturbation as an acceptable part of adulthood when coitus is not available" (Jones, Shainberg, & Byer, 1985, p. 232). As with any other activity, however, it is possible to develop a fixation on it, so that masturbation becomes the focus, excluding ties to other people. Most experts believe that such a fixation, like most fixations, would be unhealthy.

Male participation rates have always been very high, with over 90 percent admitting to having masturbated at some time in their lives. Young males often hear about masturbation before they try it, and a high proportion have observed other boys masturbating (Kinsey, Pomeroy, & Martin, 1948). Arafat and Cotton (1974) found that almost three-fourths of married college males masturbate, indicating that masturbation continues even after marriage. Most men fantasize about having sex with a partner while they are masturbating (Kinsey et al. 1948).

Kinsey et al. (1953) found that approximately 60 percent of all females had masturbated. Recent studies show the percentage of females who masturbate to be anywhere from 65 to 90 percent. Women generally do not discuss masturbation and therefore do not learn about it from their peers, as men do. They often discover it by accident. Masturbation can be especially useful for females, to increase their orgasmic capabilities and to learn more about their bodies. In fact, females have a higher rate of orgasms through masturbation than from intercourse. Masturbation has sometimes been used in sex therapy. Generally, the more educated the woman is, the more likely she is to masturbate.

PETTING

"Petting," although it is an old term, has never been replaced by a newer one. Petting, or mutual masturbation, usually involves physical contact from the neck down which stops short of actual intercourse. Petting can be heavy or light, can be done over or under clothing, and can include stimulation of the breasts or genitals. It may or may not lead to intercourse.

"Our culture is unusual in that people often engage in petting as an end in it-self. . . . Petting is important for allowing sexual expression while preserving virginity and avoiding pregnancy" (Masters, Johnson, & Kolodny, 1985, p. 627). An abrupt increase in petting occurs around puberty, with the majority of males petting at ages 15 or 16 and females' first experience of petting coming six months to a year later (DeLamater and MacCorquodale, 1979).

"Petting is usually seen as a normal step in the development of the psychosexual maturity of adolescents" (Jones et al., 1985, p. 343). While petting is intended to produce sexual arousal, it also includes some nonsexual motives, including satisfying curiosity, learning to trust a partner, attempting to be popular, and obtaining and keeping the friendship of a prospective partner (Geer, Heiman, & Leitenberg, 1984).

ORAL-GENITAL SEX

Oral-genital sex has become more popular in recent years. Fellatio is oral stimulation of the man's genitals by his partner. It usually means that the woman puts her partner's penis in her mouth and sucks it, although it can also include licking the shaft and head. Cunnilingus is oral stimulation of the woman's vaginal area or vulva by her partner.

"Couples who engage in oral-genital contact generally agree that it is enjoyable to both man and woman, whether giving or receiving. The mouth and lips are erogenous zones for nearly all people. There is, in addition, an abundance of nerve endings in the tip of the nose" (McCary & McCary, 1982, p. 219).

Oral-genital sex is prevalent among sexually active college students today. The Hunt survey (1973) found that almost three-fourths of high school- and college-educated men had experienced fellatio and slightly over two-thirds had engaged in cunnilingus. More than half of the men and women in the *Playboy* sex survey said they included oral sex most of the time they made love (Petersen, 1983).

FANTASIES

Fantasies occur frequently in sexual behavior. In a sample of college students, Sue (1979) found that slightly over one-third of the men reported fantasizing during intercourse, as compared to slightly less than one-fifth of the women. Of those who fantasized, most felt their fantasizing was normal, but slightly less than one-fourth were uneasy or ashamed of their fantasies. The primary purpose of fantasizing was to "enhance sexual arousal," while the second most frequent purpose was to increase the attractiveness of the partner. Women were more likely to fantasize about "being forced or overpowered into a sexual relationship" and having sex with a "member of the same sex," while men were more likely to fantasize an "imaginary love" (p. 303). The two most popular fantasies for both sexes were "oral-genital sex" and "others finding you irresistible" (p. 303).

Fantasies are a normal part of the functioning of the mind and often occur independent of sexual activity. "Sexual thoughts, wishes, dreams and daydreams, and turn-ons are normal, no matter how 'far out.' Behavior can be wrong, but ideas cannot be. Thoughts, images, and fantasies cannot, in themselves, hurt you" (Gordon, 1985, p. 17).

NOCTURNAL ORGASMS

Men and women may both have nocturnal orgasms. It had been thought previously that men experienced nocturnal orgasms more frequently and that a higher percentage of men than women had them. However, recent research indicates that women experience sexual excitement during rapid-eye-movement (REM) sleep just as often as men do (Fisher, Cohen, Schiavi, Davis, Furman, Ward, Edwards, & Cunningham, 1983). The frequency of nocturnal orgasms for men decreases as they age, but it increases for women as they approach their forties.

Nocturnal sex dreams and orgasms seem to be involuntary and unaffected by social forces, such as religion or education for women or religious affiliation or background for men (Kinsey et al., 1953). "In dream orgasm the hallucinated events of the dream are experienced as real and are capable of producing the same physiological responses as in waking orgasm" (Fisher et al., 1983, p. 115). This behavior seems to be an indication of the strength of the innate, biological sex drive rather than the product of culture.

YOUR DECISION

What should you do regarding sexuality? What is proper? What is right or wrong? Under what conditions, if any, should you engage in premarital intercourse? These are questions everybody asks at one time or another.

The Grammar of Sex

Only she told him that they would go to bed.
She only told him that they would go to bed.
She told only him that they would go to bed.
She told him only that they would go to bed.
She told him that only they would go to bed.
She told him that they only would go to bed.
She told him that they would only go to bed.
She told him that they would go only to bed.
She told him that they would go to only bed.
She told him that they would go to bed only.

A problem in any situation is combining experience and wisdom, and sexual situations are no exception. Unfortunately, wisdom often comes after experience. The course of wisdom seems to be that of spending more time in communication about the relationship and the possible results of various actions. Sexual activity should never be a total surprise or completely spontaneous.

Students probably have a higher personal morality today because value choices are more personal. Parents, schools, and churches are less vocal in condemning premarital sex. Therefore, young people face more choices and are more responsible for their own behavior. They must think through their decisions, control the consequences, and try out new behaviors for themselves. They are more concerned about commitment and care about what's best for themselves. All this change has resulted in greater sexual equality, less hypocrisy, more open discussion, and more concern with reality.

As Bowman and Spanier (1978) write, "If there is to be freedom of choice regarding premarital intercourse, it must be a choice *among* alternatives, not simply the choice of a given alternative. Some persons think that freedom of choice means only the freedom to *do* something. They forget that it means also the freedom *not* to do that thing" (p. 98).

Certain life events leave people in a never-the-same-again position. Once you have engaged in sexual intercourse, you will never be a virgin again. Thus, even discounting the other aspects of the event, the "first time" is a momentous occasion simply because it is a rite of passage.

Just as with choosing a mate and many other decisions, there are some poor reasons for deciding to have sexual intercourse. Pressure from your peers or your partner is one. The decision of whether or not to engage in sex is your decision and should not be made only to please someone else. Rebellion is another poor reason. To break rules imposed by parents, religion, or society by engaging in premarital sex makes no more sense than letting yourself be pressured by others into doing it. The decision should be based on your own values. Engaging in sex out of revenge and then dropping your partner demonstrates lack of respect for your partner and a lack of responsibility. "Unless freedom of choice is based on an understanding of the alternatives from which choice is to be made, it cannot be truly free" (Bowman & Spanier, 1978, p. 85).

In considering human sexuality, we must operate by some values. We must determine priorities, and eventually most people blend an ideal of sexual behavior with situational factors to arrive at a set of standards. Sexually inexperienced college students were questioned by Christopher and Cate (1985) to find out what would influence their decision to engage in sex for the first time. Three influences were found: (1) physical arousal during the date; (2) the relationship, that is, "the degree of positive affect exchanged between the partners and the degree of commitment at the time of sexual intercourse"; and (3) the circumstances, "preplanning and arousal prior to the date" (p. 268).

Another study found that "the initiation of sex seems to have been a spur-of-the-moment decision. Only 17 percent of the young women and 25 percent of the men had planned their first act of intercourse" (Zelnick & Shah, 1983).

There are several factors to consider for those who decide to have intercourse. Birth control is one. Life consists of taking risks. Some, such as crossing a busy street, are necessary. Others, such as hang gliding or having intercourse without using birth control, are avoidable. An unwanted pregnancy can change an individual's or a couple's life and is a tremendous risk to take for a brief amount of pleasure. Yet research shows that less than half of young people used birth control when they had their first intercourse (Zelnick & Shah, 1983). Those who do often consult with their significant others—parents, partners, or peers—before making their decisions. Some of the girls in the study reported that their families played an important role in their decision to obtain birth control (Nathanson & Becker, 1986).

Couples should also consider the consequences to their relationship if they engage in sex. "The moral decision will be the one which works toward the creation of trust, confidence, and integrity in the relationship. It should increase the capacity of individuals to cooperate, and enhance the sense of self-respect in the individual" (Kirkendall, 1961, p. 6). In some cases, intercourse may strengthen the relationship; in others, it may weaken it. It is likely to strengthen the relationship if both partners really want it, if the relationship is solid before the sexual relations, and if the sexual relations are enjoyable for both. Naturally, the converse of these factors may weaken the relationship. Hill, Rubin, and

---

BOX 6.1   WHAT'S RIGHT?

"Mother, he asked me to be with him for the night. Should I have gone?"
Katie's mind darted around looking for words.
"Don't make up a lie, Mother. Tell me the truth."
Katie couldn't find the right words.
"I promise you that I'll never go with a man without being married first—if I ever marry. And if I feel that I must—without being married, I'll tell you first. That's a solemn promise. So you can tell me the truth without worrying that I'll go wrong if I know it."
"There are two truths," said Katie finally.
"As a mother, I say it would have been a terrible thing for a girl to sleep with a stranger—a man she had known less than forty-eight hours. Horrible things might have happened to you. Your whole life might have been ruined. As your mother, I tell you the truth.
"But as a woman . . ." she hesitated. "I will tell you the truth as a woman. It would have been a very beautiful thing. Because there is only once that you love that way."
Francie thought, "I should have gone with him then. I'll never love anyone as much again. I wanted to go and I didn't go and now I don't want him that way any more because *she* owns him now. But I wanted to and I didn't and now it's too late." She put her head down on the table and wept.

SOURCE: From *A Tree Grows in Brooklyn,* by Betty Smith.

Peplau (1976) found no correlation between relationship breakup and having intercourse or not. About 90 percent of both college men and women who were already in strong relationships reported that sexual intercourse strengthened their relationships. A few believed it had been damaging (Strong, Wilson, Robbins, & Johns, 1981).

People might find conflict with their parents if they engage in premarital sex. The generation gap still exists, and a conflict in standards between the generations can cause problems.

Whatever your ultimate choice about premarital intercourse, it is important to remember that your choice will affect at least one other person besides yourself. To enter into the intimate life of another person through sexual intercourse and then to take no ultimate responsibility for that association is socially irresponsible.

SUMMARY

- Because sexual activity includes such a wide range of activities, everyone has experienced premarital sex.

- Sexual attitudes and behavior have undergone an evolution, with the amount of change peaking in the 1920s and the 1960s.

- Recent increases in premarital sexual behavior can be at least partially attributed to the women's movement, extensive media coverage, the youth movement, and the decline in the influence of religious authority.

- The rise in premarital sexual activity seems to have reached a plateau in the 1980s.

- Your decision about premarital sex is basically yours. However, you are influenced by societal values, the type of person you are, the characteristics of your relationship with your partner, and the opinions of others.

- Reiss differentiates four standards of sexual behavior: abstinence, permissiveness with affection, permissiveness without affection, and the double standard.

- While participation in premarital sex has increased, most relationships that include it are generally also marked by affection and stability.

- The double standard still exists in our society, with men being the initiators of sex and women the limiters.

- Because sexuality is learned behavior, we learn our sexual roles from society.

- Sex includes such activities as masturbation, petting, fantasies, and nocturnal orgasms.

- Studies have found little differences in the behavior of teenagers, college students, young adults who are not in college, and adults.

- Because morality today is more personal than previously, your value choices about premarital sex are more personal.

- Peer or partner pressure, rebellion, and revenge are all bad reasons for having premarital sex.

- In deciding whether or not to engage in premarital sex, you should consider birth control, the consequences to your relationship, and possible problems with your parents.

PERSPECTIVE: VIRGINITY

Shut your eyes and try to think of four virgins. Have them in mind? Did your list include any males? If you are like most students, you think only of females as virgins.

In truth, a virgin is anyone, male or female, who has not had sexual intercourse. Yet people tend to separate male virginity from female virginity. Berger and Wenger (1973) asked college students, "Does it make sense to say, 'A woman/man has lost her/his virginity?' " (p. 669). Less than half of both men and women respondents thought it made no sense to talk about the concept of female virginity; *over* half of the respondents thought it made no sense to talk about the concept for men.

Respondents also disagreed on the definition of virginity. Responses to "What constitutes loss of virginity for males?" included ejaculation by a woman's manipulations or by masturbation, bringing a woman to climax, and penetrating a woman's vagina without ejaculation. Responses to "What constitutes loss of virginity for females?" included bringing a male to climax, having her vagina penetrated by something other than a penis, reaching climax, and having her hymen ruptured.

Despite the variety in opinion on concept and definition, virginity does exist because of religious, moral, or personal reasons. *Playboy* (Petersen, 1982) reports that just over 20 percent of collegians say they are virgins. Some people remain virgins for fear of pregnancy or the side effects of birth control. Others want sex to be "special for marriage" or fear damaging their reputations. Others fear being exploited and left; still others simply have little interest in sex.

D'Augelli and Cross (1975) found three general classifications of virgins. (1) Inexperienced virgins have had little dating and/or sexual experience. They confine their sexual activity to kissing, necking, and light petting. They don't think about sex often. (2) Adamant virgins have strong feelings about sex but believe it should be saved for marriage. They are more likely to engage in heavy petting. (3) Potential nonvirgins are those who do not have any strong prohibitions about premarital sex but who have not yet met the right partner or become involved in the right relationship.

Women may be concerned about getting pregnant. Can you be a virgin and still get pregnant? The answer is yes. If a male and female are petting and the male's penis rubs against the female's vaginal lips, semen may drip or leak from the penis into the vaginal lips and "swim" up the vagina to fertilize the ovum. Although this phenomenon is rare, it has been reported in the popular press and documented by Stout (1977) in an article titled "The Case of the Pregnant Virgins."

Men may be concerned about their images. The expectation in our culture is that men will be sexually experienced and skillful in sexual techniques. Hyde (1986) suggests that since everyone must begin sometime, there is nothing wrong with inexperience. Brehm (1985) notes that both men and women still place more importance and value on the woman's virginity than the man's, thus perpetuating the double standard. Although virgins are a minority among young adults today, virginity is certainly an option.

QUESTIONS FOR THOUGHT AND DISCUSSION

1. There are at least four dimensions within which sexual behavior should be considered. What are they? Why are they each important? Can you think of any others?

2. What is the definition of premarital sexuality? Is there just one? What is yours? Does yours differ from your parents' or your friends'? If yes, in what ways?

3. Has there really been a sexual revolution? Discuss some supporting evidence for your answer.

4. According to the text, how does a sexual revolution usually occur? Has the so-called sexual revolution of the past two decades met these criteria? Why or why not?

5. How has religion affected sexuality historically? Are things any different today?

6. How are societal values concerning premarital sexuality a paradox for many people? How do they affect the attitudes and behaviors of young people?

7. What are some personal factors or characteristics that affect a person's sexual attitudes, values, and behaviors? How do these factors affect sexuality?

8. Are there some types of relationships that are generally more likely to result in sexual intercourse than others? If so, what are they?

9. What effects do outside influences have on attitudes and behaviors concern-

ing sexual intercourse? What are some of these outside influences? Do you feel that any of these have had an effect on your personal decisions concerning sexuality?

10. What are Reiss's four sexual standards? Which of these do you subscribe to? Which of these do you think your parents agree with? Your friends? Society as a whole?

11. Compare and contrast Reiss's four sexual standards with Rubin's six categories of sexual standards. Is there an overlap? Similarities? Discrepancies?

12. In your opinion, is there a double standard concerning male and female virginity? What is proposed in the Perspective that could change this double standard?

~ PART 3 ~

Maintenance of Relationships

Basis for a Stable Marriage

Did you ever notice how plays, movies, and especially fairy tales often end with a wedding ceremony? Beautiful Cinderella meets, fantasizes about, and finally is swept away by handsome Prince Charming. The audience is left to believe that they live happily ever after in a castle on a hill. No one looks in on the romantic couple later to see how they adjust to each other on the honeymoon and in married life. We assume their servants keep the castle clean, the peasants pay their taxes to the prince so the couple can pay their bills, the counselors of the kingdom run the country, and the minister of finance keeps the books. No one suggests that Cinderella has problems with her in-laws because the in-laws think that their son has married beneath him or that she is jealous of his devotion to his white horse. Notice how the audience is only concerned with the two lovers getting together.

Sometimes real people plan their lives with about as much forethought. An engaged couple may put untold hours into plans for showers, the rehearsal dinner, the guest list, the wedding ceremony, and a place for their honeymoon (all of which last a few weeks), but they make very little preparation for their marriage (which will last, they hope, the rest of their lives). Romantic love, the stuff on which fairy tales are built, can blind lovers to reality, but marriages must survive in the real world. A successful marriage is not guaranteed in the fine print of the wedding license; it takes time and effort and involves not simply *finding* the right person but *being* the right person. Marriage is an adult activity that can be the most rewarding as well as the most demanding relationship a couple experiences. It can be very important to spend some time, thought, and energy on such aspects of the marriage as getting to know each other, sharing expectations of one another and of the marriage, deciding on a mutually pleasing lifestyle, and even considering how to deal with feelings and problems as they arise.

THE HONEYMOON

The honeymoon is a now-or-never event, a rite of passage that marks the transition from the single state to the married one. Legally, the marriage must be consummated by sexual intercourse. In addition, the honeymoon offers the newlyweds a chance for privacy and establishes their marital identity before friends and relatives, who have time to realize that a couple, not just two people, will return from the honeymoon. Most importantly, couples on a honeymoon have the chance to begin their initial marital adjustment. The honeymoon can introduce the new partners to the realities of married life. The couple begins to learn how to compromise on things such as how to spend their money, how to pass leisure time, and even such mundane matters as who sleeps on which side of the bed and who picks up the dirty socks in the morning.

Because the honeymoon is so important for the beginning of marital adjustment, Blood and Blood (1978) believe that it should be at least a week long, allowing the couple time to be alone together away from the everyday world. "There is a very dismal aura to the thought of getting married on Wednesday and going to work on Thursday. It is almost as if someone could ask you, 'What did you do yesterday?' and you could answer 'Oh, nothing much. I just got married!' " (p. 188). Couples can choose to stay at a resort, take a vacation much like any other, or get into the car and travel as far as time and money allow.

Conversely, the honeymoon can be dysfunctional if the new partners are nervous and don't know what to say to each other. They may become frustrated if they expect a remarkable sexual adjustment within a week or two of the wedding ceremony. They may feel pressured into trying to have a wonderful time on their honeymoon because everyone expects them to enjoy it. A special effort to please one's partner during the honeymoon can add further strain.

While a majority of couples report having had a good time on their honeymoons, a significant minority report serious disappointments. This may be due to false perceptions and expectations. One study found that single people simply do not appreciate the importance of the honeymoon and do not see it as relevant to the marriage (Adams, 1980). Men and women seem to have different perceptions of their own honeymoons. The same study showed that married men considered their honeymoon "relevant and satisfying," but the women appeared "disillusioned" (p. 105). Adams suggests that because women seem to give more forethought to the honeymoon, they may have unrealistic expectations.

During the engagement period and the first few weeks of marriage, couples often feel psychologically "up" because they believe they have found the right mate and have made a good marriage. The congratulations of friends and relatives further add to the feeling of success, as do compliments the partners pay one another. However, soon the partners begin to notice each other's irritating habits—failing to put things back where they belong, leaving the lights on, falling asleep in front of the TV, or slurping soup. They may suddenly find themselves concentrating on the perceived faults and forgetting the good points that first attracted them. Criticism may lead to arguments and hurt feelings. At this point, some couples begin to feel that the "honeymoon is over." What has really happened is they have come face to face with the realities of living with another person day after day—realities that contrast sharply with the early illusions of what marriage should be. At this point romantic love is declining but mature love has not yet taken over.

Difficulties in a marriage can occur when illusion and reality collide. For example, one student reported that when she was engaged, she invited her fiancé over to her house for a dinner she and her mother had prepared. She had made a blueberry pie for dessert, which her fiancé praised highly. After they were married, she continued to bake blueberry pie for her husband whenever she wanted to do something special for him. After about two years of blueberry pies, the young man finally threw one on the floor and shouted, "Why do I always have to eat blueberry pie? I've never liked it!" She cried and said, "But I thought it was your favorite—you made a fuss about it when I served it at Mom's!" Only then did she find out that he had only been polite at that time, trying to impress his future mother-in-law and please his future wife. They now eat a variety of desserts and are living together in relative happiness. The moral of the story: It is dangerous to assume too much.

Couples who have become disillusioned with marriage frequently become bitter and feel that they have "had it" (Crosby, 1985). Much of their disillusionment is a result of their initial, unrealistically high expectations. The romanticism with which most marriages begin obscures reality and leads to unrealistic expectations. The ability to recognize problems and to work them through together can make the difference between a successful marriage and one that leaves both partners unhappy and dissatisfied. "A marriage has the potential to be one of the most significant means for either enhancing or diminishing the quality of life of one or both partners. There is an infinite variety of marital relationships and they range from living hell to a mountaintop experience for the participants. The solid foundation for one couple's union today may be their Achilles' heel five years from now" (Vincent, 1973, p. xxi).

EXPECTATIONS

People today enter marriage with varied expectations, ranging from working together in traditional husband-wife roles to pursuing individual goals of self-fulfillment. Expectations may be based on family background or situations witnessed in other families or even in the movies. Whatever their source may be, conflicting expectations between a husband and wife can lead to marital conflict.

SUBCULTURES

Everyone is influenced by culture, community, friends, and traditions, all of which have different expectations for males and females. Although many parents today are trying to rear their children in a nonsexist environment, those who grew up in a male or female subculture may react differently to the same stimuli.

Preteen boys tend to spend their time with other boys, taking an interest in such things as dogs, sports, and snakes. They can often cite statistics of their favorite baseball players and may know the standings in the NFL at any given moment. As adults, their tendency to be with the guys and their interest in sports can cause their partners to feel lonely and left out.

Young boys, also, may be able to get by with behaviors for which their sisters are punished. They find more acceptance for using profanity or for using their fists to settle arguments. Later, however, a wife may find her husband's language offensive or a husband may find it difficult to use words in settling an argument with his wife because his learned behavior gets in the way.

In contrast, girls are often taught the importance of looking pretty. When they play together during their preteen years, they often turn to dolls and dress-up games. They learn to be charming in order to get what they want from Daddy or others. Later, although a husband may want his wife to look attractive, he may be annoyed about the amount of money she spends on cosmetics and clothing. She may not understand that the communication techniques she learned as a child do not work in her adult marriage. Simply by understanding differences in subcultural backgrounds, couples may be better able to understand one another's feelings and behaviors.

MYTHS

It is important to understand your own and your partner's expectations of marriage because of ethnic, religious, family, and/or other influences. Often, a discussion of how you feel and how your spouse feels can lead you into a give-and-take agreement on many aspects of your lives together. In fact, learning to compromise can be crucial to the very survival of your marriage. However, there are several common expectations about marriage that are unrealistic and should be avoided. Let's look at some of them.

"There is a 'one and only' out there for me, and if I marry that person I will have a good marriage." The idea that you have a "soulmate" and that finding him or her ensures a good marriage is misleading. First, you could probably find happiness with any one of a number of partners. Second, marriage, to be successful, calls for constant work by both parties. Finding a partner is hardly the end of your work. It is only the beginning.

"Our marriage will succeed because we have had a long courtship." Gaining an intimate understanding of one another during the engagement period is good, but such knowledge will not be enough to carry you through the whole relationship. People change, and marriages go through different stages. The birth of children, career changes, and other factors will change your individual needs and those of your relationship. The only constant to marriage is that of change, and partners must learn to adapt to change.

"Even though many marriages end in divorce, it won't happen to us because we are different." Every person and every relationship is different, and what each couple has is special. However, many of the people who are now divorced also thought they could avoid the statistics.

"After we're married, I'll change her or him." You cannot assume that you can change your partner. Rather than marrying someone you plan to change, perhaps you should spend more time finding someone who better suits your needs. You probably don't want to marry someone who intends to change you either.

"My marriage partner will meet all of my needs." Each person has many interests, desires, and activities. You cannot expect to find a partner who shares them all. It is unrealistic to expect two people to match in all these areas. A spouse

cannot be lover, friend, counselor, jogging partner, drinking buddy, chauffeur, and whatever else is needed and still maintain his or her own life.

"Love will keep us together." Love does not conquer all. Romantic love often fades during the first few years of marriage, to be replaced by more mature love. Therefore, a reliance on romantic love to keep the marriage happy may prevent you from analyzing your problems and attempting to solve them. "There is hardly any activity, any enterprise, which is started with such tremendous hopes and expectations, and yet, which fails as regularly as love" (Fromm, 1963, p. 4).

"We won't fight." Since some degree of conflict is inevitable in any human relationship, it is normal to have some conflict in marriage. Ignoring or denying the existence of conflict can only increase problems (Bach & Deutsch, 1970). In fact, the creative use of conflict can lead to renewed growth.

"Good sex will keep us happy." Sexual intercourse is not the primary basis for marriage. Despite its importance, many couples have happy marriages in which sex plays only a small part. You and your partner may even differ on your opinion of what is good sex; one may stress frequency, the other quality. Whatever the definition, sexual satisfaction is more likely to be the result of a good marriage rather than the cause of one.

"We communicate well, so we can talk through all our problems." Although communication is important to marriage, it does not guarantee happiness. Communication takes skill and effort. It does not mean merely persuading your partner to see things your way but is a source of mutual understanding. True understanding can either bring you closer together or drive you apart. Some couples may communicate so well that they finally understand each other fully and decide on a divorce. Also, an undue emphasis on solving problems between yourselves alone may prevent you from seeking outside help until it is too late.

> *One's only real life is the life one never leads.*   —OSCAR WILDE

> *A person's character and garden both reflect the amount of weeding that has been done during the growing season.*

> *A closed mind, like a closed room, can become awfully stuffy.*

BINDS

Besides the misleading myths about happy marriages, sometimes conflicting desires and expectations created by society put us in situations that Crosby (1985) calls "binds." To be in a bind is to face a difficult choice or to be in a position where you may lose if you make the wrong decision. When you are faced with a choice between two alternatives, both with negative consequences, this is a double bind. Crosby has identified nine basic binds in marriage.

The *growth bind* is caused by conflicting desires for self-fulfillment and self-actualization on the one hand and stability and security on the other. Although change is often desirable, it is also threatening and difficult to bring about. The

Which is it going to be—a child for them, a new car for him, a career for her, or . . . ?

future-security bind relates to desire for growth and change with a guaranteed future. Pledging to stay married "till death do us part" offers security for the future, but promises made during the honeymoon stage may be difficult to keep during later stages. Staying together requires hard work.

The assumption that "we two" will face the world together with a united front leads to the *identity-in-marriage bind*. Acting, thinking, and being alike stunts personal growth and causes an imbalance in personal and couple identity. In an *ownership-fidelity bind*, the relationship is one of possession. Instead of seeking the other's welfare, the spouse caught in this bind will use the claim of ownership to limit the other's actions. "You can't do that—you belong to me."

The *double-standard bind* arises from the fact that many men may say they believe women should have equal rights in matters of sexuality and marital obligations, yet they find it difficult to accept similar behavior in women and often unconsciously seek to marry a girl with traditional sexual values. The double-standard bind reinforces the false idea that men are superior to women. The *sex-role bind* also reinforces stereotypical views of men and women. It makes some behavior acceptable for a woman (loving, bearing children, and being a housewife) and others acceptable for a man (providing for his family and protecting his home). In reality, traits considered either masculine or feminine are present to some degree in both men and women. The *good-girl–bad-girl bind* teaches men to expect that "good" girls, the women who will be good wives, do not enjoy sexual intercourse. Only "bad" girls actually enjoy sex. After he marries, the man caught in this double bind will distrust the wife who enjoys sexual intercourse or become bored with the wife who does not.

The *attraction-reversal bind* means that a person finds a quality attractive in a mate before marriage but, after the marriage, detests that same quality. A *transference bind* occurs when one partner says things to his or her spouse that are really directed at someone else. Usually the spouse represents some other figure to the partner and is not really the cause of the anger, hate, or whatever. For example, a wife may react to her husband as if he were her father; the husband may lash out at his wife as if she were his mother.

REALISTIC GOALS

While many common myths about marriage are false and binds can cause problems in relationships, the prospect of finding realistic, positive goals for a marriage is not hopeless. There are six basic obligations that couples assume when they marry (Benson, 1971). These obligations may seem simplistic, but they offer useful guidance for those entering a relationship as well as those already in one. They are as follows:

1. To be truthful and dependable. For partners to develop trust in each other, they need to have a consistent track record of honesty and of being able to count on each other.
2. To share the workload of the relationship. This obligation will vary according to the agreement of the couple. For some, it means both working at jobs and sharing household tasks. For others, it may mean one working at home and one working outside the home.
3. To be a friend to the other and to give support, empathy, and sympathy when it is needed. In order to empathize with the other, a partner needs to have experienced a similar situation. "It does, indeed, take one to know one; and it is only in an empathetic relationship that the Golden Rule has validity" (Bernard, 1972, p. 104).
4. To communicate with the partner. Notice that communication should be "with" and not "to" the partner. Effective communication requires listening as well as talking.
5. To give affection and sexual satisfaction to one another. Although this may not sound like work, maintaining monogamy without monotony does require work in order to keep variety and excitement in the relationship as the years go by. Again, an understanding of what each of you desires sexually can help improve marital sex.
6. To volunteer to help the partner. Volunteering involves being willing to do

A stable marriage is helped by a stable home. Buying a house, however, is easier than maintaining a home.

things for the spouse without being asked. Some couples expect volunteering as part of their marriage; others consider it a bonus.

POWER IN HUSBAND-WIFE RELATIONSHIPS

There is only one "state" that permits a woman to work 18 hours a day: the state of matrimony.

The real trouble about women is that they must always go on trying to adapt themselves to men's theories of women.
—D. H. LAWRENCE

When people are free to do as they please, they usually imitate each other.   —ERIC HOFFER

Power is the ability to impose your will on others. "We are powerful when we can get others to do what we wish when we wish it, and when we can avoid giving them what they want from us" (Brehm, 1985, p. 227). If a wife persuades her husband to quit smoking, she has exercised power to produce change. If a husband keeps his wife from accepting a job, he has exercised power to stop change.

The distribution of power between a husband and wife is an important factor in their relationship.

How you think a husband and wife should distribute power is part of your expectation of marriage. Therefore, it is an aspect of your relationship that you should discuss before you marry as well as throughout your married years.

BASES, PROCESSES, AND OUTCOMES

Power can be examined in terms of its bases, its processes, and its outcomes. French and Raven (1959) have identified six bases of power.

> In the *coercive power* situation, you do what the other person wants because of fear that you will be punished. The punishment could be minor, such as not being spoken to or being the target of a snide remark, or serious, such as being battered by your spouse or having your life threatened.
>
> *Reward power* is based on the expectation that the other person will do something as a reward for your compliance. The exchange may not be free or voluntary. That is, if the only way a wife can get her mate to take her out for dinner is by "performing" up to his expectations in bed, then her actions may not really be voluntary.
>
> *Expert power* is power that you attribute to your spouse because you believe that she or he knows more about certain matters than you do. If you are knowledgeable in some areas and your partner is in others, then you each may give or have expert power in specific areas.
>
> *Legitimate power* is based on the feeling or the belief that the other person has the authority to request compliance. The authority of a parent over a child is an example of legitimate power.
>
> *Referent power* is based on emotional identification with the power user. For example, a husband may not enjoy going to a company picnic with his wife, but he goes to please her.
>
> *Informational power* is based on your partner's ability to persuade you of the importance or validity of his or her message. Thus, if a wife convinces her husband that too much salt causes high blood pressure and the husband reduces his intake of salt, she has used informational power.

According to Brehm (1985), power processes vary by the way power is expressed, and the variations are almost limitless. Some people outtalk their partners; others are more effective by being silent. Language is one factor; considerable research shows that men usually dominate women in verbal conversation. Style is another factor. Several researchers have found that women are more likely to use personal or manipulative power, while men are more apt to exert authority or use coercion.

Other research has shown that men and women use different strategies in exerting power. Men are more likely to use direct approaches, such as asking, telling, and reasoning, to get what they want. Women are more likely to withdraw or to proceed without their husbands' approval (Falbo & Peplau, 1980). Perhaps the difference in strategy may be due to the expectations of the partners. That is, men expect their wives to comply, so they use a direct approach; while women do not expect their husbands to comply, so they use an indirect approach.

Power *outcome* is what is usually measured in discussions of decision making. Who won? If you won, then, according to an outcome measure, you were more powerful. In general, husbands have more power than their wives. The use of power is often hard to measure and results vary (Brehm, 1985). Sometimes no process actually takes place; that is, one spouse makes a decision and the other does not challenge it. In this case the expert spouse won by default. Ironically, spouses who demonstrate "powerful" leadership behavior in negotiating an issue (process) don't usually achieve their goal (outcome) (Szinovacz, 1981).

A Classic Study of Family Power

In the last thirty years, there have been over a dozen major sociological studies of family power. The classic Detroit study by Blood and Wolfe (1960) gave birth to the resource theory of marital power and is still one of the most popular. Blood and Wolfe studied 700 urban and 200 rural couples and found more equal decision making than was previously thought to exist. Blood and Wolfe's study was based on the idea that the spouse with more resources gains more power. Resources can include education, occupation, income, friends and contacts, good looks, status in society—anything that is valued. In most traditional middle-class families, the husband has more resources because of his higher educational level and income. In many cases, even if the wife had equal resources during courtship, she gave up her name and career opportunities and followed her husband to start his career. Therefore, what began as a situation with equal resources quickly changed into one in which the husband had more resources.

Just as spousal and family relationships are always in process, so are power relationships. Scanzoni, in his book *Sexual Bargaining* (1982), makes the point that power can shift from one spouse to the other. And, at any particular time, one spouse may have more power in certain areas of the marital relationship while the other spouse has more power in other areas.

Power in Your Marriage

What type of power distribution between a husband and wife leads to the most marital satisfaction? Available research does not point to a simple conclusion. Perhaps the answer lies within each individual relationship. For instance, if a man is the strong, silent type and his wife wants a "he-man" to take care of her, then a male-dominated relationship is likely to lead to marital happiness for them. If the husband needs a wife to mother him and his spouse is comfortable in that role, they may find happiness together. Nonegalitarian marriages are relatively easy to maintain, except that the partners may have trouble coping with crises that demand changes in their roles.

Most students today say they want an egalitarian relationship when they marry. This type of marriage is somewhat harder to maintain. Why? Simply because both partners will not always agree on every issue. Then, as each conflict arises, they must decide what to do. There are only two people in the partnership, so a vote will end in a tie. The couple must learn to negotiate, to compromise, and to fight fairly. In a sense, an egalitarian marriage is like a democracy—it requires active participation and a willingness to work at adapting to changing times. It may seem inefficient in the short run yet prove more desirable in the long run.

There are several ways to approach an egalitarian life-style in marriage. In the *autonomic* type of marriage, the couple divides the areas of power and each spouse is primarily responsible for decisions in his or her area. The couple may negotiate who is responsible not only for the decision making but also for the carrying out of the decision. For example, in owning a car, someone must decide when to buy a new one, what kind to buy, how to finance it, and where to take it for service; then someone has to carry out these decisions by actually shopping for the car, arranging the loan, and taking the car in for service.

In a *syncretic* relationship, the couple jointly make all major decisions. They must discuss each situation as it arises. In a *composite* relationship, each partner assumes responsibility for some areas, but the couple make a joint decision in others. Each spouse is likely to take a leading role in the area in which he or she has more expertise. When neither has more expertise than the other, they jointly decide. The important thing is that each couple must decide which type of power structure is best for their relationship. Agreeing on the structure is probably more important than selecting a specific type.

HUSBAND-WIFE ROLES

> Two can live as cheaply as one, but now it takes both to earn
> enough money to do it. —JOEY ADAMS

> A husband came home to find the whole house in a dreadful mess.
> "What on earth happened?" he asked his wife. "You're always
> wondering what I do all day," she replied. "Well today I didn't
> do it." —ANONYMOUS

Another set of decisions a marrying couple must face concerns who does what within the relationship; that is, what roles do the spouses play. These roles include working outside the home, doing household chores, and parenting.

The division of work between the workplace and the home has changed considerably in the last few decades. "Between 1950 and 1980 the proportion of women in the paid labor force rose dramatically, from 28 percent to 51 percent. . . . 45 percent of married women with children under six and 41 percent of those with

If a marriage is to be a true partnership, it requires teamwork or even reversal of the traditional roles in the marriage.

children under three were in the labor force" (England, 1985, p. 68). These historic changes represent dramatic shifts both in the labor force (work roles) and in the family (home roles).

In our society today, wives and husbands seem to experience their home and work roles in quite different ways. For husbands, work roles affect home roles more than the other way around, but the reverse is true for wives. For example, when men become fathers, they seldom slow down their careers. Very few men take paternity leave to care for their small children. Women, however, seem to follow a more varied career pattern (Steel, Abeles, & Card, 1982). Some women do not marry or have children; thus they may follow a career path similar to the male pattern. Of those who have children, some take short maternity leaves, having minimal negative effects on their careers. Others take leaves of up to six months, which may hurt their careers. Yet another group of women stay out of the full-time labor force until their youngest child is in kindergarten, and then they resume their careers. Table 7.1 shows some of the reasons women do and do not work outside the home.

TABLE 7.1   Factors Influencing Wives' Labor-Force Participation

In Labor Force Factors for Initially Entering the Labor Force	Out of Labor Force Factors Against Initially Entering the Labor Force
High educational level (Ferber, 1982) Absence of young children (Ferber, 1982) Plans for few children (Aneshensel & Rosen, 1980) Later age at marriage (Aneshensel & Rosen, 1980) Husband's income lower (Gordon & Kammeyer, 1980) Previous employment experience (Gordon & Kammeyer, 1980) (Huber & Spitze, 1981) Increasing opportunities in the labor market (Ferber, 1982) Wife's mother's employment during wife's adolescence (Rosenfeld, 1978)	Early age at marriage (Aneshensel & Rosen, 1980) Plans for more children (Aneshensel & Rosen, 1980) Husband's income higher (Gordon & Kammeyer, 1980) Presence of young children (Ferber, 1982)
Factors Supportive of Continued Labor Force Involvement	Factors Leading to Withdrawal from the Labor Force
Higher educational level when children are born (Waite, 1981) Changing societal attitudes (Waite, 1981)	Home or school responsibilities (in 1970, these were the reasons given by ½ of the women who quit work and by ⅓ of the women who did not seek a job) (Kinsley, 1977) Increase in husband's income (Ewer, Crimmins, & Oliver, 1979)

WORK ROLES

In general, wives who are less educated, have less labor-force experience, marry young, plan to have several children, and hold more traditional views about motherhood are less likely to enter the labor force. One study even suggests that the wife's perception of her husband's attitudes about her working outside the home is more influential in her labor-force participation than her own preference (Spitze & Waite, 1981).

Differences in wages is another factor. Females are paid only about 60 percent as much as males (England, 1985). In fact, in 1979, women with an advanced college degrees earned less than male high school dropouts (Waite, 1981). In only one out of ten dual-career marriages does the wife earn more than the husband (Rubenstein, 1982). Only about a third of U.S. wives even match their husbands' salaries (Rawlings, 1978, p. 33). These figures mean that in most families, husbands will have greater economic resources than wives.

Why do women continue to earn less than men? The reason for the disparity in wages can be attributed in part to discrimination, to wives' discontinuous labor

TABLE 7.1 (*Continued*)

Factors Supportive of Continued Labor Force Involvement	Factors Leading to Withdrawal from the Labor Force
Availability of infant care (Waite, 1981)	Birth of children (Ewer et al., 1979) Age of children (the younger the child, the less likely the mother is to be active in the labor force) (Waite, 1981) Lower educational level accompanied by birth of children (Waite, 1981)

Factors Encouraging Reentry into the Labor Force	Factors Discouraging Reentry into the Labor Force
Availability of day care and flextime (Waite, 1981)	Young age of child (Waite, 1981)
Increasing age of children (Ewer et al., 1979)	Shortage of day care and flextime (only 17% of all workers have flextime available) (Waite, 1981)
Greater demand for female labor (Waite, 1981)	Higher age of wife (Waite, 1981)
Previous labor-force experience (McLaughlin, 1982)	Higher economic well-being (McLaughlin, 1982)
Lower economic well-being (McLaughlin, 1982)	Societal attitudes (Thomson, 1980)
Rewards of working (Thomson, 1980)	Beliefs about the importance of mothering (Gordon & Kammeyer, 1980)
High job potential (Hiller & Philliber, 1980)	Tax disincentive with respect to deduction of child-care cost (Kinsley, 1977)

force participation (often due to maternity leave), and to their willingness to accept sex-typed jobs that pay less than traditional men's jobs. And even in high-paying men's jobs, women earn less than two-thirds as much as men (Waite, 1981).

Men often value their jobs as status. When a man who was the main provider for the family loses his work status, his masculinity is threatened, which, in turn, can cause problems for the husband-wife relationship (Matthaei, 1982). She maintains that if "the husband is no longer the sole family provider, he is likely to feel defensive about his position as head of the family, anxious to maintain his authority" (p. 302). In fact, even with the increasing number of wives working, husbands still like to feel that they are the primary breadwinners, that their incomes alone are perfectly adequate to meet the family economic needs, and that their wives do not have to work (Staines, Pottick, & Fudge, 1986).

In addition to lower pay for women, external forces in the occupational world combine with attitudinal influences to hinder wives' careers. For example, many companies give a maternity but not a paternity leave. Therefore, if the wife is earning less and she has access to a leave of absence, who is more likely to stay home with the new baby? The same is true if one spouse can obtain a promotion by moving to another city. Is the higher- or lower-earning spouse more apt to move the family?

Several changes in the workplace are providing some relief. On-site child care ensures proper care for children and may even allow parents to have lunch with their children. Flextime allows employees to adjust their work hours to mesh with family schedules. For example, a wife might opt to go to work later in the morning in order to see the children off to school. She would work till late afternoon. Her husband could go to work early, leaving in time to meet the children after school and prepare dinner. Sex education that stresses equality in the work and home roles, elimination of the marriage penalty in the income tax system, and jobs at home computers have been offered as other suggestions for equalizing career opportunities. Unfortunately, these options are, as yet, available in only a few places.

HOME ROLES

Housework is what a woman does that nobody notices until she doesn't do it.

The best way for a housewife to have a few minutes alone at the end of the day is to start doing the dishes.

Although more wives are working than ever before, they still do most of the housework. Now the working wife simply has two jobs—employee and home-maker. Women are responsible for the bulk of household work and child care (O'Neill, 1985), although Bird, Bird, and Scruggs (1984) say that a clear trend exists for more equal sharing of household tasks, especially when both spouses are employed.

Huber and Spitze (1981) found that wives' current employment had a greater effect on the performance of household tasks than did role ideology. They found that households were resistant to changing norms but responsive to immediate situations. Haas (1980) also found that when couples did adopt role sharing, it was for practical and not ideological reasons. They saw it as a practical way to increase their benefits in marriage.

Men who view their roles as interchangeable with those of their wives and whose wives work outside the home are more apt to share household duties. Women believe that their own job status and income influence how much their husbands help with household tasks (Bird et al., 1984).

Studies have also shown childhood sex-role socialization to have a remarkable effect on adult role performance even where sex-role attitudes have changed. Attitudes toward sex-role performance acquired during childhood may not be as responsive to cultural change as we think (Condran & Bode, 1982). Both spouses may have trouble giving up or sharing responsibilities that they have been taught are theirs (Lein, 1979).

While many women have rejected the role of being exclusively a housewife or homemaker, many combine mothering and office work while on the job.

One interesting study notes that men seem to feel uncomfortable relating to the home (Tognoli, 1979). Boys are given more freedom to wander from the home and they play at tasks unrelated to it. Girls are restricted to their homes and learn to play at homemaking.

This socialization may foster what Tognoli (1979) feels is an inside-outside dichotomy. He concludes that men's separation from the home can lead to alienation between husbands and wives and the persistence of stereotyped behavior. In summary, power, tradition, and experience in marriage can alter the allocation of home tasks.

CHOOSING A LIFE-STYLE

Many life-style options are open to couples today. The traditional role division of the wife taking care of the home and children and the husband earning the money still accounts for about one-fourth of all U.S. families. If the husband in this type of family can earn as much as two working spouses, the family can enjoy a higher standard of living because of the goods and services the wife produces for the family at home. She may garden, sew, and do home decorating and maintenance. "The two-earner family needs about 30 percent more income than the one-earner family to have the same standard of living" (Waite, 1981, p. 19).

Traditional sex roles have a good deal of support from both experts and the public. For example, "the traditional sex roles are the only patterns that are consistent with our biological heritage. No ideology can override the fact of our natures," according to Blitchington (1984, p. 23). Werner and LaRussa (1985) say that while stereotypes of women and men are changing in women's favor, "both sexes continued to view men as as more forceful, independent, stubborn, and reckless than women; and women continued to be viewed as more mannerly, giving, emotional, and submissive than men" (p. 1089). Such opinions tend to perpetuate the separate sex roles.

On the other hand, many women are working today to help support their families or for the sake of their own self-esteem. Yet the traditional task allocation of housework to the wife tends to remain, even when the husband favors sharing of housework (Lopata, Barnervolt, & Norr, 1980), because husbands do not seem to carry their egalitarian attitudes into action. Berk and Berk (1978) found that, on the average, children contribute 16 percent of the housework, husbands 21 percent, and wives 84 percent. Women who work part time report even less sharing of housework.

Employed wives have less time to themselves and for leisure than do their husbands. Haas (1980) found that employed husbands have 6½ hours more free time per week than do employed wives, while Lopata et al. (1980) found that employed wives report helping their husbands almost as much as do full-time housewives. This may be partly because wives tend to devalue their own work roles. They don't consider themselves equal wage earners and continue to take full responsibility for the home. Wives' employment is seen as "helping out" rather than as a change in the home and work role pattern of a couple (Lein, 1979), and husbands' household chores are seen as merely helping the wife with her duties.

Dual-career couples are couples in which wives and husbands pursue *careers* as opposed to jobs. A career is different from a job in that a career is a position (1) in which the individual is highly visible, (2) that is intrinsically demanding, (3) that follows a developmental sequence with evolving expertise, and (4) that requires a high degree of competence and commitment (Kilpatrick, 1982).

Wives and husbands in dual-career marriages consider it highly important for each partner to maintain a fulfilling career. Dual-career couples are often more highly educated and more liberal in their sex-role orientations than are other couples. However, many dual-career couples still practice role segregation in the home. Haas (1980) observes that "While the wife is committed to a career, her basic family responsibilities typically remain intact and her husband's career has precedence over hers" (p. 289). Even the professional pair is frequently not egalitarian (Bryson & Bryson, 1980). They divide household responsibilities along traditional lines and place differential values on their careers. What is happening here? Bryson and Bryson (1980) suggest that the goals of the couple may conflict with the external realities of societal expectations, institutional policies, and domestic demand. Often, responses to these factors are traditional because this is the easiest way to resolve the conflict.

Yoger (1981) suggests that today's career women are experiencing role expansion: They are choosing to add new role responsibilities without relinquishing old ones. She found that university faculty women married to career men perceived that their husbands devoted 12 to 16 fewer hours per week to housework than they did, and 23 fewer hours per week to child care. Research has shown that younger and more highly educated men share housework more than do others (Ferber & Huber, 1979). Career women in general do appear to devote less time to household work, but they still retain responsibility for it (Beckman & Houser, 1979). The division of household labor is less traditional but not equal. The overall pattern is that women are increasing their share of instrumental roles outside the home, but men are not increasing their share of the workload within the home (Berardo, Shehan, & Leslie, 1987). The woman in the average dual-career couple is pulled to her limit by both work and home roles, and this pull is one factor that finally leads some couples to share roles.

Role patterns change over the course of a marriage. Students often expect to move from a dual- to a single-career couple in order to have children and then to switch back again. When a couple do not yet have children, they may both work and really share the work at home. This may be a very egalitarian stage for couples who genuinely want an egalitarian relationship. However, with the arrival of children comes the possibility of the wife's leaving the labor force for anywhere from a few weeks to several years. When the children are grown and have left the home, the parents may return to more egalitarian roles, or they may remain in traditional roles.

STRESS IN DUAL-CAREER MARRIAGES

The term "stress" almost always comes up in a discussion of dual-career lifestyles. The presence of stress doesn't have to mean that the relationship will be less satisfying or that conflict will arise. In fact, some research has shown stress, conflict, and satisfaction to be separate variables and marital role satisfaction to be a separate dimension from marital role conflict or marital role stress (McNamara & Bahr, 1980).

Stress may be classified in two ways: (1) internal stress, which comes from the couple's relationship, and (2) external stress, which comes from social structures outside the family (Skinner, 1980). The four issues internal to the couple are overload issues, identity issues, role-cycling issues, and family characteristics. The external strains are normative issues, occupational structure, and social network problems.

Overload is too many things to do and too little time to do them all. Identity issues, according to Bernard (1974), are problems especially for a woman in a dual-career marriage. Usually, women have been socialized to consider parenting and homemaking to be primarily feminine tasks. Therefore, a wife must often decide whether to take a greater share of the home role, thus creating more overload, or to work hard to create a situation in which her equal-partner role is stressed and accepted by her husband. In role cycling, the problem is to arrange for the careers of the individual married persons, and their children if they have them, to fit together as compatibly as possible.

A dual-career couple separating for the day—or maybe two if his or her business requires it.

Society puts external strain on a dual-career couple by placing more responsibility for home and family on the woman. Since many of the relatives of the dual career couple—especially the older ones—are not used to women having careers, the relatives expect the dual-career couple to have time to attend family gatherings, to help each other, or to do whatever the family is used to doing. Working couples may also have to turn down invitations from friends and to limit their socializing in general. Obviously, coping with the stress and general business of dual-career marriages takes some organization and ingenuity.

Working couples often find ways of coping with chores. They may reduce their standard of housecleaning by washing windows once instead of twice a year or by keeping the living room neat and clean for guests but shutting the door to the den until they have time to clean it up. They may find ways to double up on activities. For example, she might mow the lawn and listen to the news on her Walkman. He might watch a ballgame while preparing dinner. Couples often opt to spend part of their income eating out, hiring help to do certain chores, or buying labor- and time-saving devices.

Dual-career couples need to prioritize their time so as to make time for each other and for their children. Sometimes planning specific events or setting aside

TABLE 7.2 Advantages and Disadvantages of Dual-Career Role Sharing

Advantages, Benefits	Disadvantages, Costs
Increased income and financial security	Lack of time
Stimulation, personal development for both spouses offered by careers	Taxing of spouses' energies through role overload
Utilization of each spouse's particular training	Possible restriction of each spouse's career participation
Fairness in access to society's valued resources	Possible curtailment of nonessential leisure activities
Concentration on beneficial components of ties to social network	Social sanctions when couple diverges from normative expectations
Spouse is "resident colleague" for support, takes pride in other's accomplishment	Limiting of ties to social network (friendship, kinship, and service relationships) because of lack of time
Spouse can take leave from career to pursue other interests without economic disaster	Higher divorce rate (this may be a result of less support for a less common life-style rather than of dual-career role sharing)

SOURCES: Bryson and Bryson (1980), Grieff and Munter (1982), Grossman (1982), Haas (1980), Nadelson and Nadelson (1980), Rapoport and Rapoport (1969).

a certain time period each week works well. They often learn new methods of coping with stress from other couples who are in the same situation.

COMMUNICATION IN MARRIAGE

With all the decisions husbands and wives must make, the importance of communication in marriage is evident. Spouses must discuss finances, roles, and many other aspects of their lives. In addition, it is important that they share their feelings, their fears, and their dreams. Yet few couples really understand what is involved in communication. "The demands upon marriage are constantly increasing; yet education for marriage—the most complex relationship of adult life—receives less attention than education for the relatively simple task of driving a car" (Vincent, 1973, p. 254).

Unique personalities, backgrounds, and environments filter people's perceptions of reality. We live by perceptions, not by reality itself; therefore our perceptions affect our interaction with our partner. Vincent (1973) has suggested that there are six "persons" involved in a conversation between a husband and wife:

1. Husband's impressions of himself as a husband
2. Wife's impressions of herself as a wife
3. Husband's impressions of his wife
4. Wife's impressions of her husband

5. Husband's impressions of his wife's impressions of him as a husband (what he thinks she thinks of him)
6. Wife's impressions of her husband's impressions of her as a wife (what she thinks he thinks of her) (pp. 61–62)

These six perceptions can certainly complicate the process of communication.

Nonverbal communication can help or hinder verbal communication. "What we say to each other is only part of the communication process. How we say it—with a smile, or a shrug, or a frown, or a glare—is at least as important, sometimes more" (Brehm, 1985, p. 206). Research has found that husbands and wives are quite accurate interpreters of their spouses' nonverbal communication. In fact, husbands whose wives send clear messages through facial expressions reported fewer complaints in the marriage (Sabatelli, Buck, & Dreyer, 1982).

Powell (1969) suggests that there are five levels of communication: (1) *Cliché conversation* is cocktail party conversation in which no information is shared. "Hi, how are you?" "Fine, thanks." (2) *Reporting the facts* is a simple exchange of information. "Jennifer called today." (3) *Ideas and judgments* include taking the risk of offering some ideas of your own and revealing some of your judgments and decisions. (4) *"Gut level" feelings* include your emotions or feelings about the topic. These feelings include personal feelings that underlie ideas, judgments, and convictions. (5) *Peak communication,* a goal for married couples, is based on absolute openness and honesty and is reached only rarely. A goal of good communication, according to Powell, is sharing feelings without the fear of being judged or punished by your spouse.

One thing partners can do to improve their communication is to gain adequate feedback to check that the spouse has received the right message. If a husband says that he does not want to go out to dinner, does he mean that he is too tired to go out, that he thinks they spend too much money at restaurants, that he thinks that his wife should cook more, that he is angry and doesn't want to go out in public, or something entirely different? By asking him to clarify his rejection of her invitation, his wife may learn more about how he feels.

Knapp (1984) says that we should learn to be good communicators by observing the way we and others communicate interpersonal needs and by experimenting with various ways of including others in our lives, controlling situations, and expressing affection. Good communicators, he says, generally say the right things at the right times, adapt their communication to others, avoid using offensive language, reveal some of their own feelings, are aware of the effect of their communication on their partners, and are not difficult to understand.

Although communication is not the magical answer to marital problems, it is one of the keys to a successful relationship. Because people are unique, they bring different perspectives into their marriage. Therefore, communicating one's thoughts, ideas, and feelings to a partner and understanding that partner's thoughts, ideas, and feelings is not a simple matter. Good communication includes speaking well and listening well, giving and interpreting nonverbal clues, and asking for and providing feedback. The rewards of keeping the lines of communication open may be well worth the necessary effort.

Summary

- During their engagement, couples need to spend time, thought, and energy on the various aspects of their marriage.

- The honeymoon is a rite of passage for the newlyweds, which offers them a chance to adjust to living together.

- Husbands and wives often enter marriage with differing expectations of what their married life should be. Conflicting expectations can cause marital strife.

- Some sources of expectations are the different subcultures of males and females, the many myths people accept about marriage, and the restrictions that society places on couples.

- Partners can and should develop realistic goals for their marriages.

- Power can be examined by its bases, processes, and outcomes. The distribution of power within a marriage can cause problems if it is not agreed upon in advance.

- Husband-wife roles may differ from marriage to marriage. While traditional sex roles still have a great deal of support, more and more couples have dual-job and dual-career marriages. Each style has its advantages and disadvantages.

- Even though women are working more outside the home, they still do most of the household tasks, too.

- Stress within a dual-career marriage can be caused by factors within the couple relationship as well as outside factors.

- Communication is important in a marriage not only to discuss day-to-day living procedures and experiences but also to share feelings and dreams.

- Couples talk on five different levels. They should strive for peak communication.

- Using and interpreting nonverbal communication can help or hinder conversation.

- Good communication requires asking for and providing adequate feedback to keep the lines of communication open.

PERSPECTIVE: THE MARRIAGE CONTRACT

A marriage is a legal status contracted by a husband, a wife, and the state. State laws determine under what conditions the marriage may be made and under what conditions it may be broken. In addition, a couple may wish to add their own personal marriage contract.

Marriage contracts have been around for centuries. In recent years they have been used mainly by elderly people who, upon remarrying, want to ensure that their assets are inherited by their children, and by people who are remarrying after a messy divorce. A growing number of people are drawing up marriage contracts simply because of the prevalence of divorce (Totenberg, 1985). Others may believe that traditional marriage is too restrictive or sexist and want to outline their goals for a nontraditional life-style.

The reasons may be varied, and contracts vary from couple to couple, too. The utopian marriage contract, according to Edmiston (1980), could include the wife's right to use her maiden name; the surname to be given to any children; the decision about birth control; the decision whether or not to have children and, if so, how many; child-rearing techniques; living arrangements; the division of child care and housework; financial arrangements; sexual rights and freedoms; and even possibly the husband's consent to abortion in advance. A contract may include future stipulations or divorce provisions.

You can put whatever you want into a marriage contract. However, family-law experts say that such contracts are not necessarily binding in court. A prenuptial agreement must be shown to be fair, executed voluntarily, and entered into in good faith. They suggest that each partner have a lawyer and each make a full financial disclosure. Even then, courts in some jurisdictions have the right to review the agreement and may rule a settlement contrary to the contract (Totenberg, 1985).

Experts disagree as to the value of a marriage contract. Some see it as a way to get some financial security in the marriage. A side benefit to having a contract may be that the process of drawing up the contract could be a valuable experience. "Contracts may be regarded as the product of an interpersonal process between individuals who are together identifying and working out personal problems and issues. . . . (Couples) are actually exploring and experiencing with one another the possibilities of a long-term arrangement" (Jeter & Sussman, 1985, p. 287, 291).

On the other hand, some lawyers say that marriage contracts can sometimes signify distrust and fear (Totenberg, 1985). In these cases, the marriage may be off to a rocky start with or without the written agreement.

Whether or not to have a marriage contract is a personal decision. Statistics have yet to prove if they are helpful or harmful. To the negative, one lawyer says that most of his clients who have them get divorced (Totenberg, 1985). On a positive note, one empirical study found that marriages utilizing a contract tended to be more egalitarian than those without one (Weitzman, 1981).

The following sample contract includes many of the items usually considered in a marriage contract. You may not agree with the way in which Ms. Sage and Mr. Wisdom handled certain points. If you decide to have your own contract, you and your partner need to weigh each point carefully and to add others that are important to you before signing your document.

Sample Marriage Contract

Because we believe that each marriage is individual, we have created this marriage contract to specify what we both believe should be the responsibilities of the partners in this marriage. Therefore, on June 4, 1988, this contract is entered into between Susie Sage and Willie Wisdom, who are both residents of Saybrook, Lake County, State of Wisconsin.

I. Property and Finances

All property brought into the marriage will belong solely to the party who brought said property into the marriage. Any property purchased after effective date of this contract by either party will belong to said party. All gifts are considered the property of the receiver. Each party will be responsible for personal debts. Upon the death of either party, the personal property of said party will be disposed of according to the will of that party.

The dwelling at 205 Spring Road is considered mutual property. Payments for the mortgage and upkeep of the home shall be paid by the partners in proportion to their income. At the death of either party, the other party will inherit the dwelling.

The parties will maintain individual checking accounts for their personal use and will each contribute two-thirds of each paycheck to the mutual checking account to be used for mortgage and household expenses and common purposes.

II. Occupations

Each party will be free to choose a full-time occupation outside the home, should he/she so desire. If a job opportunity requires relocation, either party shall be free to relocate.

III. Household Duties

When they are both fully employed, the household duties will be shared equally by both parties. The detailed list of which duties will be performed by which party will be separate from this contract but fully binding. If either party hires someone else to perform his/her duties, payment for that service shall come from the personal checking account of that individual. If either party should change occupational status, the household duties may be renegotiated. Household duties will include but not be restricted to: cooking, shopping, cleaning, laundry, and routine maintenance of the dwelling.

IV. Sex

Since both parties believe that sexual relations should be mutually satisfying insofar as possible, they agree not to insist on sexual relations when the other party does not agree. Each party, since sex is seen as an expression of self, shall be free to engage in sexual relations with persons other than the spouse, but not within the property at 205 Spring Road.

V. Children

Since the parties do not desire children at this time, they shall alternate on a yearly basis being responsible for contraception. Any decision to have or to adopt children must be agreed upon by both parties, who will be equally responsible for the care and support of such children. The child-care costs will be paid in proportion to the income of the parties. Child care will be shared equally. Child care is defined as feeding, clothing, attending when sick, teaching, playing, driving to activities, supervising, and disciplining. The partners are to have equal authority over the children.

VI. Names

It is agreed that Susie has the right to retain her maiden name.

VII. Domicile

Willie waives any right the legal system may give him solely to determine where the couple will live.

Executed at Saybrook, Wisconsin, June 4, 1988

Susie Sage _____

Willie Wisdom _____

Seal of Notary Public

Statement of Notary Public

Signature of Notary Public _____

QUESTIONS FOR THOUGHT AND DISCUSSION

1. Why is the honeymoon an important rite of passage for a married couple? What functions does it serve? What are some positive and negative aspects of the honeymoon? Based on what is presented in the text, do you think that couples who skip or postpone a honeymoon are hurt in any way? Why or why not?

2. What are/were your expectations for your honeymoon?

3. How can expectations make or break a relationship? How do factors such as subcultures, myths, binds, and realistic goals affect our expectations concerning relationships?

4. How many myths about marriage had you heard before you read the ones in this chapter? How many did you believe? How do myths such as these affect marital relationships? Give an example.

5. Identify some of the binds in marriage that Crosby has identified. How do these binds come about? How can they affect a marriage relationship? How can they be resolved?

6. How and why is the distribution of power important in a marital relationship?

7. What are the different types or bases of power as identified by French and Raven? How is each type of power used or expressed in marriage relationships? How can the distribution of power affect happiness?

8. Which is easier to maintain: an egalitarian or a nonegalitarian marriage? Why? How equal, in actuality, are egalitarian marriages?

9. Describe some of the different types of egalitarian relationships. Which type sounds best for you and the type of marriage that you would like to have?

10. Why are dual-career marriages difficult to maintain? How does society put pressure on couples in dual-career marriages?

11. Why is communication important in marriage? How do perceptions of self and partner complicate the communication process? According to Knapp, what is a "good" communicator?

12. What are some reasons people use marriage contracts? What can be included in a marriage contract? Do you feel that marriage contracts are beneficial or detrimental to a marriage? Why?

Maintenance Challenges

WHAT IS A SUCCESSFUL MARRIAGE?

Having a successful marriage is certainly a goal of those who marry. From their honeymoon to their sunset years, a couple may often wonder if their marriage is a success. The answer, of course, depends on their definition of success.

Those who demand little from each other and from their relationship may describe their marriage as successful. Unfortunately, they may never grow personally or together without setting new goals or trying to improve. On the other hand, those who expect bliss and harmony all the time may rate their marriage a failure merely because they are unable to attain their unrealistic goals.

Much research has been done in the area of marital success. Researchers have used concepts such as happiness, satisfaction, adjustment, and integration to try to arrive at its basis. They have measured it against all types of personal and relationship characteristics in an attempt to pinpoint the differences between good and bad marriages. Rao and Rao (1986) point out the inconclusiveness of the evidence thus far in comparing couples with different levels of formal education, those who have been married previously against those who have not, those with an employed wife to those with a nonworking wife, those with various numbers of children to those with no children at all, those with varying levels of income and occupational status, and those of different races.

Some research has found that an agreement on roles between the partners and the partner's perception of the other's role enactment has a positive affect on marital happiness (Bahr, Chappell, & Leigh, 1983). Others have identified sexual expressiveness, mutual understanding and support, determination and commitment to the marriage, and healthy egos as important personal traits for spouses (Ammons & Stinnett, 1980). Still another researcher found that good self-esteem as well as church attendance and religious influence were associated with reported marital happiness (Pittman, Price-Bonham, & McKenry, 1983). Some suggest that spouses with similar family-of-origin experiences are happier, and so are families with higher incomes (Wilcoxon & Hovestadt, 1983).

The degree of equality between a husband and wife may affect the amount of conflict as well as the ways it is resolved. Egalitarian couples generally have more conflict and more difficulty solving their problems, but they also experience more intimacy than those in nonequal relationships (Chafetz, 1985).

From all this research we can conclude that marital success is a very subjective judgment. One thing about it is certain, however: Some conflict in marriage is inevitable. While our cultural ideal is that conflict is bad, more and more scholars and counselors are finding that there is a place for controlled conflict in relationships. In fact, one recent study showed that conflict and the working out of problems were more closely related to marital satisfaction than was the level of love (Kelly, Huston, & Cate, 1985).

REASONS FOR PROBLEMS

Why can't a husband and wife avoid conflict? There are a number of reasons.

IMPERFECTION

First of all, people are not perfect and neither is the world we live in. You cannot expect your partner to be perfect in your relationship. Second, you may look to other marriages as perfect and try to meet their standards. In reality, that "perfect" marriage next door may only appear perfect in public and not be so in private. Third, society does not provide a perfect atmosphere for establishing and maintaining a perfect marriage. Particular situational conditions such as unemployment, inflation, poverty, job transfers, problems with friends or relatives, or illness can induce stress in a marriage.

INADEQUATE COURTSHIP

An inadequate courtship can lead people to marry for the wrong reasons. During courtship, individuals sometimes lose most of their judgment (Lederer & Jackson, 1981); that is, they idealize each other and don't notice each other's faults. If a couple can look at their courtship objectively, they will find that it is a good predictor of their pending marriage, because lifelong patterns are established during courtship. For instance, couples who fight before marriage will likely continue to do so after the wedding (Kelly et al., 1985).

Expecting more than you can attain can lead to dissatisfaction. Have you noticed that some people who have less than you do appear to be satisfied while others who have more appear dissatisfied? The difference comes in comparing what you have to what you want. If you expected an A on a test, for example, you may be unhappy with a B. However, your classmate who expected a C and received a B would be happy. The same logic holds for marital expectations. Some people are happy with their marital life because their expectations and reality are in balance, while others are unhappy because they expect more than they have.

Farson (1977), in his article "Why Good Marriages Fail," found some basic reasons for failure that were related to expectations:

1. While basic needs may be met in a marriage, higher-order needs are harder to satisfy because people set their expectations too high.
2. Some individuals develop unrealistic expectations for their sexual experience; for most, it just can't be "that good" all the time.
3. A couple may seek marriage counseling, psychotherapy, or other help to

improve their marriage, but these efforts may make the situation more difficult by setting a goal of improvement that cannot be met. The counselor may unwittingly be setting up an expectation that takes more effort than the couple is willing to put into solving the problem.

4. Spurred on by various encounter groups, some couples develop unrealistically high expectations of intimacy in marriage.

5. While some people may be more aware of the importance of communication, honesty, and trust in marriage, they may still fail to take advantage of them. Communication is not just one person talking to another but a mutual exchange. Others become so intent on communicating that they believe in "total honesty" and end up telling the partner things that are better left unsaid.

INCOMPATIBLE GOALS

"Intimacy requires that partners share common goals and values; that they have sufficient common experiences to be able to empathize with each other; that they care about the same things generally" (Chafetz, 1985, p. 192). Incompatible goals can create conflict between marriage partners. Often a couple can compromise on their goals. For instance, if he wants to work a great deal of overtime to acquire enough money to make a down payment on a house and she would rather he be home more often, they can compromise. Perhaps he can work some overtime and still manage to enjoy some leisure time with her. A couple can often take turns. If she wants to spend their vacation at the beach and he wants to visit relatives, they could split their time between the two or alternate vacation activities each year.

Sometimes, however, there is no way to compromise. Deciding whether or not to have children is an example. One 28-year-old woman noted that after three years of marriage her husband decided that they should start a family. She was enjoying success in her career and didn't want any children. The couple divorced, not because they didn't love each other but because they had incompatible goals.

When they have differing goals, the partners need to understand that their disagreement on goals can exist without necessarily threatening the relationship. However, if one feels exploited by the other, he or she may come to believe that the partner no longer cares about the marriage. Feeling exploited can lead to vengefulness or a power struggle between the two.

Striking a balance between individuation and mutuality is hard for many couples, according to Ammons and Stinnett (1980). They found that happy couples "appeared to have mastered the art of losing themselves in their relationship without losing their sense of self in the process" (p. 41). Paradoxically, "vital marital partners further enhance mutuality as they express their needs for individuation" (p. 41).

CHANGES IN LIFE CYCLE

Individuals and couple relationships go through many changes during the course of a marriage. A family cycle might include the transition to parenthood, child rearing, the postparental transition, retirement, and bereavement. In some cases a marital breakup and/or remarriage forces people to make adjustments. A change in career or a move to another city can cause changes in the relationship between husband and wife. The arrival of their first child compels the couple to allot time and energy not only to one another but also to the new family member. The impact of children hits husband-wife companionship the hardest, according to one researcher. "Parents of preschoolers were about three times less likely to consider their spouses as friends than were childless couples or parents of older children" (Block, 1980, p. 118).

As people grow, they often establish new goals for themselves and for their relationship. For instance, a wife who has spent years rearing her children may decide to return to school or to the workplace. This decision will affect the couple's priorities as well as their relationship. A husband may go through a somewhat opposite change.

The midlife years can be stressful for a man. He may have to meet increased financial demands if his children go to college, he faces a changing role status with his wife and possibly his children, he may be reaching a peak in his career, and he may be becoming aware of his mortality (Ciernia, 1985). Our rapidly changing society can even make him feel obsolete. Sheehy (1976) has suggested that at midlife, many men start to reassess their commitment to the business "rat race" and to look for greater fulfillment in family interaction.

Old age and retirement can bring a new set of potentially stressful situations. "Older married couples . . . are past the pressures of raising children and of earning a living. . . . However, eventually, they face the problems of accumulating losses. Friends and siblings die, and the marriage itself may be stressed first by serious illness, and finally by death" (Swensen, Eskew, & Kohlhepp, 1984, p. 94). These researchers stress that older couples do not have to suffer from a devitalized relationship. Those with strong ego development and commitment are more open and secure and better able to handle their problems.

All of these changes, whether voluntary or involuntary, cause stress. Holmes and Rahe (1967) devised a social readjustment scale of 43 items indicating the relative amount of stress that various events impose on people. The four most stressful events involve being physically separated from a spouse by death, divorce, separation, or imprisonment. Other stressful events related to marital relationships and the life cycle include retirement, pregnancy, health problems, sexual difficulties, occupational problems, and trouble with in-laws. Realizing that certain stages of life and marriage bring stress can help couples recognize the need to adapt to change.

REDUCING MARITAL CONFLICT

All relationships must weather periods of stress and conflict. To think otherwise is to be naive. Therefore, it can be very important in your relationship to know some general ways to deal with stress and conflict.

KNOWING YOU ARE NOT ALONE

First of all, the simple knowledge that conflict is inevitable can help you deal with it. When a disagreement arises, it is too easy to say, "I am a failure. My marriage is over" and do nothing about your unhappiness. Instead, adopt a positive attitude by recognizing that your situation is not an uncommon one. "We are having a conflict in our marriage right now, just as other people have. How should we go about solving our problem? How can we improve our relationship?"

Wills, Weiss, and Patterson (1974) found, not surprisingly, that unpleasant events in marriage have a major part in lowering the level of marital satisfaction. Therefore, simply giving each other positive strokes is good for your relationship. It can help keep your marital satisfaction high even while you are dealing with a problem or crisis.

ANTICIPATING PROBLEMS

Knowing that certain times of your life will bring stress and, therefore, possible marital problems may help you to plan ahead for these times. In a way, by anticipating, you are avoiding problems—not by refusing to recognize them but by planning, thinking about them, and doing what you can before they happen. For example, as a good driver, when you see a ball roll out into the street, you become alert to the possibility that a child may dart out into the street after it. You slow down the car and prepare to use the brakes if necessary. Similarly, there are common situations in marital and family relationships that may require action. These problems, which most people experience during the course of their relationships, are called "normative" problems, and they are often related to the family life cycle (Boss, 1980). For example, if you are going to start a new job in a different city, you and your spouse could discuss your feelings of apprehension. You could find out more about your new location and start early to locate a doctor, dentist, day-care center, and so on. Planning ahead and starting discussion before a time of stress arrives can help you to deal with that stress when it appears.

FACING YOUR PROBLEMS

Once you have discovered a problem, you can try to ignore it and hope that it will go away. However, avoidance allows little problems to grow into big ones and often decreases the couple's ability to relate to one another or communicate at all. Men are more likely than women to avoid conflict in marriage and to take a "wait and see" attitude. But stress from unresolved problems can actually lead to physical or psychological illness.

People with more highly developed egos—those who are aware of their own needs, fears, and wishes and are sensitive to the needs of others—are more apt to cope with problems and therefore to have happier marriages (Swensen et al., 1984). Commitment has also been found to be a key factor in long-lasting marriages.

Bach and Wyden (1970) have noted the importance of handling problems as they arise. They have suggested that people who do not handle problems quickly tend to engage in "gunnysacking," whereby all the little hurts, insults, and remarks are taken the wrong way and unfulfilled expectations and desires are piled into an imaginary gunnysack. Eventually all the gunnysack items may be dumped onto the partner—and the unresolved conflict will become a real war.

Stress can be managed better if problems are handled before they "reach the crisis stage." The use of all their resources—good self-concepts, communication skills, motivation, and commitment—can help a couple deal with a problem. It can be vital to work out some ground rules on how to ask for change in the relationship without causing new problems.

STEPS IN CONFLICT RESOLUTION

Set a Time and Place   Find a comfortable place where you will not be interrupted by children or friends. Set aside enough time to deal with the conflict at hand. One couple found that anchoring their rowboat in a quiet part of a nearby lake worked well for them. However, a room at home will do nicely.

Identify the Problem   Narrow the discussion to the specific problem that is causing the conflict. If the problem concerns money, neither partner should toss in complaints about the other's work habits, parents, or other matters unrelated to the topic of money. Also, saying "We always seem to run out of money before we run out of month" is too vague. If the problem is repeated overdrafts, the couple should focus on better record keeping. Then, if necessary, they can proceed to establishing or reworking their budget.

Brainstorm   Offer all the possible solutions you can think of. The couple with the overdraft might think of a number of remedies. One spouse could be in charge of the checkbook. They could alternate bookkeeping and check-writing duties every few months so both would understand their budget better. Perhaps one could be responsible for paying the monthly bills, the other for writing the miscellaneous checks. After all the solutions are proposed, the couple can jointly decide which one is the best for them.

Work out the Details   Once the solution has been decided on, the couple must agree on the particulars. The two discussing their checkbook might decide to take turns handling the household checking account. Next, they must decide who is going to take the duty first, for how long, and when to reconcile the statement each month.

Put the Plan into Action   A decision to wait until a later time to start the resolution may allow the couple to slip back into old habits. If they decide to take turns handling their checkbook, perhaps they could reconcile the bank statement immediately and then flip a coin to see who takes the first turn at keeping it balanced.

MANAGEMENT TIPS

When you and your spouse are trying to resolve a conflict, it is important not only to follow the steps outlined above but also to keep in mind some management suggestions:

1. Set realistic goals. Don't expect miracles just because you follow the rules. Marriage is a process; there is a constant need for communication and periodic reexamination. Each potential conflict is also a process. The couple with the checkbook problem cannot expect to end conflicts over checkwriting forever. They may want to take time, in a few months, to discuss how their new arrangement is working.

2. Learn to budget. When you hear the word "budget," you probably think of money. Couples certainly must learn to budget their money, but they need to learn to budget their other resources as well. Time is a good example. Each partner must allocate enough time to share in the work (earning money, doing household chores, caring for children, and so on) as well as to be alone with the spouse.

3. Learn to trade off. There is only so much of each commodity—time, energy, money—in a relationship. Each person in a marriage or family demands his or her share of the commodities. Each person cannot expect to receive an exact percentage of the resources each day, week, or year. There is a need for some sort of exchange in which it is acceptable for one person to get more goodies sometimes and the other to get more goodies at other times. If you have a basic trust in your partner and an overall exchange model that is mutually acceptable, you can achieve equality and balance in the distribution of resources. Keeping an exact score—"you owe me this" and "I owe you that"—can cause needless fighting over minutes and pennies.

TROUBLE SPOTS

For years, researchers have been interested in defining the major problem areas in marriage. The results of their studies vary. Some have found money to be a key problem area. Others suggest additional problems involving sex, children, friends, and relatives. Another found that sexual and affectional problems were the greatest among troubled marriages (DeBurger, 1977). In fact, DeBurger concluded, from his study of hundreds of requests for help by marriage partners, that marital problems could be grouped into eight categories:

1. A loss or lack of affectional relations
2. Problems with sexual relations
3. Conflict in personality relations
4. Problems with role tasks, such as the division of household labor
5. Problems stemming from filling the parental role
6. Intercultural relations, or problems with religion, relatives, etc.
7. Deviant behavior, such as drinking to excess, gambling, illicit sex, etc.
8. Situational conditions, such as problems due to illness, lack of money, etc.

Let's look at some of the main trouble spots in marriages.

SEX

In his study, DeBurger (1977) found that while both men and women found sexuality to be a major problem in marriage, men listed it twice as often as the major cause of marital difficulty. Women, however, were about three times as likely to mention affectional problems. From these data, DeBurger concluded that the two problems—sexual and affectional—constitute over half of all the major difficulties of those seeking help.

Couples cannot expect to continue to enjoy sexual intercourse as much as they did during their honeymoon. One study found that "coital rates were only about half as high after a year of marriage as they were in the first month of marriage. Thereafter, there was a slower rate of decline with increased marriage duration" (James, 1981, p. 114).

The myth that healthy people will naturally enjoy good sexual relations can cause problems, too. Couples need to talk about their sexual relationship. They need to tell each other what they enjoy in lovemaking and not expect their partner to be a mind reader. They should be willing to experiment and try new ways of satisfying each other. The reality of sexual experience is not always compatible with attitudes and expectations about it. Those people who expect an ideal relationship but have to accept less may feel guilty, fearful, or angry or may lose self-esteem (Wells, Lucas, & Meyer, 1980).

In their discussion of difficulties between married partners, Hott and Hott (1980) believe that misunderstandings, misconceptions, missed cues, distortions, and a complete lack of communication are at the bottom of disturbed sexual relationships. They write, "Masters and Johnson's new study demonstrated how inept men and women are in communicating their sexual preferences, frequently causing lifetimes of relative sexual frustration. Indeed, 'reading' each other's desires, instead of making them explicit, characterizes every step of the sexual process, from courtship to overture to actual sexual behavior" (p. 13).

Sexual activity is not separate from the rest of people's lives. Problems they have in other aspects of their relationship are often magnified in their lovemaking. For instance, a couple's power relationship is carried over into the bedroom.

Couples in equitable relationships are more content with their marital relationship, their lives in general, and their sexual relationship overall than are other people (Hatfield, Greenberger, Traupmann, & Lambert, 1982). Unyielding contentions of dominance/subordination, who is to be the initiator and who is to be passive, may lead to unsatisfactory sex. In reality, these roles can and should be interchangeable.

Also, if a husband or wife is angry at the other, an attempt at sex may be unsuccessful. Asking for or repressing sex might be interpreted as a punishment rather than an expression of love. Partners may also be worried about something outside their relationship. They may become bored with their sex life or disagree over birth control. One or both partners may have emotional problems that lead to inhibitions. Any one of these factors can interrupt or destroy a satisfactory sexual relationship.

As the experts say, lovemaking is more a mental process than a physical activity. Communication, again, is a key to successful sex. Satisfying sexual relationships exist only in happy marriages, not unhappy ones (Schenk, Pfrang, & Rausche, 1983). A couple's ability to relate well to one another proved to have a greater influence on sexual satisfaction than did the individuals' personality traits.

MONEY

The frequently used and often misquoted statement that money is the source of all evil is as obviously false as the statement that love conquers all. Still, studies of the family have consistently and continuously revealed that money is a prime trouble area in marriages, even loving ones.

In their classic study *Husbands and Wives,* Blood and Wolfe (1960) found that money was the major source and most frequently mentioned area of disagreement in marriage. A national survey revealed that slightly over half of the couples in the sample argued frequently about money (Yankelovich, Skelly & White, Inc., 1975). Although poorer families argued more often about money, almost half of those in higher income brackets argued about it as well.

> *Certainly there are lots of things in life that money won't buy/but it's funny/have you ever tried to buy them without money?*
> —NASH

Problems with money can be divided into two major categories: an inadequate amount of money and disagreement over the allocation of money. Sometimes an inadequate amount of money may simply be a matter of unrealistic goals. Since many young people get married at a time when their parents have reached a financial peak or they see other married couples who appear to be well off, newly married people may have high expectations of what their own standard of living should be. They often assume that they will immediately be able to afford the same comforts and luxuries that their parents have. The solution in this case may be simply to reduce their expectations.

It is helpful to their marriage if a couple can work through finances or other concerns together.

Living on a budget is the same as living beyond our means except that you have a record of it.

Money has a way of dribbling in and pouring out.

Money not only talks—in most families it keeps up a running conversation.

When both spouses are employed, the couple may be able to save a significant portion of the second income for something important, such as a down payment on a home. Although the income of the family rises when both partners work, so do their expenses. The tax bite from the second income is larger than that from the first. There may be child-care expenses, a need for two cars, two business wardrobes, eating out, and convenience foods. Sometimes couples both work hard at their jobs and still feel frustrated that their net income is not what they think it should be.

The spending of money sometimes causes marital strife, too. You can improve a financial situation by reducing expenditures and sticking to a budget. Your budget will depend on your income and your life-style. If you have a college loan to repay, you will have to figure that into your budget. You may decide to scrimp on clothes and entertainment temporarily in order to afford a new car. On the other hand, you might decide to take a Caribbean cruise before you become tied down by careers or children. Constant discussion about your budget will help you and your partner check to see if your goals for your dollars are the same.

Your budget will change as your needs and priorities change, so how and when to spend money is a constant topic of discussion. Couples should consider their motives for spending. For instance, buying a new sports car merely in order to be able to drive to a class reunion may not be a good idea. While it might be fun to show off a new car, material possessions are not a measure of self-worth nor, most likely, are they the most important aspects of your life.

The wish to control budget allocations can be another destructive force. A husband who is the sole breadwinner may think he should have total control of how the money is spent. His wife may believe that she must ask his permission before she makes any purchases, especially things for herself. On the other hand, a wife who has just gone back to work may believe she has the right to spend all her money on herself, while her husband's salary goes to the household. Be sure that your reasons for spending are positive, logical ones.

Another common problem with spending is impulse buying. If a husband impulsively buys his wife a bouquet of daisies on the way home from work, that impulse purchase is probably acceptable, even desirable. However, if he impulsively spends the family savings on a sailboat, there is apt to be trouble. Before you make a purchase, ask yourself the following questions:

1. Is this a considered expenditure or an impulse purchase?
2. Is this something we need or something we merely want?
3. Have we talked it over together as a couple?
4. Do we have ready cash for it that is not already allocated for something else?
5. Will we be just as eager, proud, and desirous of owning it next week, next month, next year?
6. Is this the best product for the intended purpose? Is this the right quality and price?

If you don't have six honest, unhesitating "yes" answers, think again.

By producing some goods and services yourselves instead of buying them, you can reduce spending. You can save a great deal of money if you can sew, grow vegetables in your own garden, do minor repairs on your car and home, or refinish your own furniture. Some enterprising couples have turned their fixing-up skills into real profit. They buy a small home that needs much repair for a reasonable price. They do all the repairs themselves while they live there. When the property is in good condition, they sell it for a profit and use the proceeds to buy a larger home. After several such sales, the couple can find themselves in their dream home. If you have a knowledge of real estate and skill in home repairs, this may be a solution for you.

Preventive maintenance is another tactic to save money. It can eliminate future problems or keep small problems from becoming large ones. For example, if you go to the dentist regularly for checkups and cleaning, you may prevent major dental work in the future. By changing the oil in your car regularly and servicing the car according to the manufacturer's instructions, you can limit major repairs later. The higher the economic level of the family, the more likely they are to practice preventive maintenance. Not having enough money to practice preventive maintenance can be very frustrating.

Some financial problems require the advice of a professional skilled in financial management and counseling (Bagarozzi & Bagarozzi, 1980). The Bagarozzis have suggested a five-step model for family financial counseling:

1. Family members identify their financial problems and outline their present spending habits.
2. With the counselor, they construct a budget.
3. After a trial period, they examine their success in following their budget and make any necessary adjustments in the budget itself or in the process for following the budget.
4. The counselor interviews the family to see if they have learned financial self-control.
5. The counselor does a follow-up evaluation in six months.

JOBS

Overall, married people claim to like their jobs more than single people do (Bersoff & Crosby, 1984). However, problems with jobs can cause problems in marital relationships. The issue of who will work outside the home can be a bone of contention for some couples. The traditional husband who thinks it is his sole responsibility to earn the money may resent his wife working. The wife who wants to stay home with her children may be frustrated at having to go to an office every day.

Sometimes problems arise due to role conflict. There are two types of role conflict that may occur in dual-worker marriages, according to Chassin, Zeiss, Cooper, and Reaven (1985). Intrarole conflict occurs when a husband and wife have conflicting expectations about their roles as breadwinners, spouses, and parents. For instance, the researchers found that women consider the wife role to be less desirable than their other roles, but their husbands underestimated their wives' discontentment with this aspect of their lives.

Interrole conflict occurs when a person occupies various roles that require incompatible types of behaviors. Women who worked outside the home considered their interrole conflict a "trade-off between the independence, freedom, and glamour of the worker role and the sensitivity, warmth, and relaxation of the wife and mother roles" (p. 308). Their husbands, interestingly, thought their wives failed to fulfill the wife role. Men, on the other hand, felt an interrole conflict too, and thought they did not do as well fulfilling the role of husband. The researchers suggest that the roles of parent and worker create immediate demands, which the spouses contend with as they arise. The role of spouse is less immediately compelling, so the partners put off dealing with its demands. This situation can lead to marital dissatisfaction.

Competition and the desire for success can lead to another problem for a married couple—workaholism. The desire to be a winner causes some people to become workaholics—to become psychologically addicted to work (Savells, 1978). Working excessively can be a problem for the family because workaholics make work a primary goal and their family relations become strictly secondary. Because they work so hard, they are frequently praised, promoted, and given more money, which encourages them to continue. Workaholics may feel guilty for not spending more time with their families, but instead of budgeting more time at home, they spend more money on the family. A workaholic's family may be well cared for materially but emotionally starved. In fact, one longitudinal study reported that the couples in which the husband had been most successful in his career were the most likely to report deterioration within their marital relationship (Dizard, 1972).

When a person has problems at work, it is hard to leave feelings of frustration or worry at the factory, store, or office. Even a bad day at work can disrupt an evening or weekend at home. When the problems are greater, the consequence is more severe.

In-Laws

There have probably been as many jokes about mothers-in-law as any other topic in history. "Definition of mixed emotions—watching your mother-in-law drive your new sports car over a cliff," for example. While in-law problems seldom cause marriages to break up, they can be troublesome. The major problems mentioned in one study were meddling in the young couple's lives, criticizing one or both of the partners, and being possessive of offspring (Duvall, 1954).

The mother-in-law/daughter-in-law relationship is traditionally more likely to cause friction than any other in the family. One reason is that the daughter-in-law, as wife and mother, is on public display. The mother-in-law can inspect the house and see how her daughter-in-law cleans, decorates the table, cooks the meals, and cares for and disciplines the children. Since she herself has been through the roles of wife and mother already, the mother-in-law can compare the way she did things with how her daughter-in-law manages. To the woman whose home is her career, criticisms the mother-in-law makes about her actions as wife and mother can be devastating.

The Duvall study found three factors related to good in-law relations. (1) Being accepted into your partner's family was the most reported reason for good family relations. If your in-laws accept you, they are less likely to be critical. (2) Mutual respect leads to less meddling, less interfering with each other's rights to privacy, more tolerance, and a lack of possessiveness. (3) Less opportunity to create problems, such as living far away, was listed as third.

LeMasters (1957) made seven suggestions for getting along with in-laws; these still hold true today:

1. Get to know them before marriage.
2. Don't try to separate your spouse from his or her family. A balance between the independence of the new unit and the love and ties of the parental family is best.
3. Don't enter marriage prejudiced against your in-laws. If you accept stereotypes, you may be the victim of a self-fulfilling prophecy.
4. Have positive attitudes toward your in-laws. If you treat them in a positive way, they will likely reciprocate.
5. Don't assume you can escape your in-laws. Usually at least one child is geographically near parents and even if you live hundreds of miles away, you may still communicate via mail, phone, and visits.
6. Remember that you will probably someday need help from your in-laws.
7. Remember that in-laws are not always wrong. Your parents and your in-laws have had more years of experience than you have, and while you may not always agree on decisions, you may benefit from what they have to say.

LEISURE/RECREATION

Before a couple marry, they frequently go to parties and movies and attend campus activities. However, after the wedding, sometimes one partner suddenly turns into a homebody. This change can be disconcerting for the other partner. Newlyweds may simply not have enough money to do all the things they used to. Sometimes partners discover after marriage that their interests are not as compatible as they thought when they were dating. Perhaps she went to the football games to be with him and their friends; he might have gone to the theater to please her. The discovery that they do not really like to share the same activities can lead to problems. On the other hand, as a couple they may find some completely new activities that they can enjoy together. Couples also need to spend some leisure time away from each other so as to retain their individuality and to grow.

RELIGION

Religion is more important to marriage than many students think. A church tie can be a form of conventionality in which the couple finds support and role models. In fact, greater religiousness is associated with less hostility between spouses (Pittman et al., 1983). However, partners with different degrees of commitment to the same religion may quarrel over the level of their religious involvement or over the amount of financial support they give their church or synagogue.

About 15 to 20 percent of marriages in the United States are between spouses with different religious preferences, not including preferences for different Protestant denominations (Glenn, 1982). Generally, people with homogamous marriages report more marital happiness than those with religiously heterogamous marriages. However, whether or not marriages between couples of different faiths actually are more vulnerable to divorce is not known.

Problems within a religiously mixed marriage may be caused, at least partially, by families who are against the marriage. Family interference or stress experienced by the couple because of their families may cause more problems than the actual religious differences. One particular problem for couples of different faiths is deciding in which faith to rear their children. This is something that couples need to consider before they begin their family.

COMMUNICATION

While communication is often a means to solve problems, it can be the cause of problems too. Small issues often accumulate in a marriage, and the way they are handled can make or break the marital bond (Hendrick & Hendrick, 1983). A survey of hundreds of marriage counselors revealed that a breakdown in communication was the number-one reason for couples to pull apart (Safran, 1979). Another study showed that the ability to express feelings and to discuss problems effectively are the best indicators of overall marital satisfaction (Snyder, 1979).

Couples need to talk with one another not only about daily situations that need to be handled but also about their feelings. "The single most important characteristic of a deep relationship is a shared personal history—problems, frustrations, tragedies, accomplishments, change, growth, hurts (including those perpetrated on each other), joys, including exchanges with other people. . . . You trade feelings

If communication has broken down, this type of togetherness will not solve anything.

with your mate, and this exchange brings on still more feelings. This trade is an important and powerful antidepressant" (Rubin, 1986, pp. 94–95).

Do husbands and wives really agree on issues? Do they truly understand each other? Actually, a wife is more apt to perceive more agreement in her marital relationship than her husband, who tends to see the disagreement that is actually there. However, in very important issues, her perception is very similar to his. At least spouses agree on which issues are important to them (White, 1985).

Couples with happy marriages are better able to express themselves and to handle their problems through communication. Distressed couples seem to perpetuate their conflicts through "negative, often punishing verbal exchanges that may just keep getting worse the longer a couple continues to talk" (Hendrick & Hendrick, 1983, p. 209). They try equally hard to solve their conflicts but are less effective.

Gottman (1979), in a detailed study of communication between married couples, found a number of differences between distressed and nondistressed relationships. Distressed couples are more apt to express feelings with negative affect, which results in sarcasm and cross-complaining. They tend to try to "read" each other's feelings and often interpret those feelings as negative, which leads to criticism and blaming. In addition, they are more likely to be negative listeners, even when the partner is talking nonnegatively, and, in turn, to be negative speakers. Distressed couples also establish a pattern of communication while nondistressed partners show more variety in their conversations. Nondistressed couples are more egalitarian in their communications, whereas in distressed relationships men tend to dominate.

Openness of communication is an excellent source of marital friendship. However, the idea of companionable marriage is a relatively new phenomenon and people have had little education for it (Block, 1980). They simply may not know how to open up to each other. There may be other reasons for lack of communication. For instance, people often bring a lot of baggage into the marriage with them. Crosby (1985) calls this baggage "antecedents of good communication." Partners may be confused about marital power and control, or they may harbor unresolved anger concerning their parents, especially the opposite-sex parent. They may have had limited models for good marital communication.

The differences between men and women has been proposed as another reason why marital partners often cannot communicate well. "Men and women do have trouble talking to each other. This is not really surprising, given their differences in communicational styles" (Brehm, 1985, p. 222). Men and women have been socialized differently in general and specifically in the way they communicate. "Masculinity is expressed largely through physical courage, toughness, competitiveness, and aggressiveness, whereas femininity is, in contrast, expressed largely through gentleness, expressiveness, and responsiveness" (Balswick & Peek, 1981, p. 90). An unexpressive man can learn through serious involvement with women, such as going steady and being engaged, to communicate with women in some situations. In fact, learning to be expressive to his wife but not to other women can actually help to preserve his relationship (Balswick & Peek, 1981).

Brehm (1985) says that by becoming more androgynous, men and women could learn to communicate better, but that process would take a long time. Meanwhile, she makes several suggestions for improving marital communication:

1. Remember your partner's good points during the bad times.
2. Try to speak each other's language. Women can be more practical and task-oriented; men, more emotional if they try.
3. If communication is failing, get a "translator," maybe a friend or relative but probably a counselor.
4. Always send and receive the messages "I love you" and "I am trying" along with your other communication.

Sometimes marriage partners don't really communicate; they merely talk at each other. They don't actually express what they are feeling or say what they want their partner to do. When one talks, the other may not be really listening. They may each be thinking ahead to what they are going to say in rebuttal rather than hearing what the speaker has to offer.

Strengthening Relationships

Whether a couple believe their marriage is a good one or they are aware of glaring problems, many seek help for their relationships.

Marriage Enrichment

For those who believe they have the basis for a good marriage, an enrichment program can be helpful. "Even in good marriages untapped marital potential may exist. Marriage enrichment programs have as their goal the discovery and utilization of this potential" (Davis, Hovestadt, Piercy, & Cochran, 1982, p. 85). They vary in their approach. Marriage Encounter Programs are one example. On an encounter weekend, couples meet with an encounter team, which consists of a religious leader and two or three married couples who serve as the team leaders. The team members present talks to the group, sharing experiences from their own lives and marriages. After each talk, the couples are asked to write answers to specific questions in their notebooks. When each person has completed his/her answer, each couple exchanges their notebooks, reads what the other has written, and then discusses their thoughts and feelings. The emphasis is on dialogue—an open, honest exchange of views in a nonthreatening environment—and on feelings, with the stress that feelings are neither right or wrong. This concept can help reduce defensiveness. The weekend begins with an understanding of the self and then progresses to an understanding of the partner and the relationship. The couples share their feelings only with their partners, not with the entire group.

Relationship Enhancement (RE) is designed to teach couples speaking, listening, role-switching, and facilitating skills so they can solve their problems and improve their marriages on a day-to-day basis. Several couples meet with two facilitators two hours weekly for ten weeks. RE is available for couples experiencing low marital satisfaction as well as for those who want to improve an already satisfying marriage (Brock & Joanning, 1983).

Couple Communication (CC) is yet another program. Three to seven couples meet with a teaching team three hours weekly for four weeks to learn how to increase clear, direct, open communication. CC is a marital enrichment program and is not recommended for people with troubled marriages (Brock & Joanning, 1983).

Which enrichment program to attend may not be an easy choice. Some research has found a weekly program to be more beneficial than a weekend one, probably because the couples had time between sessions to practice their newly learned skills (Davis et al., 1982). They also found that wives showed more initial interest in participating in the programs and reported greater improvement in their marriages after attending. Others note that those who are aware of marital strife and who are motivated to seek help and change may get more out of a personalized program, while those without specific problems might gain from a group encounter. To date, researchers have not devised a method of matching couples to the best program for them (Ford, Bashford, & DeWitt, 1984).

MARITAL COUNSELING OR THERAPY

Marriage counseling is a specialized field of counseling that centers largely upon the relationship between husband and wife. A marriage counselor has been trained to solve complex interpersonal problems. Generally, both spouses meet with the counselor to discuss their relationship. Instead of offering advice or solutions, the counselor is likely to suggest ways of identifying the problem, seeking the underlying causes of the problem, and listing the possible options for working out a solution. Most professional counselors strive to maintain a value-neutral position in relation to their clients. They try to discover the couple's goals and help them achieve them.

Although couples may need the intervention of a counselor or therapist, they are often reluctant to seek help. For one thing, they may be embarrassed and ashamed to admit they need help. However, in reality seeking help is a sign that the partners really care about their relationship and want to take steps to make it better. Another reason for not seeking help is the cost. While most people are willing to pay for medical or financial advice, they are often hesitant to spend money on their marriage. Yet when they list their priorities, spouse and family are very important.

Smart couples sometimes agree that professional help is needed for conflict resolution and reenrichment of their marriage.

When should couples call in a marriage counselor? Laswell and Lobsenz, in their book *No-Fault Marriage* (1976), note some situations or conditions when an objective, neutral referee should be sought: (1) when the couple themselves cannot figure out how to solve their difficulties; (2) when the confrontation has gone on so long that neither partner is willing to budge from his or her position; (3) when the partners are hostile and cannot reach out to each other; (4) when the relationship has deteriorated to the point that one spouse is contemplating some drastic action, such as leaving home, physical abuse, or suicide; and (5) when one partner has a personality disorder, such as chronic drinking or severe depression.

For some individuals, the decision to seek outside help pays off. The effectiveness of the counseling usually depends on the convictions of the clients themselves. They must be committed to staying together and willing to work at it. One interesting study pointed out that sometimes couples have a tendency to gang up on their referee, which, in turn, draws them closer together (Bach & Wyden, 1970). Once again being on the same side may facilitate understanding and solution of problems.

When is counseling successful? As with marriage, success of counseling is hard to define. Sometimes counseling involves getting the couple to communicate better so that they will understand each other and be able to work out their problems. At other times, it may be getting the couple to see that they are incompatible and should probably separate.

Summary

- Success in marriage depends on the couple's definition of success. Researchers have linked various factors with marital happiness.

- All marriages will have problems. Some reasons for problems are the imperfections in people, inadequate courtship, unrealistic expectations, incompatible goals, and changes in the life cycle.

- Knowing you are not the only people having marital conflict, anticipating problems, facing your problems, and learning to work toward positive solutions can help you overcome difficulties.

- Knowing how to talk about a problem can help you and your spouse work toward a solution.

- There are certain aspects of marriage that are likely to engender conflict. These include sex, money, jobs, in-laws, leisure time, religion, and communication.

- Good sex is not automatic in marriage; it takes work. In fact, it is more a mental than a physical activity.

- Husbands and wives can have money problems because there is not enough money or because they differ in their opinions on how to spend it.

- Job problems can occur when couples must decide who is going to go to work, when one person becomes a workaholic, or when a spouse brings his or her job problems home.

- Getting along with in-laws, finding ways to spend leisure time, and deciding how to handle religion are important aspects of a marriage.

- While communication can help solve problems, it can also be the cause of problems. Open, honest communication is an excellent way of building marital friendship.

- Couples may attend marriage enrichment programs to strengthen their marriages or seek help from professional marriage counselors for marital problems.

 ## Perspective: Fighting Fair

Bach and Deutsch (1970) believe that conflict is part of a vital relationship. They list 15 basic principles that can help keep marital fights instructive and constructive instead of destructive.

1. Be specific when you introduce a gripe.
2. Don't just complain, no matter how specifically; ask for a reasonable change that will relieve the gripe.
3. Ask for feedback on the major points to make sure you are understood. Give feedback to assure that your partner knows you understand what he or she wants.
4. Confine yourself to one issue at a time. Otherwise you may skip back and forth, evading the hard issues.
5. Do not be glib or intolerant. Be open to your own feelings and equally open to your partner's.
6. Always consider compromise. Remember, your partner's view of reality may be just as real as yours, even though you may differ.
7. Do not allow counterdemands to enter the picture until the original demands are clearly understood and there has been a clear-cut response to them.
8. Never assume you know what your partner is thinking until you have checked out the assumption in plain language. Don't assume or predict how she or he will react or what he or she will accept or reject. Crystal gazing is not helpful to marital communication.
9. Don't "mind rape." Ask. Do not correct a partner's statement of his or her feelings. Do not tell a partner what he or she should know or do or feel.
10. Never put labels on your partner or resort to name calling. Do not make sweeping, labeling judgments about your partner's feelings, especially about whether or not they are real or important.
11. The use of sarcasm is "fighting dirty."
12. Forget the past and stay with the here and now. What either of you did last year or last month or that morning is not as important as what you are doing or feeling now. And the changes you ask for cannot possibly be made retroactive.
13. Do not overload your partner with grievances. To do so makes him or her feel hopeless and suggests that you have either been hoarding complaints or have not thought through what really troubles you.
14. Meditate. Take time to consult your real thoughts and feelings before speaking. Your surface reactions may mask something deeper and more important. Don't be afraid to close your eyes and think.
15. Remember that there is never a single winner in a honest, intimate fight. Both either win more intimacy or they lose it.

These principles are applicable to you now in your dating relationship. In fact, learning to fight fair now will help you develop the communication skills that are vital to a good marriage.

QUESTIONS FOR THOUGHT AND DISCUSSION

1. How would you define a successful marriage? What are your criteria? What are your expectations of marriage? Give it some thought. How have they changed as you have gotten older?

2. What are some reasons for or causes of marital unhappiness and failure? How have our current views of marriage helped us to deal with these? How have our views caused additional problems? Do you think marital relationships are better now than in the past? Why or why not?

3. Describe a marital situation in which a couple experiences incompatible goals. If you were a marital therapist, how would you suggest that your clients deal with this problem?

4. Name some of the ways of reducing marital conflict that were given in the chapter. Can you think of any others that are not given?

5. What are normative problems? How can they be avoided or dealt with? What is "gunnysacking"? How can it be detrimental to problem solving and marital happiness?

6. What are the steps in conflict resolution? What are some of the key elements involved in these steps?

7. What are some of the main problems that can occur in marriage? Pick two or three that you feel are especially prevalent. How can these be minimized or dealt with?

8. Give some examples of marriage enrichment programs. How do they help strengthen marriages? If you were to choose a program for yourself and your present or potential partner, which would you choose and why?

9. What role can marital enrichment programs play in a marriage? For whom are they recommended? How does marital counseling and therapy differ from marital enrichment? When is marital counseling and therapy recommended?

10. Review the 15 principles of fair fighting in the Perspective. Which of these principles do you feel are the most important? Which do you feel are the least important? Which might you improve on? Give reasons for your answers.

Potential Family Crises

THE CONCEPT OF FAMILY

"A crisis is any decisive change which creates a situation for which the habitual behavior patterns of a person or a group are inadequate" (Burgess, Locke, & Thomes, 1963, p. 415). The concepts used to describe "decisive change" and the responses to them are numerous. Among others, the list includes stress, problems, trouble, deviance, disorganization, disintegration, maladjustment, and breakdown.

Sometimes events outside the family cause a crisis. Examples are war, floods, and persecution. Other crises, such as illness, violence, and death, have their sources within the family. Some may be a combination of events. Family stress is sometimes accompanied by financial, psychological, or other types of stress that may affect various family members differently.

An event may be considered a crisis for one marriage or family but not for another. In their pioneering work, Waller and Hill (1951) identified some of the variables that help to determine whether a given event becomes a crisis for a specific family:

1. The hardships of the situation or event itself.
2. The resources of the family, such as its role structure, flexibility, and previous history with crisis.
3. The definition the family makes of the event; that is, whether or not family members treat the event as a threat to their status, goals, and objectives.

Whenever an event produces stress or disequilibrium in the usual way a family functions, changes and adjustments become necessary. Various conceptual frameworks are used to analyze the ways families respond to such challenges. For example, Hill (1949) sees the process as proceeding from crisis to disorganization, recovery, and reorganization. He notes that some families are able to respond to a crisis situation without disorganization or with a minimal period of disorganization before recovery and reorganization set it.

According to the McMaster Model of Family Functioning, effective problem solving takes place in seven steps:

1. Identify the problem.
2. Communicate with appropriate people about the problem.
3. Outline possible alternative solutions.
4. Decide on one of the alternatives.

5. Carry out the action required by the alternative.
6. Monitor to ensure that the action is carried out.
7. Evaluate the effectiveness of the problem-solving process (Epstein, Bishop, & Baldwin, 1984).

Families differ in their abilities: Some are better at detecting patterns and organization than others; some can coordinate, cooperate, and agree more easily than others; some are more open to new information, while others delay solving their problems (Reiss & Oliveri, 1983).

Effective families tend to solve their problems quickly, efficiently, and easily. Those who do not function well do not follow the steps and therefore leave problems unresolved (Epstein et al., 1984). One recent study found that families reported that they used their confidence in being able to handle the problem most often, sought spiritual support second, and acquired social support third as coping strategies. The researchers found no difference between urban and rural families or between men and women in which strategies were used (Marotz-Baden & Colvin, 1986).

A pile-up of stressors adds to a crisis. For example, a family with a chronically ill child may be better able to cope if they do not have financial or emotional problems than would a family that does have these additional stressors. "The greater the accumulation of stressors with a resulting intensification of strains, the less family members are satisfied with the family lifestyle; the less their personal well-being; and the greater the probability of health, emotional, and relational problems in the family" (Lavee, McCubbin, & Patterson, 1985, p. 822). The type of situation—externally or internally precipitated, permanent or temporary, short- or long-term, expected or unexpected—may make a difference in procedure. Also, different families, usually based on their previous experiences, will proceed differently and at a different tempo through the adjustment process. Some families will find that the process of adaptation to stressors adds to their tension (Marotz-Baden & Colvin, 1986). Others will proceed with minimum effort.

*Happy families are all alike, but each unhappy family is unhappy
in its own way.* —TOLSTOY

*Life is not a matter of holding good cards, but of playing a poor
hand well.* —ROBERT LOUIS STEVENSON

*If all our misfortune were laid in one common heap, whence
everyone must take an equal portion, most people would be
content to take their own and depart.* —SOCRATES

All families sometimes experience crises. Crises are a natural part of life, and they produce change. Being prepared for potential changes will make adjustment easier. The orthographic character for "crisis" in Chinese is a combination of two simple characters—one meaning "danger" and the other meaning "opportunity."

The twofold meaning is significant. It is, to a large extent, up to the family what use they make of a crisis situation.

ILLNESS AND DISABILITY

Serious illness almost always represents a major threat to a family's equilibrium. However, the human capacity to deal with physical pain and/or disability is tremendous. Historical records show how people often continue to function adequately under the most harrowing life circumstances.

ILLNESS AS A CRISIS

Illness is a crisis for several reasons. First, it is usually unexpected. Having adequate health insurance is about the only preplanning a family can do. Even with insurance coverage, a single illness can wipe out all a family's savings.

Second, if the primary family provider becomes ill, injured, or disabled, the family may experience financial hardship. Worry about bringing in the weekly paycheck may, in turn, slow down the patient's recovery.

Third, people lack role prescriptions in illness situations. When you are ill, you are expected to assume a "sick role": (1) You give up most of your social obligations. You stay home from school and work. (2) You are exempted from some responsibility for your own condition. You are expected to get well spontaneously or to be cured with the help of a medical professional. (3) Since being sick is socially undesirable, you are expected to want to get well. (4) Being sick implies needing help. You are obliged to cooperate with physicians or other therapists (Parsons, 1953).

During a hospital stay, there is an additional set of expectations for sick people. King (1962) says that the subculture of the hospital (1) expects you to be dependent and compliant to hospital rules, to the daily routine, and to medical decisions. (2) Similarly, you are not expected to fulfill your normal role responsibilities but rather to concentrate on the process of getting well. (3) Your external power and prestige are deemphasized by such action as taking away your clothes. (4) You are expected to endure pain and suffering, including that caused by hospital procedures, with grace and dignity. (5) You are expected to try to get well and not malinger. If not, you are encouraged to leave the hospital.

Unfortunately, neither you nor your family are ever taught these role expectations. You have to learn them on your own through experience, which makes adjustment to the sick role or the hospital stay more difficult, at least initially. In turn, you are not likely to tell others about the roles you have learned. Families and friends may not know how to react, respond, or behave around a sick person. They may avoid confronting the situation or deny its seriousness. Little change in the typical pattern of avoidance and denial can be expected as long as our society looks upon ill health and disability as weaknesses, with the individual, somehow, being responsible for the unpleasant situation.

The seriousness of the threat depends not only upon the actual degree of disequilibrium caused by the illness but also from the resulting changes in your self-concept. All illness requires changes and consequent realignment and adaptation in the usual ways and means of functioning. "Change is the life process and adaptation is the method of change. Adaptation is the process of change whereby the individual retains his integrity within the realities of the environment" (Levine, 1969, pp. 9–10).

COPING WITH CRISIS

Warning! *This patient is a person, handle with respect.*
—SIGN BY AN ELDERLY PATIENT'S BED

It is not enough for us to do what we can do; the patient and his environment, and external conditions have to contribute to achieve the cure. —HIPPOCRATES

Lazarus (1966) has identified two general categories for adapting to and coping with a crisis. The first is to take action to eliminate or at least reduce the potential threat. The second is to think through the appraisal of the potential threat without

Crises—individual, marital, or familial—make it difficult to see straight. However, it is important to keep everything in perspective.

changing the actual situation. He calls these cognitive maneuvers defense mechanisms.

Moos and Tsu (1977) list specific tasks that patients, families, and friends commonly employ to deal with the adaptive tasks:

1. Deny or minimize the seriousness of the crisis. This includes keeping a perspective on life and isolating one's emotions when dealing with a distressing situation.
2. Seek relevant information. Often the right information can relieve anxiety caused by uncertainty or misconceptions. Organizations and publications dealing with many medical procedures and disabilities are available.
3. Request reassurance and emotional support from concerned family, friends, and medical staff. The support of those around you can be an important source of strength.
4. Learn specific illness-related procedures. Coping with an illness or disability can be devastating for you if you are used to doing things for yourself. When a newly disabled person learns to maneuver a wheelchair or a blind person masters braille, he or she achieves greater freedom and pride and is less of a burden to others.
5. Set concrete, limited goals. By breaking a seemingly overwhelming problem into small, potentially manageable bits, the problem can be conquered little by little. Achieving each small goal is an accomplishment in itself.
6. Rehearse alternative outcomes. This step includes becoming mentally prepared and discussing possible outcomes with family and friends.
7. Find a general purpose or pattern of meaning. Religion or a philosophy of life can help you to cope with difficulties and may serve as a consolation.

While these steps and the advice of experts may sound simple, following them in times of crisis is not easy. Jill Hughes (1982) explains that although she had spoken at meetings about helping long-term patients make adjustments and had served time as a student member of a chaplaincy team in a large general hospital, dealing with a personal situation was difficult for her. She says:

> There she is. Oh God, what am I going to do? How will I talk to her? What if she doesn't recognize me? She was so strong all my life and now . . . an old lady surrounded by blankets and pillows. I turned round and walked out of the ward—I hadn't even seen her close up yet. . . .
> The "she" in question is my paternal grandmother. A woman with whom I had lived off and on for many of my formative years. The woman who had cared for me up to age four and a half while my parents worked. The woman whom I look back on as one of the most important role models in my life so far. She taught me, without realizing, that women are/can be strong and must have ideals. She gave me support in all that I did, usually unspoken but always there. . . .
> My mind was in a state of anarchy and turmoil. (p. 960)

Hughes explained to the hospital staff that she wanted them to deal with her grandmother as a person and to provide, whenever possible, situations and ap-

BOX 9.1 A CRABBIT OLD WOMAN WROTE THIS

Benjamin Schlesinger, a University of Toronto sociologist, came across this anonymous poem while teaching at a summer institute in St. Francis Xavier University, Antigonish, N.S. We believe its deeply human cry deserves wider attention.

What do you see, nurses, what do you see?
Are you thinking, when you look at me—
A crabbit old woman, not very wise,
Uncertain of habit, with far-away eyes,
Who dribbles her food and makes no reply
When you say in a loud voice—"I do wish you'd try."
Who seems not to notice the things that you do
And forever is losing a stocking or shoe,
Who unresisting or not, lets you do as you will
With bathing and feeding, the long day to fill.
Is that what you're thinking, is that what you see?
Then open your eyes, nurse, you're not looking at me.
I'll tell you who I am as I sit here so still;
As I rise at your bidding, as I eat at your will.
I'm a small child of ten with a father and mother,
Brothers and sisters, who love one another,
A young girl of sixteen with wings on her feet,
Dreaming that soon now a lover she'll meet;
A bride soon at twenty—my heart gives a leap,
Remembering the vows that I promised to keep;
At twenty-five now I have young of my own
Who need me to build a secure happy home;
A woman of thirty, my young now grow fast,
Bound to each other with ties that should last;
At forty, my young sons have grown and are gone,
But my man's beside me to see I don't mourn;
At fifty once more babies play round my knee,
Again we know children, my loved one and me.
Dark days are upon me, my husband is dead,
I look at the future, I shudder with dread,
For my young are all rearing young of their own,
And I think of the years and the love that I've known.
I'm an old woman now and nature is cruel—
'Tis her jest to make old age look like a fool.
The body is crumbled, grace and vigor depart,
There is now a stone where I once had a heart,
But inside this old carcass a young girl still dwells,
And now and again my battered heart swells.
I remember the joys, I remember the pain
And I'm loving and living life over again,
I think of the years all too few—gone too fast,
And accept the stark fact that nothing can last—
So open your eyes, nurses, open and see
Not a crabbit old woman, look closer—see ME.

From *Transition,* vol. 11, no. 2, Summer, 1981, p. 10.

proaches with which her grandmother was familiar. Above all, she asked them to keep the humanness and personhood of the patient in mind.

Aging brings extra challenges to a family. "The most insistent task of the aged individual is the maintenance of integrity in spite of ever-increasing loss. Integrity implies wholeness, but losing parts of the whole tends to lead to disintegration" (Ebersole, 1974, p. 103).

Physical disability can add considerable stress to a marital relationship. This crisis dumps two very expensive—both objectively and subjectively—burdens on the couple (Thompson & Doll, 1982). Permanent disability may require changes in the family's life-style and even in the structure of the home. A family with a wheelchair-bound member, for example, will need ramps and wide doorways. Families with handicapped children are faced with special education procedures. They may also suffer guilt and anxiety over the disability.

VIOLENCE IN THE FAMILY

When you think of family violence, you usually think of physical abuse. Violence, however, can also be verbal, psychological, or sexual. It may involve any family member and every relationship. As Pedrick-Cornell and Gelles (1982) point out, "Child abuse emerged as a social problem in the 1960s and wife abuse was identified as a major social issue in the 1970s. Similarly, abuse of the elderly has become a topic of interest and concern in the 1980s" (p. 457). Other recent articles have added courtship violence (Makepeace, 1981) and husband battering (Gelles, 1983) to the list.

COURTSHIP VIOLENCE

Courtship is considered a time for moonlight, roses, and love. The idealized picture certainly does not mention violence. However, in a study of university students, Makepeace (1981) found the real-life situation to be significantly different. He found that 60 percent of the students responding had personally known of someone who had been directly involved in courtship violence. The most common forms of such violence were threatening, pushing or shoving, slapping, and punching. Jealousy over the perceived or real involvement of a partner with another person, disagreements over drinking behavior, and anger over sexual denial were the most common sources of conflict. While the most frequent locus of abuse was a residence, a significant percentage of the incidents took place in vehicles and out of doors.

The female partner was more likely to be or at least to feel victimized. In half the cases examined by Makepeace, violence occurred on multiple occasions. Only about half the relationships broke up; in fact, some of them remained intact for quite some time after single or multiple episodes of violence. As Makepeace notes, "It appears that violence is a common, albeit neglected, aspect of premarital heterosexual interaction" (p. 100).

The reasons for courtship violence are not clear. However, both male abusers and female victims seem to share similar problematic profiles, particularly in reporting lack of closeness with their fathers and lack of church attendance. Abusers and victims are also more likely to feel stressed; to be socially isolated; to come from a broken home; to have had harsh parental discipline; to have had problems with school, job, or alcohol; and to have been early daters (Makepeace, 1987).

One recent study showed that more traditionally masculine males were the most likely to abuse their dates and less traditionally feminine women were most likely to be victims, although the traditionally feminine women were less likely to report having been abused. The researchers hypothesize that male aggressors are threatened by nontraditional women (Bernard, Bernard, & Bernard, 1985).

Courtship violence is apparently not confined to a few isolated incidents; it occurs in a good many relationships. It also has further ramifications. Victims report that the more intimate the relationship between the dating partners, the more the violence increased. Violence does not end at marriage, either. Patterns of violence begun in courtship often continue into marriage (Roscoe & Benaske, 1985).

CHILD ABUSE

Physical abuse of children occurs at all the social and economic levels. The consequences typically are grave and the violence is likely to recur in the next generation—abused children are likely to become abusive parents and spouses (Gelles, 1983). The causes of violence are complex and hard to identify and the cures elusive. Stress seems to be a major factor. Parents who face other problems, such as unemployment or marital strife, are more likely to abuse their children. Similarly, problem children, who are more difficult to care for, are more apt to be abused. People with lower incomes, those isolated from family and community, and those with little understanding of child development are more likely to be abusive than are other groups (Zigler & Rubin, 1986). Studies also show that increasing numbers of unplanned pregnancies raise the chances of abuse and neglect (Zuravin, 1987).

The estimates of the extent of this problem range widely, from half a million to over two million abused and neglected children. It is also estimated that some two thousand children die each year as a result of family violence. Whatever the exact numbers and the individual definitions, most people would agree that there is too much violence in our society. Steinmetz (1977), in a questionnaire study of a broad-based but nonrepresentative sample of nearly a hundred people, most of them in their twenties, found that almost three-fourths of the families studied used physical aggression to resolve conflicts in parent-child and sibling interactions. Schuman (1983), in her article, "The Violent American Way of Life," quotes sociologist Murray A. Strauss as saying, "Violence is as common as love in the American family" (p. 182).

Incest, sexual activity including but not limited to coitus between individuals who are too closely related to ever contract legal marriage, is one type of child abuse. "Sibling incest between brother and sister who are in their early teens or younger is the most frequent type, but is rarely reported" (DeLora, Warren, & Ellison, 1981, p. 480). Father-daughter and stepfather-stepdaughter cases are by far the most likely to reach the courts (Vander Mey & Neff, 1984). However, all possible relationships, heterosexual as well as homosexual, have been noted. Other types of abuse include neglect, verbal abuse, and psychological abuse. Handicapped children are at a high risk for abuse, and such abuse can, in turn, cause additional physical and psychological disabilities (Mullins, 1986).

Whatever the means of abuse, neglect, or violence—and even though children have tremendous resilience and a great capacity for recuperation—many are likely to be scarred by these experiences. While they have a longer time to forget, they also have a longer time to remember. Consciousness raising is proposed as the most important way to increase reporting and to decrease child abuse (Vander Mey & Neff, 1984). On a personal level, Zigler and Rubin (1986) suggest that, as parents, you try to correct children's behavior without violence by learning about child development and parenting, by being consistent in your rules for your child, by talking with others about your child's behavior, and by taking a moment to calm down and assess each situation before you punish your child.

SPOUSE ABUSE

Wife beating is not a new phenomenon. However, in the last two decades there has been a social movement that has drawn it to the attention of the media and government agencies (Tierney, 1982). Numerous studies have been conducted to find the reasons for marital abuse and to pinpoint ways to stop it.

Many reasons to explain why men batter their wives have been offered. For instance, it has been suggested that an inequality between husband and wife is related to violence. In a survey of American states, it was found that "in states where the status of women is lowest, wives are most likely to be physically assaulted by their husbands. Violence does decrease as women's status increases—to a point. In those states where the status of women is highest, the level of violence against wives is also quite high" (Yllo, 1983, p. 81).

Other research points to family background. People who have observed their parents hitting one another are more likely to be involved in severe marital aggression themselves, either as perpetrators or victims (Kalmuss, 1984). Others find that being physically abused themselves, coming from a lower-class household, being under social stress, and perceiving a lack of social support is correlated with the likelihood of being physically abusive with a marital partner.

Why do wives stay with an abusing partner? Past and recent research shows that a battered woman is often economically dependent on her spouse as well as committed to their relationship, no matter how bad it is (Strube & Barbour, 1983). Others have shown that battered women have little faith in the legal system. Those in one study rarely found their husbands punished. "The criminal justice system was generally far less responsive than she desired, and it often had the effect of wearing down the victim-witness long before the defendant was due to stand trial" (Ford, 1983, p. 473).

While past attitudes have tended to lay the blame on the victim and have adapted the attitude that a man "owned" his wife, more recent attitudes have leaned toward resolving the problems more systematically. The first phase of treatment is the establishment of shelters for battered women that also provide support groups and other necessary services. The second phase is treating the male abuser (Cook & Frantz-Cook, 1984).

Shelters offer battered women a chance to leave their abusive households by finding jobs and other financial support or ways of improving their situations at home if they decide to return. Shelters can benefit children, too, because they influence women to reduce their violence toward their children (Giles-Sims, 1985).

Treating the male who batters is somewhat complicated. Since some of the violence is linked to social learning in adolescence and later, methods are being devised to help these men monitor their behavior so they can initiate change. Techniques include learning to relax, to be more empathetic to their partners' views, to rid their thinking of irrational beliefs, and to increase their expression of feelings (Edleson, Miller, Stone, & Chapman, 1985). Other researchers suggest that because the abusive husband often suffers from low self-esteem, treatment should include cognitive restructuring—so that he understands that his wife does not intend to threaten his self-esteem—as well as couple communication training and correction of other misperceptions and faulty communications (Goldstein & Rosenbaum, 1985). The abusive male is often hard to treat because he tends to be a "Jekyll and Hyde"—that is, he not only denies his abusive behavior but seems to relate well to other people and is amiable and personable. However, underneath, he "experiences intense feelings of social and personal (masculine) inadequacy and frustration arising from deep, unmet dependency needs" (Bernard & Bernard, 1984, p. 545). These researchers report success in group therapy and stressed the importance of long-term treatment.

A reverse type of situation is called "protective-reaction violence" (Gelles, 1983). In this situation "a wife will strike first (and hard) to protect herself from her husband if she believes she is about to be abused again. . . . Recently, there have been numerous cases of women who have killed their husbands and have pleaded self-defense" (p. 186).

ELDER ABUSE

The violence, abuse, and neglect perpetrated on elderly family members has also recently received attention. Despite the growing research and clinical interest in various forms of family violence, "there seems to be little discussion and no major investigation into the possibility that the aged might also be victims of familial abuse, neglect and other forms of violence" (Rathbone-McCuan, 1980, p. 296). Similarly, Turner (1980)—noting that statistics for husband-and-wife violence, the most prevalent form, are probably underestimated and are likely to increase—calls for attention to the growing incidence of child violence against parents.

Pedrick-Cornell and Gelles (1982) state that the rapid emergence of elderly abuse as a social problem is the result of two major factors. The first factor comes as a natural outgrowth of intensive research on the extent and patterns of family violence. The second factor relates to the major demographic changes of the last half century. Life expectancy has increased almost 50 percent in about as many years and the proportion of the population aged 60 and older has also increased. At the same time, there are fewer children who can share the responsibility of caring for their elderly parents. It appears, however, that for any real or definitive answers to what is going on in this area, we will have to wait for more research and, for the present, to cope as best we can.

One obstacle to stopping family violence is identifying problem families; societal rules are ineffective for situations that occur behind closed doors (Queijo, 1986). Another is attitude.

> One of the most ruthless contributors to domestic violence is our society's tolerance and acceptance of many forms of violence. Each day our children are exposed to a variety of messages which tell them that hitting other people is okay. . . . Reject violence as a normal part of family life and you begin to see that it is possible to raise a healthy, happy, and well-behaved generation that does not see the fist as the solution. (Gelles, 1983, p. 188)

DEATH AND DYING

While each new birth is proudly announced and advertised to the world, death has been somewhat removed from family life. The possibility of death is sometimes denied. If death is talked about at all, it usually involves such euphemisms as "loved ones" and "passing away." In the past, death took place in the home among family members; today, most deaths occur in a hospital or nursing home, among strangers.

Even though birth and death are opposites, they can be distinguished from other rites of passage in that both connect humanity with the unknown. "But until recently these events have been treated with either strict academic detachment—as with a halting fascination which mirrors the interest of social science in the aberrant—as in investigations of unusual aspects or circumstances surrounding birth and death" (DeVries, 1981, p. 1074). Only in the last decades has there been a shift toward more open discussion of these transitions into, and especially out of, life.

TIME OF DEATH

Death comes in various forms. Sometimes it is quick, violent, or unexpected, while at other times it may be expected, slow, and prolonged. In most cases, however, it is somewhere between these extremes. Death can also come at any

---

BOX 9.2   FOR EVERYTHING THERE IS A SEASON

For everything there is a season, and a time for every matter under heaven:
a time to be born, and a time to die;
a time to plant, and a time to pluck up what is planted;
a time to kill, and a time to heal;
a time to break down, and a time to build up;
a time to weep, and a time to laugh;
a time to mourn, and a time to dance;
a time to cast away stones, and a time to gather stones together;
a time to embrace, and a time to refrain from embracing;
a time to seek, and a time to lose;
a time to keep, and a time to cast away;
a time to rend, and a time to sew;
a time to keep silence, and a time to speak;
a time to love, and a time to hate;
a time for war, and a time for peace.

—Eccelesiastes 3:1–8

---

time. Stillbirth or the death of a child can cause particular stress. "Death has no place at birth. It is the end of life, not the beginning. For a woman to give birth to death instead of life means an overturning of the natural order of things. Such an event can have long-reaching effects on the parents and their families" (Lewis & Liston, 1981, p. 147).

COPING WITH DEATH

There is no question that dying and death are crisis situations, both for the dying person and the family. Kübler-Ross (1969) identifies five stages experienced by most dying people:

1. *Denial and isolation.* Upon being told that he or she is dying, an individual is likely to deny the fact. The dying person feels isolated because of the personal nature of dying and the feelings that no one else could understand.
2. *Anger.* The dying person's rage is expressed almost randomly at God, fate, family members, friends, and medical staff.
3. *Bargaining.* Bargaining is an attempt to postpone death. The dying person may beg for more time from God by promising to turn over a new leaf. It may also be a time when nonbelievers believe, or in reverse, believers lose faith when it becomes obvious that God will not extend their life. The dying person may also bargain with the doctor to live long enough to see an important event such as a child's graduation.

Young people can be very supportive of the elderly in their hour of need. A touch means more than a thousand words.

4. *Depression.* As their physical condition weakens, their financial expenses mount, patients see no hope in anything. At this time, they need to feel sad and to express their feelings.
5. *Acceptance.* By this stage, feelings may have been spent. Hence this can be a time of peace, rest, contemplation, and acceptance.

Some experts disagree with the stages-of-dying theory. "Even if a person does experience and express some feelings in common with any other dying person, he does so within the unique pattern of a life that no other person has lived, and within a particular environment while suffering from a particular disease syndrome" (Kastenbaum, 1981, p. 192).

Coping with the death of a family member or friend is a traumatic experience. "Grief and mourning are powerful and stressful emotional states that can touch off unconscious psychological reactions that actually jeopardize the individual's life" (Schneidman, 1984, p. 392). Grievers are often at risk for illness and accidents for a period of months or even a year.

Mourners usually respond to death with shock. They may be unable to do their daily tasks without blundering; they may cling to a child, a pet, or even an inanimate object; they may search for the dead person. They may even believe that any hate or wrongdoing of which they were guilty in relation to the dead person during his or her life *caused* the death. Later, the mourners complete the mourning process by withdrawing their emotional attachment from the deceased and learning to rely on memories about the dead person in order to talk, think, or feel about him or her (Pincus, 1984).

Children are often treated differently from the rest of the mourners. Although children usually want to talk about their feelings concerning death, parents are often either unaware of their need to talk or reluctant to involve their children because of their own confusion and fear or the belief that they are protecting them from something unpleasant. Talking with children and allowing them to participate in the grief process with the rest of the family can help children understand the death process. Children can also lend support to the rest of the family (Weber & Fournier, 1985).

Siblings are often the forgotten grievers. Their reactions to the death of a sister or brother may include nightmares, a change in school behavior and performance, depression, feelings of rejection by parents, and withdrawal (Zelauskas, 1981).

RITUALS OF DEATH

Religion and its rituals are often helpful in coping with a death. In fact, individuals who consider themselves either high or low in religiousness exhibit less death anxiety than those in the medium range (McMordie, 1981). Funerals are part of the common religious rituals tied with death, and they serve several purposes for the living. In addition to providing a formal way of disposing of the body, the funeral ritual makes it very difficult for the mourners to deny death. It is also a rehearsal of death, an expression of the worth of the dead person and of sorrow, and an opportunity both for grief to work and the restructuring of the mourner's life (Wretmark, 1981). On the other hand, interviewees in one study said they were dissatisfied with support from various institutional resources, especially clergy and religious institutions (Weber & Fournier, 1985).

ALCOHOL AND DRUG ABUSE

Broken bottles, broken families, broken dreams—a fitting description of the serious social problem of alcoholism. Estimates of the number of alcoholics in the United States range from 9 to 13 million (Leikin, 1986). "Many authorities believe that the figures grossly understate the number of people who repeatedly hurt themselves and others through the abuse of alcohol. In more meaningful terms, there are probably more people who have known and cared about someone with a drinking problem than there are people who have never been touched by alcohol abuse" (Deutsch, 1982, pp. 13–14). If drug abuse is added to alcoholism, we are talking about a significant proportion of our population.

SOCIETY'S VIEW

As with other crises, an alcoholic or drug-abusing family member is a direct source of stress for the family and all of its members. To make matters worse, such abuse is usually a contributory factor in producing such crises as unemployment, desertion, divorce, nonsupport, imprisonment, family violence, child abuse, and so on (Downs, 1982). However, our society has paid significantly less attention and has spent less money on these problems than on some other, more "socially acceptable" illnesses such as heart disease, cancer, and diabetes. Yet alcoholism and drug abuse are quite clearly illnesses and their sufferers and families need help and support.

> *A definition of intoxication: When you feel sophisticated and can't pronounce it.*

> *As kids we started smoking and drinking because it was smart. Why don't we stop for the same reason?* —EMERY

> *I'm getting sick and tired of getting up every morning sick and tired. . . .*

> *Health is what most people drink to until they collapse.*

> *You can't drown sorrow with an alcohol bottle—it knows how to swim!*

> *Lord, the greatest gift you can give me is an understanding heart.*
> —SOLOMON

While many researchers have made an effort to relate other family crises to alcoholism and drug abuse, they have not been very successful. "Alcohol literature is imprecise when it comes to defining 'conflict' and there has been little specific research on family violence in alcohol-abusing families" (Wilson, 1980, p. 106). Thus, while there is little doubt that many of these behaviors are related and frequently occur together, we do not understand the precise cause-and-effect relationship between them.

At least we now have a functional definition of alcoholism, developed by the United Nations World Health Organization, Expert Committee on Mental Health in 1951. It states: "Alcoholism is an illness characterized by loss of control over drinking which results in serious problems in any one of the following areas: job, school, or financial affairs; relationships with family and friends; or physical health" (Deutsch, 1982, p. 15). Note that frequency and quantity are not part of

Alcohol and/or drugs have never solved a crisis and typically make everything worse, not better.

the definition. Different people have different tolerances for alcohol, and these may change over time or even from situation to situation.

EFFECTS ON FAMILIES

In talking about the alcoholic marriage over time, Downs (1982) maintains that it goes through an early stage of consistency characterized by sporadic bouts of drinking and temporary sobrieties sometimes due to institutionalization. This fluctuation requires that the spouse and other family members continually adapt and readapt. Continual redefinition of the family relationships produces increased stress. In the later stages, the family can achieve some equilibrium because they recognize intoxication as the usual state of the alcoholic member and deal with it accordingly.

Continued family life and rituals during crisis are very important (Wolin,

---

BOX 9.3   SOCIAL OCCASIONS AND THE RECOVERING ALCOHOLIC

Good hosts know their guests individually and, whenever possible, their food and drink preferences and restrictions. Considerate hosts never call special attention to them, however. They do not force meat on vegetarians or try to convince teetotalers that one glass of wine is acceptable. "It's only very light, imported wine that we got especially for this occasion and you should try it" is not an appropriate comment.

Good hosts treat all guests equally. At cocktail parties, they ask, "What would you like to drink?" This applies to those who use alcoholic beverages regularly and those who have never used any alcoholic beverages, as well as recovering alcoholics. Having a selection of soft drinks and fruit juices on hand provides a choice without calling attention to specific guests. A recovering alcoholic might ask for something like coffee or tea. It should be provided without any fuss.

If nondrinkers are present at the dinner table, everyone should be given a water glass. Some of the nondrinkers may let the host fill their wine glass even though they will not drink. Others may signal, inconspicuously, "No, thank you." The host makes the offer; the guests make their own decisions.

Finally, good hosts never ask recovering alcoholics about the program. This is no more appropriate than asking other guests about their high blood pressure medications or diet pills. If guests bring up the subject, however, good hosts listen with interest and empathy.

Bennett, Noonan, & Teitelbaum, 1980). A ritual is defined as patterned behavior to which the family attributes symbolic meaning or purpose. Rituals include dinnertime, holidays, vacations, and other similar events. From their interviews with families in which one or more members were or had been active alcoholics, the researchers found that families whose rituals were altered during the period of heaviest parental drinking were more likely to transmit an alcohol problem to the children's generation than were families whose rituals remained intact.

Often families and friends don't know the best way to deal with an alcoholic member. Sometimes it is difficult to tell exactly when a social drinker becomes an alcoholic. Some signs may be identifiable only by the problem drinkers themselves. "They have to do with reasons, occasions, and patterns of drinking. Some examples are:

> Drinking to forget or to escape from problems;
> Drinking to face certain situations;
> Having several drinks before a party;
> Drinking alone;
> Drinking in the morning;
> Reserving a regular time for drinking, and looking forward to it" (Deutsch, 1982, p. 193).

Even after a person has started recovering from alcoholism, the question of how to deal with this family member or friend remains. Lack of role prescriptions is a problem. So is the length of recovery; alcoholism has to be fought throughout life.

The same may also apply to drug addiction. Drug abuse is both a problem and a symptom for individuals, families, and society. In one study, the offspring of drug abusers were seen as weak, overprotected individuals who, through most of their lives, had been allowed or even encouraged to find escape rather than to cope with their problems and frustrations realistically. In these families, fathers were typically the authority figures, and there was some tendency for them to appear as quick-tempered and/or stubborn (Cannon, 1976).

UNEMPLOYMENT

" 'Warning: Unemployment may be hazardous to your health.' It's not a sign that appears in doctors' offices, but as the recession deepens, health authorities see indications of increased emotional and physical illness in communities hard hit by layoffs and plant closings" (Trafford, 1982, p. 81). Over the past decades, the general business climate has added extra pressures and difficulty to all families but especially to those in which the chief breadwinner is out of work. Today, marriages and families cannot survive without money. A pound of hamburger or a month's electricity, for example, is likely to cost several times what it did ten years ago. Unemployment is likely to create a twofold crisis, since it involves negative consequences for the financial situation as well as the identities and roles of family members. "Other possible consequences include a decline in family goals, increased ambiguity and apprehension concerning the future, and real as well as perceived loss of control" (Moen, 1983, p. 751).

WHO ARE THE UNEMPLOYED?

Unemployment seems to affect different groups selectively. For example, Moen (1979) found that single mothers and family heads with young children (under six) were the most likely to be unemployed. In economically lean times, college graduates can experience significant trauma and anxiety when, instead of entering the profession for which they have prepared, they are faced with unemployment.

Men who have spent years or decades in a job or profession can likewise be affected both economically and emotionally by the loss of employment. In economically difficult times, it may be easier for the wife to obtain work than for the husband, although she must usually accept a lower-paying job. However, the husband who becomes a homemaker, even if he enjoys it and does a good job, is looked down upon. People may assume that he is either mentally or physically handicapped or incompetent in the workplace. As one male homemaker explained, "When a teacher calls to bring some cookies for the next PTA meeting and is referred to me, to say the least, she feels quite awkward. One day, when a salesman called about our new stove, I could hear him say to someone else at the store, 'We've got a weirdo here.' " Our society appears to have a long way to go before role reversals are accepted.

COPING WITH UNEMPLOYMENT

While unemployment does not strike randomly, no social class is immune from it. Powell and Driscoll (1973) studied a number of scientists and engineers who were suddenly unemployed and found that these men went through several predictable stages. The first was one of *relaxation and relief.* The men felt that they were simply between jobs and this was a good time to take it easy, catch up on their reading, spend more time with family, and go on vacation.

The second stage was one of *concerted effort.* After three or four weeks at home, they got bored and started making serious attempts to find work. They were generally optimistic, family relations were going well, and their wives were supportive. Things started changing in the third stage, to that of *doubt and indecisiveness.* By now they had been out of work longer than ever before in their lives and they began to think about other possible careers. They alternated between looking very hard for any kind of work and not looking at all. Their moods deteriorated, along with their family relations. They worried about being "over the hill." Finally, they entered the fourth stage, that of *malaise and cynicism.* They started protecting themselves from further rejection by staying away from interviews and responding only to ads requesting resumes. Many eventually ceased to care about anything: getting work, their families, or even themselves. They felt totally helpless.

Even if an unemployed person eventually finds work, some scars of the experience seem to remain. In those areas where unemployment is on a larger scale or longer lasting, prescriptions for antidepressants and antianxiety drugs increase along with the number of patients who require psychiatric counseling (Trafford, 1982). There is an increase in ulcers, headaches, and blood pressure, plus increased abuse of cigarettes and alcohol. Abuse sometimes extends to children, and general family tension is likely. Trafford (1982) quotes Ruth Kane, chief of child and adolescent mental-health services at a Pittsburgh hospital, as follows: "These are normal people. They are not sickies or goofies. These are working people who would have carried on their lives if they hadn't lost their jobs" (p. 81).

Now there is even a name for this crisis—the "pink-slip syndrome"—and it is most likely to hit around the sixth month of unemployment. Jahoda (1981) states, "In spite of much empirical research, knowledge in the field of work is fragmented, sometimes contradictory, and severely underused in the public debate about future levels of employment" (p. 184). She pleads for more future-oriented research—that is, research that could help prevent unemployment or at least some of the crisis stemming from unemployment.

It would be pleasant to think that families could exist without crises. However, a trouble-free life would be an unrealistic expectation. Some families face a limited number of crisis times; others seem to have one problem on top of another. Some planning can help avoid crises. Honesty and open communication can aid in the coping and adaptation process. Professional help is available in many areas. Whether the crisis a family faces is one of those discussed or another type, it can bring the family closer together or drive it apart. Much depends on the individuals involved and the family structure.

AIDS AND OTHER STDs

In the 1980s, while our society was still struggling to control alcohol and drug abuse, it was confronted with a deadly new emotional, social, and economic tragedy in the form of AIDS (acquired immune deficiency syndrome) as well as serious increases in other sexually transmissible diseases (STDs). Until recently, no marriage-and-family textbook would have included material on STDs or AIDS. Today, we can no longer dismiss these topics as inconsequential or as applying only to special populations and cases—not to the average person or "me, personally."

Neither can this text devote more than a few pages to these issues. However, we owe it to ourselves and to future generations to emphasize the seriousness of what is happening and to provide some resources for education and help. These include the following:

> The *Surgeon General's Report on AIDS* (single copies may be had free of charge by calling 404-329-3534).
> *Facts about AIDS,* U.S. Public Health Service, Washington, D.C., 1986.
> *AIDS: What Everyone Should Know,* also *Making Sex Safer,* American College Health Association, Rockville, Maryland, 1987.
> "The Facts About AIDS," *NEA Higher Education Advocate,* 1987, *4*(13), 1–16.

Also, there are several hot lines that can give you information:

> 800-342-AIDS (U.S. Public Health Service, recorded message).
> 800-227-8922 (National STD Hotline, American School Health Association).
> 800-447-AIDS (U.S. Public Health Service).
> 800-221-7044 (National Gay Task Force and AIDS Crisis).

Just as with any other topic, knowledge about AIDS and other STDs is the key to separating facts from fiction. The myths and misconceptions about AIDS have caused needless panic and concern. To become burdened by fear without facts is quite useless and only harmful to our general well-being. Nor should these concerns be taken lightly and dismissed without a careful consideration of the available information. Here we will present (1) a list of some facts in response to common myths about AIDS and (2) a summary chart of the various STDs.

Some common myths about AIDS and other STDs:

1. *Myth:* Only homosexuals, bisexuals, and intravenous (IV) drug users need to worry about AIDS. *Fact:* Heterosexuals and even children have contracted AIDS.
2. *Myth:* The AIDS virus can be caught by casual contact, as by being in the same room, touching, or using the same materials or facilities as an infected person. *Fact:* The only ways of being infected by the AIDS virus are through sexual contact with an infected person, through the injection of infected blood, or by being born to an infected mother.
3. *Myth:* The AIDS virus can be transmitted more easily than most other STDs. *Fact:* While the AIDS virus is only one of many infections

BOX 9.4   SUMMARY CHART OF THE SEXUALLY TRANSMISSIBLE DISEASES

Disease (Causative Organism)	Incubation Period	Signs/Symptoms	Complications
BACTERIAL GONORRHEA *Neisseria gonorrhoeae*	2–14 days, usually 3 days following exposure	Frequently slight, hidden or absent, especially in females. Painful urination. Pus discharge from infected site. Abdominal pains. Painful swelling of glands in genital area.	Severe infections of fallopian tubes, ovaries, lower abdomen. Chronic inflammation of ducts and glands in reproductive system. Sterility. Arthritis. Tubal pregnancy. Infection of baby's eyes at childbirth. Spread to sex partners.
NON-SPECIFIC OR NON-GONOCOCCAL URETHRITIS, VAGINITIS, "NSU, NGU, NSV, NGV" (Many possible causes; actual cause not always determined)	Uncertain; 8–14 days, varies with causative organism.	Pus discharge from sex organs. Painful or frequent urination. Inflammation of vaginal wall. Symptoms vary with organism.	Chronic inflammation of various glands and tubes in reproductive or urinary systems. Infection of infants at childbirth. Possible spread to sex partners.
Major NGU agents: *Chlamydia trachomatis*— causes about 50% of NGU	"	"	Inflammation of urethra, cervix, uterus, scrotum, rectum, eyelids, inner ear. Infant pneumonia. Trachoma. A suspected cause of liver infection. Reiter's disease and fetal and neonatal mortality.
Ureaplasma urealyticum—causes about 30% of NGU	"	"	Inflammation of urethra, fetus, amniotic sac and connective tissues. A suspected cause of low birth weight.
Mycoplasma hominis—causes 10–20% of NGU	"	"	Postpartum fever. Pelvic inflammatory disease.

Disease (Causative Organism)	Incubation Period	Signs/Symptoms	Complications
SYPHILIS *Treponema pallidum:* spirochete	10–90 days; usually 3 weeks following exposure	Frequently slight, hidden, or absent. *First-Primary:* hard, painless sore at point where germs entered the body. Swollen lymph nodes. *Second-Secondary:* rashes, white mucus patches, patchy hair loss, malaise. *Latent:* no symptoms.	Disease mimics many chronic health conditions (called "the great imitator"). Late untreated symptoms include damage to nervous, ocular, cardiovascular systems, tumors, birth defects, insanity. Transmission to unborn baby by infected female.
CHANCROID "Soft chancre" *Hemophilus ducreyi* bacillus	1–5 days	One or several small, raised painful sores with ragged, irregular edges. Hard, painful swelling of lymph glands in groin (bubo).	Secondary infection. Spread to sex partners.
LYMPHO-GRANULOMA VENEREUM *Chlamydia trachomatis*	1–12 weeks; usually 7–12 days	Small, painless pimple-like sore on genitals. Swollen, tender lymph glands in groin. Possible fever, chills, joint pains, nausea.	Swollen lymph nodes and ulcerations, enlargement of sexual organs (elephantiasis), rectal stricture. Causes different disease symptoms; usually found in tropical areas.
GRANULOMA INGUINALE *Calymmatobacterium granulomatis*	1–24 weeks; usually 8–12 weeks	Small, blister-like bump which ulcerates, becomes raised, rounded, and velvety, growing larger and somewhat painful. Possible swollen lymph glands.	Progressive destruction of infected tissue. Slightly contagious; possible spread to sex partners.
GARDNERELLA VAGINITIS *Gardnerella vaginalis*	Unknown	Vaginal discharge, with fishy odor.	Inflammation of vagina.
VIRAL AIDS (ACQUIRED IMMUNE DEFICIENCY SYNDROME) Human T-lymphotropic virus type III	(estimated) Still uncertain—2 to 5 years, up to 10	Tiredness. Loss of appetite. Fever. Night sweats. Diarrhea. Weight loss. Swollen lymph glands.	Severe weakening of immune system, frequent opportunistic infections by many kinds of pathogens, severe pneumonia, Kaposi's sarcoma—a rare form of cancer.

Disease (Causative Organism)	Incubation Period	Signs/Symptoms	Complications
GENITAL HERPES Herpes simplex virus, usually type 2 but sometimes type 1	2–20 days; usually 6 days following exposure	Single or multiple raised painful lesions. Fever. Headache. Malaise. Tender, swollen lymph nodes. Duration 2–3 weeks, often recurs.	Infection of child at birth, may be fatal. Apparent relationship to cervical cancer. Recurrence of painful symptoms. Secondary infections. Highly contagious; spread to sex partners. No known cure.
HEPATITIS B Hepatitis B virus	Range 45–160 days	Skin eruptions. Weakness. Weight loss. Vomiting. Fever. Dark urine. Jaundice. Moderate liver enlargement and tenderness.	Inflammation of liver, jaundice. Largely spread by unhygienic practices, contaminated food or water or sexual-anal practices— especially among homosexual men.
GENITAL (VENEREAL) WARTS Condyloma acuminata	1–3 months	Similar to common skin warts. Single or multiple growths around genital or anal regions; may be pink, indented and moist with a cauliflower-like texture, or hard and yellow-gray.	Location may vary. Disfigurement, benign warts in children, subject to irritation and secondary infection. Can obstruct urinary and defecatory processes. Possible malignancy.

transmitted by sexual contact, it is actually less contagious than the others. However, it is much more serious than any of the other STDs since it is incurable and generally—sooner or later—fatal.

4. *Myth:* A person who has caught AIDS will usually know this within a few days or weeks. *Fact:* Many individuals infected with the AIDS virus have no symptoms and experience no discomfort. The time between infection and onset of symptoms (the incubation period) can range from six months to six years or more.

5. *Myth:* AIDS contracted through injection or the sharing of IV needles is referred to as HIV. *Fact:* The current and preferred name for the AIDS virus is human immunodeficiency virus (HIV), whatever the means of transmission.

6. *Myth:* Some people have contracted AIDS from donating blood. *Fact:* Blood banks use new, sterile equipment and disposable needles for each donor. Today, all blood donors are interviewed, and blood is not accepted from high-risk individuals. Donated blood is routinely tested, so that giving blood is entirely safe and receiving it is relatively safe as well.

Disease (Causative Organism)	Incubation Period	Signs/Symptoms	Complications
PROTOZOAN TRICHOMONIASIS *Trichomonas vaginalis*	4–28 days	Frothy, odorous, greenish-yellow discharge. Soreness and itching of genitals. Painful or difficult urination. Symptoms usually absent in males.	Inflammation of vagina and various glands and tubes in the reproductive and urinary system; also spread by contaminated water.
FUNGAL CANDIDIASIS (ALSO CALLED MONILIA) *Candida albicans*	Organism commonly present, diseased state may be triggered by pregnancy, diabetes, birth control pills, antibiotic treatment, lowered resistance.	Intense genital itching. Thick, curd-like discharge, odorous. Inflamed vagina. Inflammation of vulva, genital area.	Frequent recurrence. Possible spread to sex partners.
ECTO-PARASITES PUBIC LICE "CRABS" *Phthirus pubis:* pubic louse	Infested from contact with infested person or linens. Eggs hatch after 7–9 days.	Slight to intolerable itching. Possible mild rash.	Nuisance. Possible spread to sex partners and household members.
GENITAL SCABIES *Sarcoptes scabiei:* a mite	Infested from close contact with infested person or linens.	Intense itching. Small, reddish, elevated track or lesion on surface of skin.	Scratching may lead to secondary infection. Spread to sex partners.

Sources: Los Angeles Venereal Disease Information Council, Los Angeles, CA, 1985; Centers for Disease Control, Atlanta, GA, 1985.

(NOTE: AN STD INFECTION MAY EXIST WITHOUT ANY OF THESE SYMPTOMS)

7. *Myth:* People infected with the AIDS virus cannot spread it if they have no symptoms. *Fact:* These people may nevertheless spread AIDS by the methods previously described.

The above list enumerates only a few examples of the many myths about AIDS. AIDS and other STDs have tended to increase so rapidly partly because of the lack of general understanding. People want answers to their questions and protection from things that they fear. If they don't get understandable answers, people will invent them in the form of myths. While this may keep them from positive action, it also creates anxiety and increases the prevailing ignorance.

SUMMARY

- Crises are changes that disrupt a family's behavior patterns. They may have internal or external causes.

- All families experience at least one crisis during their existence. Some families are better able to cope with crises than others.

- Illness can cause worry and financial drain, and there is little one can do to prepare for illness.

- Illness or disability imposes special roles on the sick person as well as on the family. However, there is little training for these roles.

- Experts offer advice on how to cope with a crisis. The steps may sound simple, but they are often hard to carry out.

- Violence in the family can be verbal, psychological, or sexual. Considerable violence is reported in American families. Victims include dates, children, spouses, and the elderly.

- Part of the violence problem lies in the attitudes of society. Teaching people that hitting is not acceptable is part of the solution.

- Dying people usually go through the stages of denial and isolation, anger, bargaining, deep depression, and finally acceptance.

- Different people handle death in different ways. Rituals can help mourners cope with death.

- Alcohol and drug abuse is a growing problem in this country.

- Different people have different degrees of tolerance for alcohol, and research has yet to discover why some people become alcoholics.

- Unemployment can cause not only financial but also emotional strain on families. It often requires the redefinition of roles within a family.

- A crisis can pull a family closer together or drive it apart. Using its resources can help a family adapt to the new situation.

- The AIDS tragedy appears to be producing more myths than positive, educated responses on the part of many people.

PERSPECTIVE: INDIVIDUAL, MARITAL, AND FAMILY WELLNESS

Scientists have begun to pay some attention to the well-being, satisfactions, and the quality of life—the wellness of the American family—in contrast to family crises. The notion of well-being and happiness is nothing new for our society. After all, Thomas Jefferson included the right to pursue happiness in the Declaration of Independence.

What makes a family a well family? "Healthy family functioning is a complex and exciting area of study that professionals have only begun to unravel"

(Fisher, Giblin, & Hoopes, 1984, p. 563). These researchers grouped family characteristics into three dimensions. *Cohesion* refers to the emotional bonding among family members. *Adaptability* refers to the family's ability to change its rules, roles, and interaction patterns. *Communication* is the means by which family members develop patterns of adaptability and cohesion. The researchers found that a blend of all three categories was considered important by therapists. Family members feel that cohesion is the most important; communication came second and adaptability a low third. However, for families to achieve wellness, they must solve their problems and crises. Glasser and Glasser (1970) present five criteria that they see as necessary for adequate family functioning:

1. Internal role consistency among family members.
2. Consistency of family roles and norms and actual role performance.
3. Compatibility of family roles and norms with community norms.
4. Meeting the psychological needs of family members.
5. The ability of the family group to respond to change.

The individual, family, and community needs, roles, and functions are involved along with the consistency and compatibility of the roles and norms and the families' ability to respond to changes in all of the above areas. The process is complicated, and no one can provide instant or simple solutions to all problems and changes that individuals or their families are likely to encounter in their lifetimes.

Despite the increasing number of marital breakups, "about seven out of ten married people say they are 'very happy' with their marriage and nearly six out of ten say they are 'completely satisfied' " (Campbell, 1981, p. 75). Marriage, of all human experiences, appears to have unrivaled potential for joy and torment, fulfillment and frustration. For most people the positives outweigh the negatives, and their feeling about the quality of their marriages contributes crucially to their perception of the quality of their lives. In fact, in one survey, researchers found that the most important factor in determining whether or not people rated themselves as very happy is marital happiness (Benin & Nienstedt, 1985).

Various groups of people rate marriage satisfaction differently. Men rate their marriages higher than women. Older people rate theirs higher than younger ones. People with more education and higher incomes are more likely to profess happiness with their marriage but less likely to claim complete satisfaction (Campbell, 1981). Satisfaction of family life parallels that of marriage. In comparing the importance of various family members to family satisfaction, the spouse is considered the most important and children make a significant contribution. Parents and siblings were rated less important. Good friends are important to people's well-being too (Campbell, 1981).

Various problems and crises have been a part of human existence from the beginning. They have also been, and will continue to be, a part of marriage and family life. However, no other relationships have given us greater satisfactions, happiness, and feelings of well-being than marriage and the family have.

QUESTIONS FOR THOUGHT AND DISCUSSION

1. Define "crisis." What are some different types and causes of crises? How can crises be dealt with effectively?

2. Think of a particular crisis that has occurred in your life. How did you deal with it? Would you deal with it any differently if it happened today? If yes, how?

3. Why does illness qualify as a crisis? What are two ways of coping with a crisis such as illness?

4. How prevalent is family violence? What is the most common form? How can family violence be avoided? How can courtship violence be avoided?

5. What are some reasons for the occurrence of family abuse? Identify those that you feel are the most valid and explain why.

6. Many believe that victims can just walk out on an abusive situation and deserve to be abused if they stay. Do you agree or disagree with this? Why or why not?

7. How long has elder abuse occurred? Why has it just recently come into public attention? Why does it occur? Is financial exploitation a form of abuse?

8. Why are euphemisms used in talking about death? In your opinion, is this a good way to deal with death? Why or why not?

9. How, according to the chapter, do people deal with death? How is dealing with your own eventual death different from dealing with the death of someone else? How are rituals important?

10. Note the definition of alcoholism given in the chapter. Is it different from the definition that you have?

11. Do you think that the AIDS crisis has significantly changed sexual behavior? Has it changed your or your friends' behavior?

12. What are some other myths or possible facts that you have heard about AIDS?

13. Has the AIDS epidemic increased concern with the other STDs? Any in particular or just in general?

14. What are some of the stages that people go through when they experience unemployment? How can families cope with the stresses of unemployment?

15. Review the criteria presented in the Perspective concerning adequate family functioning. How does your family rate according to these five criteria? How could it be improved or be made more "well"?

10

Sex in and out of Marriage

MARITAL SEXUALITY

We are all born sexual. Our sexuality grows, develops, and matures as we do. Consciously or not, we pick up cues for its sociopsychological development from our social environment. We learn what is expected of us as children, adolescents, and adults. We learn what type of sexual behavior is acceptable when, where, how, and with whom. To develop our sexual capabilities fully, we need an intimate relationship. The most appropriate sexual relationship, according to our society, is that of marriage.

Marital sexuality can symbolize the heart and soul of the relationship. In its best form, it can be a communion of the two partners. Sexuality may be a sign of commitment to the relationship, establishing an intimate bond and creating a means of communication between the husband and wife. The shared intimacy of marital sex can also enrich the lives of the couple, bringing them together for play and pleasure.

The importance of the sexual relationship to a marriage is largely a matter of perception and expectations. For couples who perceive sex as the key component of their marriage, the sexual relationship is very important. Others, who assign their sexual relations a lesser role or consider sex important only for procreation, may find it relatively unimportant. While marital closeness and pleasurable sex are positively related for both sexes, some couples report that they are not close but have a good sex life and others say they are very close but do not have an enjoyable sex life. Overall though, "the husband and wife who have a free and intensely pleasurable sexual relationship are much more likely to be emotionally close than the husband and wife who do not, and the close marriage is more likely to involve a genuinely liberated marital sex than the distant one" (Hunt, 1974, p. 232).

Married Americans seem to be happy with their sexual relations. One-third reported their marital sexual relationship to be "very good," another third found it "good," while the remaining third found it "fair to very poor" (Tavris & Sadd, 1977). Most are satisfied with the frequency of sex in their marriage. One-third of the respondents in one survey said they wanted an increase in frequency and less than 5 percent said they wanted a decrease (Hunt, 1974).

As Table 10.1 shows, generally the higher the frequency, the higher the satisfaction, or vice versa. The relationship between frequency of sex and marital satisfaction is clear; however, the cause and effect cannot be clearly established. Does

TABLE 10.1 Frequency of Intercourse and Satisfaction with Marital Sex

Estimated Monthly Frequency of Intercourse	Degree of Satisfaction (Percentages)		
	Very Good or Good	Fair	Poor or Very Poor
None	9	8	83
1–5 times	35	34	31
6–10 times	72	23	5
11–15 times	86	11	3
16–20 times	91	7	2
More than 20 times	93	5	2

Source: Levin and Levin, 1975, p. 55.

good sex account for a happy marriage, or does a happy marriage result in good sex? Perhaps each factor helps the other.

SEXUAL PHYSIOLOGY

Understanding the sexual equipment of the male and female body can help you learn how to increase your own pleasure as well as your partner's.

SEXUAL EQUIPMENT

The Female Body and Sexual Organs Women in particular often feel ambivalent or uncertain about their own sexual organs. With the onset of menstruation, they may be taught that the vagina and what happens inside it must be kept secret and that it is unattractive or even unclean. Some may believe that their breasts are too small or too large to be attractive. None of these notions, of course, is true. A woman should understand, accept, and delight in her body and her sexuality.

The labia majora are hair-covered folds of skin outside the vagina. Within the labia majora are two hairless folds of membranous skin called the labia minora. When closed, the labia minora cover the opening to the vagina. The hymen is a membrane that stretches part way across the opening of the vagina. It does not completely block it but leaves an opening large enough to allow the passage of a tampon or, sometimes, even a penis.

The vagina itself is about 3 to 3 ½ inches long and leads to a very small opening in the uterus at the far end. The vagina contains very few nerve endings. The clitoris is located outside the vagina, above the urethral opening, at the upper end

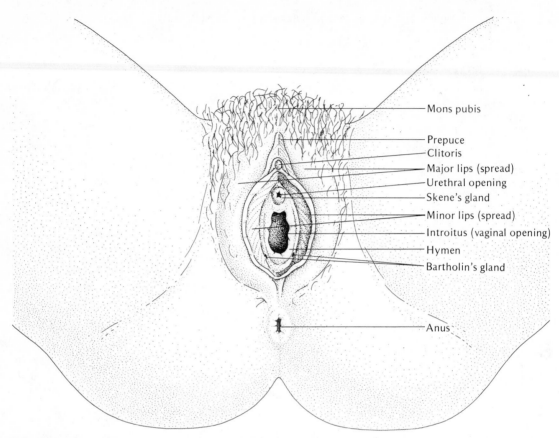

FIGURE 10.1   EXTERNAL GENITALS OF THE FEMALE.

Source: Harmatz & Novak, 1983, p. 68.

of the labia minora. The clitoris and the labia minora join to form the clitoral hood. The clitoris contains a high concentration of nerve endings that, when stimulated, aid in sexual arousal. (See Figures 10.1 and 10.2.)

The breasts also enhance sexual arousal. They contain a large number of nerve endings, particularly in the nipple. Stimulation of the breasts is pleasurable to women and exciting to men. Because the concentration of nerve endings is in the nipple, the size of the woman's breasts does not affect her capacity to be aroused.

The Male Body and Sexual Organs   In the male embryo, the penis develops from the same cells that form the clitoris in the female. The testicles are formed when the gonads descend outside the body during development and come to rest within the scrotal sac. Testosterone, the primary male sex hormone, and

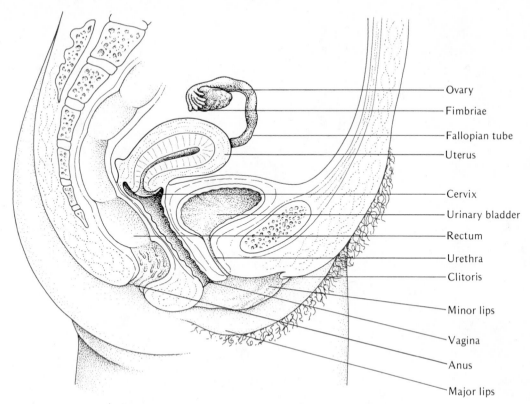

FIGURE 10.2 INTERNAL SEX ORGANS OF THE FEMALE (SIDE VIEW).

SOURCE: Harmatz & Novak, 1983, p. 72.

sperm are manufactured in the testicles. The male produces several hundred million sperm per day. These mature for about two months in the epididymis before they are ready to fertilize an egg. (See Figures 10.3 and 10.4.)

The penis contains, among other things, three tubes of spongy material that fill up with blood during arousal. As this occurs, the veins inside the penis constrict, keeping the blood there and causing the penis to grow erect. Erections are natural and sometimes quite involuntary. They first occur while the male fetus is still in the uterus. Throughout infancy and childhood, the young male continues to have erections. About half of all boys have a dry orgasm, one without the release of seminal fluid and sperm, by age five (Kinsey, Pomeroy, & Martin, 1948).

Although penile size is often a cause of anxiety, the fact is that no matter what the length of the flaccid penis, most are about the same size when erect. Penile size rarely has any effect on the amount of pleasure a woman feels during intercourse because most of her sensation occurs in the front third of the vagina.

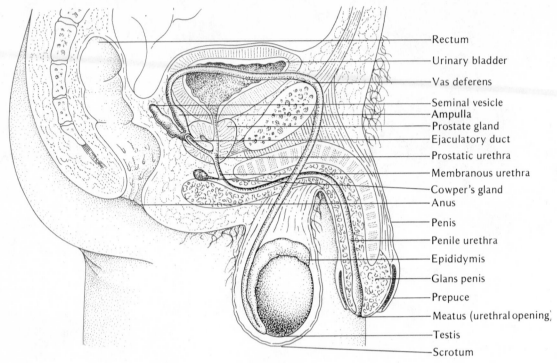

FIGURE 10.3   EXTERNAL AND INTERNAL SEX ORGANS OF THE MALE
(SIDE VIEW).

SOURCE: Harmatz & Novak, 1983, p. 80.

SEXUAL RESPONSES TO STIMULATION

Sexual arousal has been measured in a number of ways—both by physiological changes and reports of subjective sensations. In many ways it is like an emotion, and therefore hard to measure (Singer, 1984). Physiologically, both men and women go through several distinct stages of arousal. These are quite similar for both men and women.

The Female Responses   In the excitement stage, the female body undergoes several changes. The vagina begins to lubricate almost immediately after stimulation begins. It lengthens and the inner two-thirds distends. The labia majora flatten and the labia minora expand in diameter. The clitoris enlarges as it fills with blood. The uterus pulls back from its normal position. The breasts enlarge while the nipples become erect and the veins more distinct. Heart rate, blood pressure, and respiration all increase. Sometimes a sexual flush occurs and the body's muscles begin to tense.

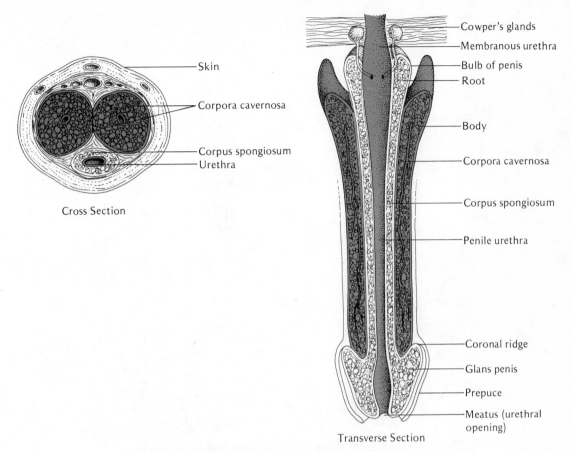

Cross Section

Transverse Section

FIGURE 10.4   THE INTERNAL STRUCTURE OF THE PENIS AS VIEWED FROM A
CROSS SECTION AND TRANSVERSE SECTION.

SOURCE: Harmatz & Novak, 1983, p. 80.

In the plateau stage, the outer third of the vagina constricts while lubrication
slows. The labia minora become darker and the clitoris retracts under the hood
for protection against too strong a stimulus. The breasts continue to enlarge by
one-fifth to one-fourth. The sexual flush extends over more of the body, and
involuntary muscle tension increases.

At the orgasmic stage, the vagina contracts anywhere from 3 to 15 times. The
uterus contracts irregularly. Increases in blood pressure, heartbeats, and respirations peak and the body experiences involuntary muscle spasms. During the final
resolution stage, the body returns to its normal state. If orgasm occurs, this
resolution process occurs quickly; if not, it takes several minutes longer (Figure
10.5).

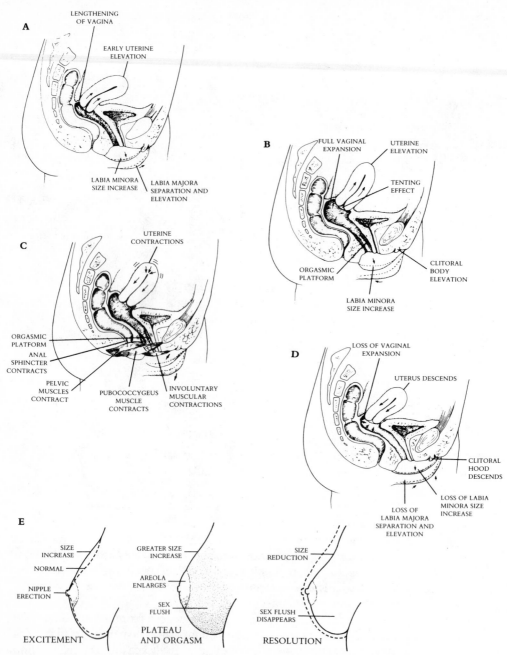

FIGURE 10.5   THE SEXUAL RESPONSE CYCLE OF THE FEMALE: A—EXCITEMENT
PHASE; B—PLATEAU PHASE; C—ORGASMIC PHASE; D—RESO-
LUTION PHASE; E—CHANGES IN BREASTS.

SOURCE: Denney & Quadagno, 1988, p. 23.

The Male Responses In the excitement stage, the male's penis becomes erect during the first few seconds, but the degree of erection may vary throughout this stage. The testes draw up closer to the body, and the scrotal sac becomes smaller and thicker. The male also experiences an increase in heartbeats, respirations, and blood pressure. Sometimes the nipples become erect and a sexual flush begins.

During the plateau stage, the glans (head of the penis) deepens in color and becomes about twice as long. The testes also increase in size and continue to rise toward the body. Muscles become tenser, and the pelvis often thrusts involuntarily. Hyperventilation often occurs late in the plateau stage.

In orgasm, the urethra is subject to involuntary ejaculatory contractions that occur at intervals of less than a second. After several contractions, they decrease in force. Heartbeats, respirations, and blood pressure peak. In the resolution stage, the penis quickly decreases in size; the full return to flaccidity takes longer. The sexual flush and muscle tension disappear quickly. Resolution of changes in the scrotum, testes, and nipples may take a longer time (Figure 10.6).

Unlike the female body, the male body experiences a refractory period after resolution during which it is incapable of becoming aroused again. The time of refraction varies with age and other factors. The refractory period is generally shorter if the man is young, not fatigued, still excited, not under the influence of drugs or alcohol, and still exposed to visual and auditory sexual stimulation or fantasy.

Using Sexual Equipment

What is the largest human sex organ? The skin. Touching of the skin is important in sexual interaction. A climate of mutually reciprocal loving rather than a focus on genital activity alone can have positive effects on sex. Foreplay allows couples to explore each other's bodies and to learn to give pleasure to one another. It does not have to be goal oriented. "Extended foreplay is to marriage what tasty soup is to a good meal: a small amount may enhance a full-course meal, while a larger amount alone may suffice in itself" (Ficher, 1979, p. 13). Foreplay can aid in developing a climate of sexuality in marriage. Similarly, afterplay can aid or hinder the climate of sensuality in marriage. "Afterplay, in essence, reveals more about the basic relationship between the partners than any other preceding sexual activity" (Crain, 1978, p. 80).

What is the most important part of the human body for a person's sexuality? The mind. It includes information, emotions, fantasies, memories, and feelings. Using the mind to stimulate and enhance sexuality is essential to good sex. Some couples become so preoccupied with sexual techniques that they miss much of the potential pleasure (Masters & Johnson, 1970).

Now, what is the most important sex act? Communication. Partners need to discuss sexuality and to tell each other what pleases them. They often bring different sexual expectations into the marriage. These expectations can only be understood and met if they are communicated. "The best expectation is not to

(a) EXCITEMENT PHASE

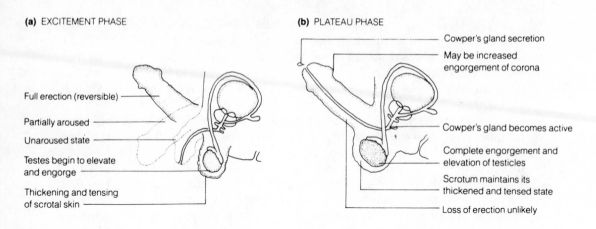

Full erection (reversible)

Partially aroused

Unaroused state

Testes begin to elevate
and engorge

Thickening and tensing
of scrotal skin

(b) PLATEAU PHASE

Cowper's gland secretion

May be increased
engorgement of corona

Cowper's gland becomes active

Complete engorgement and
elevation of testicles

Scrotum maintains its
thickened and tensed state

Loss of erection unlikely

(c) EMISSION PHASE OF ORGASM

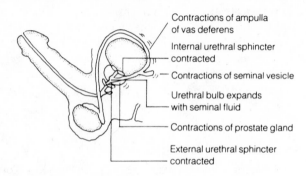

Contractions of ampulla
of vas deferens

Internal urethral sphincter
contracted

Contractions of seminal vesicle

Urethral bulb expands
with seminal fluid

Contractions of prostate gland

External urethral sphincter
contracted

(d) EXPULSION PHASE OF ORGASM

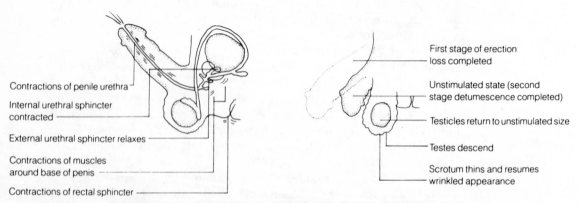

Contractions of penile urethra

Internal urethral sphincter
contracted

External urethral sphincter relaxes

Contractions of muscles
around base of penis

Contractions of rectal sphincter

(e) RESOLUTION PHASE

First stage of erection
loss completed

Unstimulated state (second
stage detumescence completed)

Testicles return to unstimulated size

Testes descend

Scrotum thins and resumes
wrinkled appearance

FIGURE 10.6   THE SEXUAL RESPONSE CYCLE OF THE MALE.

Source: R. Crooks & K. Baur, *Our Sexuality,* 3rd ed. Menlo Park, CA: Benjamin/Cummings, 1987, p. 184.

expect anything from sex" (Schimel, 1978, p. 15). Couples often develop their own language to negotiate sexual matters. Interest is usually indirectly stated. Rarely does a partner say, "Let's have intercourse" and the other answer, "Okay" or "No thanks." Instead one might suggest going to bed early or make a physical advance. The other could respond positively with a physical gesture or a smile. If not interested, the partner might say, "I'm really tired" or "I have a lot on my mind right now." Talking about sex during sexual activity as well as at other times can increase enjoyment.

SEXUAL INTERCOURSE

While sexual intercourse, or coitus, is the most commonly thought of act when sex is mentioned, it may or may not be the most important aspect of sexuality. One study found that women reported intercourse to be a more essential part of having sex than did men (Blumstein & Schwartz, 1983). The researchers think that women feel this way because "Intercourse required the equal participation of both partners more than any other sexual act. . . . Women feel a shared intimacy during intercourse they may not feel during other sexual acts" (p. 227). Men, they thought, enjoyed other aspects more because of their diversity. Conversely, another study found that married women preferred nongenital activity, specifically body stroking, to vaginal intercourse (Grosskopf, 1983).

Whatever the degree of importance they attach to it, couples perform intercourse in various ways. In addition to the number of positions available, couples may choose varying surroundings. Some prefer the privacy of their bedrooms, while others like to have sex outdoors or even in public places. Some prefer a dark room; others like a lighted area. Some couples like to vary their sexual experiences for the excitement and novelty of the variety, while others like to maintain the same routine.

ORGASM

Orgasm is the subject of much misunderstanding. It is not necessary to have an orgasm to enjoy sexual intercourse, nor does having one make sexual pleasure a certainty (Sarrel & Sarrel, 1980). In fact, "To make orgasm the be-all and end-all of sexual activity is as limiting as denying a person the right to have orgasm at all" (Gagnon, 1977, p. 199).

While for men ejaculation is usually the evidence of orgasm, women's orgasm has been the subject of much controversy. Several studies in the 1960s and 1970s concluded that women did not have to have orgasm to be sexually fulfilled and that women who did not regularly experience orgasm often reported sexual satisfaction. Some more recent research has found some differences. Surprisingly, one study showed that consistency of orgasm was related to sexual satisfaction for women but not for men. In fact, both men and women reported more pleasure when sexual activity occurred without orgasm (Waterman & Chiauzzi, 1982).

Another controversy concerns how a woman experiences orgasm. Freud

BOX 10.1   WHAT EVERYONE SHOULD KNOW ABOUT ORGASM

1. Orgasm is the climax of feelings and sensations that occurs at the peak of sexual arousal. It is followed by a release of tension and the experience of relaxation.

2. The feeling of orgasm can vary from a warm glow spreading from the genitals throughout the rest of the body to spasmodic contractions and a momentary loss of consciousness.

3. If the stimulation is appropriate and both partners are orgasmic, orgasm by one partner (if communicated to the other) is likely to bring about orgasm in the other partner.

4. It is possible for both men and women to fake orgasms. No one should feel such fakery to be necessary, since it can only be damaging to the relationship.

5. Sometimes it is difficult to tell whether or not a partner has reached orgasm, although it is a little easier to make this distinction for males because of ejaculation and the refractory period that follows. The best way to tell whether a partner experiences orgasm is to establish open, honest communication in the relationship.

6. Both men and women may suffer physical discomfort if they experience frequent and/or prolonged sexual arousal without orgasm.

7. Both men and women can have nocturnal orgasms. Men are more likely to report their experiences. Women usually associate nocturnal orgasms with erotic dreams.

8. During both male and female orgasm, the rectal sphincter, at least sometimes, undergoes involuntary rhythmic contractions. Many women also experience rhythmic contractions of the outer third of the vagina, and some experience contractions of the uterus.

9. In males, orgasm is associated with ejaculation and contractions along the penis. Prior to puberty, males experience "dry" orgasms.

10. In general, there is more variability in female orgasmic patterns, including the number of orgasms or lack of them. Males usually have a greater consistency of achieving orgasm, especially in heterosexual coitus.

11. Women can experience multiple orgasms within a very short period of time. For some women, lesser stimulation can trigger the additional orgasms, because women do not experience the refractory period that men do. All these orgasms are "real" ones.

12. It may be more difficult for older men but not women to reach orgasm. However, men are usually capable of orgasm until very late in life.

thought there were two types of orgasms for women, clitoral and vaginal. Some recent research has indicated that women have a dime-sized spot on the interior wall of the vagina called the G-spot. Stimulation of the G-spot supposedly can bring great sexual pleasure. However, other researchers say that there is no such distinct structure within the vagina. According to Kaplan (1983), it has long been known that many women have erotically sensitive vaginal areas; but the controversy of the exact structure and function of the G-spot still needs further research.

"Strictly speaking, orgasm is neither 'clitoral,' nor 'vaginal,' nor 'uterine,' but cerebral (psychic), although it may be elicited by stimuli arising from different peripheral erogenous zones" (Alzate, 1985, p. 282). While research shows that women are able to experience orgasm in a number of ways, one study found that women functioned better sexually and psychologically if they reached orgasm by penile stimulation as well as oral or digital stimulation (Taublieb & Lick, 1986).

NONCOITAL SEXUAL BEHAVIOR

Research shows that noncoital sexual behavior is not limited to premarital sexual relationships. Married people participate in and enjoy these activities too.

For instance, contrary to what many people believe, masturbation continues after people marry. Approximately three-fourths of young married men masturbate (Hunt, 1974). Husbands masturbate as a supplement to intercourse because their wives are not sexually available or to avoid intercourse with their wives.

Approximately 60 percent of the wives in one large study said they enjoy masturbating too. However, most husbands (over 70 percent) are not aware that their wives masturbate (Grosskopf, 1983). Masters, Johnson, and Kolodny (1985) suggest that more women masturbate today than in the past because negative attitudes toward the activity have softened, more women are learning about masturbation through the media than are learning it by accident, and women are becoming more aware of the positive aspects of their feminine sexuality. Some wives masturbate because their husbands are not available, because masturbation is a unique experience, because they wish to relieve tension or achieve orgasm, or because they are compensating for unsatisfactory coitus with their husbands.

Although masturbation is usually done in private, some spouses are stimulated by watching one another masturbate. Almost 30 percent of the women in the Grosskopf (1983) study say they let their partners watch. Others feel their partners' masturbation is a rejection of themselves. Guilt feelings over masturbation, as in anything else, can complicate one's life and relationships.

Oral-genital sex is becoming increasingly popular for married people. Husbands who receive and perform oral sex report being more satisfied with their sex lives than those who don't. However, wives who perform or receive oral sex say they are not happier than those who do not (Blumstein & Schwartz, 1983). In one survey, over three-fourths of the women who reported good sexual relations also reported liking oral sex (Sarrel & Sarrel, 1980). Another study found that while nearly 60 percent of the women said they enjoyed oral sex, over 60 percent rated fellatio as their least favorite sexual activity (Grosskopf, 1983).

Anal sex is not as prevalent as other types of sexual activity. Just under half of the men and just over 60 percent of the women in the Petersen (1982) survey said they had tried anal intercourse. Only slightly more than 10 percent of women said they enjoyed it (Grosskopf, 1983).

Sexual fantasies are common for married men and women. Over 95 percent of married men in one survey said they experienced sexual fantasies, and many reported that their fantasies helped them achieve sexual arousal and/or to reach orgasm during intercourse (Davidson, 1985). For nearly three-fourths of the women in the Grosskopf (1983) study, "Sexual fantasies are a positive, enjoyable, and fulfilling part of their sex life" (pp. 96–97). Most said their fantasies concerned romance and affection, lack of which was their number-one complaint in real life. Over half said they sometimes fantasized about a famous person.

FUME: Factors Undermining Mutual Enjoyment

The mutual enjoyment of marital sex may be undermined by many factors. Some of these are individual personality characteristics; others are influences from outside the relationship.

Male-Female Sexual Differences

Because of the different subcultures in which men and women grow up and the double standard that exists in our society, men and women often differ in their perception of what good sex should be. For instance, one study showed significant sex differences in sexual needs and desires. "When given a choice between foreplay, intercourse, and afterplay, women indicated that foreplay was the most important part of a sexual encounter, while men felt intercourse was the most important aspect. Women also indicated that they wanted to spend more time in foreplay, as well as more time in afterplay, than did men" (Denney, Field, & Quadagno, 1984). Men and women tend to use different words to describe genitalia and the act of sexual intercourse. There appear to be four "languages" used in discussing sex: medical/technical terminology, slang, euphemisms, and personal talk. For instance, men are more likely to use slang words such as "screw" or "fuck," and women are more likely to use euphemisms such as "make love" and "go all the way." Some researchers hypothesize that a man's tendency to use slang may have an effect on his partner's attitudes and behavior with him and that a woman's use of formal vocabulary during intimacy may have a distancing effect on her partner (Simkins & Rinck, 1982). Some couples develop a personal language, or baby talk, between themselves. They may use nicknames for body parts, sexual behavior, or feelings. If each understands the words and phrases the other uses, this new language can be special. However, one partner may introduce a word or phrase that is either derogatory or not known to the other partner, and the meaning is lost. Unfortunately, there does not seem to be a good sex language, one that includes all the necessary words and that enhances the communication between sexual partners.

Some couples may have a problem deciding who should initiate sex. Traditionally, the man has been the initiator, but recently women are taking more responsibility for their own sexuality and initiating sexual activity at least part of the time. A man who has been socialized to be the aggressor may feel threatened by a woman who initiates sex. For women who have been socialized to be passive, the challenge of being "good in bed" may pose problems. Researchers in the 1970s wondered if women's new assertiveness would cause sexual dysfunction in men—that is, whether they would become sexually impotent. However, recent studies have shown just the opposite. In one study, men who imagined women initiating sex experienced more surprise and enjoyment, while those in traditional roles experienced more disgust, fear, sadness, and anger and less sexual arousal (Sirkin & Mosher, 1985). Another study found that couples who developed a nontypical sexual orientation and allowed flexibility in their mutual responses reported more happiness and developed more commitment over time. (Stephen & Harrison, 1985). "An egalitarian sex role norm liberates both men and women" (Sirkin & Mosher, 1985, p. 48).

Unfortunately, many women are reluctant to be assertive because they think men will find their behavior unacceptable (Jesser, 1978). Wives are especially timid about making sexual advances when their husbands are troubled about work or some other area of their lives (Blumstein & Schwartz, 1983). Finally, women and men peak sexually at different times in their lives—women in their thirties or forties and men by age 20. Couples who are near the same age may find that she is reaching her peak after he has experienced a decrease in his sex drive. This difference may create a need for sexual adjustment later in the marriage.

EXPECTATIONS

People have conflicting expectations with regard to sex. On the one hand, it is viewed as a goal-oriented activity, and people often believe that they have to work at achieving the perfect orgasm. Some of the recent marriage manuals give the mistaken impression that sex is a gymnastic competition. Striving toward a sexual goal such as simultaneous orgasms can make sex more work than play.

On the other hand, our society tends to be antiplay. Meyners (1980) asks whether sex is a goal to be worked for, a means to an end, or something that is "a natural and spontaneous pleasure to be enjoyed" (p. 4). He notes, "Happiness is more often the by-product of other pursuits than a direct pursuit of pleasure" (p. 5). Couples who can relax and enjoy themselves—rather than working at the achievement of pleasure—are more likely to find pleasure in their sexual relationship.

EXTERNAL FACTORS

Nonmarital roles can have a negative impact on marital sexual interaction. Jobs can be one factor. People from lower economic classes generally have less satisfying marital relationships than those who are more economically fortunate. One reason may be that physical exhaustion from the job may leave one or both spouses tired and uninterested in sex. Even a successful business career can cause problems. A spouse may become more interested in achieving success in the workplace than in working at a successful marriage relationship. Even as simple a situation as that where one spouse has a night job while the other works during the day can interrupt a couple's quiet or fun time together.

Parental roles are a frequent cause of problems in marital sexual relationships. For example, marital satisfaction is at a low point when families have preschool or teenage children at home (Rollins & Cannon, 1974). Child-free couples report more satisfying sex lives than those who have children (Sarrel & Sarrel, 1980). Children can intrude on both the private time to engage in sexual relations and the opportunity for adult discussions. This problem can be magnified if one partner thinks the other invests too much time in the parental role.

As Vincent (1973) tells it, a husband was upset when his wife was easily distracted by their children during sex. He said that once the bedroom door was locked, she should forget everything else. One day she went to his office, and after asking his secretary to hold all calls, she locked the door, sat on his lap and said, "Okay, Honey, screw me." No matter what he did, he could not achieve an erection. He realized that simply locking the door was not enough.

Satisfaction with other aspects of their lives and their relationships can lead couples to feel good about themselves and their marriage. For instance, if one partner feels inadequate in other roles, he or she may feel unworthy of the partner's love or may be unable to perform sexually. Being angry can affect a couple's sexual relations—temporarily if the conflict is settled soon but permanently if the conflict is left unresolved. Birth control may also be a source of conflict that can lead directly to sexual problems.

SEX THROUGHOUT THE MARITAL CAREER

Statistics show that the frequency of intercourse decreases with age and length of marriage (Trussell & Westoff, 1980). The greatest decline occurs during the twenties. The frequency of intercourse at age 20 is about 12 times a month, while at age 30, it is 8.5 times a month. Respondents in another study report rates from 1 to 45 times per month (Greenblat, 1983). Two factors—the male sexual peak being at age 20 and the honeymoon effect (James, 1981)—contribute to the rapid decline.

The smallest decrease for any decade occurs during the thirties, with frequency of intercourse dropping to 7.5 by age 40. One factor may be that women reach their sexual peak in their thirties, so they may want sex more often during this time. Another is that most women have completed their childbearing by their later thirties. Those who use effective methods of birth control have higher rates of intercourse than women who use less effective methods (Trussell & Westoff, 1980).

After age 40, the decrease in frequency of intercourse becomes more marked. However, there are many people who are sexually active into their sixties and beyond.

Each stage of the marriage brings its own problems. Newlyweds must learn to adjust to sex in the new marital relationship. The crucial time is often the first five months or the first year. Often, intercourse declines by as much as one-fourth within the first five years of marriage, something that few couples expect. One study of young married women showed that the most rapid decline in frequency of intercourse was among those married the shortest length of time (Udry, 1980). Greenblat (1983) found that married couples established a pattern of sexual intimacy in their first year of marriage. "From then on almost everything—children, jobs, commuting, housework, financial worries—that happens to a couple conspires to *reduce* the degree of sexual interaction, while almost nothing leads to increasing it" (p. 294).

The middle years are the time when couples are particularly vulnerable to sexual boredom. This may occur when individuals are trying to establish themselves in careers or are rearing children. Often, they become too busy to enjoy sex to its fullest. In general, boredom results when the partners begin losing touch with one another. "Boredom can serve as a warning signal for harmful but correctable patterns in marital interaction" (Appleton, 1980, p. 73).

Somewhere after age 50, a woman reaches menopause and a man may experience a midlife crisis. What causes this crisis for a man is not certain. Fear of aging or fear of losing his sex drive are possible reasons. Actually, the notion that a man over 40 is declining sexually is a myth (Laury, 1980). He has certain advantages over the 20-year-old—he can sustain an erection longer, he feels less need to climax as rapidly, and he can spend more time satisfying his partner. He may become more concerned with the emotional rather than the physical aspect of intercourse, which should please his partner.

Does growing older have to be a detriment to sexuality in marriage? Certainly not. A middle-aged couple needs to view middle age not as a crisis but as a transitional period leading to a different but potentially very full and satisfying time of their lives (Moss, 1979, p. 110). Couples can try various ways of maintaining or reigniting their sexual relationship. They may learn new methods of expressing their sexual intimacy and may vary their sexual behavior.

Little research has been done on the effects of age on marital sex. While data show that sexual activity generally decreases with age, the decrease is often not the result of age itself but of psychological changes. This is particularly true of men, who are usually the initiators of sexual activity. Society's mistaken attitude that old age is or should be sexless and that sex among older people is somehow wrong or repulsive contributes to the decrease (Laury, 1980). For example, one study found that college students greatly underestimated their parents' marital relations, even if the parents were only in their forties or fifties and said they were in love and happily married (Pocs, Godow, Tolone, & Walsh, 1983). Nursing-home staff, who work with older people the most, had even more negative reactions toward sexual activity among older people than did the undergraduate students (LaTorre & Kear, 1977).

In truth, sexual behavior in old age has been found to be linked significantly to earlier sexual behavior, indicating that couples establish patterns of sexuality that continue into old age. Sexuality is important to being fully human; when the elderly are denied their sexuality, they are denied the right to be human.

Economics may affect sexual behavior for older people. For instance, retired people who live with their children or in nursing homes often do not have the privacy to engage in sexual activity.

EXTRAMARITAL RELATIONS

Extramarital relations are sexual relations between a married person and someone other than his or her spouse. The topic is a controversial one. Some societies allow and even expect extramarital sex (EMS), while others ban it. Even though our society holds that monogamous marriages are the ideal and three-fourths of Americans say that EMS is morally wrong, statistics show that many married people in this country have had at least one extramarital encounter.

Statistics on the incidence of EMS are varied. Data gathered some forty years ago (Kinsey, Pomeroy, & Martin, 1948; Kinsey, Pomeroy, Martin, & Gebhard, 1953) showed that half the married men and a quarter of married women admitted to some EMS experience. For college-educated women, the percentage was closer to one-third. The term "admitted" may be a significant qualifier to the available participation statistics, as people are likely to underreport this behavior. For example, Greene, Lee, and Lustig (1974) found that the percent admitting to EMS at the beginning of psychotherapy doubled after a period of intensive therapy.

During the 1960s and 1970s most research was finding the participation rates

---

BOX 10.2   ADULTERY THROUGH THE AGES

Historically, adultery has not always been condemned cross-culturally. However, the double standard seems to be quite ancient. Thus many practices, including jokes about preventing wives from having extramarital experiences by keeping them locked up in the castle under supervision or having them locked in a chastity belt, are described in historical writings. At the same time, the knights would travel, fight, and have sex whenever the opportunity permitted. Some rather strange means of proving a wife's faithfulness are described by Simons (1976). Some of these relied on magic or the supposed power of holy water. Part of such an "adultery" test is quoted from the Bible (Num. 5:27):

> And when he hath made her drink the water, then it shall come to
> pass, that if she defiled, and have done trespass against her husband,
> that the water that causeth the curse shall enter into her, and become
> bitter, and her belly shall swell, and her thigh shall rot; and the woman
> shall be a curse among her people.

In concluding, Simons remarks that "God did not trouble to institute any similar test for unfaithful husbands" (p. 139).

to be a third to a half for wives and a half to two-thirds for husbands (Hunt, 1974; Levin, 1975; Pomeroy, 1982). For the 1980s, according to Stayton (1984), "several studies estimate 65–70% of married men and 45–65% of married women engage in extramarital relationships at some time during their marriage" (p. 4). While several other studies support these percentages (Hite, 1981; Petersen, Kretchmer, Nellis, Lever, & Hertz, 1983) one study (Blumstein & Schwartz, 1983) shows figures even lower than those of Kinsey and co-workers (1948 and 1953).

Regardless of the exact percentages of EMS, enough is happening that at least one partner in the majority of marriages will have participated in such a relationship. For college-educated couples, the majority of both spouses are likely to experience intercourse in an extramarital relationship—and these rates are not likely to decline. "It is quite possible," according to Crooks and Baur (1987), "that future sex surveys will reveal pronounced increases in extramarital sexual activity. This prediction is based on the many social changes evident in contemporary American life" (p. 483).

EMS conjures up different images for different people. Much depends on the observer's values. For some, it may seem a lark, an adventure, a treat—with little or no bearing on the primary relationship. To others, it may sound the death knell of a relationship: the end of trust, love, commitment, and loyalty (Blumstein & Schwartz, 1983, pp. 267–268).

> *It has been my experience that folks who have no vices have very few virtues.* —ABRAHAM LINCOLN

> *Fidelity without a share of diversity can become an obsession and a bore; diversity without a sense of fidelity, an empty relativism.* —ERIK H. ERICKSON

> *To be a lover is easier than to be a husband. For it is far more difficult to show intelligence every day than to make pretty speeches from time to time.* —HONORE DE BALZAC

TYPES OF EMS

Clanton (1977) suggests that there are three types of EMS. *Clandestine* describes EMS in which the participating spouse believes that the marital partner does not know and would not approve if the relationship became known. If the participant is correct, this type of EMS is the most likely to have negative results upon discovery. It can set up barriers to communication, destroy trust, generate feelings of insecurity or inadequacy, and so on. The participating spouse may feel guilty, want to confess, or even ask for a divorce.

Ambiguous describes the situation in which the nonparticipating spouse may know about the EMS but is unable to prove it, tolerates it in preference to divorce, once consented to it but withdrew the approval, or approves of the idea but does not want to know the details. The consequences may be mixed. It is possible that most EMS relationships are ambiguous.

Consensual describes the EMS relationship of which the spouse both knows and approves. It may actually renew and rejuvenate the marriage and the marital dialogue. Those who are comfortable with this type of arrangement may find it beneficial.

The types of EMS can also be divided by their emotional and sexual components: emotional (in love) but not sexual (intercourse), sexual but not emotional, and both emotional and sexual (Thompson, 1984). Respondents in the Thompson study believed that the extramarital relationship that was both emotional and sexual was the most wrong and the most likely to detract from the quality of the primary relationship.

VARIABLES OF EMS

Researchers and counselors have all enumerated long lists of causes, motives, or correlates of EMS. Kinsey et al. (1953) suggested the following reasons of why people engage in EMS:

1. *Variety*—A desire for variety of experience with new and sometimes superior sexual partners.
2. *Status*—Participation in a conscious or unconscious attempt to acquire increased social status.
3. *Favor*—An almost exclusively female reason in the past; accommodation of a respected friend even though the female was not particularly interested.
4. *Retaliation*—Retaliation against the spouse's involvement in EMS or some sort of nonsexual mistreatment, real or imagined.
5. *Independence*—Assertion of independence from the other spouse or the social codes in general; may be seen as rebellion.
6. *Emotional Satisfaction*—Applicable to both spouses, but usually associated with females; the development of emotional satisfaction while maintaining a good relationship with the spouse.

Other sets of variables related to EMS experience can be found from survey of other researchers.

Low marital satisfaction has been found to be associated with EMS, especially among women (Glass & Wright, 1985), and especially in cases where the EMS is both emotional and sexual.

Low sexual satisfaction was found as a reason men, but not women, engaged in EMS (Johnson, 1970). One study found that a poor sexual relationship at home was ranked first as a reason for considering outside substitutes by husbands and third as a reason for wives (Pietropinto & Simenauer, 1979).

Sexual deprivation is another variable associated with EMS if a spouse is unable to function sexually because of an accident or illness (Edwards & Booth, 1976). Temporary incapacity, due to pregnancy or childbirth, for example, is sometimes given as a reason.

Low religiousness appears to be related to EMS involvements, since religious people seem to be more reluctant to break the commandment against adultery and are more likely to suffer from guilt. Religiousness is positively correlated with marital happiness and lack of EMS permissiveness (Reiss, Anderson, & Sponaugle, 1980).

Premarital sexual experience and general sexual permissiveness in other areas are related to EMS (Reiss et al., 1980). Women who engaged in premarital sex are about twice as likely to engage in EMS as those without premarital sexual experiences (Udry, 1974). Spouses who have been married previously are more likely to engage in EMS (Knox, 1984).

Opportunity is crucial in the analysis of EMS (Johnson, 1970). People who participate in an extramarital relationship must have the opportunity to meet someone and the time to be with that person. Therefore, perhaps the greater increase in female EMS may be related to women's greater participation in the labor force in recent decades.

Peer influence is a factor. A close married friend who has had an extramarital relationship may influence someone to do likewise. In fact, the greater the similarity between the friends, the more likely the influence (Atwater, 1982). Personality characteristics are sometimes related to incidences of EMS. Some EMS participants are trying to improve their self-esteem, to expand their self-concepts, to explore their fantasies, to develop autonomy and control, to seek defenses against anxiety, or to handle sexual performance obstacles by engaging in EMS (Eldridge, 1983).

Others may be breaking away from a perceived boredom within the marriage, seeking to satisfy curiosity, trying to reaffirm their own sexual desirability, trying to rejuvenate their sexual interest, or simply seeking pleasure for pleasure's sake.

Overall, however, researchers have not been particularly successful in isolating variables that will accurately predict EMS. This is partly because there are many reasons for EMS and each case seems to be different. Another reason is the problem of measurement due to the personal nature of the subject. People are often reluctant to admit to EMS, let alone provide realistic reasons. Due to our society's attitude toward EMS, the participants will usually go to extreme lengths to hide or deny their participation.

RESULTS OF EMS

The results of extramarital relations differ greatly from one marriage to another. According to Masters, Johnson, and Kolodny (1985), some marriages in which one partner engages in EMS end in divorce, while other couples see extramarital involvements as no source of concern. They also note that solid marriages are not especially likely to break up because of EMS alone. Usually those that do break up over EMS do so more because of the partner's *emotional* involvement with another rather than because of the sexual activity.

Experts take different views of EMS. On the one hand, some say it is not natural for people to be monogamous and that therefore they should be able to have a variety of sexual partners. "If sex is relief, there is no reason for anyone to be denied it. If sex can be the expression of a joyful emotional understanding, well, all the more reason to liberate it" (Wallach, 1971, p. 108).

On the other hand, extramarital sex can sometimes be damaging. "The involvement of one or both marital partners in romantic or sexual relationships outside the traditional marriage dyad often produces unmanageable bitterness, irreconcilable hurt, and destruction of both affiliations" (Eldridge, 1983, p. 1). In one study of couples who were seeking marital therapy, researchers found that those who presented EMS as an issue reported higher rates of depression and lower levels of commitment to their marriages than did the other couples. The spouse who was participating in EMS was more likely to suffer from depression than the nonparticipating partner (Beach, Jouriles, & O'Leary, 1985).

SUMMARY

- Marital sexuality can symbolize commitment, bonding, and communication; however, it is more important for some couples than others.

- Most Americans seem to be satisfied with their marital sex relations.

- Understanding the sexual equipment of the male and the female can help you learn how to increase your pleasure in sex.

- Sexual responses can be measured in physiological changes and perceived sensations.

- Both females and males experience the excitement, plateau, orgasmic, and resolution stages of arousal.

- The skin is the largest sex organ, the mind is the most important sex organ, and communication is the most important sex act.

- Sexual intercourse, while usually thought of as the most important sex act, may actually be less important for some couples.

- Orgasm, especially women's orgasm, is the subject of much misunderstanding.

- Masturbation often continues after people marry.

- Married couples often enjoy oral-genital sex and, to a lesser extent, anal sex. Sexual fantasies are common and harmless.

- Enjoyable sex may be undermined by many factors, including differences in the ways men and women feel and talk about sex, people's expectations of what good sex should be, and events and worries outside the sexual relationship.

- Although statistics show that sexual activity usually decreases with age and the length of marriage, older people can and do enjoy good sexual relationships with their spouses.

- Statistics vary as to the prevalence of extramarital sex, but researchers believe that the incidence of EMS is likely to rise.

- People differ in their views of EMS, and researchers have noted a variety of reasons for its occurrence.

PERSPECTIVE: THREE DOZEN "SUPERLOVER" COMMANDMENTS

Although there are no rules controlling sexuality, a few suggestions about maintaining a good sexual relationship in marriage might be in order. Here, then, are a few general guidelines about what might help or hurt marital sexuality.

General Considerations

1. A good lover is a combination of many things: appeal, imagination, tenderness, affection, and confidence coupled with esteem for self and partner.
2. Treat your partner as a unique individual who has personal, physical, and emotional preferences. Likes and dislikes may change over time and/or vary from situation to situation.
3. Be each other's best friend. After all, sex (if it is to be limited) should at least occur between friends.
4. Remove your "masks" or facades. If the relationship is to last, these will come tumbling down sooner or later—the sooner the better.
5. Recognize that the mind is the most important sex organ, the skin is the largest sex organ, and communication is the most crucial sex act. Learn to get past the body and make love to the total person with your total being.
6. Treat sex as a natural function and process, letting go of any guilt you may have internalized or developed.
7. Recognize that concerns and problems unrelated to sex can cause sexual problems and difficulties.
8. Recognize that while there are many gender similarities, there are also some differences (i.e., males tend to be more genital-oriented; females more oriented toward body, the emotions, and the personalities). Be conscious of and try to integrate your and your partner's gender characteristics.
9. Any act that is pleasurable, does not offend or hurt either partner, and is not witnessed or heard by an unwilling party is okay.
10. While sex should primarily be play (as in "fore*play*" and "after*play*"),

accept the idea that sexual pleasure at least sometimes requires effort. Make the effort to enjoy each experience to the utmost.

11. Become sexually educated and knowledgeable about your own and
your partner's body. Remember, there is no "norm" for sexuality; every
person is unique.

12. Sexual freedom for both men and women means the right to say no to
something or someone, as well as the right to say yes.

The "Dirty Dozen" or Spoilers

1. Don't just have sex; make love in the true sense. Celebrate in the giving
and receiving of physical sensations and interpersonal awareness.

2. Don't ever take your partner for granted. Respect your partner's dignity, pride, and selfhood. Appreciate one another as persons, not objects.

3. Don't force or withhold sex as a threat, weapon, or exchange medium
for security, goods, or services.

4. Eliminate emphasis on techniques and goals (i.e., orgasm). The goal
should be to enjoy the whole experience—appetizer, main course, and
dessert.

5. Eliminate perfectionism, jealousy, possessiveness, and overcontrol before they have a chance to bring ruin.

6. Don't attribute your characteristics, desires, or preferences to your
partner or make assumptions about him or her.

7. Don't expect your partner always to take the initiative. As in all else,
that should be shared!

8. Don't expect spontaneous interest and arousal from your partner when
you are in the mood. Be prepared to romance and seduce him or her.

9. Don't be in a hurry; slow down and explore. It will extend your interest
and will likely increase your partner's interest.

10. Abstain from sexual conventionalism, indirectness, rigidity, and ul-
traromanticism.

11. Eliminate the notion that some body parts or sexual acts are dirty,
vulgar, unnatural, or immoral. Establish acceptable bounds to sexual
activity by mutual consent.

12. Enjoy your grand fantasies, but also bring them into the realm of
reality so that they don't constantly lead to disappointment and eventual disinterest.

The "Pleasure-and-Joy Dozen"

1. Talk. Social intercourse enhances sexual intercourse. Your partner
does not automatically or intuitively know your preferences and tastes,
nor how they may change over time.

2. Stay in touch physically, emotionally, and mentally with your partner

from the beginning of excitement/arousal until you are both satisfied and fully at rest.

3. Keep in mind that whatever you do should be fun. Think of yourself as both a pleasure-producing and -receiving person.

4. Remember, a touch, a kiss, or some other physical or verbal act that expresses joy, love, and satisfaction is heightened by mutual sharing.

5. Imagination, creativity, and experimentation should continually be held in high regard.

6. Keep in mind that there is more to the human body than genitals and more to sex than orgasm.

7. Learn the value of positive "stroking" and praise. Be generous and genuine in giving and appreciative in receiving looks, sounds, words, and body language.

8. Allow yourself to be an "effect"—that is, allow your partner to possess the power and capacity to excite and satisfy you. Committed lovers should be minimally concerned with vulnerability.

9. Adjust to the speed of your partner and recognize that your excitement, when communicated, will excite your partner.

10. The woman should be allowed to judge when she is ready for intercourse and she should indicate this to her partner.

11. If both you and your partner are willing, try multiple stimulations and recognize the possible value of noncoital activities either as an addition to or sometimes a substitute for coitus.

12. Be attractively neat and clean, and respect your own and your partner's body.

QUESTIONS FOR THOUGHT AND DISCUSSION

1. How are sex and marriage intertwined? How do they relate to each other? How important is sex in marriage?

2. What is the relationship between frequency of sex and marital happiness? Which causes which?

3. Why are some women uncomfortable about their bodies and their sexuality? How does this affect their sexual relationships?

4. Describe both the male and female response to sexual stimulation. How are they similar and different? How are orgasm potentials different or similar?

5. What is the largest human sex organ? What is the most important one? How is foreplay important in sexual intimacy? Afterplay? How does communication fit into the picture?

6. How important is orgasm? Why is there so much controversy surrounding it?

7. How does guilt affect sexual enjoyment and sexual relationships?

8. What are the four different "languages" used in discussing sex? Which gender is more likely to use which language? Does use of these different languages affect the relationship at all? How?

9. How does everyday life affect sexual relationships? What effect do the expectations of others and the demands of other roles have on sexual relationships? How can these be dealt with?

10. What happens to the frequency of sexual activity during marriage? What are some of the factors that contribute to these changes in frequency?

11. How prevalent is extramarital sexual activity? Are rates going up or down?

12. What constitutes extramarital sexual activity? What is your definition? What are the different types? How do you feel about EMS? What are some reasons why people engage in EMS? Can you think of any others?

13. What would you do if your husband or wife (present or potential) admitted that he or she had participated in EMS in the past? What would be your reaction? What would be the future of the relationship? Give reasons and support for your decision.

14. The three dozen "superlover" commandments in the Perspective section of the chapter cover a wide range of things. Are all of them limited to marital sex? Which are not? How do you feel about these?

PART 4

Relationships in Transition

11

Fertility Control

Nice round pebbles, gold balls, half a hollowed-out lemon, a mixture of crocodile dung and honey, disks of beeswax, oil-saturated paper—these are all among the early methods of birth control used by such peoples as the ancient Arabs, Romans, and Greeks (McCary & McCary, 1982). Birth control, in one sense, can be considered a very old practice because methods such as these have been around since the beginning of humankind. On the other hand, it is also a relatively new field, since it is only recently that research has focused on birth control, that reliable methods have been available, and that issues about it have come to the attention of the public.

Social imperatives, rather than science, determined the downward trend in the American birthrate since 1800, according to Reed (1978). In the early 1800s, English economist and sociologist Thomas C. Malthus was the first to sound the alarm about limiting population growth. Although there was some information about reasonably reliable methods of contraception before the Civil War, Victorian legislation suppressed it and its use during the 1800s (Reed, 1978). The Comstock Law of 1873 prohibited the mailing, transporting, or importing of "obscene, lewd, or lascivious" materials, including information and devices concerned with "preventing conception."

Margaret Sanger became a pioneer of birth control in the early 1900s. In 1914 she founded the National Birth Control League and wrote about birth control in her magazine *Woman Rebel*. In 1916 she opened a birth-control clinic in Brooklyn. "At 7 a.m., the line of women waiting to get in stretched around the block; they saw 140 women that first day" (Clinch, 1981). Reaction was harsh. Sanger was sentenced to 30 days in jail for "maintaining a public nuisance" and New York laws made it a misdemeanor to "sell, lend or give away" contraceptive devices (Clinch, 1981.)

The American Medical Association did not recognize contraception as a medical service until 1937 (Reed, 1978). In fact, when Sanger died in 1966, at the age of 86, the Comstock Act was still in effect. It has only been over the last three decades that birth control has become reliable—and available—in most areas of this country.

SOCIETAL VALUES

Societal values are even slower to change. Many individual and institutional (religious, family, legal, and other) values are basically pronatalist—that is, encouraging reproduction and exalting the role of parenthood.

"A key element in pronatalist thought is the age-old idea that woman's role must involve maternity—that woman's destiny and fulfillment are closely wedded to the *natal*, or birth, experience. . . . Pronatalist prejudice, or bias, exists at all stages of life" (Peck & Senderowitz, 1974, pp. 1–2).

Our society's pronatalist attitudes and values show up in many different ways. A mother gives her small daughter a baby doll to play with. A young woman is urged to have a cute little baby to give meaning to her life. Orthodox Freudians tell the woman that she feels compelled to have a child to compensate for her unfortunate lack of a penis. The Internal Revenue Service tells her that she can deduct so many dollars a year on her tax return for every child she has. Nulliparous ("not having given birth") wives and couples are typically referred to as "childless" in both everyday language and scientific writings, including most marriage and family textbooks. The obvious implication of the term is that the wife and/or the couple are missing something, that they are less than they should be. In her study, Polit (1978) found that voluntarily childless individuals and parents of only one child were perceived most negatively, while parents with eight children and involuntarily childless individuals were rated high in terms of social desirability. Mothers of large families (five or more children), however, do not agree with this evaluation. Many of them say that they had actually wanted fewer children (Gurel, 1978).

In recent decades, the term "child-free" has been used to describe women or couples who do not have children. This is also a value-laden term, but with positive implications. More and more couples are debating whether or not to have children, but little help has been available for those struggling with this decision (Prochaska & Coyle, 1979).

PERSONAL DECISION

In actuality, the decision whether or not to have children and when to have them should be a couple decision. Reasons for wanting children can include wanting to carry on the family name, the desire to have a close relationship with children, fulfillment, identity, companionship, and many more. Reasons for not wanting children are numerous too. Some reasons are wanting to pursue a career without the burden of child rearing, avoiding medical risks, postponing starting a family, and spacing children. "The question of why people have babies is amusing and simple-minded at the same time that the answer is unclear, complex, and profound. . . . As my office janitor put it, 'That's simple—they slip up!' " (Scanzoni, 1975, p. 18).

Whatever the reasons for or against having children, the decision is a couple decision and it should be made conscientiously and thoughtfully, together. Responsible people have responsible sex, and one aspect of responsible sex is taking the trouble to avoid unplanned consequences. Otherwise, according to a Planned Parenthood poster, you may find that "The stork is a dirty bird."

Literature is mostly about having sex and not much about having children; life is the other way around.

A COMMON METHOD OF BIRTH CONTROL,

THAT DOESN'T WORK.

You can't be an ostrich about birth control. Unwanted pregnancy will occur if you don't take proper precautions.

An ounce of prevention can avoid nine months of shame and a lifetime of regret.

The latest word on birth control is "No"; the only problem is that you can't use it forever.

TERMINOLOGY

Population control is the broadest term relating to fertility control. One of the earliest statements about increasing population is God's instruction to Eve and Adam to "Be fruitful, and multiply, and replenish the earth, and subdue it" (Genesis 1:28). More recently some people have noted that the charge was to "replenish" the earth, not to destroy it by overpopulation. Generally speaking, population control includes a great variety of economic, social, and natural events. War, depression, and drought, for example, limit population.

Fertility control, or birth control, can be defined as any behavior, method, or procedure that prevents conception or live birth. Thus the term would include such methods as "the pill," rhythm, sterilization, and abortion but not methods advocated by Malthus (1816), such as celibacy or deferred marriage, where no opportunity for conception or birth would exist. Contraception means any deliberate attempt to prevent the access of sperm to ovum or to interfere with fertilization. Contraception includes the examples mentioned under birth control methods with the exception of abortion.

The terms "fertility" and "fecundity" are often used interchangeably and thus incorrectly. "Fertility" refers to actual reproduction and parity (the number of children one has had). "Nulliparous" means having no children; hence "multiparous" means having several children. "Fecund" refers to reproductive potential and describes a woman who is capable of producing children. Therefore, a 25-year-old mother of two has a fertility of two and a potential fecundity of several times that many children—theoretically as many as one a year until menopause.

Social-Psychological Decision Factors

There is no perfect method of birth control. Clinicians in the field of fertility control recommend that you choose a method or methods on the basis of factors maximizing health benefits and/or contraceptive effectiveness. Various of these factors have been identified; however, you and your partner must decide which are important. You may also change your priorities under differing circumstances.

You will want to consider five factors in deciding which method to use. The higher you rate these characteristics, the more desirable the method will be for you.

1. *Effectiveness and reliability* are the criteria most often cited for judging the acceptability of a birth-control method. These criteria involve the extent to which any particular method will avoid fertilization, conception, implantation, or birth and with what regularity it will do so. They are not, however, entirely objective data because, with most methods, the human factor may alter the laboratory or theoretical effectiveness. Therefore, the "theoretical effectiveness rate" refers to the percentage of women who do not become pregnant in a year's time of using the method correctly and consistently. The "use effectiveness rate" represents the typical rate of effectiveness, including those who neglected to use the method or used it improperly.

2. *Safety* factors can be described as cautions, risks, contraindications, side effects, and so on. They may be short-term, like a temporary weight gain due to water retention from taking the pill, or serious threats to a user's health and well-being, such as problems with blood clots. You will want to weigh the risks against the benefits before making a decision about a specific birth-control method.

3. *Reversibility* refers to the option of terminating the use of a contraceptive method and resuming the potential for reproduction. Sterilization is usually not reversible, so couples must decide very carefully that they do not want any

children or any more children before they have a sterilization operation performed.

4. *Ease and cost of use* can be measured in two different ways. An initial measure involves the difficulty of teaching proper use of the method (for example, the diaphragm) and the initial cost of purchasing or obtaining the method (the doctor's visit and the device itself). The other aspect is the ongoing ease and cost of use. This involves physically continuing to use the method (for example, inserting foam) as well as the continued procurement of the method (buying condoms, for instance). Therefore, intellectual, mechanical, financial, and motivational factors are all involved in this aspect of the decision.

5. The *aesthetic acceptance* of the method and its use is the most subjective variable. You must consider your own as well as your partner's particular attitudes, feelings, values, and experiences directly and indirectly related to the method. To get an idea if a method is aesthetically acceptable, consider the following questions:

> Am I afraid of using this method of birth control?
> Has my mother, father, sister, brother, close friend, partner or spouse
>   strongly discouraged me from using this method?
> Am I opposed to this method because of my religious beliefs?
> Will the use of this method embarrass me?
> Will the use of this method embarrass my partner?
> Will my partner or I enjoy sexual activity less because of this method?
>   (Hatcher, Guest, Stewart, Stewart, Trussell, Cerel, & Cates, 1986).

THE USE AND MISUSE OF BIRTH CONTROL

Many people who profess not to want children do indeed have children. In fact, there are over three million unintended pregnancies per year in the United States (Edmondson, 1986). Yet today birth-control methods are available and relatively effective. Why the disparity? Many other factors are involved. Some researchers believe that how people feel about having or not having children is a good indicator of whether or not they will actually produce children. For instance, Townes, Beach, Campbell, and Martin (1977) found that those couples who expected maximum benefit from having a child did actually conceive a child within a year. Those who expected a maximum benefit from not having a child did not conceive. This represents a classic example of the exchange theory.

Similarly, at the actual time of sexual relations, some women consider the disadvantages of contraception more pressing than the consequences of a pregnancy that might not even occur (Luker, 1975). The women in this study cited, as reasons for neglecting birth control, loss of spontaneity and intimacy and a concern that only promiscuous women use contraceptives. Once pregnant, however, they typically changed their assessment and sought abortions.

Ambivalent feelings about pregnancy can cause contraceptive failure, according to Lehfeldt (1971). He says that certain tendencies inherent in human nature may thwart the protective action of contraception. Reasons why people who profess not to desire pregnancy fail to use methods to prevent it may be both conscious and subconscious (Sandberg & Jacobs, 1972). Some common reasons include denial that pregnancy could occur, guilt about sex, and embarrassment in obtaining and/or using contraceptive devices.

Researchers have found that people who are mature, independent, high in self-esteem, successful in other aspects of their lives, motivated, and intelligent are more apt to have success in contraceptive usage. Communication between partners also contributes to proper use of birth control.

> —*A woman's body belongs to herself alone . . . and (she) has the right to dispose of herself, to withhold herself, to procreate or suppress the germ of life.* —MARGARET SANGER

> —*Every human being has the right to express himself or herself sexually and in his or her own way as long as she or he does not infringe on the rights of others. If there is a right to have babies, so is there a right to have sex without babies.*

STAGES OF VULNERABILITY

A woman's vulnerability to pregnancy varies throughout her life. Miller (1973) has identified eight stages when a woman is especially likely to have an unwanted pregnancy:

1. Early adolescence, a transition period between the inability to conceive and the point of fecundity.
2. The start of the sexual career, when a woman is not likely to use contraception. It may take a while for her to acknowledge that she will continue to be sexually active and to start using contraception.
3. The beginning of a stable sexual relationship, when a contraceptive pattern may not yet be established. A breakup of the relationship may cause a temporary lapse in birth control and an increase in vulnerability.
4. A geographical move from parents' home to her own living quarters or from one subculture or psychosocial area to another, which may change the social and sexual demands on a woman.
5. Just before the wedding, when the couple may be more careless about using contraceptives. Similarly, right after the wedding, during conflict and/or separation, and after divorce are vulnerable times.
6. After termination of each pregnancy, when a woman is likely to feel that because fertility is lower, contraception is not as necessary. Even after abortion, there may be psychological conflict or ambivalence about becoming pregnant again.
7. The end of the childbearing career, which may bring changes in feelings regarding birth control, changes in circumstances, and ambivalence about stopping the procreative career.

8. Menopause, a high-risk time because fertility does not stop at one precise moment. A woman may suspect that she is not fertile and therefore relax her contraceptive vigilance. Or she may be afraid that she is losing her self-worth or womanhood and be careless about contraception for that reason.

BIRTH CONTROL AMONG TEENS AND STUDENTS

Birth control for teenagers is a specific problem and is of special concern to experts, families, society, and teens themselves in this country. Statistics show that the rate of teenage pregnancy has been increasing in recent years, with the rate for 15- to 19-year-old girls now at 96 per 1000. This rate is more than double that of other developed countries: England and Wales (45), Canada (44), France (43), Sweden (35), and Netherlands (14) (Murray & Parks, 1985; Scales, 1987).

The numbers for the United States are alarming. One out of ten teenage girls in America becomes pregnant every year, and nearly half of these pregnancies result in births (Stark, 1986). Four-fifths of teen pregnancies occur out of wedlock. Over 80 percent are unintended (Zelnik, Kantner & Ford, 1981). Studies show that teenagers wait about a year after their first intercourse before first using a prescription contraceptive. The younger they are, the less likely they are to use an effective method.

The societal cost of teen pregnancies is high. In dollar amounts alone, the public cost in 1985 of teen childbearing was estimated at over $16 billion. Of

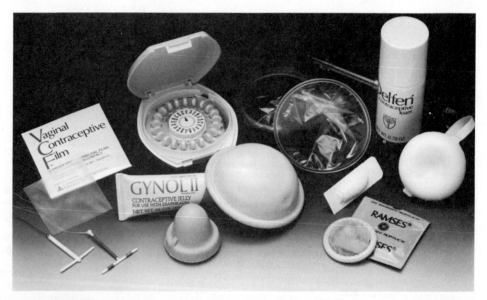

A few examples of available contraceptives. Clockwise from upper left: vaginal contraceptive film, "the pill," female condom, contraceptive foam and inserter, sponge, male condom, contraceptive insert, diaphragm and contraceptive jelly, cervical cup, and copper and progestasert IUDs. In order to use a prescription method such as the pill or a diaphragm, it is necessary to see a physician.

course, money alone is not the measure. Teenage out-of-wedlock pregnancies cause drastic disruptions in the lives of adolescents, their children, their parents, and society as a whole (Smith & Kolenda, 1982). Although the adverse consequences of teen childbearing are more social and economic than physical, studies show that babies born of teen mothers have lower birthweights, slightly higher late fetal death rates, and markedly higher perinatal death rates. They are also more likely to have health problems during their first year of life and to be slower in cognitive development (Makinson, 1985).

A study of teenage fertility in the United States and five other countries revealed some interesting facts. It found that (1) teenagers in other countries are not too immature to use contraceptives effectively, (2) the availability of welfare benefits and services does not act as an inducement to teenagers to have babies, (3) low teen birthrates in the other countries are not achieved by greater access to abortion, and (4) teen pregnancy rates are lower in countries with greater availability of birth control and sex education (Murray & Parks, 1985). The authors conclude that "increasing the legitimacy and availability of contraception and sex education (in its broadest sense) has been effective in reducing teenage pregnancy rates in other developed countries, and that there is no reason to believe that such an approach would not be successful in the United States" (p. 4).

The overall goals of programs to reduce teen pregnancy should include a decrease in adolescent pregnancy, abortion, childbearing, and school failure as well as an increase in contraceptive use, knowledge about reproduction, contraception, and the consequences of pregnancy; psychosocial skills for decision making; and job skills and placement (Dryfoos, 1985). When parents and adolescents share values that stress responsibility, the adolescents are less likely to experience an out-of-wedlock childbirth (Hanson, Myers, & Ginsburg, 1987).

These factors apply to males as well as females. The male partner must see himself as responsible. He must develop a more caring and respecting attitude toward females and realize that sex is only "one component in a more inclusive relationship" rather than a demeaning favor that a girl grants him. It is further suggested that teen girls must change their perceptions of themselves as weak, inferior individuals and develop self-esteem and confidence in a variety of activities (Smith & Kolenda, 1982).

Sex education has been a subject of controversy in recent years. Some people believe that an increase in sex education, like an increase in the availability of birth control, will cause young people to be more sexually active. Research shows otherwise. "Study after study shows that sex education does not stimulate sexual behavior" (Scales, 1987, p. 13). Instead, it fosters responsibility.

FEMALE CONTRACEPTIVE METHODS

A good decision about birth control can be encouraged in part by an understanding of the various methods available. You will want to consider the factors mentioned earlier as they relate to each method to decide if that method is a good one for you and your partner. You may elect to use one method or methods for a particular time of your life and another as your circumstances change.

TEMPORARY PRESCRIPTION METHODS

"Temporary" refers to the reversibility of the birth control method. This simply means that you may stop using the method when you wish to have children. This can be an important factor for couples who do not want children now but may in the future or for couples who want to space their children a few years apart. "Prescription" means that the method is given to you by a doctor or clinician after appropriate testing and examination.

"THE PILL"

In the early 1950s hormonal substances, particularly progestin (synthetic progesterone) and synthetic estrogens, were found to inhibit ovulation. By the mid- to late 1950s, the first oral hormonal contraceptives (commonly called birth-control pills) were marketed in Puerto Rico. Since their introduction in the United States in 1960, they have become a very popular prescribed method of contraception. There are several different types (Figure 11.1).

Sequential pills were among the first hormonal contraceptives. A package of these pills sequences the hormones and the relative amounts of hormone in each pill, releasing first synthetic estrogen and then progestin to mimic the woman's body's release of the natural progesterone and estrogen. These products were taken off the market temporarily but are available again in various dosages and combinations.

Combination pills contain progestin and synthetic estrogen. When they were first introduced, these pills contained much higher dosages than they do now. Present dosages can vary according to the user's needs. To aid the matching of pill prescriptions to patients, currently available combination pills also vary in the nature and amount of the synthetic hormone (progestin or estrogen) they contain.

Minipills are different from the usual combination pills and contain only progestin. They are somewhat less effective and have to be taken every day, even during menstruation.

The primary mode of action of hormonal contraception is to inhibit ovulation. When a woman takes birth-control pills, she probably does not ovulate. The estrogen portion of the pills is primarily responsible for this change, although progestins may also inhibit ovulation. Other effects of hormonal contraception are to (1) increase "hostile cervical mucus" (progestin), (2) incapacitate the sperm, and (3) inhibit implantation (estrogen and progestin).

In order to maintain a sufficiently high level of hormones in the woman's body so that ovulation is inhibited, the pill must be taken regularly, generally every day at nearly the same time. If a user forgets to take a pill, she can make it up the next day. However, if more than one day is missed, another backup method must be used. Sequential and combination pills are taken for 21 days, with a week break between packs. The minipill is taken continuously.

How birth-control pills affect a woman's physical and/or psychological functioning has been the subject of extensive study in the years since they became

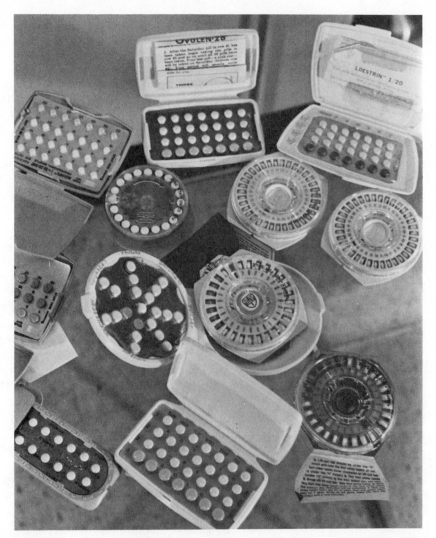

FIGURE 11.1 MANY DIFFERENT BRANDS OF BIRTH CONTROL PILLS
ARE AVAILABLE. MOST COME IN CASES THAT ARE SPE-
CIALLY DESIGNED TO MAKE PILL COUNTING EASIER.

available. In the 1960s, use of the pill was linked to increased risk of cardiovascular disease, blood clots, certain types of cancer, and strokes. However, the lower
dosages and greater medical supervision of use today has, for all practical purposes, eliminated these risks. In fact, "most recent studies indicate that they do
not increase the risk of any cancer, including breast cancer, and actually decrease
the risk of both ovarian and endometrial cancer, even after a woman goes off the
pill. Pill users also experience less benign breast disease, fewer ovarian cysts, and

fewer pelvic infections" (Wilbur, 1986, p. 57). Also, psychological risks of pill use are lower than related physiological risks of pregnancy (Hatcher et al., 1986).

Advantages of contraceptive pills include high effectiveness (95 to 100 percent), reversibility, separation from the act of intercourse, ease of use, and moderate cost. Disadvantages include effects on hormonal and other body systems, the inability of some women to use them, human failure or forgetting to take them, and the need to see a doctor regularly while using them.

Diethylstilbestrol, better known as "the morning-after pill," received FDA approval in 1975 as an emergency postcoital contraceptive preparation. It is not intended to be a primary birth-control method because of the many possible side effects that the user may suffer on repeated use as well as the effects that the fetus can suffer if the drug is not effective in preventing fertilization or implantation. The drug must be prescribed within 72 hours of intercourse if it is to be effective.

Injectable Hormonal Contraception ("The Shot") The shot is another highly effective method of contraception. It has been widely used throughout the world and now has FDA approval in the United States for some medical uses and for some special populations. It is not currently available to the general public for contraception.

Its mode of action is that of other progestin substances—production of "hostile cervical mucus," incapacitation of sperm and ovum transport, and inhibition of implantation. Physical risks are the same as those for other progestin products. Advantages of the shot include high effectiveness, separation from the act of intercourse, ease of use, low risk of human error, and moderate cost. Its disadvantages are its effect on hormonal and other body systems, unknown period of time before it is reversible, possibility of irregular menstrual bleeding, and the necessity to see a doctor.

The Intrauterine Device (IUD) The IUD is one of the oldest methods of contraception, probably first used to prevent unwanted pregnancy in female animals and adapted for human use in the early 1900s. An IUD is a small plastic device inserted into the uterus. Some IUDs can be left inside the uterus indefinitely; others must be replaced at certain intervals. The search for a "perfect" IUD continues.

The Lippes Loop, Safety-Coil, Copper 7, and Copper T types of IUDs were removed from the market in late 1985 and early 1986 because of financial considerations (lack of profit due to lower user levels and high costs of production and distribution) and costs of litigation and court suits. By the time you read this, a new Copper T should again be available. Most of these types of IUDs are still available outside the United States, and some users are planning trips to Canada, Mexico, or Europe at replacement time.

The progestasert is the only IUD now available in this country. This device contains progesterone, which is time-released to act locally on the uterine lining. It is good for 12 to 18 months.

The IUD is as effective as the pill, but how it works is not really known or understood. The most often cited explanations fall into two categories: (1) the presence of an IUD makes the lining of the uterus unsuitable for implantation and (2) most probably it causes the egg to travel more quickly through the fallopian tube, so that the chances of the sperm and egg uniting in conception are reduced. It may be that all IUDs cause chemical changes in the uterus and fallopian tubes that inhibit sperm mobility and viability. It is fairly certain that the combination copper and hormonal IUDs work this way.

Both birth-control pills and IUDs are very effective means of birth control. The major difference is that the pill inhibits ovulation and the IUD most likely inhibits implantation. Because of this difference, some people consider an IUD an abortifacient (something that causes an abortion). In fact, there are legislative moves to define life as beginning at fertilization, which would make IUDs illegal. However, whether or not IUDs are legal, couples may have philosophical or psychological reservations about the IUD because of its disadvantages or because of the possibility of conception.

Advantages of the IUD include the following:

It requires only one act of motivation for the length of its effectiveness.
It is separate from the act of intercourse.
It carries little risk of human failure.
It is highly effective (mid- to high 90 percentiles).
It does not inhibit ovulation.
It has a moderate cost.
It can be used by women who cannot use the pill—those over 35, smokers, and those with physiological risks such as cardiovascular problems.

Its disadvantages are as follows:

It may be philosophically unacceptable.
It involves a higher risk of infection, especially if the woman has multiple partners.
A skilled doctor/practitioner is needed to insert it.
It may cause moderate pain at the time of insertion, possibly heavier periods or cramping, and irritation from the string.
It may have to be replaced every 12 to 18 months.
It involves a higher risk of ectopic pregnancy.

The Diaphragm The vaginal diaphragm is a rubber cup-shaped device with a spring rim which is inserted into the vagina and covers the cervix. It comes in a range of sizes and in several kinds of rim styles, such as arching spring, coil spring, and flat spring. These variations affect fit and usage but not mode of action. For the most part, your doctor will be the one who chooses the type as well as the size of the diaphragm based on a physical exam and the ease of learning to use the method (Figure 11.2).

Because the diaphragm is not a form-fitting device, it must be used with a contraceptive jelly or cream. A number of products are made specifically for use with a latex diaphragm. Choice of a particular product is usually made on the basis of the amount of lubrication needed, esthetic acceptability, and possible skin sensitivity.

The diaphragm with cream or jelly acts as a chemical and physical barrier

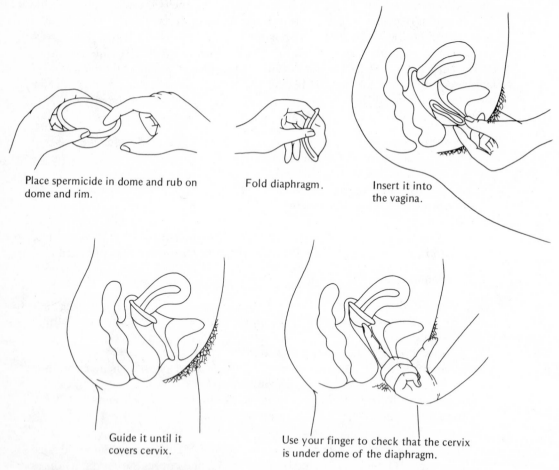

Place spermicide in dome and rub on dome and rim.

Fold diaphragm.

Insert it into the vagina.

Guide it until it covers cervix.

Use your finger to check that the cervix is under dome of the diaphragm.

FIGURE 11.2 THE PROPER METHOD FOR INSERTING A DIAPHRAGM.

SOURCE: Madaras & Patterson, 1981.

to the fertilization of the egg. In order to assure maximum effectiveness of the chemical substance, it is suggested that the diaphragm be inserted a maximum of 1 hour before intercourse, that additional applications of cream/jelly be made (with a plunger type applicator and without disturbing the diaphragm) if intercourse is repeated, and that the diaphragm be left in place for at least 6 hours after intercourse. The diaphragm should be removed within 24 hours of intercourse to prevent odor and irritation of the vagina and/or bladder.

While, theoretically, the effectiveness of the diaphragm approaches 100 percent, use effectiveness is actually 80 to 95 percent. The use effectiveness of the diaphragm depends on many factors, including the fit and condition of the diaphragm, the consistency of use of the diaphragm and cream or jelly, vaginal muscle tone (usually related to the number of pregnancies), and movement and position during intercourse.

The advantages of the diaphragm are as follows:

> It does not change hormonal or other bodily functioning. Its mode of action is easily understood.
> It can be used only when needed.
> It is effective if used consistently.
> Nearly all females can use it.
> Its cost is low to moderate.
> Users require little ongoing medical care.
> It can be used during a female's menstrual period in order to prevent menstrual fluid from interfering with sexual activity.

The disadvantages of the diaphragm are these:

> It requires high motivation.
> Partners may need to plan sex more and/or interrupt it more often.
> It is necessary to touch the body in order to insert it.
> The cream or jelly is somewhat messy.
> The diaphragm may be dislodged in some sex positions.
> It requires moderately high cooperation of the female's partner.

The Cervical Cap The firm rubber cervical cap is very similar to the diaphragm except that it covers only the cervix, not the whole upper portion of the vaginal canal, and is held in place by suction, not spring tension. The cap is much smaller and harder to insert than the diaphragm. However, it may be left in place for up to three days and does not require reapplication of spermicide before each act of intercourse. Currently available sizes fit only about half of women well; they can cause cervical abrasion, discomfort during intercourse, and odor. Manufacturers show little interest in producing this product (Wilbur, 1986).

TEMPORARY NONPRESCRIPTION METHODS

Other temporary methods are available without prescription.

The Sponge   The vaginal contraceptive sponge is a polyurethane mush-room-cap-shaped sponge which the user moistens with water and inserts it into the vagina in much the same way as a diaphragm. It may be left in place for 24 hours and is effective for multiple acts of intercourse. It works in three ways—it contains a spermicide to kill sperm, it blocks the passage of sperm to the uterus, and it soaks up semen, thus collecting sperm. The use effectiveness rating is rather low (about 83 percent) and some women are allergic to the spermicide, have trouble removing the sponge, or find it uncomfortable (Hyde, 1986).

Others   Vaginal creams, jellies, and foams offer a substantially less effec-tive method of birth control (80 to 97 percent use effectiveness rate) but are easily available over the counter. These vaginal contraceptives act as chemical barriers to sperm. Primarily, they impede mobility so that the sperm cannot swim to the egg or are not viable enough to fertilize it. Foam is available in an aerosol form with a reusable applicator, in prefilled applicators, and in vaginal suppository form. It should be inserted no more than 20 minutes before intercourse and reinserted with each act of intercourse. The user should not douche for two hours after intercourse. Vaginal spermicides that contain nonoxynol-9 have been shown to reduce the female's vulnerability to sexually transmitted diseases, including AIDS (Masters et al., 1988).

The advantages of nonprescription methods are as follows:

No prescription or physical exam is necessary.
They are used only when needed.
They do not affect hormonal or other bodily functions.
They are relatively easy to use.
They are moderate in cost.

Disadvantages include the facts that:

They require high motivation.
They require touching of the body/genitalia.
They may be esthetically unpleasant and messy.
They have low effectiveness if used alone.
They require moderate to high partner cooperation.
They may irritate female or male genital tissues.

PERMANENT METHODS

Voluntary sterilization is a very popular form of birth control. In the United States, it is the most popular method for couples who want to end their childbear-ing years (Mumford, 1983). In fact, worldwide, over one-third of all couples who practice an effective method of birth control now use sterilization (Camp, Speidel, & Barberis, 1986).

Sterilization has the advantage of being nearly 100 percent effective but the disadvantage of being irreversible. Therefore, couples who are sure that they do not want to have children or any *more* children may opt for sterilization. Experts warn, however, that although surgeons can occasionally reverse female sterilization, the procedure should not be undertaken without ample consideration.

A number of female sterilization methods are commonly performed. They include (1) *hysterectomy*, the removal of the uterus and sometimes the fallopian tubes and ovaries—a procedure usually performed for medical rather than voluntary reasons; (2) *tubal ligation*, major surgery done under anesthesia during

---

BOX 11.1   THE BIRTH-CONTROL PARTNERSHIP

Many women are unhappy about the fact that birth control usually turns out to be exclusively their responsibility. The typical male response, that most of the methods have been designed for females, is of little help. What we would like to suggest is that contraception is a partnership responsibility. Since most contraceptives are designed for females, we will emphasize the male part in general and in the use of some of the more common types.

First, it is the male's responsibility to find out if his partner is protected. Often a simple question like "Are you on the pill?" is all that is required to show both one's concern and one's responsibility.

Second, the male can offer to accompany his partner to a family planning clinic and to help pay for the exams and the chosen method. He can also keep an eye on the supplies to make sure they don't run out.

Third, the male can offer to use a condom if his partner is not on any regular method of contraception or if that method for any reason is interrupted. A woman may, for example, miss taking the pill or may be in the initial period of starting the pill or using of the IUD. The males using the condom should do so without complaining.

Last, the male partner's participation can be part of sexual foreplay. The female can help with the proper placement and removal of the condom, and both partners can experiment with different brands until they find one they like. If the woman is using an IUD, her partner can check the string during lovemaking. If a diaphragm is being used, the male partner can apply the jelly or cream and learn how to insert it properly. Both of you may get turned on in the process. If you would like to repeat intercourse, remember that foam, cream, or jelly must be added for the "second round."

A contraceptive partnership can turn a tedious, lonesome, and even uncomfortable activity into one that includes play, togetherness, and even fun for both. Instead of concern and pain now or later, why not elect to go for pleasure now and knowledge of safety for now *and* later?

which an abdominal incision is made and the fallopian tubes are cut and tied (this can be performed any time, but it is sometimes done following routine childbirth); and (3) *laparoscopy,* or surgical closure of the fallopian tubes under general or local anesthesia using a laparoscope. The laparoscope is inserted into a small incision below the navel to visualize the fallopian tubes, and a cauterizing instrument is then inserted through a small incision above the pubic hair to seal the tubes. Laparoscopy is called Band-Aid sterilization because Band-Aids are used to close the small incisions. This can be performed in a hospital or outpatient clinic.

Voluntary sterilization, tubal ligation, or laparoscopy prevent the egg from being fertilized by the sperm. The reproductive process is permanently interrupted but not halted, as in the case of a hysterectomy. Research has been under way for some time to discover a reversible method of blocking the fallopian tubes, but no reliable method is yet known. Because the release of hormones and eggs is unaffected by voluntary sterilization, the female still experiences a normal menstrual cycle and all primary and secondary sexual characteristics remain unchanged.

Advantages of sterilization include its permanence, its high effectiveness rate (about 99 percent), its low incidence of human failure, its lack of alteration of other body functions, and its long-run inexpensiveness compared to temporary methods. Its disadvantages are irreversibility, need for hospitalization and recovery, risks associated with surgery and anesthesia, and considerable one-time expense.

MALE CONTRACEPTIVE METHODS

CONDOMS

Condoms (prophylactics or rubbers) are thousands of years old. Early ones were made from linen cloth, and later sheep intestines, and were not very effective. They are popular today not only as a birth-control method but as a means of protection against sexually transmitted disease. Besides a wise choice of a partner, the condom currently is the best protection against AIDS. Condoms are thin sheaths that are rolled over the erect penis. The majority are made of latex rubber, the rest of animal membrane. Condoms can be purchased over the counter without a prescription, at clinics, drugstores, and some department stores. They are available lubricated, wet or dry, or unlubricated. In addition, recent additions to the variety of condoms have included assorted colors and other features including ribbing, contouring, scents, and flavors. Although condoms come in only one size, there are variations in shape and elasticity. Assistance from a clinician or pharmacist may be helpful in selecting a condom (Figure 11.3).

The primary mode of action of the condom is to prevent sperm from entering the vagina. In addition, many of the lubricated kinds are coated with the same spermicidal agent as that in vaginal jellies, creams, and foams.

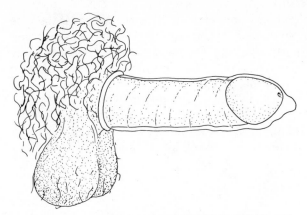

FIGURE 11.3   THE CORRECT POSITIONING OF
THE CONDOM ON THE PENIS.

SOURCE: Harmatz & Novak, 1983, p. 198.

The effectiveness of the condom is maximized by (1) usage as soon as sexual activity involves genital closeness, since preejaculatory fluid may contain sperm; (2) maintenance of sufficient lubrication to prevent tearing (vaginal foams, saliva, or non-petroleum-based lubricants can be used; however, petroleum jelly, hand cream, and many other petroleum-based or perfumed products can damage the rubber); (3) maintenance of space at the end of the condom for semen to collect—this is where shape of the condom is applicable; and (4) care in removal of the penis from the vagina following intercourse. The penis should be withdrawn prior to its return to the flaccid state and the male or his partner should hold onto the rim of the condom so that it does not slip off. While the theoretical effectiveness of condoms is about 98 percent, the actual use effectiveness of a condom used alone is only 80 to 90 percent.

Advantages of condoms are that they do not affect bodily functions, are used only when needed, give some of the responsibility of contraception to the male, require no prescription, cost relatively little, and prevent the spread of sexually transmitted diseases. Their disadvantages include that they must be used with each act, they require moderate to high partner cooperation, and they may cause embarrassment or guilt because of their image as a back-alley product.

VASECTOMY

Vasectomy is a permanent male birth-control method that involves cutting and tying the vas deferens, or the sperm-carrying tube. This procedure is usually performed under local anesthesia in an outpatient setting. It is considered irreversible, although a few successful reversals have been recorded. The side effects are the same as those of female sterilization.

Male and female sterilizations are now performed in about equal numbers. Among couples who are in agreement about sterilization, it is usually the man who undergoes the procedures, while among those in disagreement, it is the wife who is sterilized (Bean, Clark, Swicegood, & Williams, 1983). One reason is that men require a lot of social support in making the vasectomy decision. Some may be concerned, given today's remarriage patterns, that they might someday be widowed or divorced and choose to marry a younger woman who will want to have children. Men tend to take a long time deciding—anywhere from two to more than ten years. In fact, men seem to pass through stages in their information-gathering and decision-making process (Mumford, 1983). Many men who seek vasectomy say they would choose a male pill if such an alternative existed (Goldstein, 1986).

COUPLE METHODS

ABSTINENCE

The most effective method of birth control is abstinence. If you don't have sex, you won't get pregnant. Abstinence works 100 percent of the time. However, abstinence also includes "outercourse," or touching of genitals.

Advantages of abstinence are that it is always available, highly effective, couple-oriented, safe, reversible, and inexpensive. Its disadvantages are that it requires very high motivation and willingness to abstain by both partners and it may cause one or both partners to become emotionally and/or physically frustrated if no alternatives are available.

FOAM AND CONDOMS

When combined and correctly used, vaginal foam and condoms can be 99 percent effective. In addition to this improvement in effectiveness, this couples combination method reduces the disadvantages of the two individual methods. Less motivation is required by either individual as these methods are to be used at roughly the same time, so one person need not always act and/or interrupt. In addition, the couple method can more easily be incorporated into sex play, thus further reducing embarrassment and interruption. Finally, this combination is an excellent way of preventing the spread of sexually transmitted diseases.

NATURAL FAMILY PLANNING

Natural family planning refers to rhythm or periodic abstinence methods. These methods involve the need to ascertain the probable fertile period of the female and to abstain during this time. Most frequently used ways of determining fertility include (1) the *calendar rhythm method,* recording the dates and length of the female's cycle for some six months and then mathematically calculating probability given the shortest and longest cycles; (2) the *basal body temperature method*, recording of the female's waking temperature for about six months to determine the preovulatory drop and ovulatory rise (a "basal body" thermometer measures to a tenth of a degree); and (3) the *mucus method* (sometimes referred to as the Billings method), which records the cycle of changes in cervical mucus.

The advantages of natural family planning are that it does not alter body functions, has no medical side effects, is couple-oriented, is acceptable by all religious groups, and can easily be reversed to aid in conception for couples desiring pregnancy. Its disadvantages are that it requires high motivation and possibly substantial abstinence, is difficult for women with irregular cycles to use, requires substantial planning during recording time, is difficult for women without a steady and open relationship, and means that the times of desire for intercourse may not match the allowable days.

FERTILITY AWARENESS METHOD (FAM)

A recently introduced couple birth control method is a combination of natural family planning and the use of female or male barrier methods during fertile times. This combination is felt by its adherents to maximize the advantages of each, particularly medical safety and couple orientation. Effectiveness is claimed to be at the high 90 percentile level.

INEFFECTIVE METHODS

There continue to be many myths about birth control. Some often cited myths are: You can't get pregnant

> if the female does not experience orgasm.
> if the female urinates right after intercourse.
> if you do it standing up.
> the first (or second, or third) time you do it.
> if the male pulls his penis out before ejaculating.
> if the male does not insert his penis all the way into the vagina.

Another nonmethod is douching. Douching is *not* a method of birth control. No matter what substance is used, douching washes out the vagina too late to prevent sperm from entering the cervix and swimming up the fallopian tubes to fertilize the egg. Withdrawal of the penis prior to the sensation of orgasm is sometimes listed as a birth-control method. However, the method is difficult to use because the male's instinct at the time of orgasm is *not* to pull back. In addition, enough sperm to fertilize the egg may, by that time, have entered the vagina in the preejaculatory fluid.

A summary of the various methods of birth control is presented in Table 11.1.

TABLE 11.1 Contraceptive Methods, Effectiveness, Advantages, Disadvantages, and Causes of Failure

Method	Effectiveness*	Potential Advantages	Potential Disadvantages	Possible Causes of Failure
Combination Oral Contraceptive (birth control pill containing estrogen and progestin)	98%	Reliable Increases regularity of menstrual cycle Reduces menstrual cramping Lower incidence of breast and ovarian cysts and pelvic inflammatory disease	Nausea, weight gain, fluid retention, breast tenderness, headaches, missed menstrual periods, acne (usually in the first several months) Mood changes, depression, anxiety, fatigue, decreased sex drive Circulatory diseases	Inappropriate use or improper supervision by physician Skipping pills
Minipill (progestin only)	98%	Reliable Increases regularity of the menstrual cycle Reduces menstrual cramping Lower incidence of breast and ovarian cysts and pelvic inflammatory disease	Irregular menstrual periods	Not taking pills as directed or skipping a pill Improper supervision by physician
Injectable Hormonal Contraceptive ("The Shot")	98%	Highly effective Separate from act of intercourse Ease of use Low risk of human error Moderate cost	Affects hormonal and all other body systems Unknown period of time before reversible	Failure to obtain replacement
Intrauterine Device (IUD)	95%	Reliable Can be left in place so that nothing must be remembered or prepared prior to intercourse	Possible irregular menstrual bleeding Uterine cramping, abnormal bleeding, and heavy menstrual flow Pelvic inflammatory disease or perforation of the uterus during insertion of the IUD; violent allergic reaction; infection of the uterus	Failure to notice that IUD has been expelled by uterus
Diaphragm (with spermicide)	81%	Negative side effects are rare Inexpensive; can be reused	Allergic reaction to the rubber (plastic diaphragms are also available) or spermicide Increased risk of toxic shock syndrome Bladder infection or vaginal soreness because of pressure from rim Infection from keeping diaphragm in place too long	Improper fitting or insertion Removal of diaphragm too soon (within 6–8 hours after coitus) Using insufficient amount of spermicidal jelly with the diaphragm Leakage in or around diaphragm or slippage
Cervical Cap (with spermicide) (Not approved for contraceptive use in the United States)	87%	Can be left in place for considerably longer periods of time than the diaphragm	Possible risk of toxic shock syndrome Allergic reaction to rubber or spermicide Abrasions or irritation to vagina or cervix	Improper fitting or insertion/placement
Sponge (containing spermicide)	80–90%	Ease of use Inexpensive Protection lasts over 24 hours, for several acts of intercourse No odor or taste Available without prescription	Increased risk of toxic shock syndrome Allergic reaction to polyurethane or spermicide	Difficulty of proper insertion and placement Internal anatomical abnormalities that may interfere with placement or retention

TABLE 11.1 (*Continued*)

Method	Effectiveness*	Potential Advantages	Potential Disadvantages	Possible Causes of Failure
Spermicidal Foam, Cream, Jelly, or Suppositories	82%	Available without prescription Minimal health risks Easy to carry and use	Allergic reactions to the chemical Unpleasant taste of chemical during oral-genital sex	Failing to use enough spermicide or additional spermicide when activity lasts several hours Inserting spermicide too long before intercourse Douching within 6–8 hours after intercourse Failure of suppositories to melt or foam properly
Tubal Ligation, Laparoscopy	Nearly 100%	Permanent Very reliable Minimal health risks	Rarely, postsurgical infection or other complications Psychological implications of being infertile	Procedure improperly performed by the physician
Condom	90%	Available without prescription Offers protection from sexually transmitted diseases The man can take full responsibility Easy to carry and use	Allergic reactions to rubber (natural "skin" condoms are also available) Some reduction in sensation	Breakage of condom Not leaving space at tip Lubrication with petroleum jelly, which can weaken rubber condom Seepage of semen around opening of condom Condom slipping off in vagina Storing condom for more than 2 years or in temperature extremes Not placing condom on penis at beginning of intercourse
Vasectomy	Nearly 100%	Permanent Very reliable Minimal health risks	Psychological implications of infertility can sometimes lead to some sexual problems	Unprotected intercourse before reproductive tract is fully cleared of sperm (may be several months) Healing together of the two cut ends of the vas
Abstinence	?	No cost or health risks Freedom from worry about pregnancy Accepted by Roman Catholic Church	Sexual frustration	Inability to continue abstaining
Natural Family Planning/ Fertility	76%	May increase chances of pregnancy No health risks	Sexual frustration during periods of abstinence	Insufficient time period for charting the menstrual cycle; lack of complete understanding of the method Ovulation at an unexpected time in the cycle Intercourse during the unsafe period of the cycle
Withdrawal (coitus interruptus)	77%	No cost or preparation involved No risks to health (if sexually transmitted diseases are absent)	Inability to fully relax Frustration caused by inability to ejaculate in the vagina	Sperm present in preejaculatory fluid Lack of ejaculatory control Ejaculating semen too close to vaginal opening

*In 100 typical users, over a year, the % that will not produce pregnancy. Effectiveness figures based on Hatcher, et al. (1986).

NEW METHODS

A number of new methods of birth control are now being developed. However, extensive testing is necessary before new drugs and devices can be made available to the public. For example, it takes an average of over seven years for any new drug to be developed, tested, and approved by the Food and Drug Administration. Norplant (described below), one new development in birth control, has already been in the works for 18 years and is not ready yet (Clifford, 1986).

A number of new products are now being researched and tested (Clifford, 1986; Wilbur, 1986). They include the following:

1. A hormone-releasing plastic or rubber vaginal ring that remains in place for three weeks of each month and is removed during menstruation. The hormones are absorbed directly into the bloodstream, so dosages can be lower than those of the pill.
2. Contracap, a custom-fitted rubber cap that fits on the cervix. It has one-way valve that allows blood and uterine discharges to flow out but prevents semen from flowing in. It can remain in place for months.
3. Gossypol, the first birth control pill for men. A derivative of cottonseed oil, it seems to disable sperm-producing cells.
4. RU486, a drug blocking the effects of progesterone, which is needed for implantation and maintenance of the fertilized egg.
5. Prostaglandins, which cause uterine contractions to bring on menstruation or a very early abortion. They may be used once a month.
6. Norplant. It consists of two very thin silicone rubber rods that are implanted beneath the skin of a woman's arm. They release low doses of progestin and last five years without attention. Similar hormone-releasing rods have been produced and tested for men, but various problems have delayed their development.
7. LH-RH analogues, which tell the pituitary gland to intercept the message to ovulate in women or to shut down testosterone and thus sperm production in men. They would be taken via shots or nasal sprays.
8. Antipregnancy vaccines—yearly shots of human chorionic gonadotropin (hCG)—which lead to the production of antibodies against hCG in order to thwart implantation or destroy an implanted egg.
9. The levonorgestrel IUD, a plastic IUD that releases a synthetic progestin. It remains effective for five years.
10. Sterilization plugs, or liquid silicone that is injected into the fallopian tubes, where it hardens, blocking fertilization. This is a simpler, less expensive method of sterilization.
11. Fimbrial hoods, or tiny plastic tubes by way of a small abdominal incision, over the openings to the fallopian tubes so eggs cannot enter. This procedure is generally reversible.

Experts tend to agree that the more contraceptive options there are, the better the choice is for each individual and each couple. As long as these new, promising methods remain in the developmental and testing stages, people will have to choose from the methods currently available.

SUMMARY

- Although people have tried various often absurd methods of birth control for centuries, reliable methods for both men and women have been available only in the last several decades.

- Our society strongly emphasizes the importance of having children and the positive values of parenthood; hence deciding not to have children or to limit family size has been a hard choice for many women.

- In reality, the decisions whether or not to have children and how many to have are personal ones that involve many factors.

- Your choice of birth control should be based on your priorities concerning the characteristics of the method. These characteristics include effectiveness and reliability, safety, reversibility, ease and cost of use, and aesthetic acceptability.

- Sometimes even those who profess not to want children may, for a number of reasons, not use birth control effectively.

- There are eight stages in women's lives during which they are especially vulnerable to pregnancy.

- Female methods of contraception can be divided into temporary prescription methods, temporary nonprescription methods, and permanent methods. Each type has its own advantages and disadvantages.

- Male birth control methods are, to date, quite limited. Use of the condom is a temporary method; vasectomy is a permanent one.

- Abstinence, a combination of foam and condoms, and natural family planning are examples of couple methods.

- There are many myths about birth control and many ineffective methods have been proposed.

- New scientific methods of birth control look promising but are still in the stages of development and testing.

 ## PERSPECTIVE: THE ABORTION CONTROVERSY— BELIEFS AND BEHAVIORS

"Abortion. It is, without question, the most emotional issue of politics and morality that faces the nation today" (Isaacson, 1981). It involves religious, legal, medical, moral, and social concerns. Some people are proabortion because they believe that women should have control over their own bodies and should have the choice of whether or not to carry a conceived fetus to full term. They stress people's right of personal choice. At the opposite end of the spectrum, antiabortionists feel that fetuses are human beings and are thus entitled to protection of their lives; hence it is argued that abortion at any time during a pregnancy is murder. The disagreement between "pro-choice" and "pro-life" groups often gets heated and is likely to continue for the foreseeable future.

One of the basic conflicts stems from the disagreement as to when human life actually begins. A number of views have been presented throughout the centuries.

1. *Gametes.* These are the mature male (spermatozoa) and female (ova) sex cells. Some people believe that life actually begins before conception, with the individual male or female sex cells, mainly because researchers have been able to induce an ovum to grow by mechanical, chemical, or electrical irritation in experimental situations.

2. *Conception.* A common belief today is that human life is complete at the time of conception because the fetus at that time has a full set of chromosomes and is a distinct genetic entity.

3. *Nidation.* This is the embedding of the fertilized egg in the uterine lining. At nidation, scientists can discern activity. When the heart begins beating (fourth week), when reflexes are evident (sixth week), or when the fetus is recognizable as a human being are other stages people pinpoint as the beginning of life.

4. *Animation or ensoulment.* This is the moment at which, according to various religions, a person receives a soul. Jewish religious writings put animation at 40 days of development for males and 90 days for females. Early Christian writings talk about 41 and 81 days, sometimes 90 days for females. In the Shinto religion, which is widespread in Japan, a newborn is recognized as human life when he or she sees the first light of day. In China a baby is considered a year old at birth.

5. *Quickening.* This refers to fetal movement that can be felt by the mother. This theory, which would put the beginning of life at 16 weeks of development, is based on the common-law tradition and was prevalent from colonial to Civil War times.

6. *Viability.* This would put the beginning of life at five to seven months after conception, when the baby would have a reasonable chance for survival and functioning outside the mother's body. The age at which a fetus is viable has declined with medical advances, and some researchers believe they may someday be able to keep all fetuses alive. The U.S. Supreme Court used this definition of human life in its 1973 ruling that the states cannot regulate pregnancy termination in the first trimester but *can* regulate it to some degree in the second trimester and can exercise more control in the last trimester.

7. *Live birth.* The time of birth is legally considered the start of a new human life. Birth is when a person is granted certain rights by society and government.

Public Opinion

Public opinion varies not only on when life begins but also on the circumstances under which an abortion may be acceptable. Thirty years ago, the majority of Americans approved of abortion if a pregnancy seriously endangered the woman's health, if the woman had been raped, or if there was good reason to believe that the child might be deformed. Fewer than one-fourth approved of not being married, not being able to afford another child, or simply not wanting more children as reasons for abortion. In short, abortion has been considered more an emergency measure that an elective method of regulating birth. By the late 1970s, approval for elective reasons rose to almost 50 percent. Interestingly, there seems to be little difference of opinion between

Some groups feel that women should have a choice between reproduction and no reproduction and that every child should be a wanted child.

men and women, political parties, age groups, or Catholics and Protestants. However, people living in the Midwest and South are less accepting; those with more education consider abortion more of a personal choice.

Actual Behavior

A substantial increase in legal abortions followed the 1973 Supreme Court abortion decision—from approximately 750,000 to 1.5 million per year. However, in the last years, this increase has leveled off. Part of the apparent increase stems from the fact that more abortions are now being performed legally and are thus being reported.

Who are the women having abortions? Henshaw and O'Reilly (1983) list the characteristics of those who obtained abortions in 1980 as follows:

Age—Thirty percent were teenagers, 35 percent women aged 20 to 24, and 35 percent women aged 25 and older.

Race—Seventy percent were white.

Marital status—Seventy-nine percent were unmarried.

Other children—Nearly 60 percent were childless; about 3 percent had had four or more live births.

Education—Over 30 percent had attended college, nearly 45 percent were high school graduates, and the rest had not completed high school.

About one-third had had a previous abortion. Over half of the abortions were obtained within the first eight weeks of pregnancy.

Abortion Procedures

The length of the pregnancy usually determines the procedure used. Brief descriptions of the surgical procedures and the medical methods are as follows:

Vacuum aspiration or curettage is the typical method used in the first trimester, that is, up to 13 weeks of pregnancy. This procedure involves a quick, complete suctioning out of the uterus by means of a minimal dilation of the cervix. During the first trimester, this procedure can be done in an office setting using local anesthesia.

Dilation and curettage (D&C) is a traditional method that is seldom used today. A sharp metal loop is inserted into the uterus to scrape out the contents. The advantage of this method is that older doctors are more familiar with it. Its disadvantages can include more pain and blood loss, greater risk of uterine perforation, greater dilation of the cervix, possible incomplete emptying, and more expense. It can be used beyond the first trimester but usually requires general anesthesia.

Dilation and evacuation, a procedure that is an extension of the other two methods, is considered especially appropriate for the early part of the second trimester, 13 to 16 weeks, but is used throughout the second trimester. It involves greater dilation of the cervix and may require either local or general anesthesia.

Hysterotomy and hysterectomy involves an incision in the abdomen and removal of the uterus. This type of surgery may be performed late in the second trimester or in the third trimester when abortion is necessary to save the mother's life. Laws require the availability and use of all lifesaving techniques for both mother and child.

While it is usually better to wait until a positive diagnosis of pregnancy has been made, women who wish to avoid an ethical dilemma or who are uncomfortable with the notion of abortion may find menstrual extraction or menstrual regulation an attractive option. This procedure may be performed if the patient's expected period is a day or so late. One of the disadvantages of this method is that many unnecessary procedures will most likely be done.

Myths

Abortion is surrounded by a number of myths. Here are a few:

1. "Abortion is dangerous to the woman's life or health." Actually, abortion is less dangerous than carrying a fetus to term and/or giving birth. Childbirth is eight times riskier to a woman's life than a legal first-trimester abortion and somewhat riskier than a legal second-trimester abortion. Studies have found that abortion does not cause sterility (Luria, Friedman, & Rose, 1987).

2. "A woman who has an abortion will always have guilt feelings and psychological problems." Although the decision of whether or not to have an abortion can be emotionally draining, the predominant mood of women after abortion, according to Hyde (1986), is relief and happiness. Those whose request for abortion is denied have higher rates of psychological disturbance than those who have an abortion. The children resulting from denied abortions are more susceptible than average to sickness, handicaps, and social and emotional problems (Diamond & Karlen, 1980).

3. "Abortion is a lower-class phenomenon, related to uneducated, irresponsible, indiscriminate sexual attitudes and actions." First, people with negative attitudes toward sex are less likely to practice contraception (Sandler, Meyerson, & Kinder, 1980) and thus more likely to be put in a position of considering abortion. Abortion is more common among women with at least some college education (Diamond & Karlen, 1980). Abortions among lower-class women are more likely to affect the statistics because they may receive state or federal support and may be forced to wait until later in the pregnancy before being granted an abortion.

Some groups insist that all abortions are murder, and all pregnancies should be brought to term.

4. "Women who get abortions are careless about contraception and will likely have repeated abortions." Abortion repeaters are not abusing a "privilege," are not a "special" population, and usually practice better contraception than women having their first abortion (Lake, 1981). Women who have had one abortion are typically more careful about birth control (Luria et al., 1987). About 15 percent of women who have abortions have more than one (Diamond & Karlen, 1980).

5. "Widespread abortion is the result of today's generally permissive, immoral life-styles of the teenagers." Abortion has historically been the most widely practiced method of birth control (Sandler, Meyerson, & Kinder, 1980). Today the typical woman having an abortion is in her middle twenties and is living with or going steady with a man (Diamond & Karlen, 1980). Women over forty have the highest percentage of abortions per 1000 live births for any age group (Smallwood & Van Dyck, 1983).

QUESTIONS FOR THOUGHT AND DISCUSSION

1. Why has it taken so long for society's views of birth control to change? How much have they changed?

2. What are the differences between population control, fertility control, and contraception? What are some special concerns that teens and students have concerning birth control and contraception?

3. Many teen parents report not using birth control because it indicates that sex was premeditated. How would you address this issue?

4. What are some important considerations in determining a birth-control method for you? Are some more important than others?

5. What are the most probable times that a woman will have an unwanted pregnancy?

6. Imagine you are a female considering using a contraceptive. Name three of your top choices, give advantages and disadvantages of each, and state the reasons why you chose these. Which one would you ultimately choose and why?

7. Imagine you are a male considering trying one of the contraceptive methods mentioned in the text. Would you choose any? Which would you choose and why?

8. Who do you feel is responsible for contraception in a sexual relationship? Why? How should this decision be made?

9. Review the list of new contraceptive methods that is given in the text. Pick out those that you feel would be the best. Why did you pick these? What are some problems with them?

10. Why is there such an emotional controversy over abortion? State your views on abortion and give *logical, rational* support for your views. Now, take the other position and give *logical, rational* support for that view.

11. Can you imagine under what conditions abortion will no longer be such a controversial issue? Explain.

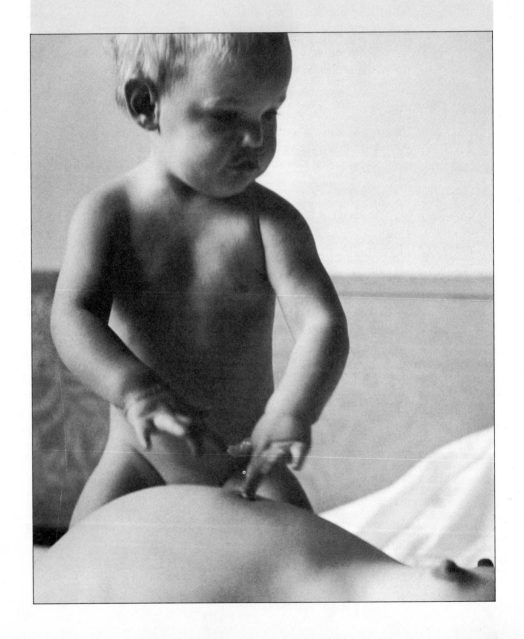

Having Children and Being Parents

We are born as males or females, and as we grow up we develop the ability to reproduce. The female is born with close to half a million maturing egg cells, which her two ovaries start releasing, one at a time, when she reaches puberty. From approximately ages 15 to 50, the female has the potential of becoming pregnant. The male, from puberty to old age, releases several million sperm each time he ejaculates. Thus the female could hypothetically produce thirty to forty children and the male could be fertile for more than three-fourths of his life.

However, for humans, reproduction and parenting is not simply a matter of biology. Each society and culture has established a set of expectations, customs, and laws about who should have children, when they should become parents, and how many children they should have. Although some people are forbidden to marry and reproduce, once marriage has been legally approved in any culture, "parenthood is an accepted normal feature of the adult role" (Callan, 1986, p. 261).

THE DECISION TO HAVE CHILDREN

"It has been suggested that biologically, socially, and psychologically we have little choice in having children" (Callan, 1986, p. 261). Some people believe that an innate biological drive leads couples to procreate. They may believe that women possess a "mothering instinct" that makes them want to have children. Certainly society fosters this notion. "The childless woman has been portrayed as selfish, irresponsible, immature, abnormal, unnatural or neurotic" (Hoffman & Levant, 1985, p. 197). Many parents have children for psychological reasons, such as fulfillment, companionship, the need for someone to carry on the family name, social status, giving meaning to their lives, or the desire to have a family similar to (or different from) the one in which they grew up. Although most of the women in a recent study did not view parenthood as mandatory and one-fifth expressed no desire for children of their own (Cook, West, & Hamner, 1982), only about 5 percent of couples in our society actually remain child-free voluntarily (Leslie & Leslie, 1980).

Many factors play a part in the decision to become a parent. Some have a positive and others a negative effect. LeMasters and DeFrain (1983) observed a number of these influences:

1. Modern medicine has decreased the number and severity of childhood diseases. Therefore, parents can assume with some certainty that their

children will live to adulthood and may not feel the need to have so many children.

2. The affluence of our society allows parents to provide more material goods for their children. Some may want children because they can provide for them. Others may delay parenting or limit their families in order to provide more for one or two children.

3. Contraception allows couples to regulate the number and spacing of their children.

4. Two factors—higher standards for parents and marital instability—make parenting more difficult. Feminism and the women's movement have had both a negative and a positive effect on parenting. Early feminists denounced motherhood as unfulfilling, burdensome, and noncreative. More recent attitudes have redefined motherhood as a worthwhile endeavor and are asking why the role of the father should not be expanded.

A few couples decide before marriage how many children they want (Ory, 1977), particularly those who do not want any children at all. People who want more than the two-child norm are usually the ones who discuss their goals before marriage (Oakley, 1985). Generally, though, those who have children see the benefits of having parenting as outweighing the costs. Educated, professional women who had decided not to have children perceived that the restrictions, disruptions, and general life-style costs associated with child rearing greatly outweighed the emotional and psychological satisfactions. Those who were postponing parenthood rated emotional factors such as making them feel closer to their spouse, bringing more fulfillment, and giving more incentive to life higher than those who wanted no children. They were also less enthusiastic about the value of work (Callan, 1986). Education level is the factor that most affects the age at which a woman has her first child. The average age of first-time mothers in 1980 was 23.5 (Bloom, 1986).

Husbands may have their own reasons for wanting children. Because of men's increased interest in becoming active fathers and participating in child-rearing duties, parenthood is having a bigger impact on their lives. However, although many men may want their wives to become mothers, they do not necessarily want to share equally in the work of parenting. Stammel (1982) asks, "Why do men suddenly want to be fathers? Especially when a lot of women don't want to be mothers" (p. 109). While some men are interested simply in becoming fathers, others—childless and already in their thirties—may be concerned about spending their later years sick and alone. Quoting a psychologist friend, Stammel (1982) suggests three possible explanations for the increased male interest in parenting: (1) as a reaction against the women's movement and women's careerist goals, (2) males' longing to recapture childhood, and (3) their wish to enjoy the kind of intimate connection they feel they are living without in this decade of opportunism.

For women, societal pressures to have children are strong, and those who do not want them may find it extremely difficult to explain their feelings to their spouses (Carter, 1984). The main reason some women do not want to have children is that they want to have careers. Along with age at marriage, working has the biggest influence on the timing of first-time motherhood. Women who work outside the home are more apt to delay the birth of their first child (Teachman & Polonko, 1985).

PREGNANCY AND BIRTH

Pregnancy can be an exciting time for the expectant mother and father. However, they both must work at keeping this a happy time. While many women enjoy a healthy pregnancy, some are plagued with problems ranging from morning sickness, fluid retention, heartburn, fatigue, hemorrhoids, and sleeplessness to severe depression. One of the best ways to ensure that pregnancy is a healthy time is to establish healthful eating and exercising habits before conception (Walker, Yoffe, & Gray, 1979). Pregnant women should also see their doctors regularly.

Attitude can make a big difference both for the mother and the father. Often the planning and excitement of pregnancy give the expectant mother a positive outlook that carries over into her feelings about herself. Some women, however, feel concerned about their appearance, do not really understand the changes taking place in their bodies, and may have a hard time accepting their pregnant selves. They may have fears about the childbirth process and concerns about their

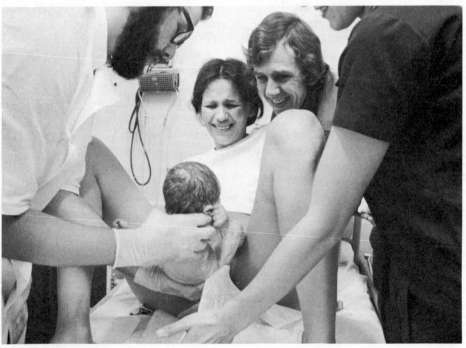

"She's ours, all ours. . . . Isn't she beautiful?"

abilities as mothers. Husbands, too, reflect such attitudes. Those who are excited about the new child are apt to be more positive and more helpful to their spouses. Those who did not want the pregnancy or feel that everyone's attention is now focused on the expected child may feel resentful and neglected. The husband may be worried about his wife's health or about adapting to the new role of father.

A husband may feel that his only duty is to provide financial support for the new baby. While one sometimes hears that a pregnancy can bring a couple closer together, the opposite often happens.

One way to alleviate the difficulties is to learn more about childbirth and parenting. Preparation for childbirth, Lamaze classes, for example, offer the expectant parents an opportunity to learn about the process. The mother learns exercises and breathing routines to use during labor. Her partner serves as her coach and becomes part of the birth process, monitoring his wife's progress, coaching her efforts, and giving her emotional support. The couple functions as a team. Being present at the child's birth also gives the father an opportunity to participate in the bonding that is said to occur shortly after birth. In bonding, the infant and parent are said to react to one another's smell, touch, body warmth, and voices, so that they form an attachment (Ambron, 1975).

A father who was present at the birth of his child tends to see himself as having a greater number of functions than one who was not (Cordell, Parke, & Sawin, 1980). Such fathers feel more supportive and helpful and participate in more child care.

All mothers do not react in the same way to the birth process. On the one hand, some find the pain of labor and birth very hard to bear while others find it to be minimal. Reactions to pain may depend on the length of labor, the preparation for childbirth, the emotional state of the mother, the mother's attitude toward pain, and whether or not sedation or anesthetic is used. Some mothers are ecstatic about the actual experience of giving birth, while others are simply anxious to get the ordeal over with so they can see their new baby.

The birth process takes place in three stages. The transition stage is the series of contractions before the birth. It may take anywhere from two to thirty-six hours. During this time the baby moves into position and the head enters the birth canal. Sometimes the mother may feel despair, anger, isolation, or loss of control over the management of her contractions during this stage. During the second stage, the baby moves through the birth canal and is born. Some mothers find this the most difficult part, but others feel elated during the actual birth. The third stage, after the birth, involves the expulsion of the placenta or afterbirth (Figure 12.1).

While most births take place in the delivery room of a hospital, some hospitals now offer a birthing room, which is decorated to look like a home bedroom. Some parents prefer this reassuring atmosphere to the stark look of the traditional delivery room. Some hospitals allow the baby to room with the mother during their stay. A few couples are choosing to have their children at home with the help of a midwife. However, it is generally considered prudent, when childbirth is imminent, to be in or very near a hospital in the event that unforeseen complications should arise.

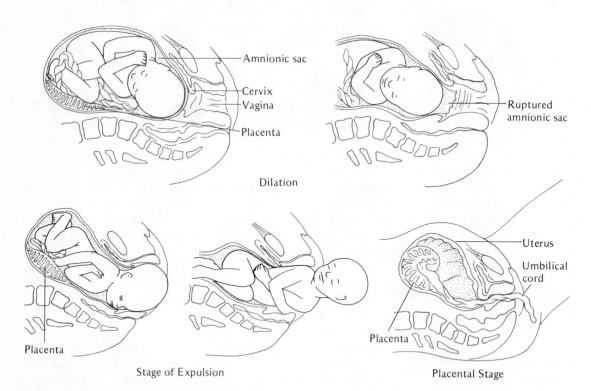

FIGURE 12.1   THE BIRTH PROCESS.

SOURCE: Harmatz & Novak, 1983, p. 165.

ADJUSTING TO PARENTHOOD

Cultural myths portray the period following childbirth as an idyllic one (Gilliam, 1981), and it is certainly true that having a new baby in the home is an exciting, happy time. However, the transition to parenthood is not simple. "New parents face two critical challenges: making the transition to parenthood successfully, and giving their babies the care and guidance needed to thrive" (Cudaback, Darden, Nelson, O'Brien, Pinsky, & Wiggins, 1985). These researchers contend that although experts know much about these two challenges, parents themselves are receiving little information. In fact, it has been found that mothers know little more about child development than do fathers (Kliman & Vukelich, 1985). Fathers tend to turn to professional and written material for information, while new mothers rely on their own mothers and their physicians for advice. These researchers suggest that having realistic expectations about their child's development can help both mother and father become better parents.

Expectations about how a newborn will affect their lives may play a part, too. While most couples predicted the changes in their lives fairly well, those who found that their new lives were not what they had expected felt a decrease in marital satisfaction and love, an increase in conflict and feelings of ambivalence, and a decrease in efforts to work at the relationship (Belskey, Lang, & Rovine, 1985).

Often new parents face crises they do not know how to handle, such as infant illness or injury. They may not know what to do if their child cries a great deal or is otherwise difficult. What's more, they may find advice from doctors, books, and family to be less than adequate. To compound the problem, they may feel inadequate as parents if they have to admit that they have questions or concerns (McKim, 1987).

One aspect of the transition to parenthood that has received considerable attention from researchers in the past decade is the change in the couple's relationship as a result of a first child. Most research has found that marital satisfaction tends to decrease after the first child arrives, especially for women (Belsky et al., 1985). Also, mothers, especially those with two children or male children, reported less marital satisfaction and cohesion than did child-free wives, primarily in the areas of sex and affection (Abbott & Brody, 1985). They suggest that young boys are more demanding than young girls. Not surprisingly, mothers of one child who feel less positive about the benefits of that child to the marriage, who feel bored in the care of the child, who feel they received little help from their husbands, or who feel incompetent are less likely to want another baby (Callan, 1985).

When new babies arrive home from the hospital, they need constant care. Usually the mother assumes most or all of this responsibility—feeding, diapering, doing laundry, and picking up as well as holding, cuddling, and playing with the baby. Motherhood is romanticized, but in reality there is a lot of drudgery involved. Bernard (1974) observes that motherhood is "often tremendously disappointing on a work a day basis, in some vital way promising renewal, and then often letting you down, or, perhaps more exactly, weighing you down with the minutiae of the child care routine" (p. 77).

The drudgery can have numerous consequences. It may cause distinct stereotypical sex-role divisions, since a mother may care for the baby around the clock and any "help" from her husband is often seen as a gift (Green, 1976). The new mother may become physically and emotionally drained, leaving her less energy for her husband and other aspects of her life. Therefore, interaction between the couple is decreased—they may spend less time together and participate in fewer social outings. Their frequency of intercourse often decreases as well, and they may have to arrange their time to maintain their sexual lives. In addition, a mother may feel isolated if she has given up her job or has little contact with other adults. While new mothers have more negative responses about parenthood, such as depression and decreased marital satisfaction, than new fathers, they also report more positive items and view themselves as better parents (Wilkie & Ames, 1986).

The father's transition may be quite different from the mother's. His transition is likely to be slower; his first step may be becoming aware of his role as provider. While he may participate in the birth and early child care, it may not be to the extent he expected (Cowan, Cowan, Heming, Garrett, Coysh, Curtis-Boles, & Boles, 1985).

For some families, the adjustments may result in a crisis; for others, they may

The birth of a child may disrupt the aspirations and ambitions of a young couple.

BOX 12.1   "NOT NOW, HONEY, THE BABY'S CRYING . . ."

This is the title of an article by Hester Mundis (1983) in which she discusses how lovemaking sessions do not need to become only a memory when you have children. She feels that romance can be put back into marriage without shortchanging the kids. Not all of these suggestions will be acceptable to all parents. However, all parents need to weigh the importance of their sex lives carefully for the continued happiness of their marriage. Without a happy marriage, neither you nor the children will have a happy family life. "You should know it's [your marriage] in trouble if your kid asks, 'Mom, where did I come from?' and you can't remember" (p. 97).

Some ideas for your consideration are:

Keep your bedroom door locked at all times. You are entitled to your privacy and the children will come to respect it once they are part of the household routine.

"Saturday morning cartoons can do more for your sex life than Masters and Johnson" (p. 97). After some juice and cold cereal with milk by the TV, you may be able to spend a couple of hours together without interference.

Trade off baby-sitting with other parents in a similar situation. For older ages, this may even include some overnights, thus providing you with a whole night of romance. Grandparents and a portable crib can also be very handy.

An occasional night out, with a baby-sitter at home, may be well worth the price of a dinner and a motel room. The cost may be much less than that of a marriage counselor and definitely much more beneficial and enjoyable.

be only transitional. Whatever the view of the adjustment period, new parents have a number of tasks to accomplish. They must devote time to the new baby yet allow themselves time to be alone and together as a couple. They must find space in the home to accommodate the new baby and all the paraphernalia necessary for the baby's care. They must adjust their budget to allow room for the child's mounting needs. They must develop patience for a child who may or may not be cooperative.

Jimenez (1984) suggests setting aside at least one evening a week to work on the couple relationship. "After all," she says, "this is where the family began" (p. 123). In addition, the couple should think of each other as man and woman, as husband and wife and not only as father and mother; they should communicate openly and express love for each other.

Most new parents report their new roles as positive ones. They find a sense of fulfillment, a new meaning to their life, and an expansion of their view of the world. Some find that their marital bonds are strengthened. Some feel they have better family cohesion because they can now understand their own parents better (Miller & Sollie, 1980). The interaction of the mother, father, and child can engender affection and warmth and add a feeling of contentment and happiness to the marriage. Parents may derive pride and satisfaction in identifying with their child.

Good advice—something your children disregard but save to give to their children.

"The thing that impresses me about America is the way parents obey their children." —DUKE OF WINDSOR

Second thought: Giving children everything they want, when they want it, is a form of child abuse. —FRANK TYGER

BEING PARENTS

In general, the parent's goal is to assist the child in meeting and accomplishing developmental tasks or goals, so that eventually the child has the skills and competencies to function sufficiently in the adult world. According to Benson (1968), this "parentwork" includes a number of elements. First, parents must provide for the physical needs (food, shelter, clothing, and so on) of their children. Second, they must provide positive guidance, teaching and modeling socially and morally acceptable attitudes and behaviors. Third, they must provide discipline and help in matters which go beyond basic survival. Fourth, they must love, want, and respect their children as they mature. Last, parents need to train their children for eventual independence and release them from the proverbial "apron strings."

The trouble with being a parent is that by the time you're experienced, you're unemployed.

One youngster to another: "Want to have a big laugh? Ask your parents where you came from."

Adult education is what goes on constantly in a household containing adolescents.

TEAMWORK

Parents can make their roles somewhat easier if mother and father work together as a team. For one thing, fathers can provide unique experiences for their infants and an extra source of stimulation. Babies 7 to 8 months of age can become as attached to their fathers as they are to their mothers (Ricks, 1985). For another, consistency in parenting is important if children are to understand what is right and wrong and what is expected of them. In addition, parents who work together can bolster each other in their roles and reinforce each other's confidence through cooperation (Benson, 1968). Generally, parents who agree on child-rearing practices are likely to be better parents—even if their parenting practices are not the best.

OBSTACLES

Parents today are faced with a number of obstacles in their efforts to do what they feel is right for their children. For instance, society promotes consumption of material goods, so parents often feel pressured to buy toys, clothes, and other items that their children don't need. In fact, parents may become so concerned with being able to provide material goods that they fail to provide adequate nurturance and emotional security for their children.

The media, particularly television, pose other problems for parents. In addition to encouraging children to want to buy products that they do not really need, programs can influence children in other ways. Small children may take what they see literally and uncritically. They may use violent or stereotypical "heroes" as their role models. TV can become a substitute for active play and can impede creativity (Singer & Singer, 1981). Parents need to regulate their children's viewing and discuss the programs they do watch with their children so the children gain a good perspective.

TV may have an influence on parenting patterns too. Dail and Way (1985) found that, in family programs, the parental role is exhibited almost 32 times per hour and child-rearing patterns nearly 28 times per hour. Moreover, the shows portray men as more active, nurturing parents than women and children as responding more positively toward men.

Because of competition in today's society, parents may be tempted to push their children into excelling in school, social skills, and sports. This can be harmful for the child who has less interest in the activity than the parent might like. Expectations to excel are placed on parents, too. Society seems to say that good parents have good children, so parents are often blamed for their children's deviant behavior. Books offer a variety of models for good parenting and suggest that with certain techniques, the job can be accomplished. However, experts differ on their approaches to rearing children and opinions change from one decade to another. Even if a technique works for one child in a given family, it may not work for another. In truth, children experience many influences other than that of their parents which may contribute to their attitudes and behaviors.

PARENTING MODELS

"Two false assumptions have pervaded American attitudes toward families and child rearing: that the ability to raise children wisely is a natural talent possessed by most parents, and that child rearing is always a joyful, positive experience. Parenting is a complex and difficult task" (Larsen & Juhasz, 1985, p. 823).

A fallen woman today is a mother whose children didn't pick up their toys.

It had been a trying day for the young mother and housewife. As she tucked her small boy into bed, she sighed. "Well, I've certainly worked from son-up to son-down today."
                                                        —HENRY LEABO

A friend of ours says that her children are just the right age: Too old to cry at night and too young to borrow the family car.

Fathers are a biological necessity but a social accident.
                                                        —MARGARET MEAD

A youngster complained to a friend: "My dad wants me to have all the things he never had as a boy—including five A's on my report card."

A teenager is a youngster who has a father to tell him what to do—and a mother who does it for him.   —DAN BENNETT

Numerous experts in child development and parenting have offered theories in good parenting. They range from authoritarian to permissive models. Authoritarian parents consider obedience very important and physical force as a reasonable means to achieve it. Your parents probably grew up in this type of environment. Permissiveness allows children to regulate themselves as much as possible. Parents offer themselves as resources but do not actively modify or shape the child's behavior (Carter & Welch, 1981). Because this model was popular in the 1960s, perhaps your parents reared you with this theory in mind.

More recent approaches have taken a middle ground and stressed certain special aspects of the parent-child relationship. Behavior modification, for example, stresses the use of praise and reinforcement when children behave in ways that parents approve. This positive view of the child will contribute to his or her positive self-image. It is hoped that in this way children learn to understand that their parents love them for themselves rather than for their behavior. This approach means that parents must decide what behavior is good, must be attentive to what their children are doing, must decide what types of reinforcements to use, and must be prepared to exercise lots of patience. In other words, they must be highly motivated to work together and to be consistent.

Parent Effectiveness Training (PET; Gordon, 1970) stresses good communication with children, especially good listening techniques. Parents need to pay careful attention to what their children say and to try to understand the feelings contained in the message. For example, a child may slam the door behind him, throw his books down, and exclaim, "School is the pits!" The parent might respond, "It seems you are upset by what went on at school today." In this way, both the content of the child's message and the feeling behind his actions are acknowledged and validated, and the parent has given the child both opportunity to

Facial expressions express most eloquently the quality of this father-son relationship.

elaborate upon his feelings. Through this technique, it is felt, parents can establish and maintain good relationships with their children and be supportive and accepting. They learn to maintain an active and genuine interest in their children and never use things that their children may say against them at a later time. Gordon (1970) says that PET encourages children to express their feelings openly, to work through their feelings, and to be less afraid of negative feelings and that it promotes a warmer relationship between children and parents; causes the parent-child relationship to become a reciprocal one in that children learn to listen to their parents and accept their feelings; and encourages children to think for themselves and solve their own problems.

Other researchers have observed that while some families spend a lot of time in the same room, they are not really spending time together. These researchers concluded that the amount of time families spend together is not as important as what they do together (Muenchow, 1983). Quality time with children can be enhanced if parents plan some time alone with their children, so that they are able to interact rather than merely sitting side by side. Activities should be the kind that both parents and children enjoy; children can sense if their parents are not enthusiastic or are forcing themselves to participate. A relaxed attitude can be important. Sometimes just being there—sitting down with a child right after work or school to share joys and problems—can be more rewarding than an expensive family vacation. Doing projects together—raking the yard or doing the dishes—offers time to accomplish a chore, to talk, and to teach children how to work together and to accept responsibility.

"Empathy—the ability to step outside yourself and share the feelings of another person—is the central concept underlying much of the recent work in parent-child communication" (Schuman, 1983, p. 142). Schuman says that being able to express empathy does not come naturally. Parents must work hard to place themselves in their children's shoes and understand why they are angry, upset, or uncooperative. For example, if a small child begins to cry about having to leave friends to come in for dinner, instead of saying, "You have to eat. Dinner will get cold," say, "Oh, it makes you very sad to quit playing now, doesn't it?" This way, your child knows you understand. Just the understanding may be enough to stop the uncooperative behavior. In turn, parents can tell their children how *they* are feeling and what they expect from their children.

Giving children support and encouragement can sometimes go too far. Parents may feel anxious that their children won't be the best in activities ranging from giving up the bottle and being potty trained to achieving the best grades and becoming a super athlete in school (Spock, 1985). Children who are pushed too hard, who are driven by their parents' desire for them to excel, he says, "may become somewhat self-centered, humorless, joyless and unsociable" (Spock, 1985, p. 150). The children, in turn, may feel that their parents only love them for what they can accomplish and not for themselves. They may have a sense of failure if they don't live up to parental expectations.

Overall, children should be allowed to explore and learn new things for themselves yet have parental support to help them set goals and to provide help when necessary. Children need to have limits set for them by parents, so they know what behavior is acceptable and what is not. Yet they also need the freedom to make their own mistakes and to learn from those mistakes. Parents can often be effective by pointing out the consequences of certain behavior. Parents have a number of resources available to them. Family-structure resources include parental income, education, and occupation; family-process resources include parental help, time, and attention (Amato & Ochiltree, 1986). These researchers found that both sets of resources contribute to a child's ability to develop competence. The family-process resources of both the mother and father are especially important to the development of a child's self-esteem.

There seems to be a need for parenting education and parenting models accessible and understandable to average parents. Such information should be uniformly available to all classes, races, locales, and so on. However, most parent-education efforts originate in the middle class; hence the values of that class are dominant (Harman & Brim, 1980). Unfortunately, those who need help the most may not seek it at all. Generally, parents seek help with specific problems; they do not look for information about parenting models.

PARENTING THE GROWING CHILD

There are many books in the libraries and bookstores on caring for newborns, child development, and dealing with behavior problems of small children. Numerous home economics and psychology courses are available at the high school and especially college levels dealing with these subjects. Learning about child development, in fact, is a very important aspect of being a good parent.

You can tell that a child is growing up when he/she stops asking where he/she came from and starts refusing to tell where he/she is going.

Adolescence is like a hitch in the army—you'd hate to have missed it and you'd hate to repeat it.

Youth is such a wonderful exciting time, it is a shame it has to be wasted on the young people. —G. B. SHAW

Compared to the parenting of small children, little information is available about the parenting of adolescents. Yet this can be a trying time for both parents and their offspring. Although the early teen years may seem like a long time ago in your life, you probably remember some of the feelings you experienced during high school. Imagine—the next time you go through this experience will be from a parent's point of view.

Gaining independence is an important goal for teens. They must come to an understanding and acceptance of themselves as independent people, separate and distinct from their families. Families that allow young people increasing amounts of responsibility as they grow in age and ability while also offering support and understanding when needed, will usually have little difficulty accepting and supporting their youngsters' moves toward independence in adolescence. However, a family that is authoritarian will be less accepting of this move toward independence and may make the process difficult.

As part of their quest for independence, teenagers begin to turn away from their families as sources of information and support and to turn to their friends. While they may continue to rely on their parents for financial, educational, and career matters, they turn to their peers in social matters (Sebald, 1986). Often adolescents embrace the values and styles of the peer group with such fierce loyalty that parents feel threatened. "There may be a lack of fit between adult expectations of adolescents, adolescents' expectations of themselves, and adolescents' capabilities" (Newman, 1985, p. 643). What happens is that the adolescent is trying to achieve control while the parents are trying to maintain control. Both need to adjust to the shifting responsibility. As reported by adolescents in one study, the greatest conflicts with parents centered around parental orders or demands, disapproval of their friends, and disagreement regarding parental preferences for the teen's hairstyle and clothing (Clemons & Rust, 1979).

In general, adolescent values are different from adult values but not necessarily antagonistic to the values of the majority of adults. This difference can cause difficulty when adolescents are continually held dependent and deprived of rights granted to adults (Klein, 1975) or when they receive little positive attention from their parents. Sometimes, when whole groups of teens are made to feel very different from and unacceptable to society, they may adopt delinquent patterns of behavior. For example, Duncan (1978) found that delinquent suburban adolescent males held significantly more negative attitudes toward their parents. Smith and Walters (1978) found delinquency among adolescent males to be related to lack of a warm, loving, and supportive relationship with the father.

> *A definition of a teenager: A young person who gets blamed for acting the way his parents did when they were his age.*

> *Cosmetics are beauty products used by teenagers to make them look older sooner, and by their mothers to make them look younger longer.*

> *Husband to wife as they leave baby-sitter with young son and start out for the evening: "I still say that when they begin asking for a blonde instead of a brunette, they're old enough to stay alone!"*

For the most part, teens choose styles, fads, and activities with their peers as part of their effort to achieve independence. Parents who can tolerate such exploration yet remain open and accepting are likely to have closer parent-child relationships. Adolescents who perceive their parents as supporting, willing to let go, and prepared to spend time with them have higher self-esteem (Gecas & Schwalbe, 1986). Those who grow up in a warm and accepting environment develop lower rates of anxiety and higher rates of extroversion (Kawash, 1982). Parents need to realize that their influence and values are still important to their children and that ultimately their children will accept values and life-styles similar to those of their parents. Interestingly, socialization can be a two-way process. Adolescents, it is found, often affect their parents' attitudes on such subjects as sports, leisure, minority groups, youth, drugs, and sex (Peters, 1985).

PASSAGE TO ADULTHOOD

The teen years may be confusing for adolescents. They are trying to progress from childhood to adulthood. Yet no specific event marks that transformation. "Adult" privileges and responsibilities are granted at different ages and by different groups (parents, legislators, teachers, and so on). For instance, the rights to obtain a driver's license, seek employment, sign contracts, vote, join the military, marry, leave school, and buy alcoholic beverages may all come at different times, depending on locale.

The discrepancy between puberty (biological maturation) and the societally

"Look Mom, Dad. We grew up!" To what extent do clothes make people?

accepted age of maturation (usually 21) is eight to ten years. During this period, the young person appears to be an adult physically but is restricted socially. Occupational access is limited, academic pursuits are mandatory, and interpersonal relationships, including sexual ones, are not taken seriously by adults unless they produce some unexpected, undesirable consequences. Teens may be expected to serve in the armed forces, but they may not have the right to drink beer. When they are receiving such contradictory messages, it is little wonder that adolescents have difficulties deciding where they fit in.

Teens often turn to certain behaviors to exhibit their ability to act as adults. For example, Klein (1975) points out that adolescents are especially attracted to sports cars for several reasons: Advertising for such cars promotes an image of autonomy and power; sports cars are symbols of status during a time when status is difficult to attain; and teens in an affluent society often have more disposable income to spend on such luxuries than do many adults.

Drinking is another way to identify with an adult life-style. Adolescents see a can of beer in the hand as a sign of independence and a method of being accepted into peer groups. Young people who are more likely to use alcohol have been found to place a lower value on achievement (and to expect it less), to have less parental support and control, to experience lower compatibility of their views with those of their parents but greater influence from peers and friends, and to value independence more highly (Jessor & Jessor, 1975).

Sex is another activity that becomes important to young people in their transition from childhood to adulthood. Adolescents are seldom told by parents or other adults that sexual thoughts, fantasies of a variety of sexual activities, and nocturnal dreams to the point of orgasm are a natural and normal part of growing up. Instead, they are merely informed that sex is reserved for married people. This may make sexual activity more attractive for teens seeking independence and adult status (Jessor & Jessor, 1975).

While decisions and behaviors regarding driving, drinking, sex, and many other activities are difficult for teenagers, they are also worrisome to parents. Their worries are threefold: (1) they want their children to be safe; as a car accident or a pregnancy can be devastating to both the teen and the family; (2) they may fear that their children will be arrested or get into trouble; and (3) they want their children to learn to make responsible, mature decisions that will lead them to a happy life. Yet parents often feel helpless to intervene. They can't accompany a teenage daughter on her dates or ride along when a son goes to a party with friends. They can, however, be available for their children; they can talk about issues and express their views. Even if the parent and teen can only agree to disagree, they have accomplished a great deal. Parents can lend support to their teens in making decisions, comfort them during trying times, and praise them for accomplishments. Perhaps by remembering how they felt about growing up when they were in junior high and high school parents can more easily relate to their children when they, in turn, face similar problems.

Adolescents as Individuals   In addition to becoming adults, adolescents are becoming individuals. They are absorbing the values they have learned from family, friends, church, school, and media and are deciding for themselves what they believe and value. The perceived values of the adolescent, according to Jessor and Jessor (1975), include a more mature status, a sense of independence and autonomy, the capability for interpersonal intimacy, respect from the peer group, the feeling of being sexually attractive, rejection of conventional and societal restrictions, and affirmation of sexual identity.

Autonomy can be perceived in three overlapping but distinct categories—emotional, behavioral, and value-oriented (Douvan & Adelson, 1966). "Emotional autonomy" refers to giving up childhood dependencies and learning to regard parents as friends and confidants instead of models. "Behavioral autonomy" refers to behavior based on decisions that the adolescent has made. Parents have

BOX 12.2   FOR MY PARENTS

I am a teenager and this is what I want:

I want time to be alone—alone with my thoughts.
I want to be accepted for what I am.
I want to be loved by those who brought me into this world.
I want a home that is rich in honesty, sharing, and caring.
I want to be heard: I just might have something to say that you need to hear.
I want to know more about myself—my sexuality, my desires, my goals.
I want to know God and worship Him in my own way.
I want to live my life one day at a time; for only then will I know its fullness.
As I would live my life for me, so would I have you live your life for you.

—Anonymous

BOX 12.3   FOR OUR TEENAGERS

Someday when my children are old enough to understand the logic that motivates a mother, I will tell them:

I loved you enough to ask where you are going, with whom, and what time you would be home.
I loved you enough to insist that you save your money and buy a bike for yourself even though we could afford to buy one for you.
I loved you enough to be silent and let you discover that your new best friend was a creep.
I loved you enough to make you take a Milky Way back to the drugstore (with a bite out of it) and tell the clerk, "I stole this yesterday and want to pay for it."
I loved you enough to stand over you for two hours while you cleaned your room, a job that would have taken me 15 minutes.
I loved you enough to let you see anger, disappointment and tears in my eyes. Children must learn that their parents aren't perfect.
I loved you enough to let you assume the responsibility for your actions even when the penalties were so harsh they almost broke my heart.
But most of all, I loved you enough to say NO when I knew you would hate me for it. Those were the most difficult battles of all. I'm glad I won them, because in the end you won something, too.

—Anonymous

to set limits for their teens yet keep in mind both the changing times and the changes in their growing offspring and allow them to gradually make their own decisions. "Value autonomy" refers to an adolescent's examination of the values held by parents and peers and ultimately selecting a set of values for his or her own life.

Teens and parents both may suffer from growing pains during this time of their lives. However, overall, teens provide a positive psychological self-portrait of themselves (Offer, Ostrov, & Howard, 1981). These researchers focused on five aspects of the self in a study of over 20,000 teens. The psychological self appears generally strong, with a positive self-image and a general feeling of being in control. The social self is work-oriented (that is, reflects a wish to work rather than be supported), makes friends easily, and enjoys the company of peers. The sexual self likes the recent bodily changes and finds having a friend of the opposite sex to be important. The familial self perceives no major problems between parents and self, perceiving the parents' pride as well as a sense of closeness with the parents. Over three-fourths of these teenagers say they would like their own families to be similar to their families of origin. The coping self shows a little more negativism. Males have more faith in their coping abilities while females rate higher on the affiliative aspects. About one-fifth feel empty emotionally and confused about their coping selves.

Adolescents, then, seem to be functioning quite well in a rapidly changing society and are managing to adapt admirably to the problems they encounter on their way to adulthood.

THE END OF ACTIVE PARENTHOOD

Your goal as a parent is to work yourself out of a job by rearing children to be independent adults and make lives of their own. However, the time when they actually move out of the home can bring mixed emotions for parents. The term "empty-nest syndrome" suggests that parents whose last child has just left home may suffer depression and have to make readjustments.

> *A definition of middle age: The difficult period between juvenile delinquency and senior citizenship when you have to take care of yourself.*

> *Our generation never got a break. When we were young they taught us to respect our elders, and now that we are older they tell us to listen to the youth.* —SEITTER

> *Time the subtle thief of youth.* —MILTON

> *Fun is like insurance—the older you get the more it costs.*
> —NANCE

It may be true that "Life begins at forty," but everything else starts to wear out, fall out or spread out. . . .

For the most part, mothers are more likely to experience the symptoms of the empty-nest syndrome. Denied important roles outside the home, many women have made a career of parenting. They have put most of their time and energy into rearing their children, and now that role is removed. To complicate matters, they are apt to be experiencing menopause at approximately the same time. Therefore, they may experience not only emotional stress of loss of self-esteem but also physical changes and the feeling that old age is upon them. The lack of children in the home brings social changes as well. The mother may no longer face the work and responsibility of full-time parenting, but she also loses her social position. Activities such as school club meetings, committee meetings, and sports, drama, or music events are gone. Therefore, she must find a new niche. She may turn to community, volunteer, or political work, go back to school, develop skills and hobbies, begin a new career, or resume a former job. In many ways these difficulties are a twentieth-century phenomenon and are somewhat limited to white women (Borland, 1982). In any case, this period of adjustment is relatively short-lived (six to eighteen months) and is not necessarily a stressful time or a major threat for most women (Harkins, 1978).

The father is less likely to feel as great a sense of loss as his children leave home. While he may feel saddened by the decline of his parental role, his primary role is usually that of breadwinner. Therefore, he may feel a greater loss when he retires later in life. However, the empty nest may trigger a sense of regret that he has fed too much energy into his job and not spent enough time with his family over the years. His opportunity to interact with his children on a day-to-day basis is gone. His feelings may be compounded if he believes that he has reached his peak, or even a stalemate, in his career. Like his wife, he may turn to other activities to fill the void.

If the children go off to college and return home for the summers, the transition to the empty nest may occur more gradually. However, students moving back home can cause stress in the family. They have no doubt established themselves as adults, because they have been living somewhat on their own. They have established their own routines and life-styles. Their parents, on the other hand, may still claim at least some authority over their behavior and a great deal of say as to what goes on in their home. Therefore, parents and college students need to establish some ground rules about guests, parties, hours, noise level, and the sharing of household duties before the students come home so as to avoid as many disagreements as possible.

Since families tend to be smaller today, children often leave home while their parents are still quite young. This gives the average couple more than twenty years together after their children are grown. The result is a diamond-shaped pattern of interaction between married couples over the span of their lives together (Spanier & Lewis, 1980). As young couples, they are generally very close, but as children come into their lives, their roles differentiate and they drift further apart.

After their children leave home, they have a chance to reestablish the closeness that characterized their early relationship.

Becoming close again does not automatically happen nor is it necessarily easy. "Marriage in the later years is not merely the extension of marriage in the early years. . . . Not only do the circumstances differ, but it appears that marriage partners too differ in some very important ways" (Zube, 1982, p. 147). These may include differing goals, values, world views, and patterns of social interaction, any of which could affect the marital relationship. The husband may tend to move toward interpersonal commitments while the wife now focuses her attention outside the home. These changes can be exciting opportunities for both if the husband and wife can understand and appreciate each other. With improved lines of communication and information sharing, most stress can be alleviated and the couple can confidently look forward to sharing their sunset years.

Summary

- Even though our society is pronatalist, the decision of whether or not to have children is up to each couple.

- There are many reasons to have children and many reasons not to have them.

- A positive attitude, preparation, and couple closeness can help make the times of pregnancy and birth go more smoothly.

- A couple will find that their life-style changes upon the arrival of a child. They need to adjust to their new roles and still maintain closeness between themselves.

- Parents are expected to provide for their children's physical needs, as well as to teach, discipline, and love them.

- Parenting can be made easier when a couple works together as a team and avoids societal pressures.

- Several parenting models have been proposed. Most of those accepted today rank somewhere between authoritarianism and permissiveness and stress a good parent-child relationship.

- Overall, parents should provide guidelines for their children but also allow children opportunities to learn.

- A child's teen years may be especially trying for parents because teens turn away from their families to gain independence and establish their own identities.

- Teens are often confused because they are granted some adult privileges but denied others.

- The end of active parenting is another change for couples. Some adapt to the empty nest more easily than others.

PERSPECTIVE: PARENTHOOD—COSTS AND BENEFITS

LIMITED 1-YEAR WARRANTY

This product is warranted for 1 year from date of purchase against defects in material and workmanship. This warranty does not cover damage caused by misuse or negligence. If the unit fails to operate during the warranty period, notify (name of company) for repair or replacement without charge at the manufacturer's option. If any components must be replaced, the transportation costs for returning the defective components are the responsibility of the consumer. This warranty gives you specific legal rights, and you may also have other rights which vary from state to state.

Children do not come with a warranty—limited or otherwise. A child may be born with a mental or physical handicap. A child may contract a disease that will require long, expensive hospitalization. A few children die because of an illness or accident; the fact that such events are rare is no consolation to those who have lost a child. To be a parent is to make a lifelong commitment. You may change majors and become ex-biologists, ex-home economists, or ex-sociologists. And about 40 percent of you will become ex-spouses through divorce. However, once you are a parent, you are a parent forever. Think about it—parenthood in our society is a much longer commitment than marriage.

As any economist will tell you, good decisions are based on a careful weighing of costs and benefits. Therefore, in deciding whether or not to have children, you need to become aware of the costs and benefits of parenting and then weigh them for yourself. One recent study analyzed the reasons couples gave for wanting or not wanting children and categorized them under pluses and minuses (Ramy & Tavuchis, 1986). The positive values pertaining to the children themselves include:

1. Affect—children are a source of happiness and pleasure.
2. Religion—Religion dictates procreation.
3. Security in old age—a child is someone to depend on in later life.
4. Continuity of family name.
5. Continuity of society.

Positive values related to parenthood include:

1. Civic responsibility—duty to the nation and society.
2. Maturity—childbearing and rearing are signs of adult status.
3. Biological drive—the innate need to reproduce.
4. Generativity—expansion of self through reproduction.
5. Expression of sex roles—fulfillment of one's masculinity and femininity.

The negative aspects associated with having children include:

1. Restriction of freedom.
2. Limit on self-actualization.
3. Competition with conjugal ties.
4. Prevention of child-free life-style.
5. Ecological concerns—zero population growth, population problems.

The authors note that these negative aspects of having children become positive aspects of choosing a child-free life-style because they seem to contribute to the value of the intimate couple relationship.

The financial burdens of having and rearing children, according to economic criteria, can also be divided into direct costs and opportunity costs. Direct costs include dollar amounts spent in caring for children, as on housing, clothing, food, medicine, and so on. Estimates range from $85,000 to nearly $250,000 for each child from birth through college and/or time of marriage. Opportunity costs are the costs involved in spending time and energy caring for children rather than on some other activity, such as work or pastimes. Although children are expensive, direct costs seem to have little bearing on a woman's decision as to whether or not to have children.

Other costs are hard to measure. For instance, studies show that marital happiness declines after the birth of the first child and does not pick up again until the children leave home. Emotional stress can take various forms during the child's growing-up years. Parents of newborns are often overwhelmed by the total dependence of an infant, they may have difficulties adjusting to being a family of three, or they may simply become worn out from lack of sleep. As their children grow, parents often identify with the hurts and traumas their children experience. They feel sad when their child is cut from the basketball team or is the brunt of a bully's prank. As teens develop enough independence to be out on their own, parents often worry about their children's behavior. Those parents who are still in high school themselves are often forced to compromise their own educational futures and may face particularly serious financial problems.

The factors involved in becoming a parent are many. The decision to have or not to have children is certainly not an easy one for those who do make it consciously. And all couples who plan to be responsible parents are obliged to make such a choice. This decision, however, is a personal one that can only be determined by the partners themselves after careful consideration of the benefits and costs of parenting.

QUESTIONS FOR THOUGHT AND DISCUSSION

1. Describe some of the myths that are associated with pregnancy and childbirth. How do they affect the attitudes of the expectant mother and her partner? How do they affect their self-concepts? The way they deal with the pregnancy?

2. What are some of the realities of childbirth and child care? What are the consequences for the mother and father? For their marriage? For their roles?

3. What types of changes take place in a family when a child is born? What kinds of adjustments must be made? Decide which are positive and which are negative.

4. What are some of the factors that play a part in making the decision to be a parent? Are some more powerful than others? Are some more important than others? Explain.

5. What are some of the primary sources of parenting information? How can some of these sources cause problems for parents? Do "different" types of parents select or use different sources? Explain.

6. Why is parenting a difficult task? In answering this question, in addition to the information in the chapter, draw upon your own observations and experiences from your family life.

7. Has parenting become easier or more difficult today than in the past? Explain.

8. Describe the different parenting models. How do they differ? How does each see the parent-child relationship and the role that each person plays?

9. What are some of the problems that parents and teens experience as children grow and move toward independence? How can these problems be handled?

10. What are some benefits of middle age? What are some of the problems or major changes?

11. What is the empty-nest syndrome? How can this syndrome affect a woman in midlife? Why doesn't it usually affect men as much?

12. List some of the most serious costs of parenthood. What do you consider the greatest benefits for parents?

Separation, Divorce, and Remarriage

The royal wedding of Prince Charles and Lady Diana in 1981 captured many people's hearts. Why? Was it the romantic aspect of the gala event? Was it because so many of us want to believe in marriage? What if the princess of Wales were to decide that marriage to the future king of England was not what she thought it would be and file for divorce? What would the reaction be?

Marriage and divorce in our society are legal, emotional, and usually religious processes involving couples. The acts of establishing and terminating marriage are part of the basic framework of practically every society. Both marriage and divorce are surrounded by a variety of values, beliefs, and customs. They indicate the importance of marriage to society and exemplify one way of relating.

WHAT IS DIVORCE?

In Chapter 1, marriage is defined and broken down as follows:

Components	*Definition*
1. Ties to social norms	"A socially sanctioned . . .
2. Action and actors	union of one man and
	one woman . . .
3. Societal/cultural ongoing influences	expected to play the roles
	. . .
4. Definitive cultural labels	of husband and wife."

Marital dissolution involves the same components and can be defined as follows:

Components	*Definition*
1. Ties to social norms	"A socially sanctioned . . .
2. Action and actors	process of legal separation
	of a married man and
	woman . . .
3. Societal/cultural ongoing influences	who are expected to
	redefine their adult roles
	in the following ways:

Components	*Definition*
4. Definitive cultural labels	by learning a new 'single-again' role, by reemphasizing the occupational role, and often by redefining the parent role."

It is important to note that both of these definitions refer to a process and not just an event. "When divorce occurs a decision is made by two people to end the legality and intimacy of their relationship. The legal issue is resolved in the courtroom, but the intimacy must be unwoven piece by piece" (Daniels-Mohring & Berger, 1984, p. 17). The legal dimension of divorce involves the state, which, through the judicial system, allows the marriage contract to be dissolved and declares the individuals free to enter into another marriage—should they so choose. In addition to the legal dimensions of divorce, Bohannan (1971) has identified five other dimensions. The emotional dimension involves the deteriorating interpersonal relationship between the husband and wife. The economic dimension centers around the settlement and bargaining over such items as money, property, alimony, and child support. The co-parental dimension involves child-custody arrangements, visitation rights, and the working out of a new relationship as co-parents. Since the now divorced individuals have related to neighbors, co-workers, and educational and religious institutions as a couple, the community dimension of divorce includes changing relationships with friends and community. Finally, there is a sixth dimension, the psychic divorce, in which the man and woman reestablish individual identities.

The divorce process not only includes components of our society but is also influenced by the norms and values of our culture. And as our cultural values have changed, our attitudes toward marriage and divorce have changed too. As mentioned earlier, the institution of marriage is changing, not dying. Similarly, attitudes and behaviors in relation to divorce are changing—divorce is becoming more widely accepted and practiced. Two themes in 1980s culture—a lack of stability and permanence on the one hand and an emphasis on self-fulfillment on the other—contribute to these changes.

In the 1930s, when your grandparents were getting married, there was a strong emphasis on the durability of products and the belief that things should last a long time. Prized possessions were often handed down from one generation to the next. That philosophy was carried over into the kinds of relationships that people established. Most people believed that marriage should be a lifelong commitment; therefore it was hoped that marriages, like other valued things, would be durable.

Some now see the development in our society of a "throwaway" mentality, where planned obsolescence is the norm and where manufacturers want "no deposit—no return." In a society where it is possible to achieve overnight success and where there is instant everything, people may develop an "if at first you don't succeed—quit" mentality that is likely to carry over to quick divorces rather than efforts to work problems through.

Some people today enter marital relationships with the expectation that they may last for some years but not necessarily a lifetime. This, of course, places a significantly different perspective on marriage, making it more disposable and vulnerable to dissolution.

In today's society, many of our relationships with others are transitory. That is, we often tend to relate to others on the basis of part or parts of their personality or life-style. In many of these relationships, we really don't know much about the other person. It is a functional type of relationship, one that works well in certain settings, such as paying a cashier for your groceries. However, in the relationship of marriage, your failure to know your spouse intimately can lead to big trouble.

From another perspective, we might think of divorce trends as paralleling the growth of the "me" generation. The seventies were years of increased attention to self-actualization and self-fulfillment. People were encouraged to strive for career satisfaction, total sexual fulfillment, healthy bodies, and perfection as parents. One aspect of all this self-fulfillment was a concentration on the self and personal happiness and well-being. Some lines from an article in *New Woman* shows how this attitude carried over to the permanence of marriage:

> Letting go of your marriage—if it is no longer good for you—can be the most successful thing you have ever done. Getting a divorce can be a positive, problem-solving, growth-oriented step. It can be a personal triumph. . . . You have a responsibility to yourself to make the most of your life. (Adam & Adam, 1982, p. 74)

Some experts view this change of attitude as destructive, charging that it is selfish and that it destroys marriage. Other sociologists praise it. They believe that in our society, marriage is so important a source of emotional satisfaction that few people would be able to endure a poor one (Udry, 1974). In fact, it can be argued that the divorce rate has risen *not* because people care less about marriage but because they care *more*. That is, they won't stay in a poor relationship. Remember, marital stability and marital success are not the same. Many stable marriages are not successful in meeting individual needs, and many marriages that end in divorce were successful for a time (Figure 13.1).

APPROACHES TO DIVORCE

Practically all societies have some way of dealing with unsatisfactory marriages. Before the advent of Christianity in the western world, divorce tended to be available primarily for the male. Later, the brutality of some husbands was recognized and a limited divorce allowed the abused party or parties to live in separate residences but not to remarry.

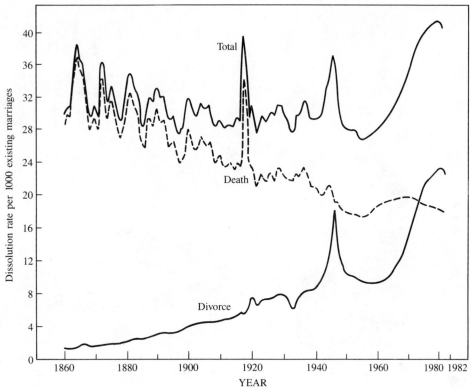

FIGURE 13.1   THE MID-1970s MARKED THE FIRST TIME IN AMERICAN HISTORY
THAT MORE MARRIAGES ENDED IN DIVORCE THAN BY DEATH.

SOURCE: Kent, 1984.

ADVERSARY SYSTEM

The philosophy of divorce in the United States was based on the principles that divorce should be granted only for grave and serious reasons and only if it could be legally demonstrated that one party and one party only was guilty. Under this adversary system, divorce was granted to the wronged or innocent party. The desire to find one guilty and one innocent party was so strong that, if a countersuit was filed alleging wrongdoing by the supposedly innocent party, a divorce might not be granted on the grounds that both parties were guilty of some wrongdoing and thus did not deserve a divorce. The adversary system specified grounds for divorce which, of course, did not fit all of the individual divorce situations. A divorce lawyer might advise the client to claim grounds that fit the state law and that would arouse the sympathy of the judge.

It is important to remember that each state has its own grounds for divorce, and there are about 40 different grounds for divorce among the 50 states. Adul-

Friendly breakups did not fit the adversary system of divorce, and often a couple's hostility toward one another was increased, not lessened, by the divorce.

tery, as a ground for divorce or evidence of irreconcilable differences, is the only one recognized by every state. Other common grounds for divorce include cruelty, desertion, nonsupport, alcohol and/or drug addiction, conviction of a felony, impotence, and insanity. In Canada, the same grounds hold for all the provinces and territories. They include adultery, sodomy, bestiality, rape, homosexual act, subsequent marriage, physical cruelty, and mental cruelty. They also include marriage breakdown because of separation of a specified duration due to imprisonment, desertion, nonconsummation, addiction to alcohol or narcotics, and "whereabouts of spouse unknown." The choice of a friendly separation simply did not fit the adversary system.

NO-FAULT DIVORCE

A turning point in divorce law came in 1970. The California Family Law Act was the first law in the country to abolish the establishment of fault in divorce proceedings. Commonly called no-fault divorce, this system has spread to nearly every state in the Union. The law also substituted the term "dissolution" for the term "divorce" and removed evidence of marital misconduct from consideration in settlements (Dixon & Weitzman, 1982). In general, community property—that is, property jointly owned by the couple—is divided equally and support is awarded on the basis of financial need and ability to pay. The California law was a model for the country in that it established the right of one marriage partner to request and be granted a dissolution whether or not the other party wanted it. It also substituted "irreconcilable differences" as grounds for a dissolution in place of accusations of wrongdoing. Its goal is to amicably work out a settlement of custody, property, and child support during a time of great stress.

With some of the bitterness taken out of divorce by this change from the adversary to a no-fault divorce system, some thought that there would be an explosive increase in divorce. No such explosion has taken place. There has, however, been a significant difference in who files for divorce. It appears that men are much more likely to file for dissolution and to complete the process under the no-fault than under the adversary system. Dixon and Weitzman (1982) found that a husband's likelihood to file is increased with his greater education, occupation, and prestige. They offer two explanations: (1) The resource model, which predicts that relative costs/benefits will determine who asks for the divorce, and (2) the normative model, which predicts that the spouse with the least investment in the relationship and the most options outside it will file. In practice, divorcing mothers tend to be awarded less under the no-fault system. They receive less alimony and less child support and are expected to become more self-sufficient (Welch & Price-Bonham, 1983).

CHILD CUSTODY

In early nineteenth-century America, custody of a child was almost always awarded to the father, presumably because of his greater ability to support offspring. Not until the late 1800s were mothers awarded custody. Most of the decisions regarding children took into account only the parents' rights and preferences. In the 1880s, however, courts shifted the emphasis to the rights of the child. The "tender years doctrine," which gives more consideration to a mother than a father when a child is young, has been prevalent for about one hundred years and is still a major influence on divorce custody decisions. Today 90 percent of mothers in contested cases receive custody of their children. A more recent approach is the "psychological parent" theory, which encourages courts to give more consideration to the adult (not necessarily a biological parent) with whom the child has established a mutually gratifying, continuing relationship (Alexander, 1977).

A number of different custody arrangements are currently in use; among the newest is joint custody. Under joint custody, both parents have equal power and authority in decisions regarding the child's upbringing, education, and general welfare. In one version of joint custody, the children stay in their old home and the parents take turns living in. More commonly though, the children spend approximately equal amounts of time living with each parent.

Joint custody has been found to have both advantages and disadvantages for children. One benefit of joint custody for children is that both parents are involved in child care on a regular basis. It also gives both parents some time alone to develop their own new lives and to build new relationships. Since children are with both parents regularly, they are likely to feel loved and wanted by both parents (Roman & Haddad, 1983). They do not have to choose between one parent or the other or be in a situation in which one parent has custody most of the time. Also, the joint custody arrangement provides them with reasonably consistent role models of their own gender.

On the other hand, the logistics of working out the physical arrangements can be difficult. It is easy for a child to leave a coat or a homework assignment behind at one parent's house in making the move to the other parent's. Also, because children see both parents on a regular basis and since the parents get together in person or over the phone to plan for the welfare of the children, it is easy for children to develop false hopes that their parents will remarry. Inconsistencies between the way the parents enforce discipline and in their personalities and life-styles can confuse children. For the parents, joint custody may mean that they must live in the same locality. They may also find it difficult to see each other while trying to establish their new lives.

Divorce often creates other "victims without crimes" in addition to the children—that is, the grandparents. For example, Jack and Jill get married and Jack's parents become very attached to little Joey. When Joey is four, Jack and Jill divorce, and Jill, who has sole custody, leaves California with her son and moves to New York. Where does this leave the grandparents? Often, hundreds or thousands of miles away from their grandchild. Even if she stays nearby, the grandparents may be uncomfortable visiting little Joey in their former daughter-in-law's house. If Jill remarries, will her new husband want the parents of her ex-spouse visiting? This continues to be an emotional issue, and some states have recently enacted laws that give certain postdivorce visitation rights to grandparents.

THE SETTLEMENT: PROPERTY, ALIMONY, CHILD SUPPORT

The property settlement depends on the skill of the lawyer, the types of records one has, the views of the judge regarding what is fair, the need of the spouse to receive property, who has child custody, and many other factors. Among the poor or college students with little joint property, there may be no property settlement at all, while property settlements among "jet-setters" may involve enormous amounts of money. Alimony, which means "sustenance" in Latin, was originally the money a man paid a woman so she could sustain or support herself after a divorce or separation. The "unwritten marriage contract" derived from English common law held the husband/father responsible for the economic support of his wife and children. Thus, alimony was a way to continue the patriarchal system of males being responsible for females. In recent decades, with the women's movement and with a majority of married women now working, the judicial system has no longer viewed alimony as it once did. Now, the courts have ruled that alimony should be gender-free and, in practice, alimony has been greatly deemphasized.

While both legal and public support for alimony has declined considerably, our society is still very child-centered, and child support is more likely to be approved by the public and granted by the courts. Usually, the courts still hold the father responsible for more than half the financial support. However, the courts are beginning to see child support as a responsibility of both parents. Since the

Learning to do without his wife and their mother: "Nobody seems too happy, but we are managing. I try to make things OK."

average woman earns considerably less than the average man, many people feel that an equitable division of child support should require a contribution proportional to each parent's income.

The joint custody arrangement often results in a more equitable and realistic child-support system, with the parents sharing child-rearing expenses. For some couples, the no-fault divorce itself may reduce bitterness and allow them to cooperate for the good of their children. Others may simply continue to argue over child-care expenses after the divorce.

DIVORCE: THE RATES

There are two problems regarding the incidence of divorce or the divorce rate. The first is the incompleteness of the data. For most of our history, divorce data were based on estimates at the national level. However, marriage and divorce are regulated by state not national laws. Although all states report the number of divorces to the National Office of Vital Statistics, only about three-fifths of the states report information on the characteristics of the divorces granted. Thus, information on such factors as age, race, and whether the divorce is a first or second one are reported by some states but not by others.

The second problem with divorce statistics is the way the rates are calculated. One of the most common, simple, but misleading ways is to divide the number of marriages in a year by the number of divorces. The problem with this figure is that it compares the marriages in one year with divorces from that year's marriages plus the divorces from marriages begun in all previous years.

The crude divorce rate per thousand people compares the divorces in a given year to the total population. The problem with this calculation is that it could change due to a decrease in the population and not because of an increase in divorce. It also includes persons not "at risk" for divorce, such as single persons and even infants.

The refined divorce rate figures the number of divorces in a given year per each 1000 married women over age 15. This is an improvement over the crude divorce rate. However, it can be skewed by the rate of cohabitation (a breakup of a cohabiting relationship is not counted as a divorce) and by the presence of women in marriages broken by desertion, particularly among the low-income groups.

One last way to express the divorce rate is to calculate the percentage of all married couples that divorce in a given year.

Once divorce rates are calculated, how do you interpret them? On the one hand, the divorce rate doubled between 1965 and 1975, and the divorce rate is now about seven times as high as it was in 1900. Considering these facts, the divorce situation seems alarming. On the other hand, one could look at the other side of the picture—the marriage survival rate. In any one year, 98 percent of married couples do not experience divorce. "Viewed in this perspective, the institution of marriage seems strong and healthy" (Brown, 1982, p. 150). Because of our high remarriage rate, only about 5 percent of the adult population is divorced at any given time. These facts make the divorce situation seem less drastic.

The trends in divorce may provide a more useful picture. Statistics show a slow, rather steady increase in the divorce rate from 1860 until today. Several major events, however, have been responsible for variations in the pattern. The Great Depression of the 1930s caused a temporary decrease in the divorce rate. World War II again brought an increase in the rate, and the conservative familistic period of the 1950s brought it back down. The liberal movement of the late 1960s and early 1970s corresponds to another rise in divorce rates.

> Since 1979 the divorce rate has leveled off. But because the population base is growing, the *number* of divorces continued to climb. . . . While the recent leveling of the divorce rate provides hope that the upward spiral of the 1960s and 1970s is over, this may only be temporary. If the divorce rate of the late 1970s were to continue, nearly half of all marriages can be expected to end in divorce. (Kent, 1984, p. 2)

REASONS FOR DIVORCE

> *No marriage is one person's failure any more than one person's success. . . .*
> *The best reason for divorce is that the man and woman cannot function together without serious damage to one or both, physically or emotionally.*
> *Divorcees are people who have not achieved a good marriage—they are also people who would not settle for a bad one.* —PAUL BOHANNAN (1971)

> *The big problem is not to keep people who want one from getting a divorce but to keep all from wanting one.*

Much research in recent years has focused on factors related to divorce. Some factors are correlates of divorce, that is, they have corresponding or parallel characteristics. For example, early age at marriage correlates with probability of divorce. The age of marriage, however, cannot be said to *cause* divorce. Other factors are causes of divorce—that is, reasons for divorce. Falling out of love is an example of a cause of divorce. You'll notice that correlates are characteristics of the individual or society. They are generally descriptive in nature. Causes are more closely related by behavior or attitude to the actual interpersonal marriage relationship. It is important to note that no one cause can be attributed to divorce or to divorce rates. Certainly multiple causation is at work, and researchers have yet to pinpoint who will divorce and who won't.

CORRELATES OF DIVORCE

A number of individual correlates increase the risk of divorce. Women who marry when they are age 20 or younger are most likely to divorce; second are those who marry after age 25. Men who are 0 to 4 years older than their wives are less likely to divorce than those who are 5 years older or who are younger than their spouses (Heaton, Albrecht, & Martin, 1985). Marrying at an early age reduces the opportunities for an individual to establish his or her own personality and for a couple to learn about each other as different personalities and as prospective marital partners. Also, marrying at an early age can hinder a couple in adequately preparing for husband, wife, and parent roles or in attaining the sort of education or training that leads to financial security.

Premarital pregnancy increases the likelihood of divorce. It seems that premarital pregnancy may lead to marriage and parenthood before the couple are prepared for it either emotionally or economically (Coombs & Zumeta, 1970).

Instability of the husband's employment is related to a higher incidence of divorce. In fact, how regularly a husband brings home a paycheck may matter more than how much he brings home (Cherlin, 1979).

A wife's employment outside the home increases the probability of divorce. "Wife's employment seems to set in motion a number of structural and psychological processes that increase the chance of marital dissolution. These may include the wife's increased financial independence, marital role conflict and status competition, and husband's perceived loss of status" (Spitze & South, 1985, p. 325).

Couples of lower socioeconomic status are more likely to divorce. While the literature supports this relationship, it also highlights a change in this pattern. The increase in divorces has been greater in higher socioeconomic groups, which means that differences in socioeconomic groups are growing smaller (Glick & Norton, 1977).

Blacks have a higher unemployment rate, are more likely to live in poverty, often have lower-status occupations, and are more likely to become premaritally pregnant than are whites. All these factors have been shown to relate to a higher divorce rate. Therefore it is logical that blacks would have a higher divorce rate than whites (Norton & Glick, 1979).

The receipt of welfare has been proposed by some as a correlate of divorce (Bahr, 1979) but Draper (1981) has proposed that this relationship is actually reversed; that is, divorced women are more likely to need welfare.

Education correlates with divorce. Women who did not graduate from high school have the highest rate of divorce. Women with five or more years of college have the second highest rate (Houseknecht, Vaughan, & Macke, 1984). These researchers conclude that the strain of balancing work and family roles causes the disruption.

One recent study found that partners who talk to each other and share an emotional relationship are less likely to disrupt their marriage. It also found a pleasant home environment to correlate with a stable marriage (Palisi, 1984). Researchers have found that the problems of age at marriage, husband's age relative to his wife's age, wife's religion and religious homogamy affect the risk of divorce no matter how long the couple has been married (Heaton, Albrecht, & Martin, 1985).

People with no religious preference have the highest divorce rates; Protestants have the next highest rates. Catholics, Jews, and Mormons have the lowest rates (Heaton et al., 1985).

The most commonly identified cultural correlates of divorce are changes in the organization of the family, industrialization, the women's movement, and liberalization of religious attitudes and divorce laws (Kitson & Raschke, 1981). Cross-culturally, as female status in society increases, divorce increases (Pearson & Hendrix, 1979). In the United States, divorce rates tend to be higher in the West than the East and somewhat higher in the South than the North. The rate is also higher in regions in which people move their residence more often than in areas in which people live in the same locality for long periods of time (Glenn & Shelton, 1983).

CAUSES OF DIVORCE

While correlates of divorce can be measured rather easily because they are descriptive and often more objective in nature, causes are more difficult to measure. Models or theoretical frameworks are often used to organize proposed causal relationships.

Marrying for romantic love and later falling out of love probably is one of the most important causes of divorce. It is logical, given our cultural emphasis on love, for a person no longer in love to leave the marriage by divorce to be free to enter another relationship in which love will be strong. Individuals who are in relationships that many would consider ideal end up divorcing because their high expectations have not been fulfilled (Cuber & Harroff, 1965).

Ira Reiss (1980) proposed that a primary cause of divorce in this country is a courtship system in which mates are selected by the young people themselves rather than by parents. This is probably related to the romantic love phenomenon, in that young people tend to choose partners for love rather than for homogeneity.

"The intergenerational transmission of divorce" refers to the way in which children from divorced families may transmit the tendency to divorce to their own marriages. Three different explanations have been proposed.

Children may learn inappropriate marital role behavior because their parents are divorced (Kitson & Raschke, 1981). Children of divorced parents may select mates very casually and enter into unstable marriages because they perceive that their parents were very casual about mate selection (Mueller & Pope, 1977). Finally, these children may simply have a more accepting attitude about divorce because their parents divorced (Greenberg & Nay, 1982).

The term "myth of the romantic divorce" has been used by some authors to identify the tendency to romanticize divorce as an answer to all problems. "Contagious divorce" refers to the ideas that divorce is a more possible option when peer-group support is available and that the rising divorce rate allows couples to think about divorce more freely (Olds, 1981). If your parents, several neighbors, and two or three of your best friends have divorced, you might feel that divorce is a normal way to solve marital difficulties. People you know may encourage divorce as a solution. On the other hand, if virtually none of the significant others in your life have divorced, you are more likely to question the advisability of divorce. Your family and friends may try to help you patch up a quarrel.

Increasing opportunities for women to support themselves is thought by many to be a major factor in the increase in divorce. That is, the decreased economic dependence of women on their husbands has substantially broadened the non-marital options for many women. Fifty years ago, a woman in an unhappy marriage often had only two options—to move back home to mother or to remain in the marriage. Now, women with the ability to be self-supporting have a third option—to move out and take care of themselves.

When divorcing people are asked what caused their marital breakdown, their answers may be different from the correlates or model causes of divorce. For instance, Kitson and Sussman (1982) found that although premarital pregnancy is correlated with divorce, only 1 percent of those they surveyed listed it as a cause of divorce. The most often cited complaint was lack of communication and understanding. Men also listed joint conflict over gender roles, different backgrounds, and changing interests and values. Almost one-fifth said they were not sure what had happened. Among the causes listed by women were internal gender-role conflict or their husbands' extramarital sex, untrustworthiness, immaturity, or drinking. Almost three-fourths of the respondents blamed their spouses for the breakup.

Models of divorce causation are theoretical in nature; they attempt to explain divorce from a societal, individual, or combined perspective. A model may consider the rewards and costs as determinants in the decision to divorce.

In general, divorce is likely when the rewards for staying in a marriage are lower and the costs higher as compared with those available outside the marriage, either in another relationship or living alone (Kitson & Raschke, 1981). Levinger (1979) describes attractions and barriers as material, symbolic, and affectional rewards or costs. Alternative attractions or barriers would be the perceived rewards or costs of an alternative situation. An individual may compare the present relationship with either a new paired relationship (new marriage or living-together arrangement) or with a single-again situation. One person may weigh all the attractions and barriers while another may use only one factor (say religious constraint against divorce) to make the decision. Throughout marriage, partners are thought to be in a fairly constant state of reevaluating their attractions to the marriage, the barriers to its dissolution, and the alternatives available to them elsewhere.

Udry (1981) hypothesizes that your marital resources are related to your alternatives, and that the more resources you have, the more alternatives you have. Conversely, the more resources your partner has, the less alternatives are available to you. Udry found that marital alternatives were good predictors and that partners who both had many alternatives had several times the disruption rate of other couples. He does, however, modify this conclusion by stating that it probably applies well only to a society where barriers to divorce are fairly low.

In summary, causes and correlates of divorce are different. Family scholars have not identified or isolated all the correlates—and certainly have not answered the "why" of divorce. However, they have provided useful frameworks, such as the exchange model, with which to examine the divorce phenomenon.

DIVORCE: THE PROCESS

Divorce dates from just about the same time as marriage; I think marriage is a few weeks older. —VOLTAIRE

Seldom, or perhaps never, does a marriage develop into an individual relationship smoothly and without crimes; there is no coming to consciousness without pain. —CARL JUNG

My wife and I tried two or three times in the last forty years to have breakfast together, but it was so disagreeable we had to stop. —SIR WINSTON CHURCHILL

How do couples move from marital problems to separation and divorce? Exactly what is the process? Just as many individuals have difficulty telling why, when, and how they fell in love and decided to marry, many have trouble defining exactly why their relationship deteriorated and they divorced.

Various researchers have created models to describe the process of divorce. There appear to be five key segments of the process that are common to the literature.

1. The marriage breaks down, the individuals think about divorce, and they may talk about it openly.
2. The couple separate and try to reconcile, bargain, and negotiate. Finally they reach a decision to divorce.
3. They obtain a legal divorce and arrange child-custody responsibilities, living situations, and economic support.
4. Both partners make some immediate postdivorce adjustments.
5. A long-term postdivorce adjustment phase may involve remarriage, establishment of a new identity, and other changes. The length of time between deciding to divorce and filing a petition to divorce varies among couples. Some take only a few weeks while others take several years (Melichar & Chiriboga, 1985).

In one study, researchers found that more wives (about a third) than husbands (about a fourth) had ever considered divorce. The younger the wife was at marriage, the more likely she was to have thought of divorce. Wives who perceived the marital division of household tasks to be more equitable were less likely to have considered divorce. For husbands, thoughts of divorce increased with religious differences between spouses and decreased with the presence of young children. Increasing duration of marriage decreased thoughts of divorce for both partners (Huber & Spitze, 1980).

Some couples do carry these thoughts of divorce through to the separation stage; Kitson (1985) found that one in six couples is likely to separate at some time during their relationship, and Weiss (1975) estimates that about half of all married couples separate. Research indicates that separation is the period of greatest marital stress (Bloom, Asher, & White, 1978). Kitson and Raschke (1981) propose that this stress may be a result of the ambivalence of the partner's status, being neither married nor legally free of marriage. Bloom et al. (1978) also found that the average length of separation is about 14 months for those who divorced, and that almost 90 percent of separations are resolved by divorce. Persons who reconciled had much shorter separations, about six months on the average. However, not all divorced persons go through separation before they divorce. A study based on court records indicates that about four of every ten who divorce have previously separated and reconciled before a final divorce (Kitson & Raschke, 1981).

A recent development in divorce counseling has been the contractual, working separation. This separation (of honor only, not legally specified) provides a written document that spells out separate living arrangements, child care with the parent most likely to gain custody, interaction times, and evaluation dates for meeting with the counselor as a couple (Hight, 1977). The goal of this type of separation is to help couples "during their critical decision-making either to divorce or maintain the marriage" (Granvold, 1983).

Next, those who decide to divorce hire lawyers, negotiate the settlement points, and take the matter to court.

Divorce Mediation

Divorce mediation, in conjunction with the no-fault divorce process, seems to be a growing method of arriving at agreeable terms for the divorce and arrangements after the divorce, particularly with regard to the children involved. "Divorce mediation is a family-centered conflict resolution process in which the two parents in conflict meet with an impartial third person who will help them sort out what issues need to be decided and how to go about resolving those issues" (Hale & Knecht, 1986, p. 11). It is designed for couples who need help in controlling their anger or in communicating with each other during this trying time.

The divorcing partners each hire their own attorneys. Then they meet with a mediator to discuss the issues of custody, visiting rights, child support, and other matters that pertain to the welfare of the children. The partners can usually resolve all the issues in three to eight hours if they are working only with a parenting plan. As the process continues, the parties can consult with their attorneys about the legalities of the decisions they make in mediation.

Mediation seems to be beneficial in that it can reduce hostility and stress, aid in the "constructive disconnection" that often leads to personal growth (Elkin, 1982), preserve good relationships between father and child and mother and child, keep divorced couples from coming back to court to settle unresolved issues (Pearson & Thoennes, 1982), preserve family functions, give power back to the family where some feel that it rightfully belongs, and provide a cultural ritual for divorce that is helpful in dealing with the changes affecting the family.

The benefits of mediation seem to outweigh the costs. The concept is growing; there are now a number of professional organizations and providers of training in family mediation across the country.

ADJUSTMENT TO DIVORCE

As part of the divorce process, divorced partners are expected to redefine their adult roles. McPhee (1982) defines divorce adjustment as the successful transition from predivorce to postdivorce familial roles for spouses and children. He

It started with such beautiful dreams. . . . Now I'm even more alone than ever before. If he at least called, maybe . . .

predicts more difficult divorce adjustment if normative changes required in role transition are high, if role strain is great, and if roles are ambiguous. He predicts easier role and divorce adjustment as positive occupational involvement increases. The redefinition of parent, career, and spouse roles can present many difficulties that might hinder adjustment. For example, if the single-again role is perceived to be ambiguous by the former partners, adjustment to divorce is more difficult. The roles of a dating single or of a grieving former spouse and the parent role may seem incompatible, causing role strain and making the adjustment to divorce difficult. However, if ex-partners can increase their career participation in what they perceive to be a positive way, adjustment to divorce is easier.

Kitson and Raschke (1981) describe adjustment to divorce as an ability to develop an identity for oneself that is not tied to the status of being married or to the former spouse and an ability to function adequately in the role responsibilities of daily life. A redefinition of roles does not always mean complete rejection of old roles; it may, instead, mean simply a modification of roles. "The process of coparental redefinition requires that divorced spouses separate their spousal and parental roles, terminating the former while redefining the latter" (Ahrons, 1981, p. 415). As a result, the divorced couple may be forced to see each other to discuss aspects of child rearing and may, therefore, have to continue their altered relationship for many years. In addition, at least 25 percent of divorced people have trouble completing the psychological divorce and remain attached to their ex-spouses for significant periods of time (Berman, 1985). This research found that those who had the most difficulty included parents of minor children (especially male children), women with little education, women in low-status jobs, those who did not want the divorce at the time of separation, those with more positive feelings toward the ex-spouse prior to separation, and those who experience tension and conflict in their contacts with the ex-spouse. In general, parents have more frequent interaction with their ex-spouses than nonparents, and those who have been married longer have more postmarital contacts than those who have been married shorter lengths of time. For women, friends seem to play a part in trying to get the separated partners back together during the early months of separation. The greatest decline in frequency of contact takes place between 6 and 18 months after separation. It seems that during this time span the spouse who did not want the divorce becomes resigned to the idea (Bloom & Kindle, 1985).

EFFECTS ON INDIVIDUAL PARTNERS

Often we hear that the divorced become victims of psychiatric problems, suicide, and health problems. Divorced and separated people do have the worst health status and highest rates of acute and chronic conditions (Verbrugge, 1979). They also rank higher in automobile fatality and alcoholism rates than persons of other marital statuses. Divorce—along with age, race, median income, and migration data—has been shown to explain two-thirds of the variation in suicide rates (Stack, 1980). The self-concept of divorced individuals often suffers, and they may experience intense loneliness (Trotter, 1979).

The relationship between divorce and distress is not completely understood. Some researchers suggest that those who divorce had emotional or physical disabilities before they married. Others suggest that such handicaps arise after the couple marries, which causes marital disruption. Still others say that marriage helps prevent these stressors and/or that divorce itself causes them (Weingarten, 1985).

One recent study (Menaghan & Lieberman, 1986) followed couples over a four-year period and found that those who divorced during that time and had not remarried suffered more depression that the others, mostly because of a decline in their standard of living, increased economic difficulties, and less availability of intimate, reliable supports. People who remain divorced seem to suffer continued depression, partly because those who offer support to the newly divorced tend to dwindle away after the initial crisis. Those who remain divorced usually continue to face economic problems.

Economically, women tend to lose in divorce. They generally seem to receive an equitable share of the property, but two-thirds experience a lowering of income. Men, however, tend to have as much as or more disposable income following a divorce as they did before (Albrecht, 1980).

Sexual readjustment after divorce appears to happen rather rapidly. Hunt (1974) notes that during the year following divorce, 100 percent of men and 90 percent of women under age 55 are sexually active with an average number of eight partners for men and four for women. These data for the 1970s show a significant increase in sexual activity for both men and women as compared to the Kinsey data reported in the 1950s. The average frequency of intercourse for divorced men is slightly higher than that for married men and slightly lower for divorced women than for married women. Cleveland (1979), in her study of divorce in the middle years, found that sexual activity between spouses had ceased for some time before the actual divorce and that the current sexual partners were either serial or concurrent short-term partners. Some persons had monogamous partners with whom they were likely to have been sexually involved before the divorce. Some divorced partners continue a sexual relationship with each other for a time. It appears that heterosexual activity may, in fact, assist in role adjustment. Spanier and Casto (1979) found that less than 10 percent of divorced persons who were sexually involved had problems adjusting, while almost half of those not so involved had problems. The number of sexual partners tends to peak during the first year after divorce and then returns to a more typical level as partners move toward remarriage.

Although divorce is certainly a major stressor, its effects appear to be modified with time. Spivey and Scherman (1980) found that though there is psychological maladjustment in women who divorce, it diminishes over time and becomes no different from that experienced by continuously married women. It appears that time, as one might suspect, is a good healer.

Individual Characteristics Affecting Divorce Adjustment

Some people seem to adjust better to divorce than others. Research shows that divorced people who are significantly better adjusted are high in dominance/assertiveness, self-assurance, intelligence, creativity, social boldness, liberalism, self-sufficiency, ego strength, and tranquillity (Thomas, 1982). Other researchers have found that women with more egalitarian sex-role attitudes are significantly better adjusted than less egalitarian women (Granvold, Pedler, & Schellie, 1979). Brown and Manela (1978) found a positive relationship between nontraditional sex-role attitudes, less distress, and higher self-esteem after divorce. Overall, Albrecht (1980) found that the divorce process was more stressful for the woman.

Social or Interpersonal Factors Affecting Divorce Adjustment

Affective ties with the former spouse are often maintained, particularly by the partner who did not want to divorce and among those for whom divorce has been more recent. Almost 90 percent of those sampled by Kitson (1982) exhibited some signs of attachment to the former spouse, which was a primary cause of social distress. Many authors feel that the "psychological" and "emotional" divorce phases break these ties and aid in adjustment. That is, making a "clean break" that allows one to build a new life is better than trying to cling to a bad relationship.

Families of divorced people offer emotional and often material aid (Johnson & Vinick, 1981). Women often turn to their families for their social network (Leslie & Grady, 1985). However, "developing a sense of autonomy and expanding one's learning and realm of social activities" (p. 672) is more important for postdivorce adjustment, and women could benefit more by interacting with other divorced women than limiting their social life to their kin, the researchers conclude.

Social support and social participation are recognized as positive ways to decrease the stress of divorce. Work is a positive force in helping women manage their lives (Davis & Dawson, 1985). Participation in clubs, community organizations, dating, and church or synagogue have been found to be inversely associated with divorce stress. That is, as participation goes up, stress goes down. Divorced people who adjust more easily tend to have a small group of family and friends who meet their emotional needs and help them maintain a feeling of self-worth (Daniels-Mohring & Berger, 1984).

Effects of Divorce on Children

The effect of divorce on children has been the subject of much study in recent years. The major long-term effect seems to be simply a more favorable attitude toward divorce than found in their counterparts from intact families. An unhappy intact family appears to be more negative for children than living in a single-parent family. Four decades of research have not provided conclusive information that children reared by one parent are at risk for psychological maladjustment (Blechman, 1982). In fact, "In the long run social adaptation skills may be enhanced" (Clingempeel & Reppucci, 1984). Landis (1960) identified seven potentially traumatic situations for the child facing the divorce of his or her parents:

1. Adjusting to the probability of divorce
2. Adjusting to the fact of divorce
3. Being used by one parent against the other
4. Redefining relationships with parents
5. Readjusting to peer group
6. Recognizing the implications of parents' marriage failure
7. Adjusting to stepparents

Looking back on their parents' divorces, half of the college students studied whose parents had divorced before they were 16 remembered initial parent conflict (predivorce) as the worst stressor; another fourth recalled the postdivorce

Where do I belong now? Will anybody see that I'm hurting? I'm miserable . . .

phase as the greatest stressor. Less than one-tenth viewed the actual divorce as the most stressful time, and one-sixth said that they were not stressed by the divorce but were glad because the "bad" parent left (Leupnitz, 1979). A study measuring effects on adolescents at the time of the divorce found that pain, anxiety about parents' future marriages, changed perceptions of the parents (saw parents more as individuals and as sexual), financial worries, loyalty conflicts, and withdrawal to avoid pain were perceived as major events. Some adolescents responded to these effects with regression because of lack of external values and controls, premature heterosexual activity, and trouble entering adolescence (Wallerstein & Kelly, 1974).

Children who have experienced parental divorce, especially boys, have problems with external behaviors such as acting out, aggression, and distractability and with internal behaviors such as dependency and withdrawal (Kinard & Reinherz, 1984). Stress seems to be greater when the mother does not work, probably because of financial strain. Boys not only seem to be more affected by divorce than girls but also take longer to recover from the stress (Francke, 1983). The long-term effects of divorce seem to be smaller than one might expect. Grossman, Shea, and Adams (1980) measured level of ego development, locus of control, and identity achievement in college students whose parents had divorced during their early childhood. Divorce backgrounds were not predictive of lower scores on these items. Remarriage also did not affect the scores.

The way children are told about the divorce may be important to their adjustment. McCoy (1984) suggests that both parents tell the child together before one leaves and that they explain why, without blame, in words the child can understand. They should stress that the child has nothing to do with the divorce and that both parents still love him or her. They should also explain the living and visiting arrangements. Cottle (1981) describes the reactions of a young girl whose parents had cried together and held her and each other when they told her. She felt then that her parents' relationship had mattered, and that they did mean something to each other even if they couldn't live together. He quotes her as saying, "They were two destroyed people with broken hearts. You can't stay angry at people like that, even when you're hurt yourself and very frightened" (p. 97).

Children and one or both parents are placed in the single-parent-family role after divorce, at least temporarily. Although mothers are most often granted custody of children, they usually receive less general support than married mothers. Divorced mothers have less support in the areas of care arrangements, housing, household chores, aid during illness, financial aid, child-care information, and support from people in general than do married mothers (Colletta, 1979).

Divorced fathers with custody often find themselves and their children playing nontraditional roles. The lack of role models may be a problem for some single-parent families. Studies show that children living with their father do less housework than children in two-parent families. Older daughters seem to help out more than older sons (Greif, 1985). However, studies have found no difference in the eventual adjustment of children reared by mothers versus those reared by fathers (Rosen, 1979). In general, single-parent households have been found to be more isolated from neighbors than married households and have scored lower on a scale of parental power and control (Smith, 1980). This maintenance of community participation could be a valuable key in role adjustment.

Many authors have lamented the lack of normative prescriptions for adjustment to divorce. This lack of shared cultural prescriptions may be one factor in the 80 percent remarriage rate of divorced persons. In most cases divorce leads to a search for a better relationship, typically through remarriage.

SUMMARY

- Divorce is a process comprising the same components as marriage.

- Attitudes and behavior in relation to divorce have changed as our society has adopted an attitude that stresses personal satisfaction and the idea that relationships are "disposable."

- The process of divorce has progressed from an adversary system to a no-fault system.

- While in most cases child custody is awarded to the mother, a growing number of fathers are being awarded custody of their children and many parents are turning to joint custody.

- Although divorce statistics are sometimes interpreted as alarming, the trends actually show more of a steady increase than a dramatic jump in rates.

- Correlates of divorce are characteristics of one or both partners, the relationship, or society; causes are reasons for divorce. All causes are correlates, but correlates are not necessarily causes of divorce.

- Generally, divorce is likely when the rewards for staying in a marriage are lower and the costs higher than those available outside the relationship.

- Mediation can help couples resolve issues in obtaining a divorce as well as improve their adjustment to a divorce.

- Divorced people must redefine their roles in order to adjust successfully to their new lives. They must learn to adjust emotionally, financially, and sexually.

- The divorce of parents can be traumatic for their children, but research shows that its long-term effect is minimal.

- Three-fourths of those who divorce eventually remarry and report that their second marriage is better than their first. However, remarriages are more vulnerable to divorce than initial marriages and they bring a different set of problems.

PERSPECTIVE: REMARRIAGE—A VOTE OF CONFIDENCE IN MARRIAGE

To marry a second time represents the triumph of hope over experience.

There's this little tidbit that hangs in the courthouse in Springfield that we might all identify with: "There's a lot to be learned from experience— if you ever recover from it."

If the second marriage is a success, the first one really isn't a failure.

"If I died, would you remarry?" Unendingly women keep asking their husbands and then are not sure which answer insults them most: "Yes!" or "Positively no!"

Despite the inherent problems, divorce and remarriage seem to be effective ways of dealing with marital dissatisfaction. Although most divorced persons remarry, older women may find it difficult to do so because of the dwindling number of single men their age and because men tend to marry women younger than themselves. Gurak and Dean (1979) have found markedly lower probabilities of remarriage and longer intervals between divorce and remarriage for educated women with children who divorced at an older age.

There is a significant increase in serial monogamy. That is, about three-fourths of people who leave a monogamous marriage by divorce will eventually marry again (Glick, 1984). Today, remarriages make up over one-third of all marriages (Price-Bonham & Balswick, 1980). Of all marriages in existence, it is estimated that nearly half include at least one person in a second marriage (Weed, 1982).

Albrecht (1979) asked remarried partners about their remarriages, and almost all said the remarriages were better than their first marriages. About two-thirds said that their previous experience had made adjustment easier the second time around and that their present marriages were better than they had expected.

Remarrieds "experience equally high levels of self-acceptance, self-esteem, personal control, feelings of zest, and no higher levels of worry, anxiety, and immobilization than their first-married peers" (Weingarten, 1985, p. 658). Remarriage, she concludes, seems to be more critical for readjustment after divorce than does time.

Remarriages, however, are more vulnerable to divorce. Several factors may contribute. First, some people refuse to terminate a bad first marriage (Glenn & Weaver, 1977). Second, low marital homogamy—that is, spouses with little in common—is most apt to lead to divorce. Marriages that end in divorce are less homogamous than intact marriages, and remarriages are less homogamous than first marriages. Third, the selection process for spouse characteristics does not seem to be altered in the remarriage market, so if poor mate selection was a problem in the first marriage, it could be a problem in the second (Gurak & Dean, 1979). Fourth, people who are liable to divorce simply may have characteristics that do not favor marital stability. In general, however, remarriage has become an accepted and apparently effective method of role adjustment following divorce. When children are involved, even more role adjustment is necessary. Stepfamily roles are ill defined and often dual in nature. Parents relate to the current partner as spouse and the ex-partner as co-biological parent, while children sometimes maintain residence in two households and must adjust to two stepparents, two ways of life, and two or more sets of grandparents.

How large a group is the blended family in our population? Over 35 million adults are stepparents and one out of every six children under age 18 is a stepchild (Pink & Wampler, 1985). Even with large numbers of persons entering blended families, they still make up only 13 percent of all families.

Reconstituted families seem to have different sets of problems than do initial families. Remarried partners list children and money as the two top problems, while these are usually at the bottom of the problem list for first marriages (Messinger, 1976). Berstein and Collins (1985) suggest that remarriages face the following problems: The complexity and ill-defined roles for the added relationships involved, unresolved emotional issues from the prior marriage and divorce, the children's adjustment to the new marriage, financial considerations, and legal considerations. These researchers suggest that remarrying couples consult a therapist to determine what unresolved issues and ambiguities create stress and to help the couple find a lawyer who can clarify these points through a premarital or postnuptial agreement (one written somewhat after the remarriage).

Research differs on the quality of relationships between stepparents and children. Clingempeel and Brand (1985) suggest that couples in complex stepfamilies (those with biological children of both the wife and husband) may confront greater role conflicts, which may cause disharmony and stress.

Other research has found stepfamily relationships to be relatively good. Duberman (1973) found stepparent–stepchild relationships to be reasonably good. Only 1 percent of the men and just over 10 percent of the women in her study felt that their relationship with their stepchildren had worsened. She offers two possible explanations: (1) Either parent socialization is so powerful that it is transmissible from one's own child to another or (2) primary ties within a family are weak enough that anyone can be a mother or father. Duberman found no relationship between parents' educational level and their relationship with their stepchildren, but she did find Protestants more successful in stepchild relations than Catholics. Younger children adjusted better to a stepmother than did older children, while age made no difference in adjustment to a stepfather. Finally, Duberman found that the presence of natural children in a reconstituted family enhanced the overall family relationships.

It appears that once interrelationships have been worked out and the new roles learned, blended families can function very effectively. Wilson, Zurcher, McAdams, and Curtis (1975) found that stepfather families could provide all the pluses of relationships that natural families could. Visher and Visher (1979) note that individuals growing up in stepfamilies do not differ in social functioning from individuals growing up in original nuclear families.

As our society is developing the norms surrounding the family re-formation phenomenon, new roles are being defined and accepted. Many more people in your age group than in your parents' have grown up as a part of two families, a natural and a blended family, and perhaps will become members of two more families, their own initial family and a later blended family. The roles of son or daughter, mother or father take on new meanings; learning and adjusting to these roles presents challenges and rewards. In the past this was more likely because of the death of one parent, while now it is more likely to be due to divorce. The exchange-theory framework would predict that as long as rewards balance costs, the process will continue.

QUESTIONS FOR THOUGHT AND DISCUSSION

1. What is divorce? What does it mean legally? Socially? Individually? What does it mean to you?

2. What are the different dimensions of divorce? How do they describe the processes and effects of divorce?

3. How have views of marriage and divorce changed from times past? In your opinion, are these changes positive or negative? How have they affected the way relationships progress? Explain.

4. How has the process of divorce changed over the years? What has contributed to the change? How have the roles that people play in divorce changed? How has the legal system changed the divorce process? Have these changes been for the better or the worse? Explain.

5. How have child custody laws changed over the years? How have these changes reflected changing views of sex roles? Have these changes been positive or negative?

6. How much has divorce actually increased? In your opinion, what do you think are some of the reasons for increasing divorce rates? What are some of the reasons given in the chapter? How are your reasons similar to or different from those given in the chapter?

7. Are there certain types of couples who are more likely to divorce than others? Explain.

8. How do people handle or adjust to divorce? How are men and women different in adjusting? What are some key elements in the adjustment process for both?

9. How does divorce affect people? In general, do divorced people have certain characteristics? Does divorce affect men or women more? Explain.

10. How does divorce affect children? How can parents help children cope? If you are a child of divorced parents, how did their divorce affect you? How did you cope? Could you help other children deal with the divorce of their parents? How?

11. As compared to first marriages, how do remarriages rate (i.e., satisfaction, divorce, length of duration, etc.)? What are some of the unique problems in remarriage and stepfamilies?

The Sunset Years

The number of older people in the United States is growing rapidly. Today, over 10 percent of the population is over age 65, and this figure is projected to increase to 20 percent by the year 2050. People today are living longer and staying healthier (Bulcroft & O'Conner-Roden, 1986). The popular press adds that the over-55 population is also wealthier and better educated (Brewer, 1981).

While Americans place an emphasis on the youth, perhaps their views of older people are changing for the better. For example, in a study of feelings about older adults, children's attitudes were more positive than their elders had expected them to be (Nishi-Strattner & Meyers 1983). As the proportion of senior consumers increases, markets and services will increasingly have to be geared toward them.

The elderly are breaking out of the stereotypical role of being totally dependent on family or living isolated in nursing homes. Most seniors report that they are satisfied with their lives, especially with friendships and housing, although they are least satisfied with their health and income (Rempel, 1985).

Most people in their sunset years live in their own homes and "cope well within the community without an inordinate amount of assistance" (Chappell & Havens, 1985, p. 227). Many rely on their spouses as their most dependable caregivers. Some turn to their children, especially their daughters, for help when they become ill or incapacitated; however, "elderly people in our society prefer not to live with their children and, at any one time, only a small percentage of elderly live with adult children in the same household" (Fischer, 1985, p. 105). Some of those living with their children or other family members go to day-care centers at least some of the time in order to let the caregivers go to work or do other things. Only a small portion of the elderly are institutionalized.

It appears, too, that the elderly are active. Contact with family and friends usually continues into the eighties, and many seniors participate in volunteer groups, and church organizations, and politics. A few even increase their social activity as they age (Palmore, 1981).

Whatever an older person's level of activity and living arrangements, the sunset years bring about changes in people and in their life-styles. As with other phases of life, successful change requires successful adjustment. Figure 14.1 shows the changes that take place throughout a person's life. While each person experiences these changes in different ways and at different times, everyone does progress through fairly predictable stages of the life cycle, aging, occupational activities, and family relationships.

FIGURE 14.1 RELATIONSHIPS AMONG AGE, LIFE CYCLE, OCCUPATIONAL
CYCLE, AND FAMILY CYCLE.*

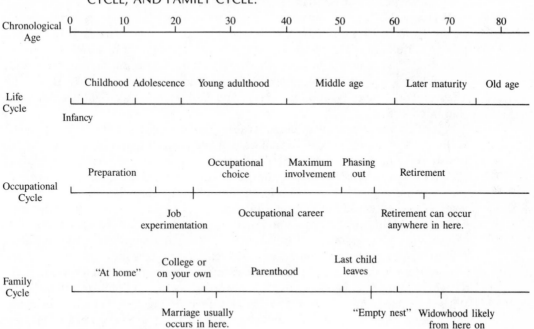

*These relationships fluctuate widely for specific individuals.

SOURCE: Atchley, 1976, p. xii.

RETIREMENT

You have probably already heard and read a great deal about retirement. Retirement benefits may be an important thing for you to consider in relation to a long-term job. Perhaps your grandparents talk about their retirement or your parents are planning to retire in the next few years. "Retirement can be viewed in several ways—as a process, as an event, as a social role, or as a phase of life. It can be viewed as both a cause and an effect. It is a complex social pattern that touches the lives of almost everyone" (Atchley, 1976, p. 1).

Definitions of retirement vary. A dictionary definition is "withdrawal, usually permanent, from a job or occupation." More serious students of the topic may add other qualifications. Langston (1978) states: "Retirement is the institutional separation of an individual from his occupational position" (p. 101). Atchley (1976) says, "Retirement is a condition in which an individual is forced or allowed to be and is employed less than full time (whatever that may mean in his particular job) and in which his income is derived at least in part from a retirement pension earned through prior years of service as a job holder" (p. 1). He adds that in both of these conditions, "employed less than full time" and "income from a pension," have to be met for an individual to be considered retired.

Perhaps the most positive and forward-looking description of retirement comes from McCluskey (1981), who states: "retirement is a 'transfer point' in a person's life—*point* for the event and *transfer* for the implication of dynamic change. . . . The transfer, in sum, is a transition into a new phase of mature adult life with its own special expectancies, tasks, and challenges" (p. 64). It directly affects income, activity, and interaction and subtly affects health and satisfaction (Palmore, 1981).

Age of retirement can vary considerably from one person to another. While 65 is the most common and often mandatory age, retirement at ages 55, 62, or 67 is also frequent. About 90 percent of all workers have retired by age 70, two-thirds involuntarily because of health or mandatory retirement policies (Palmore, 1981). Some organizations, such as the armed forces or other government services, place retirement after 25 or 30 years of service, people in their forties may be retired. Some professions and many crafts have no retirement rules. For example, employees in small businesses and the self-employed often have no pensions or retirement rules. Thus, a medical doctor or a shop owner can work as long as he or she is able. The social security system requires that a person spend ten years in a job covered by the system before being eligible for any benefits. With the increasing strain on the social security budget, the age for receiving retirement benefits is gradually being increased from 65 to 67 and benefits at early retirement are being reduced.

There is nothing magical about age 65, nor is any specific age an automatic time when a person is no longer useful.

> Our sixty-fifth birthday would not have special significance if society had not made an arbitrary decision. It was Otto von Bismark of Germany in the last century who established 65 as the age of retirement. At that time life expectancy was under 50, and most people who reached 65 were in poor health. Today life expectancy exceeds 70 years, and most people over 65 are still vigorous and active. (Kinzel, 1979, p. 2)

In fact, many executives are now taking early retirement from their companies not to sit in a rocking chair but to start new businesses or to try their hands in a different field of work.

Whatever the perspective of retirement and the rules that govern it, retirement involves change—change for both the individual and his or her family. What is happening to retired people? Do they see retirement and aging as periods of crisis or opportunity? What are some of the implications for the family in its later stages? Do people adjust easily and are they satisfied with their retirement years? What can you expect for your parents and eventually for yourself?

PLANNING FOR RETIREMENT

Retirement need not be a crisis event if it is preceded by adequate and appropriate planning. Retirement does not mean retirement from all of life—only from an occupation, job, or career. Therefore, it is important to plan ahead for the other aspects of your life. In fact, people who plan for their retirement have been found to feel better about their retirement adjustment than people who do not.

There are three considerably overlapping areas for planning: finances, time expenditure, and social or other activities. As with all planning, the earlier you begin financial planning for retirement and old age, the better. However, it is not easy to keep this in mind at the beginning of your career or even during its height. When things are going great, there are too many other, more immediate expenses and a certain amount of "conspicuous consumption" to let you pay much serious attention to the last part of life. When you get within five or ten years of retirement, anxiety about retirement may set in and lead to immobilization and confusion.

> Until that anxiety begins to recede, no serious planning can occur. Fortunately, the simple process of *beginning* to gather data often causes the stress to recede sufficiently. On the other hand, if the retiree postpones action and instead tells himself that he will "get around to it soon," the anxiety begins to increase dramatically. (Kinzel, 1979, p. 17)

Finances A financial analysis is the first step toward planning your retirement life-style. You and your family should begin by summarizing all your assets (all things of value that you own) and liabilities (your outstanding obligations or debts). Your assets might include such things as pensions (social security or other pension plans), annuities, and cash value of insurance policies. Some of your assets, such as investments or savings accounts, may continue to earn money for you, while others, such as your car and house, may involve expenditures for maintenance.

After listing all your assets and liabilities, summarize all of the income that you expect after retirement. While you will have to eliminate your former salary, other income will serve as at least a partial replacement. Then, figure your yearly income tax. Remember that personal exemptions on your federal (and sometimes state) income tax return double after age 65 and that some retirement income, such as dividends and interest, is taxable, while other income, such as pension payments on which you have already paid tax, is not. Subtract your estimated income tax from your total income to see how much is left. This net figure will be the amount that you will have to live on, and you can plan your budget based on your net income. A professional financial expert may be able to help you get a clearer picture of where you stand.

Time Curiously, time can be a problem for retirees who have made no provision for large amounts of free time that come with retirement. While going to school or working a 40-hour week, most people look forward to weekends and vacations, which provide extra free time. If you include the time it takes to prepare for work, to travel to and from work, and to work overtime, you may be faced with some 50 to 60 extra hours of free time a week upon retirement.

Planning can help in this area, too. So can a positive attitude. Unfortunately, some retirees don't acknowledge that they have earned their free time but instead feel a lack of worth or guilt about doing nothing, being lazy, or cheating on society

Which couple looks like you expect to be when you are retired? For a happy retirement, it's best to start your planning early. Good health, life satisfaction, and a happy marriage all contribute to successful retirement.

and family—feelings similar to those experienced in earlier years of going to school. Studies show that retirees who have strong work values are not as satisfied with retirement as those who have weaker work values (Hooker & Ventis, 1984). Kinzel (1979) says that he likes to remind such people that "by working all those years, and while usually fulfilling the parallel obligation of raising a family, they have amply paid their debt to society. Having paid their dues fully, they should have a clear conscience" (p. 65).

Some type of overall goal and plan for a structured daily routine can help retirees adjust to their new lives. Often, retirees tackle projects that they have wanted to do for years but never had the time for. Some may want to include exercise or sports in their daily routine as well as time for reading or meditating.

Social or Other Activities   The types of activities you plan for your retirement will depend considerably on the result of your financial and time planning. For instance, if you have accumulated enough money, you may want to travel or indulge in an expensive hobby. If not, you may turn to activities within your own community: volunteer work or a part-time job. You may start that novel you have always wanted to write or learn to play the piano. Retirement is the loss of the worker role, but it is also a challenge to diversify and learn and to participate in new activities.

You want to keep in mind the need for that self-respect which comes from social acceptance and the admiration of others as well as your need for self-satisfaction. You must consider your spouse and other family members who may be affected by your choices. The most successful adaptation to this role transition is contingent on a dual process of anticipatory socialization into your new role and psychological readiness to leave your old role (Atchley, 1972). You can expect retirement success if you plan ahead and work to put your plans into action.

SATISFACTION WITH RETIREMENT

Early gerontological research concerning retirement viewed aging and retirement as crisis situations (Friedman & Orbach, 1974). For example, Cavan (1949) perceived retirement as problematic for most workers, not only because of economic loss but also because of the loss of status and a meaningful role. Barron, Streib, and Suchman (1952) found that the loss of the work role often led to physical and mental breakdowns as well as to numerous lesser psychological difficulties. Ash (1966) found that the attitude toward retirement was becoming more positive, at least among steelworkers. His study showed that in 1951 the most prevalent justification for retirement was ill health, but in 1960 retirement was considered a reward for a lifetime of work. In summarizing the research over the past thirty years, Beck (1982) found that it "has resulted in inconsistent findings regarding the relationship between the loss of the work role and the psychological well-being of older people" (p. 616). Note, however, that even in this assessment, the word "loss" points to the negative connotations of retirement.

Research in the last decade seems to indicate that other aspects of older people's lives have more impact on their happiness and satisfaction with retirement than the retirement itself. Health, recent widowhood, and income have the greatest impact on life happiness; poor health, lower income, and earlier-than-expected retirement lead to negative evaluations of retirement (Beck, 1982). "The unpredictability of change in later years—illness, unanticipated economic changes, forced retirement, death of significant others—creates its own stress. Control of at least some aspects of one's life has been found to be critical to successful adjustment" (Zube, 1982, p. 154).

ADJUSTMENT TO RETIREMENT

The transition and adjustment to retirement can be compared with the transition and adjustment to adolescence. "Life after 60 shares with adolescence an intensification of the intimate and self-reflexive. At both times of life the question, Who am I? assumes poignant relevance . . . as both adolescent and elder become absorbed in the workings of their own bodies and minds, watching these internal changes with a mingling of wonder and dismay" (Clark & Anderson, 1967, p. 78). For the young, adolescence is a time of considering a 40-hour-per-week commitment for the next 40 or so years. For the elderly, retirement is a time of considering a new time dimension—time left to live (Neugarten, 1968). For both, the adjustment includes pain as well as pleasure and joy. Fortunately, people do make the adjustment over time. Retirees report more satisfaction with retirement the longer they have been retired (Streib & Schneider, 1971).

For a married couple, retirement can have various effects on the spouse who is retiring and also on the spouse who is not. Housewives whose husbands have recently retired report both positive and negative aspects of their new life-style. On the one hand, they have more time to do what they want, increased companionship, a greater flexibility of schedule, and an increase in their husband's participation in the household chores. On the other hand, they also report financial problems, not enough for the husband to do, and too much togetherness. The wives said they were the most satisfied if their husband's health was good, they had adequate financial status, they experienced joint decision making about entertainment, and especially if the husband participated in the household chores (Hill & Dorfman, 1982). Rural housewives are particularly interested in joint decision making and the ability to pursue their own individual activities as well as share time with their spouses (Dorfman & Hill, 1986). "Some wives welcome their husband's increased time spent around the house. Others do not. As one woman puts it: 'I married my husband for better or worse, but not for lunch'" (Atchley, 1976, p. 72).

Overall, the effects of the wife's retirement on the marital relationship are positive. "Many couples feel relieved from the stresses associated with their dual

---

BOX 14.1   WOMEN ON AGING

"Old age is not an illness, it is timeless ascent. As power diminishes, we grow toward the light."   —MAY SARTON

"Don't hide the lines in my face when you photograph me. I suffered too much to get them."
—ANNA MAGNANI, A MOVIE ACTRESS

"Age puzzles me. I thought it was a quiet time. My seventies were interesting and fairly serene, but my eighties are passionate. I grow more intense as I age."
—FLORIDA SCOTT-MAXWELL

"What all my work shall be, I don't know that either, every hour being a stranger to you until you live it. I want a busy life, a just mind, and a timely death."
—ZORA NEALE HURSTON

"Let me not forget that I am the daughter of a woman who bent her head, trembling, between the blades of a cactus, her wrinkled face full of ecstasy over the promise of a flower, a woman who herself never ceased to flower untiringly during three quarters of a century."   —COLETTE

"Age is a problem to many people. It isn't for me. I've not the time to bother with it. I think it's just a matter of genes and luck."   —MOLLY PICON

"Living in the past is a dull and lonely business; looking back strains the neck muscles, causes you to bump into people not going your way."   —EDNA FERBER

From *Ms* (January 1982)

work and family obligations and enjoy their new togetherness and joint leisure time activities" (Szinovacz, 1980, p. 423).

Women vary in how they perceive retirement. Those who are strongly committed to their work, particularly professional women, tend to have a more negative attitude toward ending their careers (Price-Bonham & Johnson, 1982). "The importance of family commitments in women's lives renders their employment histories more discontinuous than men's and this fact, as well as continuing sex discrimination in the labor market, makes women more vulnerable than men to economic loss at retirement, as it may also prevent them from reaching the occupational goals to which they aspired" (Szinovacz, 1982, p. 232). Those who can identify and use a wide variety of options, such as "their ability to enter into new 'careers,' their friendship networks, their linkage systems to family members, financial security, good health, satisfactory use of leisure time, and preretirement preparation for a transition period that may seem hazardous even if one has anticipated it" (Jewson, 1982, p. 179), seem to adjust more easily. Leisure roles seem to be the most important factor in explaining older women's life satisfaction (Riddick, 1982). Women seem to spend less time in preparation for retirement than men do (Kroeger, 1982), but they have a larger social support network with a larger inner circle of very close relationships after they retire than do men (Depner & Ingersoll, 1982).

MARRIAGE DURING THE SUNSET YEARS

"Marriage in the later years is not merely the extension of marriage in the early years. It is a unique and often lengthy period" (Zube, 1982, p. 147). Marriage has the potential of providing a number of benefits to couples, such as longer life expectancies, better health, less chance of being institutionalized, and less disability than the single life (Ferraro & Wan, 1986). However, seniors have less energy, more health problems, and more changes in their economic situations than younger people; usually, they are less able to cope with the demands of their environment (Zube, 1982).

MARITAL SATISFACTION

Research has revealed two different patterns in satisfaction with married life in the later years. Some researchers believe that marital satisfaction declines steadily during the lifetime, while others conclude that marital satisfaction is generally high in young adulthood, low in the middle years, and high again in the late years (Blieszner, 1986). On the whole, recent research finds that older spouses are satisfied with their marriages during old age. In fact, many report an increase in marital happiness during the early stages of old age, but a decline in happiness as the couple reach the later stages (Gilford, 1984).

Numerous factors influence how happy older people perceive themselves to be. Health status has been found to be the strongest predictor of life satisfaction, followed by certain family strengths and job prestige (Sanders & Walters, 1985). Almost 80 percent of the couples in one survey said they were happy with their marriages and over 90 percent said they would marry the same person again if they could live their life over. It was found that those who said they were satisfied with life and happy with their marriages confided almost everything to each other, showed little struggle for dominance, were interested in each other's expressive qualities (such as kindness, patience, and understanding), and were concerned about the impending death of their spouses. Over half were sexually active. Being independent—that is, living in their own homes—was a big factor, as was being in good health and being able to see their children. While most indicated that their marriages had their ups and downs, they said they considered this normal and had not considered divorce. Several said, "Divorce, no; murder, yes" (Roberts, 1979, p. 267).

A study of couples who had been married more than 50 years and who were living in a retirement community found that all were happily married and had high morale. However, they did not socialize as much with other couples nor have as high a level of sexual interest as those who had been married shorter periods of time (Ade-Ridder, 1985).

Satisfaction with marriage in the later years may depend a great deal on skills and relationships developed well before retirement. Cole (1986) says that couples in high-quality, long-term marriages will already have accomplished certain developmental tasks. These tasks include establishing effective communications, being responsive to one's own as well as one's partner's needs, being able to express one's emotions, being aware of one's own as well as one's partner's sexuality, and managing conflict and solving problems. "For couples who have attained the requisite interpersonal relationship skills and have continued to maintain and upgrade them at each stage of the life cycle, later life will be an enjoyable time of sharing and rediscovery of each other" (pp. 392–393). The way a couple relates in earlier life is a good predictor of their relationship in later life (Brubaker, 1985).

MARITAL ADJUSTMENT

As with the start of a marriage, the arrival of children, or some life crises, the ability to adapt to change is critical in later life, too, especially because of health problems (Ferraro & Wan, 1986). Cole (1986) notes that such problems can lead to changes in relationships—with spouses, children and grandchildren, siblings, and friends. For example, older people need to relate to their children on an adult-to-adult basis rather than on a parent-child basis. They need to cultivate new friendships as their friends die or move away. At the time of retirement, they need to adjust their daily routines and patterns, simplify their life-styles, develop healthful personal habits, develop and manage their resources, and rebalance their workloads.

Several factors can adversely affect a couple's happiness in later life. Income is one. If a couple has limited resources, they may be unable to engage in all the activities they had hoped to. They may be worried about having enough to live on or to see them through a health crisis. But "Couples who have been able to handle the important developmental task of establishing a positive marital relationship will be able to *help each other* to maintain well-being in the face of poor health or personal problems" (Ferraro & Wan, 1986, p. 435).

Although there is a degree of continuity in personality, behavior, and life-style from early life to later life, people do tend to experience gradual changes. Women and men seem to change in different directions that account for "differing goals, values, world views, and patterns of social interaction" (Zube, 1982, p. 147). Generally, men as they age experience a decrease in aggressiveness, less concern for masculinity, and an increase in interpersonal commitment, while women display more assertiveness and dominance in later life. In fact, it is said that older people tend to become more androgynous as they age; that is, they each exhibit both traditionally feminine and masculine traits (Sinnott, 1984).

This crossing of roles can cause friction between some marital partners. The husband may become more interested in the home and family and thus interfere in a domain that the wife has considered hers. On the other hand, the wife may be interested in moving her focus of attention from the house to the work world or the community just at a time when her husband wants to stay home with her and share more domestic activities. Couples may also have problems if their children were their only common bond. They may find themselves growing further apart as their children leave home.

Along with the other changes, attitudes about marriage and roles within marriage may also change as men and women grow older. One study found that people become more egalitarian in their attitudes toward their role relationships and that there is a declining interest in the husband's dominance in the relationship. There is also agreement that the wife should be financially independent and that they should frequently express their love for each other in words (Holahan, 1984). Men tend to be more satisfied with aging than women, and more satisfied with marriage as well. Bernard (1972) suggests that women contribute more to a marriage than they get out of it, so they would naturally be less satisfied with the relationship. While Ferraro and Wan (1986) found that those women who had been married longer reported a decreased sense of well-being, no such correlation was found among men.

SEXUALITY

Sexuality among older people has been a topic of some recent research. Although college students rarely think of their parents as sexually active and drastically underestimate their parents' frequency and variety of sexuality (Pocs & Godow, 1977), most older people do remain sexually active. About 65 percent of women and nearly 80 percent of men report being sexually active after age 70 and more than half of those over 70 say they have intercourse at least once a week. Of those who are sexually active, over 70 percent of the women and 75 percent of the men say they enjoy sex (Brecher, 1988).

Most studies show that sexual activity declines during later adulthood, although some (George & Weiler, 1981) show that it remains relatively stable. Certainly physical changes among both men and women may cause a decline in sexual activity in later years. However, these changes do not occur all at once. In fact, for men, most occur gradually from the age of 20 or so to the end of the life cycle. For women, the decline begins about 10 or 15 years later. An older man usually takes longer to get an erection and requires more stimulation to reach orgasm. He may not be able to sustain an erection until orgasm and may experience a longer refractory period. An older woman usually experiences a decrease in vaginal lubrication during arousal.

The best predictor of sexual activity among older couples, according to Masters, Johnson, and Kolodny (1985), is not physical abilities but the level of sexual activity in earlier years. As with people of other ages, desire is related to many other aspects of life, such as satisfaction with the relationship, worries, illness, or emotional problems. Overall, men tend to be more interested in sex and to remain more sexually active than do women. However, both men and women often report that the cessation of sexual activity is attributable to the male partner, mainly because the man is typically the initiator of sexual activity between the partners (George & Weiler, 1981). These researchers point out that the concepts of the asexual older person and the appearance of irreversible impotence and other sexual problems in later life are virtually myths. "Men and women are as sexually active when they can be for as long as they want to be" (Brecher, 1987, p. 184).

WIDOWHOOD: THE UNROLE

"The loss of a spouse is widely recognized as a source of intense emotional stress, perhaps the most severe stress an older adult may encounter" (Breckenridge, Gallagher, Thompson, & Peterson, 1986, p. 163). Although older people who lose a spouse seem to suffer less distress than those who lose a spouse at a younger age, they do face a traumatic change in their lives that requires adjustment.

Problems of adjustment to widowhood have led to elevations in suicide rates, morbidity rates, mortality rates, and mental disorders (Clark, Siviski, & Weiner, 1986). One of the biggest problems seems to be loneliness. For widows, loneliness is correlated with having no or few children, having physical health problems, losing the husband suddenly, being widowed less than six years, being withdrawn from social activities, and having little support from friends (Lopata, Heinemann, & Baum, 1982).

Widowed men report that they tried to cope with their loneliness by doing things with their families, reading, believing in God, keeping themselves in shape and well groomed, and going places with friends. Half of these widowers sought a confidant to whom they could express their emotions (Clark et al., 1986).

WIDOWS AND WIDOWERS

Most of the elderly widowed population (nearly 85 percent) is female. Several reasons account for this fact. First, since a woman's life expectancy is about eight years longer than that of a man, there are simply more older women than older men. Second, on the average, a woman's first marriage is to a man about 2½ years

Those who were happily married and had a great family life may be the ones for whom the loss of a spouse and subsequent loneliness are hardest to bear. It helps when people remember them with a letter, a phone call, a visit, or a few nice words.

older than she is. Therefore, merely by combining these two factors, we see that wives can expect to be widowed for over ten years. Finally, a widower has a greater chance of remarrying than a widow because he can choose among women of his own age as well as among younger women. In short, a woman who is widowed in middle or late life is unlikely to remarry.

Because they experience marriage in different ways, men and women experience widowhood differently, too. A widow who has been part of a traditional marriage—in which her husband was the principal breadwinner and she was responsible for the home and children—often loses the central source of her identity when her husband dies. His death may mean the loss of her major source of income, social status, and personal identity. She has even been linked to her husband by giving up her maiden name and taking his surname.

Widows may also suffer economic problems, and many are unable to maintain the standard of living they enjoyed when their husbands were alive. As many as half of all widows live at or below the level of income considered adequate by the Social Security Administration (Lopata, 1978). There seems to be a consistent pattern of "poverty and deprivation" among widows (Morgan, 1981). If she has been working, a widow may be able to continue her job; however, if she has spent her life being a homemaker, she may lack the necessary skills to secure a job. She may experience frustration at not being able to find needed employment, apprehension about returning to the job market, and dissatisfaction with employment that is dull or underpaid. These feelings only add to her distress.

A widow may suddenly be faced with a variety of dollar decisions that she is unused to making—decisions concerning insurance claims, veterans' pensions, probate of her husband's will, and social security benefits.

She may also be faced with doing household chores, such as fixing a leaky faucet or repairing the car, which she has never done before. She may have inadequate funds to pay for outside help and may be fearful of scams perpetrated on the elderly.

Men, on the other hand, often face a completely different set of problems. They do not usually lose their major source of income or social status upon being widowed. However, "widowers appear to be just as likely to experience economic hardships as are widows, other things being equal" (Smith & Zick, 1986). The researchers suggest that women's better economic preparations offset men's greater sources of income. They found that widows who had been married longer and had more years of work experience were less likely to experience poverty than others.

Widowers do not fare as well socially and emotionally as do widows. After loneliness, widowers list domestic chores and acceptance of their loss as their main problems (Clark et al., 1986). The men in this study sought professional help for aid with domestic chores but shunned counseling and psychological support services for their emotional needs.

Widows in good health and with adequate income are more likely to continue to engage in social activities and to feel fulfilled than do those who experience a loss of health and income as well as the loss of spouse (Creecy, Berg, & Wright, 1985). The cumulative effect of these stressors may deprive the elderly person of meaningful relationships and lead to isolation. In addition, the tasks involved in adjustment—making new friends, finding new activities, securing a job, or moving to less expensive housing—can in themselves produce additional emotional stress, mental illness, and even heart attacks (Hiltz, 1978).

SUPPORT

Rebuilding one's life after losing a spouse often requires a support system. In building support groups, the widowed rely especially upon friends. Friends and neighbors seem to be more effective in filling this role because of their availability and because peers are likely to have shared the same life history, have the same interests, and have some spare time. Often the widowed do not want to feel dependent on their children.

Widows find that other widows are a particularly valuable source of help because they share the experience of widowhood and can listen sympathetically as well as offer advice from personal experience. The widow-to-widow program is an example of an organized effort in this area. The "experienced" are able to serve as role-models for the inexperienced widow. The program gives widows a chance to talk to someone else who can empathize and who is an example of successful adjustment. It also provides help in acquiring the instrumental skills to do chores that were formerly carried out by the partner or in job training or retraining.

RELATIONSHIPS WITH ADULT CHILDREN

With the many changes in our society in the past decades, there has been concern about the relationship between the elderly and their adult children. Do the two generations still interact? Do the children provide for their parents on a regular basis and in times of crisis?

First of all, people today are having fewer children than they did generations ago. Therefore, elderly people have fewer children to rely on in their old age. Second, more women are working outside the home, so that young and middle-age daughters, who have traditionally been a primary source of help for the elderly, do not have as much free time as they used to. Third, people live longer today; therefore, they spend more time in their sunset years. Their children may even enter the sunset phase of their lives while their parents are still alive. However, evidence shows that adult children are providing at least some portion of their parents' support and services (Cicirelli, 1984).

In general, research shows that "parent-child interactions are fairly frequent, that adult children provide a great deal of aid and support to parents, that parents often reciprocate the aid and/or support, that both affection and a sense of obligation motivate the relationship participants, and that the relationships are perceived as generally satisfactory" (Blieszner, 1986, p. 558). Older people usually live near their children or at least one child, and the two generations play an important part in each other's lives (Lee & Ellithorpe, 1982). Adult children make 50 to 120 telephone and letter contacts each year with their parents (Atchley & Miller, 1980).

Intergenerational ties today, however, are more voluntary than obligatory. Parents may choose to spend more time with and money on their adult children whose needs are greater, such as those who are single parents (Aldous, 1987).

The idea that adult children should help their aging parents seems to be consistent among various age groups. One study of three generations of women found that all three groups thought that elderly people should be able to depend on their grown children for various kinds of help, but they did not think a daughter should have to quit her job to care for her mother (Brody, Johnsen, Fulcomer, & Lang, 1983). In fact, the daughters and granddaughters were less accepting of formal services for the elderly than the elderly themselves.

Another study revealed that most adult children believed they should care for their sick parents or help them financially if necessary, but they did not think they should invite their parents to live with them or even be obligated to live nearby or visit frequently (Blieszner & Mancini, 1987).

Three generations of smiles certainly make adjusting to life's later years much easier.

Also, women often turn to their children, particularly their daughters, for emotional support as they grow older, and daughters often become the primary emotional support for their mothers when their fathers die (Lopata, 1979). Daughters are more likely to participate in activities with their mothers and to view this relationship as enjoyable, while a son tends to see his relationship with his widowed mother as an obligation (Adams, 1968). Interestingly, widows are more likely to turn to their children when they are worried but to their own brothers and sisters when they are ill or in need of money (Anderson, 1984).

The exchange of various resources between adult children and their parents—visiting time, financial aid, and physical help—does not necessarily have a positive effect on the elderly (Lee & Ellithorpe, 1982). In fact, older people who have never had children report that they are just as satisfied with life as those whose children have grown and left home (Bell & Eisenberg, 1985). Society tends to view the childless elderly as isolated and lonely; however, this may not be the case. While they seem to have fewer friends than others, the childless are "somewhat more satisfied with their income and standard of living and are more able to afford major necessary items" (Rempel, 1985, p. 346), which may compensate for the companionship and aid that children might have provided. It seems that the ability to reciprocate is more important to the morale of the older person than the receiving of help (Stoller, 1985).

Seniors, not surprisingly, are more apt to receive help from their children when they are physically and financially less well off, and some studies show that older persons as a whole give more help to their children than they receive (Stoller, 1985). Conversely, those who are more able provide more help to their children. Parents who have provided financial help to their children throughout their lives usually continue to do so into their sunset years and after widowhood (Morgan, 1983).

DATING AND SEX FOR SINGLE SENIORS

Because of rising divorce rates, decisions not to marry or remarry, widowhood, and the imbalance in numbers of men and women, the unmarried represent one of the most rapidly growing population groups in America. Likewise, the unmarried elderly are projected to make up an increased percentage of the elderly in the future (Keith, 1986). For older singles, this means that they are more isolated from society than are their married peers, and they must make efforts to secure and maintain ties with families, friends, and neighbors.

For many senior citizens, dating is a hedge against loneliness in later life (Bulcroft & O'Connor-Roden, 1986). For them, dating is very similar to dating for young people. First, the main purpose of dating in the sunset years is mate selection. "In reality, however, most do not choose to marry the dating partner for a variety of reasons" (p. 399). Dating also provides companionship. It provides someone to talk with and someone with whom to share leisure time. Dating may offer different experiences to men and women. Women derive increased status from dating, while men report that dating provides them with an outlet for intimate exchanges.

Older people who date are serious about their dating. For the most part, seniors have monogamous relationships and tend to form long-term commitments. The dating partner often assumes the roles of friend, confidant, lover, and caregiver (Bulcroft & O'Connor-Roden, 1986).

Older daters are similar to younger daters, too, in that they get first-date jitters, worry if their date will call again, and experience sweaty palms and beating hearts. They differ from younger daters in that while romantic love is important, they are aware of the value of companionate love. They have had more experience in a variety of activities during their lives and have determined their own tasks and values, so they can be more adventurous on dates. They are more concerned

At any age, doing youthful things helps one stay younger and happier.

about neatness, cleanliness, and energy in their partner than his or her good looks.

Happiness in a relationship may include physical contact. Couples can derive pleasure and comfort from just holding each other. Many also enjoy an active sex life. While men and women undergo certain physical changes in their later years, for both "sex drive and interest are closely tied to attitudinal or psychological factors. The important factors in continued sexual responsiveness and coital capacity of men in later life appear to be having a lifelong interest in sex plus a willing sexual partner" (McCary & McCary, 1982, p. 333). Seniors with good health may be able to continue their sex lives into their nineties. Sexual enjoyment for seniors seems to be a strong predictor of life satisfaction (Palmore, 1981).

Because many seniors fear the loss of retirement income should they marry or remarry in later life, older couples sometimes live together or at least share the same bed part of the time. Some are afraid of what their neighbors and friends will think about their clandestine relationships; others do not want their children and grandchildren to find out that they are having sex without being married. As one man noted, "When my girlfriend spends the night she brings her cordless phone, just in case her daughter calls" (Bulcroft & O'Conner-Roden, 1986, p. 69). As one author noted, there is no retirement age for the feeling heart.

Summary

- The population of elderly people in the United States is growing rapidly; this segment of the population appears to be relatively independent, happy, and active.

- Planning for retirement finances, time expenditure, and social and other activities can make the adjustment to retirement easier.

- Often other factors, such as ill health or widowhood, have more negative impact on the elderly person's life satisfaction than retirement.

- Most married seniors are happy with their marriages, especially if they have developed good interpersonal-relationship skills during their early years of marriage.

- Older couples may encounter difficulties adjusting to their later married years if they find their interests growing in opposite directions, if they have built their lives entirely around their children, or if their attitudes about marriage and their roles within marriage have changed.

- Although sexuality declines over the years, most elderly couples remain sexually active.

- The biggest problem facing widows and widowers is loneliness.

- Because of their different roles within marriage, men and women seem to face different problems when a spouse dies. Contact with other widows and widowers seems to be the best source of support.

- People in their sunset years often turn to their children for financial, physical, and emotional help and offer similar help in return.

- Dating in later life is very similar to dating among teenagers and young adults. Most older daters have monogamous relationships and are interested in long-term commitment.

- Sex for senior citizens sometimes continues until very late in life; however, for a number of reasons, some single older people do not marry their sexual partners.

PERSPECTIVE: BEING A GRANDPARENT

Today, approximately 70 percent of people over age 65 are grandparents, and in the future children will have an even greater chance of having two or three living grandparents than they have had in the past. Children today can expect to spend half of their own lives as grandparents (Barranti, 1985).

The life-styles of the elderly are changing as Americans live longer and stay healthier. With high rates of divorce, families moving from one end of the country to the other, and grandparents establishing their own identities and social networks, has the role of grandparent gotten lost in the shuffle? Some people say yes. Grandparents, according to Galloway and Avery (1985), have become America's forgotten resource. Part of the reason, they say, involves changes in the life-styles of the younger generation but many older people have estranged themselves from their children and grandchildren as well by moving to retirement communities, traveling, pursuing other leisure activities, or working to supplement their pension income.

Research has shown that perhaps this situation is not as critical as it may at first appear. About three-fourths of grandparents over age 65 actually maintain contact with their grandchildren (Palmore, 1981). Grandparents often serve as secondary parents or backups and help maintain the family system as a whole. While grandparents vary considerably in their interactions with their grandchildren, they are definitely a part of family dynamics (Troll, 1983).

The benefits from grandparent-grandchild relationships can be seen from both perspectives. For grandparents, being a grandparent provides a central role in their lives, allows them to be the wise and esteemed elders and to indulge their grandchildren, gives them a feeling of immortality, and provides a chance to become reinvolved in the past by relating stories of their experiences to the grandchildren (Kivnick, 1982). From the grandchild's point of view, the grandparents are historians, mentors, role models, wizards (that is, they can tell stories and kindle their grandchildren's imaginations), and nurturers (Kornhaber & Woodward, 1981). Grandparents make good confidants; relationships between grandparents and grandchildren constitute not only emotional bonds between the two individuals but also a link between the generations. Grandparents can help children develop positive attitudes toward aging and older people in general.

Studies overall confirm that grandparents are significant to the lives of their grandchildren. The maternal grandmother-granddaughter bond seems to be the strongest. This is partly because a grandmother and her daughter usually spend more time together than do a grandmother and her son; therefore, granddaughters have more contact with their maternal grandmothers and thus the opportunity to develop a closer bond.

Not surprisingly, grandparents as a rule tend to become closest to the grandchildren who live nearest to them and to those with whose parents they have the most contact. A study of grandfathers found that the most frequent type of association between grandfathers and grandchildren was visiting, followed by getting together for holidays and other special occasions and going to church together. Almost 90 percent of these grandfathers said they felt very close to the grandchild with whom they had the most contact, even though they rate their role of grandfather as much less important than other family, work, and social roles (Kivett, 1985).

The potential for bonding, interaction, and reciprocal benefits between grandparents and grandchildren is great. Each generation can provide physical, mental, and emotional assistance to the other. To let the relationships slip away, as some people fear might be happening, would be a shame. For the elderly in particular, "The grandparent role may be one of the few social roles that does not diminish in importance in later life" (Kivett, 1985, p. 565).

QUESTIONS FOR THOUGHT AND DISCUSSION

1. What are some common misconceptions about older people? How are they and their lives different from the stereotypes?

2. What is retirement? What effect does it have on people who retire? On their family life? On their self-image and self-esteem? Do you feel that people should be forced to retire at a certain age? Why or why not?

3. How can a person plan for retirement effectively? What are the major areas in which planning is needed? Why is planning a necessity?

4. How is marriage in the sunset years different from marriage in the earlier years? Are people more or less satisfied in the later years of marriage? What factors contribute to this state?

5. What role does sexuality play in marriage during the sunset years? Does it increase or decrease? Get better or worse? What is the best predictor of sexual activity in older married couples?

6. What are some of the individual consequences of widowhood? The social consequences? How do men and women experience widowhood differently? Why do they experience widowhood differently?

7. How does the relationship between parents and children change as all of the parties age? During widowhood?

8. Is dating in later life similar to or different from dating earlier in life? Explain.

9. How does dating in later life fulfill different needs for men and women? Why do some couples not remarry?

10. What are some of the benefits of grandparent-grandchild relationships from the standpoint of the grandparents? Of the grandchildren?

11. Why is maintaining the role of grandparent important for most older people? How are changes in society threatening this role?

PART 5

Alternatives and Future

Alternatives to Traditional Marriage

When you think ahead to the life-style you will establish, you will probably consider a traditional marriage—that is, a union between a man and a woman who live together as husband and wife. You may think of many alternatives within the marriage—who works outside the home, whether or not to have children, how to divide the workload, how to make the decisions, and how to handle crises. You probably think of marriage as lasting a lifetime. Perhaps you are even realistic enough to think about the possibility that your marriage might end in divorce and that you will live as a single again or remarry later in life. These are all choices that you will face soon and throughout your life. They are by no means all of your options.

There are many alternatives to the so-called traditional marriage. Some people will either choose or be relegated to the ever singles. They may choose to live alone. At the other end of the continuum, some people will choose to live in communes. Communal living is varied, too. Sometimes participants merely live together as singles or marrieds in order to share work and a common goal; others are members of a group marriage in which there is open sex.

A significant percentage of the population whose preference is for homosexuality or other nonmarital relationships will establish their own ways of life. These life-styles, too, will vary. Some will never acknowledge or tell others about their sexual preference. They may live as singles or marry and have children. Others will practice homosexuality by developing relationships with people of the same sex or by frequenting the gay scene.

Life-style preferences and the ways of expressing these preferences are endless. No two people are alike. Preferences and practices are also dynamic; they are constantly changing. What is most important for you today may not be as significant later in life. Other goals may replace your current ones.

SINGLEHOOD

Singlehood. What image does this bring to mind? A successful woman executive who lives in a luxurious apartment and travels all over the world, or an old maid who sits in front of her TV knitting and wishing she had a companion for the evening? A dejected man who eats his dinner from a can or an eligible bachelor who has women flocking around him in a singles bar?

Marriage has many pains, but celibacy has few pleasures.
—SAMUEL JOHNSON

*I live in that solitude which is painful in youth but delicious in the
years of maturity.* —ALBERT EINSTEIN

*The American becomes uneasy when he finds himself alone. To be
left alone is a situation to be carefully avoided.*
—JURGEN RUESCH

Solitude is terrible even when drowning. —A RUSSIAN PROVERB

In truth, the gamut of singles includes people at both ends of the spectrum, with
the majority somewhere in between. Whatever individual singles may be like, the
singles population is growing. Currently there are nearly 55 million single Americans over age 18. This is a nearly 80 percent increase in the last decade (Cockrum
& White, 1985).

However, this number is still a small percentage of the population. Less than
5 percent of the 18-year-olds questioned in a large metropolitan study planned to
remain single. Among high-school respondents, 10 percent of the males and 5
percent of the females said they didn't expect to marry (Thornton & Freedman,
1982).

WHO ARE THE SINGLES?

Singles who have never been married, as opposed to those who are widowed
or divorced, can be classified into several groups. "Transitional singles want to
find a mate. They attempt to make the most of their singleness, but accept their
eventual coupling and, generally, parenting as a natural progression" (Barkas,
1980, p. 42). They may be delaying their marriage voluntarily because they want
to wait until later life to marry or they may be delaying involuntarily because they
have not found a suitable mate. Others view singlehood as a permanent state.
"These permanent, committed singles are content to be unattached. They find
satisfaction in their family, friends, work, hobbies, outside interests, and romantic liaisons" (Barkas, 1980, p. 43). Still others had planned on their singlehood
being temporary, but have come to realize that it is permanent.

What types of people are more apt to remain single? Do they have any distin-
guishable characteristics? While those who opt for singlehood are quite diversi-
fied, some characteristics seem to correlate. One study (Spreitzer & Riley, 1974)
found some interesting ones. White females are more likely to remain single than
black women; Protestant women more than Catholics. People with a lot or very
little education tend to remain single. Men with higher levels of intelligence
and/or higher occupational achievement are the least likely to remain single,
while women with higher levels of intelligence and/or high levels of occupation
are the most likely to remain single. Concerning family backgrounds, these researchers found that only-child males were significantly more apt to remain
single; first-born females, especially those from large families, were slightly more
likely to remain single. Men who grew up in a democratic type of family were
more apt to marry, but women who grew up in similar families were more apt

---

BOX 15.1   TYPOLOGY OF SINGLEHOOD

	Voluntary	*Involuntary*
Temporary	The never married and formerly married who are postponing marriage by not currently seeking mates but who are not opposed to the idea of marriage	Those who have been actively seeking mates for shorter or longer periods of time but have not yet found mates
		Those who were not interested in marriage or remarriage for some period of time but are now actively seeking mates
Stable	Those choosing to be single (never marrieds and formerly marrieds)	Never marrieds and formerly marrieds who wanted to marry or remarry, have not found a mate, and have more or less accepted singlehood as a life status
	Those who for various reasons oppose the idea of marriage	
	Those who have taken religious vows of celibacy	

SOURCE: Adapted from Stein, 1981, p. 11.

---

to stay single. Women who were reared by a single parent were more likely to remain single, and so were males reared in a foster home. Women who leave their parents' home and live on their own in their early adulthood are more likely to remain single (Goldscheider & Waite, 1987). While these factors cannot be labeled as causes of singlehood, they do correspond with the decision to remain single.

Several stages of adult singlehood based on age are noted by Stein (1981). As you might expect, never-married singlehood is at its peak among those in their twenties. Young adults often leave their families of orientation and strike out on their own. Many attend college; others start jobs or careers. This group has increased significantly in the last several decades, as can be seen from Table 15.1.

"A majority of the singles population is concentrated in large cities and in specific areas of such cities" (Stein, 1981, p. 13). Single people's goals of finding meaningful work, satisfying living arrangements, and congenial friends seem to be best achieved in large cities.

Age 30 is seen as the age of transition (Stein, 1981). Among many 30-year-olds, there is significant evaluation of life-style, with intensified social and parental pressures to find a mate, while an almost equal percentage have already separated or divorced. "A major source of difficulty during these years was work-related" (Stein, 1981, p. 14).

TABLE 15.1 Percent Ever Single (1960–1986)

	1960	1970	1980	1986	Percent Change
Women					
Ages 20–24	28	36	50	58	+30
Ages 25–29	10	11	21	28	+18
Ages 30–34	7	6	10	14	+7
Ages 35–39	6	5	6	8	+2
Men					
Ages 20–24	53	55	69	76	+23
Ages 25–29	21	19	33	41	+20
Ages 30–34	12	9	16	22	+10
Ages 35–39	9	7	8	11	+2

SOURCE: Adapted from U.S. Bureau of the Census, *Current Population Reports,* March, 1986. Series P-20, No. 418. Washington, D.C.: U.S. Government Printing Office, 1986.

For the middle years, Stein (1981) notes significant his and hers differences in singlehood. Age 35 to 44 shows less than 10 percent ever-single men and women, a slightly greater percentage of males separated or divorced, and about twice as many women as men in the single-again category. While males seem to be more satisfied with their marriages than females (Bernard, 1982), the impression from those who remain single is just the opposite. "Long-term singlehood tends to be experienced as a more positive state for women and a more negative state for men. This is particularly true of the older never-married singles" (Stein, 1981, p. 15).

The last stage of singlehood, those aged 55 and older, is more and more made up by the widowed, especially widowed women.

ATTITUDES TOWARD SINGLES

In the past, singlehood was viewed as the state of those who could not find mates. People who chose such a life-style were considered odd. Terms for single people such as "unmarried," "never-married," "spinster," and "old maid" reaffirmed this negative view, emphasizing that something was missing.

Attitudes seem to be changing. One study found nearly a 180 percent increase in the number of articles that appeared on singlehood in popular magazines from the mid 1960s to the mid 1970s compared to the previous decade (Cargan & Melko, 1982). These researchers noted a reduction in the sexist, stereotypical references to old maids and swinging bachelors and an evolution from a defensive, negative attitude to a positive, objective one. However, another study noted that magazine articles, even those in the liberal magazines, focused on coping strategies and problems associated with living alone rather than on techniques of enjoying or taking pleasure in living alone (Clark, 1981).

In our society, attitudes about the importance of marriage as a way of life have changed markedly over the past several decades. Singleness as a life-style is increasingly recognized by young people and even their parents. "Most Americans no longer regard getting married as necessarily better than remaining single and do not disapprove of those who eschew marriage" (Thornton & Freedman, 1982, p. 297). While our society still discriminates against singles by assessing them a high income tax rate and by fostering the stigma of eating alone in a restaurant or renting to a single, single people are now more independent than ever. Few single adults live with their parents, and most earn their own living.

Attitudes among singles themselves vary. Some like it, some don't. Some are preoccupied with the search for a mate yet harbor a "prevailing doubt" about marriage itself (Barkas, 1980). Others praise its advantages.

About 85 percent of the single women in one study report that they are satisfied with their lives. Their satisfaction was found to be related to such factors as good health, not being lonely, living with a female housemate, having many casual friends, and being invested in work. While half of the respondents said they had sexual needs (which were or were not fulfilled) and the other half reported no sexual needs, this factor did not seem to correlate to life satisfaction. Although one-fourth reported regrets about not having had children, this factor did not correspond to lack of satisfaction either (Loewenstein, Bloch, Campion, Epstein, Gale, & Salvatore, 1981).

> *The man who thinks he can live without others is mistaken; the man who thinks others can't live without him is more mistaken.* —HASIDIC SAYING

> *The spinster pooh-poohed her friend who suggested that it was too bad she did not have a husband. "I have a dog that growls," she said, "a parrot that swears, a fireplace that smokes and a cat that stays out all night. Why should I want a husband?"*
> —L. J. GOODYEAR

> *A bachelor is a man who not only has bad habits but is allowed to enjoy them.* —HAL CHADWICK

REASONS FOR MAINTAINING A SINGLE LIFE-STYLE

Stein (1981) proposes seven social developments that contribute to the increased tendency among young adults to postpone marriage:

1. The number of women enrolled in colleges and professional schools tends to take women temporarily out of the marriage market.
2. Expanding career opportunities for women have made it less necessary for women to seek economic and personal stability through marriage. Even

though women are still paid considerably less than men, they are capable of making their own living and buying a home on their own. A rewarding career can provide personal satisfaction and status that was once only attainable through marriage.

3. The impact of the women's movement has made women step more carefully into marriage. More young women are pursuing their personhood before joining with a mate in marriage.

4. The shortage of educated young men of marriageable age has made it statistically more difficult for college-educated women to find suitable mates. This numbers problem has led to more relationships between older women and younger men.

5. A more realistic portrayal of marriage by the various media has made people question the desirability of marriage and the perception that marriage is the only way to a happy life.

6. The increase in the divorce rate and the number of young adults who grew up in broken homes may cause some people to delay marriage until they have their own lives in order. Seeing those around them go through divorce may lessen the appeal of marriage even more.

7. The increased availability of effective birth-control methods, more permissive societal attitudes regarding premarital sex, and increased privacy allow singles to satisfy their sexual needs without marriage.

LIVING ARRANGEMENTS AND ECONOMICS

Right now you are probably living in a dormitory or sharing an apartment with other students. However, after you leave school, living alone will certainly be an option. The number of people who live alone rose to 20.6 million in 1985, nearly triple the number living alone in 1960. These persons make up over 10 percent of all American adults, and they represent almost one-fourth of all U.S. households (U.S. Bureau of the Census, 1986).

Single persons living alone compared to those sharing expenses with roommates often must pay high rents in order to maintain suitable apartments. They may find it difficult to save enough money for a down payment on a condominium or a house, but an increasing number are doing so. The real estate market is adjusting to the increase in single-person households and marketing to these individuals. The construction industry is designing for singles. In New York City, new residential buildings contain more studio and one-bedroom apartments. In San Francisco, condominiums are being designed for two single people to share. The floor plans include two master bedrooms, baths, and sitting rooms. The same is true of most other cities.

Other industries are affected by the growing number of singles, too. For example, small appliances are designed to cook a single hamburger or hot dog. Many food items are packaged in one-serving containers. The microwave oven is designed to prepare small amounts of food quickly.

Finances for single people can cause problems. Single women are particularly susceptible to money woes simply because they do not earn as much as men. Even women who have reached a supposedly comfortable executive salary level find it difficult to afford the expensive life-style that supposedly goes with their positions. Books often offer advice on how to dress for success, travel, or entertain, but single women may find it difficult to afford these things. Additionally, single women who make good salaries are less likely than men to make investments to secure their economic stability (Jacoby, 1974).

SOCIAL SUPPORT

Social support is important for everyone. Those who are married or who live with their families of origin have a built-in support system within their own homes. They have people with whom to share their thoughts and feelings and to turn to for help. Being part of such a network is important for reassurance that one is loved and esteemed. Single people must turn to relatives who live in other households or to people outside their families for such support.

Supportive relationships with other singles serve a vital function. Such relationships assure singles that they are "enacting appropriate and desirable adult roles" (Cockrum & White, 1985, p. 552). They also provide a feeling of self-worth and approval from society. Of course, they help prevent loneliness. In fact, social support seems to be a better predictor of life satisfaction than marital status (Austrom, 1984).

While single people, on the average, are lonelier than their married counterparts (De Jong-Gierveld & Aalberts, 1980), being single does not necessitate being lonely. "Loneliness is caused not by being alone but by being without some definite needed relationship or set of relationships" (Weiss, 1981, p. 157). A lonely person may feel the need for an intimate relationship, close friends, or community ties. Some singles seek out relationships of all kinds to alleviate their feelings of loneliness. They may turn to their families of origin, co-workers, friends, neighbors, others who they feel are similar in situation to themselves, and organized support groups. Some even turn to pets for companionship. Success in being a creative single (one who gives a positive meaning to singlehood) can be attributed in part to good social skills and in part to an ability to overcome the prevailing norms concerning marriage and the nuclear family (De Jong-Gierveld & Aalberts, 1980).

ADVANTAGES AND DISADVANTAGES

The joys and problems of single people are often the same as those of married people, yet some can be dramatically different, too. "Single life is a mixed bag, an ambivalent, bittersweet, confused and sometimes desperate medley of experiences" (Simenauer & Carroll, 1982). Singles, according to these authors, list freedom as the number-one advantage. They also cite the opportunity to make new

BOX 15.2   SINGLE VS. MARRIED LIFE

Advantages of Being Single

No pressure to have children

Opportunity for a wider variety of experiences

No necessity to explain where you're going or with whom

Lack of criticism for habits, actions, or decisions

Freedom to spend as much time or money as desired doing what you want to do

More opportunity for a varied sex life

Opportunity to set your own schedule without worrying about what your partner will think

More opportunity to try new things, new ways of life, new places

More peace and quiet—no bickering and tensions

Freedom to keep the house as messy or clean as you want

No one to hassle you when you're tired and out of sorts

Opportunity to cultivate friendships with someone of the other sex without arousing a mate's jealousy

More privacy and freedom to pursue one's own interests

No one else's bad habits to put up with

Freedom to eat what you like, when you like

Advantages of Being Married

Societally approved parenthood

Opportunity to share yourself and your growth with the most important other

The security of having someone to count on

Dependable companionship

Access to partner's economic resources

A regular sex partner

Participation in a couple-oriented society

A loved one to grow old with

Praise for your successes from your loved one

Someone to share in the tasks of daily living, such as shopping, cooking, and cleaning

Someone to care for you when you're ill

Opportunity to develop an emotional bond with someone of the other sex

Someone to come home to

Someone with whom to share your dreams and plans

Someone with whom to share your meals

friends and to expand one's social life. In addition, singles say they have more energy to devote to their jobs, so they can do well in their careers. Many also see their sex lives as exciting and rewarding.

On the negative side, singles say the worst disadvantage is loneliness. Many are unhappy with the public ways of meeting people today; that is, they dislike introducing themselves to others in a bar or other public place rather than being introduced by friends or family members. Some are disappointed with the dating scene because of unrealistic hopes and the influence of media portrayals of the single life. Many are confused over their sex roles and dissatisfied with "the sexual rat race" as well as with casual sex (Simenauer & Carroll, 1982). They also listed prejudice against single people as another disadvantage. Women tend to suffer more financially because they often do not have the skills needed to survive in the business world. Men, on the other hand, tend to suffer more on an emotional basis because they lack the skills necessary to start new relationships.

Stein and Fingrutd (1985) note that "single life is, at first glance, incompatible with the sociologist's notion that human beings are social animals" (p. 85). Marriage seems to be a more social existence. Yet, paradoxically, single people have more time and energy to become involved in their communities and to think more deeply about their society and ways of becoming involved in it. Single people are often accused of having no sense of responsibility and are assumed to be rather selfish. Yet because they are perceived as free of family responsibilities, they are often called upon to do more for families and friends and others (Stein & Fingrutd, 1985).

COMMUNAL LIVING

Communes are an American tradition. The Old Order Amish, the Oneida community, the Shakers, and numerous other groups have developed communes for their adherents since this country began (Kephart, 1982). Thousands of communes were started during the second half of this century.

Communes are composed of individuals and/or nuclear families who share a common life-style, belief system, or goals, living and working together as an extended family. Some call themselves "The Family." Some people join a commune to work toward a specific cause or to develop intimate or community relationships. Others are trying to escape from a society they see as too materialistic or personally isolating.

"People live together for many varied reasons: professional, craft, agrarian, philosophical, political, therapeutic, religious, or some combination thereof" (Stayton, 1984, p. 2). Property is usually held in common, with the possible exception of personal belongings, and family responsibilities are assigned in various ways. Religious communes are usually the most highly structured, disciplined, and longest-lasting. Drug-culture-oriented communes are unstructured, undisciplined, and typically quite short-lived (Ramey, 1972).

Sexual patterns in communes range from complete celibacy to monogamy to polygamy or group marriage to free love. Ramey (1972) lists five distinct sexual patterns:

1. Celibacy requires that the commune recruit new members or die out.
2. Exclusive monogamy is found in most religious communes, and those who disobey are usually expelled.
3. Free-love communes do not have pairs or couples but require a bonding to the whole group.

Some see the togetherness of a community as a beautiful thing, no matter what the weather is like.

4. Intimate friendship is the most commonly practiced intimacy pattern, found especially in evolutionary and utopian communes.
5. Group marriage usually involves a commitment among three to six members of the total group.

Usually communes are short-lived. Cornfield (1983) found that the duration of communes increased when the members carefully planned their expenses in line with their income, they knew each other prior to forming the commune, parents in the group assumed most of the responsibility for their own children, and members felt they had enough free time to themselves. In addition, commune members were more satisfied with the endeavor when they also set a time limit for the duration of the group's existence and when they did the housework regularly. Sharing of property or the absence of monogamy did not seem to affect the duration of the communes or the satisfaction of their members.

VARIANTS WITHIN MARRIAGE

No two couples are exactly alike in the ways they communicate, live, work, dress, act, and interact with each other and society. Each couple establishes a life-style that is somewhat unique and suited to their own needs and wants. At one end of the spectrum is the traditional couple who believes in strict lifetime monogamy. At the other end, with tenuous, often temporary ties, is the couple that emphasizes individual freedom and pleasure. Many options exist between these extremes: open marriage and swinging are two examples.

OPEN MARRIAGE

O'Neill and O'Neill (1972) first publicized the idea and the practice of open marriage. They suggest that the real problem with the traditional closed marriage is that it is "a static state of being, a pattern that, once established, will mean the fulfillment of all expectations" (p. 83) and will continue as such for life. In contrast, open marriage is perceived as a process, and realistic expectations are based on change and growth. The O'Neills offer eight guidelines for a good open marriage:

1. Living for now and realistic expectations
2. Privacy
3. Open and honest communication
4. Flexibility in roles
5. Open companionship
6. Equality
7. Identity
8. Trust (pp. 72–73)

The emphasis is for partners to make joint decisions that allow for personal growth as well as marital change and growth. For some, the change may result in freedom and growth for the partners while they maintain a satisfying marriage; for others, it may result in a termination of the marriage for the good of one or both. For some couples, the openness allows for both partners to have sexual relations outside the marriage; others stop short of extramarital sex (EMS) in their ground rules.

While the concept of open marriage has been very popular, this type of arrangement is not easy to maintain in practice, especially for people with a traditional upbringing. Such people have difficulty allowing their partner to engage in sex with someone else without becoming hurt or feeling jealous. Five years after she coauthored *Open Marriage,* Nena O'Neill (1977) wrote that people have placed too much emphasis on personal growth and individualistic aspects of marriage and not enough on the marital relationship. "We have downgraded the 'us' in marriage because we were so dedicated to the search for 'me'" (p. 27). As in all aspects of life, and perhaps especially in intimate relationships, a continually changing and adjusting balance of individuality and togetherness needs to be maintained to sustain the relationship.

SWINGING

Swinging is another example of an alternative life-style within marriage. "Swingers are couples who meet other couples with the intention of pairing off for sexual and/or sensual experiences with someone new" (Stayton, 1984,

p. 3). It is estimated that there are about 10 million swinging couples in America today. Usually the husband suggests the idea of swinging, but it is the wife who enjoys the activity once they begin. Many couples who discuss the possibility never attempt to carry it out. Sometimes couples are introduced to the idea by other couples they know, but usually they answer an ad in a swingers' magazine or newspaper to find other couples. Sometimes two couples get together for the evening. They may have drinks and show pornographic movies as mood setters. Sometimes the couples exchange partners and go off to separate bedrooms for sex (closed swinging). Other times they engage openly in sexual activity and invite others to join in (open swinging) (Masters, Johnson, & Kolodny, 1985).

Sometimes the women in the swinging couples also engage in bisexual activity (three-way swinging). Many of these women are introduced to lesbianism through their swinging activities (Dixon, 1984). Dixon studied 50 married women who were currently involved in swinging, who enjoyed sex with men, and who had had no prior history of sexual attraction to women. The research showed that other swingers, the swinging environment, and particularly the women's husbands influenced them to participate in bisexual activity.

Palson and Palson (1972) have established a typology of swingers on the basis of their observations:

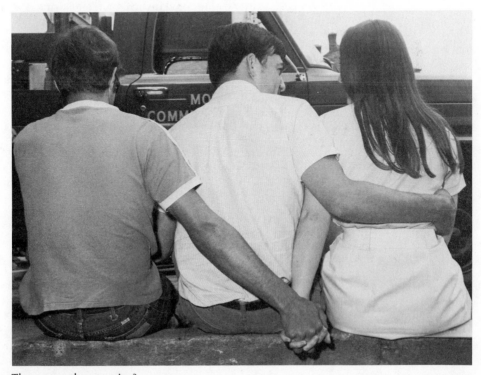

The more the merrier?

1. *The Eversearchers*—Couples who married quite young, with little sexual experience, seek swinging because they see marital sex as routine and they find swinging rewarding. It is kept secret from their friends.
2. *The Close Friends*—Swinging activity comes as an extension of long-time friendships. This type usually includes emotional involvement. Relationships are seen as second marriages in conjunction with the primary marriages.
3. *The Sharers*—People who have previously been involved in clandestine EMS eventually introduce their spouses and friends to swinging. These couples often swing exclusively with another couple for extended periods.
4. *The Racers*—Couples who are highly competitive and quite successful turn to swinging as an outlet. Racers are prone to jealousy of each other and may break off outside relations in order to keep their marriage intact.
5. *The Successes*—These are older couples with established jobs or careers and comfortable homes. Having succeeded in these areas, they are looking for fun and excitement. They view swinging as a new, more interesting life-style.

Noting that swingers vary greatly in the types of physical and interpersonal experiences they seek in their sexual activities, Varni (1972) divides mate swappers into these categories:

1. Hard-core swingers want no emotional involvement and swing whenever and with whomever possible. Variety is seen as its own reward.
2. Egotistical swingers seek sexual-sensual experiences with little or no emotional involvement, primarily to satisfy their own emotional need to be desired. They are fairly selective, see swinging as a separate part of their lives, and have no social contacts with swinging partners.
3. Recreational swingers are largely concerned with the social aspects of swinging and become members of a fairly stable group of swingers. Swinging is seen as a hedonistic activity in which emotional involvement is neither sought or desired.
4. Interpersonal and communal swingers, as opposed to most other swingers, seek close emotional relationships with their swinging partners. They usually are quite selective, seeking friends as well as sexual partners with whom they can have open and honest relationships and interaction. What distinguishes the communal swingers from others is that they advocate some form of group marriage, an idea quite unacceptable to almost all other swingers.

The general public has many mistaken notions about what kinds of people are swingers, what goes on, and how often. For example, swingers, while liberal in their sex lives, are not necessarily liberal in other areas. "People who enjoy this lifestyle come from every economic, educational, religious, and racial group in our society" (Stayton, 1984, p. 3). Many are very conservative in their political views and in other areas.

Swingers are not necessarily obsessed with sex, nor are they especially energetic and action-oriented. Many swingers engage in swinging about twice a month

(Gilmartin, 1975); many have few interests outside of TV and swinging (Bartell, 1970).

While many swingers at least try to represent themselves as successful and sexy, their descriptions of themselves may be exaggerated to attract new couples. Some couples may continue to swing into later life and hardly fit the stereotype of young, sexy swingers.

Another common notion about swingers is that their marriages are in trouble, so they turn to swinging. This is usually not the case. In fact, swinging couples often report greater sexual satisfaction and pleasure from their marital sex than do monogamous couples (Wheeler & Kilmann, 1983). However, the swinging couples in this study also displayed more disagreements and less ability to solve conflicts than did monogamous couples.

Couples react differently to the experience of swinging. Studies show that less than half of those who try swinging continue it on a regular basis. Others find swinging a healthful, fulfilling life-style. In a study of sexually exclusive couples and sexually open couples, researchers found no difference in the overall marital adjustment between the two groups (Rubin, 1982). Some swingers say that ties with their spouses are strengthened from sexually open marriage. Others either quit swinging or separate. Those who divorced after experiencing a sexually open marriage said they had attempted an open marriage "as a way to temporarily leave an unfulfilling and unsatisfying marriage" and that they experienced possessiveness and jealousy as a result (Watson, 1981, p. 16).

CELIBACY

At the other end of the spectrum from engaging in sex with a number of partners, some married couples choose to remain celibate—that is, to abstain from sexual activity altogether. Some couples have an otherwise excellent relationship but choose not to have sex. Sometimes people choose celibacy as a permanent state; others opt for it as a temporary way of life. For those who get little or no pleasure out of sex, celibacy may be a welcome relief. "Others may choose celibacy even though they enjoy sex because they find that abstinence rejuvenates their lives or creativity. Of course, some people find celibacy to be a frustrating and unfulfilling choice and may quickly reject it" (Masters, Johnson, & Kolodny, 1985, p. 453).

Although people often speak of the sex drive as a need that must be satisfied, celibacy has never been shown to be damaging to anyone's health and is recognized as a valid alternative life-style (Hyde, 1986).

HOMOSEXUALITY

Homosexuality, like heterosexuality, is a life-style that is neither new nor exclusive to any one society. While homosexuality has always existed, "Homosexuals have responded to being homosexual differently in the past than they do today because different psychosocial, cultural, and historical factors were at work"

(Bullough, 1984, p. 4). Homosexual activity occurs in all human cultures and among animals other than humans.

While, generally speaking, homosexuality can be described as a sexual preference for members of the same sex, it can be divided into three components: (1) homosexual behavior includes sexual activity with another person of the same sex, (2) homosexual attraction includes erotic and emotional interest in people of the same sex, and (3) homosexual identity means a person's acknowledgment of his or her preference for sexual partners of the same sex (Geer, Heiman, & Leitenberg, 1984).

Approximately 10 percent of American men and women are primarily homosexual, yet relatively little is known about homosexuality. Until 1973, the American Psychiatric Association classified it with several other behaviors as a "sociopathic personality disturbance." The radical political movements of the 1960s; liberalization of religious and legal positions on sexual conduct between consenting adults; gay demonstrations; research studies showing no differences between behaviors, characteristics, or problems in heterosexual and homosexual samples; and the position that illness was more a matter of social malfunctioning and client discomfort than a pathological problem—all these helped change the APA's terminology. Since 1973, there has been an increase in the number of articles that

Some people prefer to relate intimately to people of their own sex.

portray homosexuality as a positive life-style and more psychologists are helping their homosexual clients cope with a hostile environment rather than trying to change them into heterosexuals (Schwanberg, 1986). However, "Gay persons are primarily recognized in the literature not as individuals first who also happen to be gay, but rather primarily as homosexuals, even though the range and diversity of gay culture remains undescribed and misunderstood by health care practitioners" (Schwanberg, 1986, p. 68).

ATTITUDES TOWARD HOMOSEXUALITY

Most of society still seems to be negative about the homosexual subculture. A great many people consider homosexuals to be "loathsome, freakish things—criminals at worst or pathetic strangers at best—whose conduct must be curbed for society's protection" (Weinberg, 1982, p. 40). This irrational, obsessive fear has been labeled homophobia.

People who do not support equality between the sexes but maintain traditional sex roles are especially negative, according to a number of studies. Masculine males and feminine females tend to be more negative than masculine females and feminine males. However, one recent study found that females with masculine traits were accepting of homosexuals, probably because they themselves have broken tradition in their behavior and are willing to accept others who have done likewise. The same study found that males with feminine characteristics were less accepting of homosexuality, perhaps because they felt defensive about their feminine characteristics (Black & Stevenson, 1984).

It is not an easy task to change social attitudes. "It is not enough to state that black is beautiful or gay is good; it is necessary to emphasize black power and gay power" (Bullough, 1984, pp. 3–4). Bullough says that part of the problem lies in the fact that individuals who are homosexuals, like other stigmatized groups, have to define themselves in homosexual terms to be distinguished from others.

However, "Attitudes toward homosexuality are also in flux . . . perhaps as more factual information becomes available to the general public, attitudes will change" (Black & Stevenson, 1984, pp. 92–93). Gay marriages are still illegal. "Although there has been no legal legitimation of same-sex marriage, there is accumulating evidence of the acceptance and viability of marriage-like liaisons within the gay community" (Macklin, 1980, p. 914).

REASONS FOR HOMOSEXUALITY

A number of diverse reasons have been proposed as to why some people are homosexual rather than heterosexual. Early theorists, including Freud, suggested that homosexuality was "the result of sex role inversion—that is, having or desiring to have characteristics of the opposite sex, including sexual attraction towards one's own sex" (Storms, 1980, p. 783). Other researchers have added the suggestion that homosexual men, for example, are attracted to the sex role characteristics of their own sex either because they themselves have weak masculine characteristics or because they have strong masculine traits and therefore identify with other males. This line of thinking would suggest that a person's sexual orientation is part of his or her total sex-role makeup. However, research has found that homosexuals and heterosexuals do not differ on measures of masculinity and femininity. They do differ sharply "in the extent to which they reported sexual fantasies involving men and women" (Storms, 1980, p. 789), which suggests that homosexuality is limited to sexual desires rather than overall characteristics.

Homosexuality has also been thought to be a mental disorder, and counselors have tried to change the sexual orientations of many patients. Others have considered the possibility that homosexuality is an inherited trait, but this theory seems unlikely, because homosexuals are less likely to reproduce and therefore pass the genes to their children. Yet homosexuality remains present in all societies. Other theorists propose that disruptive relationships between a parent and child can cause or enhance the development of a homosexual orientation (Shavelson, Biaggio, Cross, & Lehman, 1980). However, Bell, Weinberg, and Hammersmith (1981) found no correspondence between a person's sexual orientation and his or her relationship with mother, father, or siblings. Still other theories propose that a lack of hormones or an imbalance of hormones causes homosexuality. Researchers have been unable to isolate which hormones may contribute to a person's sexual orientation. To date, none of these theories has been proven.

Other researchers conclude that "Homosexuality is one example of the immense flexibility of human behavior. It requires no more explanation than a preference for blondes or brunettes or for music or sports" (Futuyma & Risch, 1984, p. 166). Seaborg (1984) proposes that individuals—people as well as animals—that possess greater "behavioral plasticity in general will also have greater sexual plasticity . . . [which] in turn, will allow the development of either the heterosexual or homosexual orientation" (p. 155).

It has been suggested that homosexuals go through a set of stages in assuming their homosexual identity (Cass, 1984). First, individuals perceive the possibility that their behavior is homosexual. At this point, they may be confused and bewildered; they may reject the possibility or accept it. Second, they note the difference between themselves and heterosexuals and usually face feelings of alienation. Third, they feel a need, not necessarily a want, to identify with other homosexuals to fulfill their social, sexual, and emotional needs. They develop a tolerance of the homosexual self-image. Fourth, they gradually develop a network of homosexual friends and take a more positive view of homosexuality. Fifth, they develop a feeling of pride toward their own homosexuality and a fierce loyalty to homosexuals as a group. They become angry about society's stigmatization of homosexuals and may flaunt their sexual orientation before heterosexuals so as to promote their equality. Finally, they see themselves as people with many sides to their characters, so that while their homosexuality is no longer hidden, neither is it an issue.

Those who assume a gay identity "exhibit the following characteristics: homosexual behavior, homosexual attractions, homosexual self-conceptions, social as well as sexual affiliations with the gay world, and same-sex romantic attachments" (Troiden, 1979, p. 372).

LIFE-STYLES OF HOMOSEXUALS

He killed ten men and they gave him a medal; he loved one man and they gave him a dishonorable discharge . . .

Although many people today view homosexual behavior as an oddity and assume it to be very different from heterosexuality, research has shown that "The values and experiences of homosexual couples are similar to those of heterosexuals in many ways. . . . Most people strongly desire a close and loving relationship with one special person" (Peplau, 1981, p. 28). Homosexual couples derive love and satisfaction from their intimate relationships.

Partners, friends, and lovers.

Some people tend to think that homosexuals pattern their partnerships after traditional heterosexual relationships, with one partner dominant over the other. It has been suggested, for example, that a gay masculine male will be attracted to a feminine male and vice versa, or a younger to an older partner. Neither holds true in most cases (Harry, 1982). The relationships between lesbians or between gay men involve less gender-role playing than do those between heterosexual couples, possibly because gays and lesbians do not follow the role models provided by heterosexual couples, and they endorse feminist values and the ideology of gay liberation. They are, in effect, trying "to create new forms of relationships that are distinct from those of heterosexual couples" (Marecek, Finn, & Cardell, 1982, pp. 46–47).

"Instead, gay relationships resemble 'best friendships,' with the added component of romantic and erotic attraction" (Peplau, 1981, p. 29). Lesbians and gay men say that the lack of rigid role playing is an advantage to their relationships, and they strive for egalitarianism. The Peplau (1981) study found that two-thirds of the lesbians and two-fifths of the gay men in the study were involved in a romantic/sexual relationship, and the rest of the participants had all been in a similar partnership at least once during their lives. Other studies show between 50 and 90 percent of homosexuals to be in a gay couple relationship (Winkelpleck & Westfield, 1982). Most reported they were very satisfied with their relationships, were in love, and were committed to their partnerships.

Partnerships, like those of heterosexuals, may not last forever, no matter how much in love the partners are or how committed they are to their relationships. Studies show that young homosexual couples stay together for two or three years, but many older couples report being with the same partner for decades. Since marriage between two people of the same sex is forbidden by law, homosexual couples find "fewer barriers to calling it quits" (Peplau, 1981, p. 34). They have no legal ties, no children, and little encouragement from family and friends to stay together. They are less apt to be financially dependent on each other.

Gay couples have strengths and weaknesses that may be different from those of heterosexual couples. Participants in one study of gay males listed their strengths as "commitment, based on oppression, to explore and develop alternative relationship styles," greater emotional strength and understanding, and greater individual freedom of choice (Winkelpleck & Westfield, 1982, p. 294). They listed the major issues for gay couples as discrimination and prejudice; lack of role models; inadequate communication; dealing with parents and other family and "in-laws"; and sexual problems of finding information, alternative styles of expressing their sexuality, sexual dysfunction, and monogamy; and dependency and personal development within their relationship.

Men and women in general appear to be dissimilar in their sexual attitudes and behaviors, whether they are homosexual or heterosexual. For example, homosexual men are more likely than lesbians to have sex with people other than their primary partners. Over half the gay men in the Peplau (1981) study reported having had sex with someone other than their partners in the last two months, as compared to 13 percent of the lesbians. Lesbians, like heterosexual women, are more likely to become emotionally involved before engaging in sexual behavior; gay men were "more variable in their behavior" (p. 37). Nearly half the men said they became friends with a partner before having sex, another fourth had sex with casual acquaintances, and another fourth reported having sex with men they had just met.

In recent years, however, there has been a change in this life-style, with increased emphasis on more long-term monogamous relationships among gay males. This change has been attributed to the concern over the fast-spreading disease known as AIDS (acquired immunodeficiency syndrome).

Interestingly, lesbian women report more frequent sex, more frequent orgasm, and more sexual satisfaction than do heterosexual women. Reasons may include the fact that lesbians use methods of sexual activity that are more likely than penile stimulation to produce orgasm and that they have "gender empathy, i.e., lesbian women may be more adept sexually because they know firsthand what feels arousing to the female body" (Coleman, Hoon, & Hoon, 1983, p. 70).

Aging can bring on added problems for homosexual people. It is estimated that there are 1¾ million older gay men and lesbians in the United States. The myths that older gay men are apt to molest children, that they age faster, and that they are socially isolated adds to their problems. In truth, however, the aging gay man bears little resemblance to this picture. He is satisfied with his sex life, desires adult male partners of his own age, and does not seek sexual encounters in public rest rooms. Most lesbians report that they have overall good mental health, that they enjoy their lesbianism, and that they feel positive about aging (Berger & Kelly, 1986).

Some older homosexuals still conceal their sexual orientation from people; others have "come out." Many of the older homosexuals find their relationships more important than heterosexuals because they have fewer social supports. Because same-sex partners have the same average life expectancy, they are less apt to encounter "widowhood."

Homosexuals still have a long way to go before they will be accepted into American society. A recent study of two states in Australia, one in which homosexuality is illegal and one in which it is legal, showed that "Decriminalization did not include an increase in the negative aspects of homosexuality, such as public solicitation or sexually transmitted disease" (Sinclair & Ross, 1986, p. 119). Instead, it showed an increase in the psychological adjustment of homosexual men and a decrease in solicitation and STDs. This study concludes that there is "room for cautious optimism that decriminalization may provide significant benefits to society in general, as well as to the homosexual" (Sinclair & Ross, 1986, p. 127).

SUMMARY

- Although the traditional marriage is the most prevalent life-style in America, many people choose one of the many alternatives: singlehood, communal living, nontraditional marriage, or homosexuality.

- The number of single adults in America is growing at a rapid rate, and society's attitude toward singlehood is changing from basically negative to more positive.

- The single life offers many advantages and rewards, but it also has its own set of problems. The biggest advantage appears to be freedom; the worst disadvantage seems to be loneliness.

- Communal living involves a group of people living and working together for a common goal. Although communal living has been in existence for centuries, most communes are short-lived.

- Even within the marriage, some couples opt for alternatives to strict lifetime monogamy. Open marriage and swinging are two examples of such variations.

- Open marriage stresses change and growth within the relationship and may include sexual relations outside the marriage.

- Swingers—married couples who meet with other married couples for sexual stimulation and experience—come from all backgrounds and walks of life. Some find this life-style rewarding, but others either quit swinging or divorce after trying it.

- Some married couples choose to remain celibate for all or part of their lives.

- Approximately 10 percent of Americans are homosexuals. Within this group is a wide variety of life-styles. However, for the most part, homosexuals, like heterosexuals, strive for a close, loving relationship with one special person. This is especially true for lesbians and is becoming more true for male homosexuals, especially with the threat of AIDS.

PERSPECTIVE: WHAT IS NORMAL ABOUT NORMAL?

Is what we have done, are doing, are thinking about doing, or desire to do normal? Or is it abnormal? Practically any activity, especially in the area of sexuality, can fit under the heading of normal or abnormal—depending on who is doing the defining or, more correctly, the labeling.

The term "normal" is typically and often erroneously used to imply that the majority of individuals conform to that particular sexual behavior or pattern. Often it does not seem to be based on anything more than the speaker's preference. Abnormal behavior is behavior that springs from irrational sources, behavior that represents "a displacement or mischanneling of emotions that generates a need that can be met only through behavior that forces one to suffer the unnecessary pain of social ostracism" (Goldberg, 1982, pp. 121–122).

Pomeroy (1966) has identified six bases that are used to apply the concept normal to sexual behavior.

1. *The statistical definition.* By this standard, behavior which is commonplace or frequent is considered normal and that which is not is considered abnormal. According to this criterion, masturbation, premarital intercourse, and oral-genital sex would be considered normal. Virginity would be considered statistically abnormal.

2. *The phylogenetic definition.* Humans are a species of mammal, so if you considered sexual behavior found among mammals, it would be quite difficult to find human sexual behavior that was abnormal.

3. *The moral definition.* Because of the restricted and inhibited set of sexual codes that our society has inherited, about the only normal sex act under this standard would be marital intercourse. While many people verbally, and possibly ideally, subscribe to this definition, their actual behavior is nowhere close to their own definition of normal.

4. *The legal definition.* This definition closely parallels the moral definition, with a few curious exceptions. For example, masturbation is considered morally wrong but is not illegal in any state. On the other hand, oral-genital activity is against the law in many states but not forbidden by any of the major religions. Most laws pertaining to sexual behavior are based on the idea of consenting adults.

5. *The social definition.* This definition basically says that sexual activity between consenting adults is permissible or normal, but that it is abnormal when force or coercion is used or the sex involves acts by an adult directed to a child.

6. *The psychological definition.* The determining factor under this definition is based on how a person feels about a particular act, partner, or circumstance. Any factor that produced guilt or lowered self-esteem would be abnormal. This would allow a difference in definition of normal and abnormal from one person to another.

In all six of these definitions, a crucial question remains—who is to be the judge, the definer, the individual in charge of labeling? What do you do in cases where your definition is different from your partner's or when you disagree with your religion, law, or society? Ellis (1962) wrote that whichever definition is used, normal sexual behavior still boils down to human cultures and subcultures making sexual acts healthy or unhealthy, mature or immature, adjusted or maladjusted, disturbing or nondisturbing.

Since there is probably no sexual activity that could not be termed deviant or abnormal at some time or place or in some relationship or circumstance, Pomeroy (1966) suggests that it makes more sense to banish this entire concept from our vocabulary and thinking. Reiss (1986) says that "the label abnormality imposes a pressure in the direction of change" (p. 133). He offers the term "nonconformity" to apply to sexual behavior that is not in line with societal norms.

QUESTIONS FOR THOUGHT AND DISCUSSION

1. What comes to your mind when you think of a single person? Is your image close to the stereotype? Is the stereotype close to the reality?

2. Who are single people? How are they different from married people? How are they not so different? What are different types of singles? Which sex is more apt to stay single? Why?

3. Why do some people remain single and others marry? What effects do culture and society have on this decision?

4. Have attitudes toward singles changed over the years? If so, how? What are some advantages and disadvantages of being single? How do they compare to the advantages and disadvantages of being married?

5. Describe the stages of singlehood throughout the life cycle. How are they defined? What things characterize movement from one stage to the next?

6. What are some reasons for staying single? Do you agree with any of them? Why or why not?

7. What is a commune? Why do people join? What are some advantages and disadvantages of communal living? Would you consider joining one? Why or why not?

8. Describe some of the variations within marriage. What are the advantages of these types of marriage as opposed to traditional marriage? Disadvantages? Would you consider one of these life-styles? Why or why not?

9. What are some proposed reasons for or causes of homosexuality? What are advantages and disadvantages of the homosexual life-style? Be objective. How does it differ from the other alternatives to traditional marriage?

10. What are your definitions of "normal" and "abnormal" behavior? Now, review the definitions discussed in the Perspective and see how different or similar your definitions are. Which definition is most commonly used?

11. How do the concepts of normal and abnormal put pressure on members of society to behave in certain ways? Do you notice this pressure in everyday life?

Future Directions

A baby is born of four biological parents through gene splicing.

Families do their banking and shopping via computer from their own homes.

A fertilized egg in a test tube is represented by a lawyer in an estate-settlement dispute.

Someone takes a pill to increase his or her attraction to another.

Do these events seem like scenes from a science fiction movie? Or situations that will confront generations in the distant future? Chances are the scenes are real, and if the questions have not already been raised, they will be soon—at least at some point during your lifetime.

Exactly what will happen in the future, of course, is hard to say. The future depends on events that have already taken place and things that are occurring right now. The future is directly related to the available technology and numerous other coexisting factors, such as economics (Are the times affluent or depressed?), politics (Is the country at war? Are there government funds for family studies and social support?), meteorology and biology (Has the weather affected crop production? Has a new disease affected health or death rates?), and education (Is sex education being approached logically and thoroughly?). The list is endless. And closely related to these factors are the values that people hold as a result of the times in which they live.

PERILS OF PREDICTION

"What if?" How many times have you asked that question? What if it rains Saturday? What if I change my major? What if my spouse is offered a job in another city? Forecasts of the future have always been valued—and always attempted.

However, prediction is difficult, and in areas that are affected by highly emotional forces both within and without, such as intimate relationships and family, the process becomes even more difficult. The well-known psychologist John Watson predicted in 1927 that marriage would no longer exist by the 1970s (Kinsley, 1927). Yet in the 1980s there are more marriages in America than ever before (Glick, 1984) and over 90 percent of young people say they include marriage in their future plans (Thornton & Freedman, 1982). Pitirim Sorokin (1937) predicted that there would eventually be no distinction between marital and nonmarital sex. Today, although most people engage in premarital sex, they do not give it the same sanction as sex within marriage. Likewise, although statistics show that over half of all married people engage in extramarital sex at least once, about three-fourths of Americans believe that extramarital sex is wrong (Thornton & Freedman, 1982).

To consider the future of intimate relations, marriage, and families, you must

BOX 16.1   PREDICTIONS FOR MARRIAGE AND FAMILY
                   IN THE YEAR 2000

Without a crystal ball, tea leaves, tarot cards, or some other type of magic, predicting the future is quite precarious. The following predictions for future directions in marriage and family life are based on current trends and statistical analyses. The only prediction that is guaranteed, however, is the last one.

1. The period from 1985 to 2000 will be more stable, with less change than in the 1960s and 1970s.
2. Attitudes toward premarital sex and sexual behavior in general will remain quite similar to those of today.
3. The vast majority of people will marry, although at a somewhat later age than in the past 20 years.
4. Experimentation and more options in marriage and family life will increase, but there will also be continuity.
5. Cohabitation will continue to increase, not as a substitute for marriage but as an advanced form of dating, although only a small percentage of the population will be cohabiting at any given time.
6. There will be an increase in singlehood among both the young and the elderly.
7. Women's employment will continue to increase, but at a much slower rate than in the past 20 years.
8. Couples will have fewer children; they will have them later in life and in a more compressed time period. Therefore they will have more couple time during the family life cycle.
9. Household size will continue its slow, century-long decrease. The number of households will increase slightly.
10. There will be an increase in serial monogamous marriages mainly because of a stable or slowly rising divorce rate and a subsequent increase in remarriage.
11. There will be an increase in certain family types, such as single-parent and blended families.
12. The proportion of children cared for outside the home will increase.
13. There will be an increase in widowhood, especially for women, who will generally spend their later years living alone.
14. In some families there will be an increase in associations between the generations, while in others the generations will grow further apart.
15. The percentage of the population over age 65 will continue to increase.
16. Technological innovations will continue to produce opportunities and changes in family life.
17. Although women will make some gains toward equality with men, there will still be a pattern of inequality—especially in the home—for the typical couple.
18. Divorce rates will level off before beginning a slow upward trend in the twenty-first century.
19. Happy couples will become happier and unhappy couples will become unhappier unless they terminate their marriages.
20. The institutions of marriage and the family are healthy and will continue to be healthy, although there will be more forms or structures of marriage and family functioning with varying degrees of openness and success.
21. Some people will agree with these predictions; others will not. Most of the predictions will come true; a few will not.

consider them not in isolation but in a social context. You must consider the educational, religious, economic, and political climate of the times and, in turn, realize that the disposition of the intimate relations—marriage and the family— may have an impact on these other situations as well.

The most commonly used and one of the safest methods of prediction is the projection of statistical trends—that is, studying the overall trends in a particular area and presuming that the trends will continue in approximately the same way or in a slightly altered way because of a certain force. Sometimes it is necessary to qualify predictions and say "If A happens, then B will happen; but if C happens, then D will occur."

Some predictions are confounded by events that are difficult or impossible to anticipate. Jessie Bernard (1982), following the lead of Robert Nisbet, calls these variables "change agents." She lists four—the maniac, the prophet, the genius of technology, and the random event. The ultimate maniac to fear today is the person who might push the button to initiate a nuclear war.

The prophet is one who presents a vision of the future and initiates change through his or her ideas. The leaders of the women's movement are examples in that they have supported more equal roles within marriage and convinced many people to live accordingly.

Examples of geniuses of technology are those who created contraceptive methods that are virtually 100 percent effective, who devised surgical procedures that can extend people's lives, and who have found cures for previously deadly diseases.

The random event is a seemingly isolated happening that triggers a sequence of changes affecting the lives of all people. For example, the Soviet Union's launching of the Sputnik satellite in the 1950s led to major changes in American education as the United States rushed to educate a generation of scientists and engineers. This wave of scientists, in turn, gave rise to the current hi-tech age of computer programming and satellite communication.

Television is another bit of technology that subtly affects everyone. "Today's Americans are turning to the mass media in their search for new models for marriage and other intimate relationships" (Francoeur, 1980, p. 4). The sitcoms, the soaps, and the dramas display a variety of relationships, and the frequent portrayal of a singles life-style, cohabitation, or multiple sex partners tends to make viewers see these situations as acceptable. In addition, talk shows and newscasts present the pros and cons of controversial personal problems.

FROM THE PAST TO THE FUTURE

"Many students mistakenly feel they know the facts about the past, or feel that the past is irrelevant to an understanding of their own lives" (Hendrix & Brown, 1980, p. 39). The myth persists that the American family was once large, extended, patriarchal, self-sufficient, and happy. Therefore, many people are holding up a picture of "the American family" that never existed, let alone one that can stand as a model for the modern family. In addition, the "sudden changes" that took place during the industrial revolution were not sudden at all. The patterns that have emerged since the colonial days have all represented a gradual change. Therefore, these trends can serve as a basis for prediction, and the knowledge that "Many major changes in the family were less recent and less rapid than is often believed, the current state and future of the family look less dismal" (Hendrix & Brown, 1980, p. 41).

RECENT DECADES

The future that we study and plan for begins today.
—CHESTER O. FISCHER

My interest is in the future because I'm going to spend the rest of my life there.   —CHARLES F. KETTERING

Hats off to the past; coats off to the future.

The best thing about the future is that it only comes one day at a time.

The changes that have taken place during the last several decades make more sense considered in the light of the overall trends in marriage and family. The 1950s were a time of "happy days" and growing wealth. Young people rushed into marriage, the birthrate was high, familism and pro-family values held sway. Young adults were interested in their jobs, their families, and their possessions.

The 1960s somewhat reversed these trends. Social issues became news. "Ask not what your country can do for you, but ask what you can do for your country," President John F. Kennedy challenged. So the idealistic, affluent generation became involved in politics and social movements. The civil rights movement broadened opportunities for minorities. College students began to question all authorities—government, the military, religious leaders, and university systems. The young established new morality featuring sexual freedom and independence. With the benefit of affluence, young people moved away from their homes and away from their parents' control. College students and other young people questioned religious values and stressed situational ethics. They asked for more "space" and the freedom to "do their own thing." They wondered if the nuclear family was important. Attitudes toward premarital sex became more liberal— what Reiss (1967) had labeled "permissiveness with affection" appeared—and many young people behaved accordingly. Effective contraception became widely available, often at college health clinics, for the first time. Also, living in their own apartments for the first time and having won recognition of student rights, the young enjoyed added freedom to experiment.

THE WOMEN'S MOVEMENT

Perhaps the most influential event of the 1960s and 1970s—at least in terms of shaping personal relationships and family life—was the emergence of the women's movement. "The Women's Movement is, for me, the most radical and potentially most transforming movement of our times," says Leonard (1983, p. 23). During the 1970s women voiced their dissatisfaction with their roles as second-class citizens. They raised such issues as equal household and childrearing responsibilities for husbands and wives, no-fault divorce, paternal and joint custody of children of divorce, legalized abortion, premarital contracts, open marriage, cohabitation, communal living, the right of unmarried women to bear and rear children, and the legitimacy of homosexual and transsexual marriages (Levine, 1981).

Women entered the work force in greater numbers, which, in turn, gave them

Women don't necessarily want what men think they do. They may hear a different drummer.

the economic independence and hence the option to remain single or to divorce. The divorce rate doubled between 1965 and 1975. There was a significant rise in single-person households and families. The prevailing attitude toward marriage and parenthood became less positive. Noted sociologist Jessie Bernard (1982) summarized the period as follows:

> Between roughly the mid to late 1960s and the mid to late 1970s, civil-rights movements, antiwar movements, consumer movements, student movements, antiestablishment protest movements of many kinds, recession, oil crises, and public scandals, among other social events, had left the whole structure of our society "trashed." Marriage itself was not spared. Marriage rates declined; so did fertility; divorce rates doubled. In 1973–1974 for the first time in our history the number of marriages terminated by divorce exceeded the number terminated by death. Female-headed households increased by half. There was widespread alarm at the prospect of the imminent demise of marriage altogether. (Bernard, 1982, pp. 295–296)

Today the women's movement is credited with helping women to feel good about themselves, to be optimistic about their future, and to see themselves as growing and taking risks.

The 1980s

The 1980s thus far have seen a leveling off in the precipitous conflicts of the previous decades. "We may have entered a period in which American families can adjust to the sharp changes that occurred in the 1960s and early 1970s" (Cherlin & Furstenberg, 1983, p. 10). Bernard (1982) notes that "the statistical trends seem to have moderated their precipitous rise and decline and appear at this moment to be in a holding pattern if not wholly stabilized. Negative attitudes toward marriage have been countered by a strong 'pro family' movement with wide ramifications" (p. 297).

Attitudes and behavior seem to reflect this leveling phenomenon. The divorce rate is leveling off. From the mid 1960s to the mid 1970s the rate rose from 2.5 to 5 percent and remained at that level through 1985. The birthrate, which had been decreasing for 20 years, has leveled off and has shown some very slight increases. There were a record number of marriages in 1982, with the average age of newlyweds higher than it had been in the 1950s.

People seem satisfied with marriage and family life. Despite changes in family structure and relationships, most Americans still regard the family as central to their well being and happiness (Kent, 1984). For example in a study of several hundred couples married more than 15 years, Lauer and Lauer (1985) found that both partners in 85 percent of the couples said they were happily married. This is not to say, however, that all marriages are happy—merely that the majority of those who are married and who are staying married are happy with their lives in general.

A look at intimate relationships, marriage, and family in the late 1980s shows three distinguishing characteristics that have emerged from the preceding decades, characteristics that will probably continue into the next century. They are continuity, diversity, and legitimation of choice. Continuity means that the traditional family structures in force today will still be in existence in the future. That is, the nuclear family, the extended family, the blended family, and the single-parent family will continue to be part of American society.

Diversity will be characteristic of the late 1980s and the years beyond simply because the changes of the 1960s and 1970s have left their mark. In addition to the prevalent nuclear family, a large minority of young people will live together without being married; some of them will never marry. The never-married parent-child household is here to stay. Single-parent households are increasing. Many gay men and lesbians are finding relationships with partners and establishing households. New attitudes will join, not replace, traditional attitudes, "thus making American society and culture much more pluralistic where sex, love, marriage, and family are concerned" (Clanton, 1984, p. 43).

Tolerance for a variety of life-styles and family relationships has become a key issue too. People are more willing to accept other people's choice of life-style without placing a stigma on those who differ from the social norm. Not all the issues will be solved in the near future, however. Abortion is likely to remain a controversial topic for the next decades. It is doubtful that society as a whole will be totally accepting of gay rights or allow homosexual marriage in this century.

DEVELOPING RELATIONSHIPS

PREMARITAL SEXUAL ATTITUDES AND BEHAVIOR

"Patterns of marriage and sexual values in the United States have historically followed the cyclical movements of the economy, with innovative freedom during expansions and conservative retrenchment during contractions" (Francoeur, 1980, p. 3). However, a swing completely back to conservatism in the 1980s and beyond is not likely. "Future economic downswings will be less likely to trigger a reversion to previous traditional values" because the "flexible attitudes and alternative life-styles" of our recent past have taken a firm foothold (Francoeur, 1980, p. 3).

The 1960s and 1970s have certainly left their mark on premarital sexual behavior. Studies vary as to what percentage of teenagers and college students have experienced sexual intercourse. The trend is toward an earlier age for first coitus and toward more sexual partners. Teenage pregnancies are up. Again, however, sexual permissiveness may be leveling off. One study shows that the percentage of female college students who had had premarital intercourse rose from 20 percent in the 1960s to 80 percent by the mid-1970s and then dropped to 50 percent in the early 1980s (Clatworthy, 1985).

What overall effect the "religious right" and the "moral majority" will have on the attitudes and behavior of young people remains to be seen. How the liberal young people of today will change when they have children of their own will also affect the general attitude.

The "sexual revolution" of the 1970s has brought both good and bad consequences, according to some experts. Leonard (1983) says that it would be beneficial if we could keep some of the elements of the changing attitudes and behaviors and eliminate others. For instance, he approves of the freedom to talk openly about erotic matters; the accessibility of information on physiology, venereal diseases, and birth control; the availability of abortion; and freer communication concerning sex education between children and parents. However, he sees the pressures and demands of sexual performance, the quest for never-failing arousal and climax, the neglect of surprise, the pervasive dogma about how sex is supposed to be, and the depersonalization of relationships as the negative results of the recent changes.

> *The trouble with burning the candle at both ends is that you always get caught in the middle.* —ALLEN M. SCHAEFER

> *Success in dating or marriage is much more than finding the right person: it is a matter of being* THE RIGHT PERSON.

> *Coming together is a beginning; keeping together is progress; working together is success.*

COHABITATION

Cohabitation in the United States is up in recent years, and it will probably continue to rise. It is estimated that up to a third of college students cohabit now, and half to three-fourths of the rest say they would elect to do so if the right circumstances arose (Stayton, 1984). In addition, more middle-aged and older couples are choosing this life-style, and Stayton (1984) suggests that two trends accompany it: (1) more parents are encouraging their children to cohabit before they marry, in hopes that living with a partner before marriage will help them make a better selection of a lifelong marriage partner, and (2) more people are cohabiting before they enter a second marriage, presumably to assure that their decision on a second partner is a good one. However, research findings in the future may alter this pattern. To date, research has not proven that cohabitation before marriage either increases or decreases a couple's chances for a successful marriage. If research should turn up conclusive evidence concerning the value of cohabitation on marital adjustment, the number of couples who cohabit may take a corresponding upward or downward swing.

It does appear that cohabitation for most people is viewed as a test period or a temporary life-style. It has not yet become a substitute for marriage, as was once predicted, but rather a step in the courtship process and a transition between first and second marriages (Cherlin & Furstenberg, 1983). There is no indication that it will replace marriage in the near future either.

SINGLEHOOD

In 1985, 20.6 million people in the United States lived alone. The percentage of women age 20 to 24 years who had not yet married has been larger in the 1980s than ever recorded previously. In the late 1980s, 13 million women lived alone. By 2001, it is expected that 18.5 million nonfamily households will be headed by women (Exter & Barber, 1987). The proportion of never-married men rose significantly too.

While some of these people will eventually marry, it is likely that singlehood will continue to become more popular. For some, the postponement of marriage to acquire an education or establish a career may turn into a satisfying life-style that they may continue indefinitely. The longer a person delays marriage, the less likely he or she is to ever marry (Glick, 1984). Another aiding factor in remaining single is the acceptance of singlehood as a legitimate alternative to marriage—whereas the attitude in past generations had been that something was wrong with any adult who could not find a mate or did not want to be married and to rear a family.

Glick (1984) estimates that 10 percent of men and 12 percent of women now aged 25 to 29 may never marry. If so, this means that today three times as many young adults—as compared to their parents' generation—will remain single. Associated with these figures is the fact that the number of children born out of wedlock has tripled in the last three decades.

Along with the numbers of Americans who are remaining single permanently, the age at first marriage is rising. The rising percentages of men and women who are still single in their twenties "may mean only that more young adults are postponing marriage. On the other hand, it could mean that a growing proportion of adults are committing themselves to staying single or cohabiting" (Glick, 1984, p. 22). Remarriage after divorce is becoming less frequent as well, thus increasing the number of single adults (Norton & Moorman, 1987).

The women's movement has contributed considerably to these statistics. As more women choose to complete their college educations and develop careers, fewer of them need to depend on a husband for their support.

Marrying too young is like taking a cake out of the oven before it's done and trying to frost it.

Many young people (and their parents) may be ready for the wedding but not the marriage.

When you find something that satisfies—you stop looking.

Many a good marriage is ruined in an attempt to make it perfect.

ALTERNATIVES TO TRADITIONAL MARRIAGE

Intimate relationships of the past were narrow in definition: they were virtually limited to the traditional marriage pattern. However, the key word today seems to be "choices." Intimate relationships today include homosexual cohabitation, marriage of more than two people, and communes in which groups of people consider themselves all married to one another.

Within the traditional marriage of a husband and wife, the options are endless too. A number have been proposed and tried over the past decades. For example, in a *term marriage,* a couple agrees to live together for a set period of time—say two or three years—with the option to renew their agreement. In the *two-step marriage* advocated by Margaret Mead (1966), the first marriage must be childless and would be easy to enter into and exit from. If a couple felt that their marriage was working on the couple level and they then wanted children, they could take the second step and start a family.

Suggestions such as these were popular in the late 1960s and early 1970s. However, such formalized forms of marriage have never really materialized. Some couples, though, agree less formally to an arrangement in which both are free to establish other independent, significant relationships. They may or may not agree to sexual exclusiveness. Some couples draw up a marriage contract that not only establishes the division of monies and property but also sets up expectations for each partner in terms of household duties, children, and work outside the home. Some couples engage in swinging; others maintain celibacy within their marriage.

None of these options has become popular enough to be used by a majority of married people, but all are available to those who marry. A pattern that has become the norm and is likely to continue to grow is that of serial monogamy— that is, entering a monogamous marriage in the hope that it will last a lifetime but finding that marriage unsatisfactory, divorcing, and remarrying. "The majority of those who go from one monogamous relationship to another are, however, looking for one which is more mature and fulfilling than the first" (Stayton, 1984, p. 22).

Predictions concerning new life-styles within marriage would be precarious. Some generalizations about marriage in the future are relatively sound. The number of first marriages contracted per year in the United States is likely to fall during the closing years of this century, in part simply because those born during the baby boom of the 1950s have already reached the age at which they are most likely to marry. The number of those between 18 and 26, the age at which they are most likely to enter a first marriage, is declining. Also, most people will eventually enter a monogamous marriage and spend more years in such an arrangement than in any other.

"By the year 2000, three kinds of families will dominate the personal lives of most Americans: families of first marriages, single-parent families, and families of remarriages" (Cherlin & Furstenberg, 1983, p. 8).

Marriage and Family Life

Husband and Wife Roles

The changes that have taken place in husband and wife roles in the past few decades have, in large part, been the result of the women's movement. There has been a great deal of media coverage on the changing roles of women in the community, in the work world, and in the home. As a result, the media have also

Men are gradually taking on more household chores, but statistics show that even women who work outside the home still do most of the housework.

focused on changes in the relationships between men and women and on men's roles as fathers and in the home.

Certainly some changes have taken place in this regard. The biggest change, perhaps, is the increased opportunity for women to gain satisfaction, fulfillment, and salary in careers outside the home. More women than ever before are working. "By 1990, well over half of all mothers of children under age six are expected to be in the labor force" (Phillips, 1986, pp. 63–64), the most rapid increase being for women with children under age two. Therefore, it is safe to predict a continuation of the upward trend in two-earner and dual-career families. Also, more women are obtaining advanced education, which qualifies them for better jobs.

However, while it is true that more women are moving into middle-management positions and the United States has now had a female vice-presidential candidate and has a female Supreme Court judge, top-management positions and top salaries are still primarily reserved for men. Women today still earn only about two-thirds of what men earn for the same work.

There has also recently been a lot of hype about the sharing of household chores and child-care duties between husbands and wives who both work outside the home. Numerous examples have been written up in popular magazines showing how a particular couple achieved a satisfactory balance in handling their work and personal lives. However, statistics show that in reality most women are simply taking on the work role in addition to their role as homemaker and primary parent. Husbands whose wives enter the workplace take on few extra duties at home to compensate for their wives' extra efforts outside the home.

While the average woman who works outside the home may not have all the advantages her husband has, in many cases she is in a more powerful position to negotiate for the equality that she wants and as a result may feel more free to leave a marriage that she finds unsatisfactory. Women's movement into the work world has been given credit—and blame—for at least part of the rising divorce rate.

> *There are two things to aim at in life: first, to get what you want;*
> *and after that, to enjoy it. Only the wisest of mankind achieve*
> *the second.*   —LOGAN PEARSALL SMITH

> *Observation: A man who won't let his wife work is probably*
> *married to a woman who doesn't want to.*
> —FRANKLIN P. JONES

> *The perfect spouse adjusts the marriage knot so that the couple are*
> *tied up without being tied down.*

> *From a Thanksgiving Day prayer:*

> *. . . and I thank Thee for a wife/husband who knows all about me*
> *yet still loves me.*

REPRODUCTION

Statistics show that most individuals marry and most married persons have children. The long-term trend over the past two centuries has been toward a lower birthrate, with a slight upward movement in the last decade. In the future there will probably be fewer children per family and these will be spaced more closely together (Grotberg, 1980).

Attitudes toward including children in one's life will affect reproduction. Women's movement into the labor force has influenced couples to have fewer children. Also having an effect is the pride parents take in their children and their children's accomplishments. The focus has shifted from simply bearing many children to providing adequately for a few.

Technology, likewise, has been instrumental in lowering the current birthrate. Effective temporary and permanent methods of contraception allow couples to plan the number of children they want and to control the spacing of those children. Recent developments in new contraceptives—such as rings and caps, vaccines, injections, and birth-control pills for men—promise couples a greater variety of choices in easy-to-use and reliable methods. Testing is slow, however, so—what with the threat of lawsuits—manufacturers are likely to be cautious before they make these new contraceptives available.

On the other hand, couples who want children but have been unable to conceive are being aided by new fertility research. "Cold and clinical as these advances may sound, the results of scientists' tinkerings with life in the lab are bringing real-life warmth to thousands of once-childless couples" (Alsofrom, 1984, p. 64). Many babies have been produced by fertilizing an egg and sperm from a given couple in a petri dish and then implanting the embryo into the mother's womb. (This process is known as in vitro fertilization.)

Carrying this process a step further, it is now possible to transfer a fertilized egg from one woman to another. One woman can be artificially inseminated with the sperm from a man whose wife who cannot conceive a baby. Then the donor's uterus is flushed and the fertilized egg is transferred to the wife's uterus through a tiny tube threaded through the cervix.

In addition, doctors can now perform microsurgery or use lasers to untangle kinks and twists in a woman's fallopian tubes or to clear away obstructions; they can also use lasers to treat precancerous conditions of the cervix, vagina, or vulva. In addition, they can insert balloons into blocked fallopian tubes and inflate them, much as they do in clearing blocked arteries to the heart. In some cases, ovarian cancer can now be treated without destroying a woman ability to bear children.

Advances have been made in testing to determine if a man's sperm is capable of fertilizing a woman's egg. Doctors can also inject a man's healthiest sperm into a woman's uterus through a tiny catheter to increase the chances of fertilization. Researchers are working to understand varicoceles (varicose veins in the testicles) and destructive immunologic responses (such as a man's allergy to his own sperm) that can cause infertility.

In addition, doctors can use a hormone pump to cause a woman to ovulate, and home fertility-check kits now enable women to tell when ovulation is about to occur.

No doubt research will continue in both contraception and fertility enhancement. However, so will the controversy over such procedures. Already moral issues have been raised and legal battles are being fought over rights to children produced by alternative methods. The abortion issue will no doubt continue to be a major one in the coming decades. People not only disagree on the basic issue of abortion but are raising new questions. Is it ethical to determine the sex of the fetus and then to have an abortion because you would rather have a child of the other gender? If many parents opt to choose the sex of their children, will that cause an imbalance in the overall sex ratio?

Other issues arise with surrogacy through artificial insemination. Does the surrogate mother have any rights to the child? Can a surrogate mother change her mind and keep the child? Should children conceived by artificial insemination or other methods be told? How will the news affect them? Does a male donor have visiting rights to children he has created with his sperm? Should a baby born with physical and/or mental defects be kept alive by elaborate medical procedures? If so, who will pay the costs?

The outcome of court battles and public opinion will direct the future of further testing and experimentation. Gone is the idea that creating life by artificial methods is purely science fiction. People today believe that anything is possible; now they must decide whether it is also desirable. Perhaps the best time to consider the consequences is before the procedures are implemented rather than after all sorts of emotional and legal problems have already arisen. As Blank (1985) notes, "As we acquire the capacity to control and direct the human condition, we also assume an awesome responsibility, whether willingly or not, for the choices we make" (p. 17).

BEING A PARENT

The way parents relate to and discipline their children has changed throughout history. Some generations of parents have shown strict discipline and have expected children to work on the farm or in the family business from the time they were able. Other generations have pampered their children and protected them from the world outside their homes until they reached late teens or early twenties.

With the decrease in family size, one aspect of parenting today is the effort to provide generously for each child in material goods and opportunities for education and travel.

"Both the popular press and the social science literature show a growing interest in the meaning of fatherhood" (Eggebeen & Uhlenberg, 1985, p. 251). These researchers point out that the voluntariness of fatherhood today makes parenting a more important aspect of men's lives. Although today a man spends less of his time in a household with children, it is expected that fathers will interact more with each child than they have in the past.

The secret of dealing successfully with a child is not to be its parent. —MELL LAZARUS

Children need love, especially when they don't deserve it.

This is her year to go to work and his to stay home with the children. In another year, the children will all be in school and both parents at work.

The parents who want their children to get an education these days may have to pull a few wires—the television wire, the VCR wire, and the radio wire.

The trouble with today's young people is they all want to look different in the same way.

Child Care   With young mothers moving into the world of work, more and more children are being cared for in settings other than the home. In the next few years, over half of all mothers of children under age six will be working. Because parents often do not live close to relatives who can help with child care—or *have* relatives that would be able and willing to help with child care—many of today's children attend day-care centers. At least two problems arise. One is that there are not enough day-care centers to accommodate all the children who need them. Waiting periods for openings can run 18 to 24 months (Phillips, 1986).

Another problem is that the quality of care is generally uneven. Almost 90 percent of family day-care providers earn less than the minimum wage (Phillips,

1986). Some experts question the capabilities of such personnel. In addition, some say that licensing provisions are inadequate and stress the need for workplace policies (Phillips, 1986). Some suggestions are infant-care leaves, day-care facilities at the workplace, and flex time for parents.

It is more likely that steps will be taken to improve day care for children than that mothers will return to the home to care for them.

Being a Single Parent   Recent years have seen a decrease in the percentage of children living with both parents. Over half of all divorces involve minor children living at home, which means that these children will live with only one parent, usually the mother. Still others are born to unmarried mothers (Cherlin & Furstenberg, 1983). Nearly 60 percent of children born in the early 1980s can expect to live with only one parent for at least a year before they reach age 18 (Glick, 1984). The problems that surround the single-parent family will have to be faced in the years to come.

FAMILY SUPPORT SYSTEMS

"The decline of extended and nuclear families has left many people without traditional support groups" (Rossman, 1985, p. 19). Therefore, people need to turn to alternative sources of help in times of crises. Government-funded agencies are one source of help, and many experts are calling for more public policies and helping agencies for the diverse families that are emerging in the American society. People also rely on health insurance to get them through medical emergencies financially. They send their children to free public schools. They rely on government police and fire protection. They seek counselors and social workers for emotional problems.

Many people are turning away from professionals and are learning to form their own networks or their own extended families for their personal problems. On the model of Alcoholics Anonymous, families with similar problems band together. "Such families can meet together regularly to share and evaluate their successes and failures and to encourage and help each other" (Rossman, 1985, p. 20). Others turn to local community and church volunteers for help.

RELATIONSHIPS IN TRANSITION

DIVORCE AND REMARRIAGE

The long-term trend throughout U.S. history has been an increase in divorce, although major events have altered that pattern along the way. For example, the Great Depression of the 1930s and the familistic era of the 1950s slowed down the rising rate, while World War II and the liberalism of the 1960s and 1970s caused upturns. Many other factors, such as the decreased stigma of divorce, women's greater economic independence, and unrealistically high expectations of marriage may also be contributing to the rising rates.

"In 1980 the proportion of men aged 30 to 34 who had ended a marriage in divorce was already as large as that for men aged 45 to 54, even though the older men had been exposed to the risk of divorce for many more years" (Glick, 1984, p. 23).

This overall upward trend is likely to continue. "At current rates, half of all American marriages begun in the early 1980s will end in divorce" (Cherlin & Furstenberg, 1983, p. 7). However, a number of factors may work in the opposite direction to help lower or at least maintain the current rate. Kemper (1983) lists them as follows:

> Decline in marriage rate; older age at marriage; higher proportion of single persons; mental health improvement in the population; upper limit on women in the labor force; slowdown in geographic mobility; end of the "cultural revolution"; end of "anomie of affluence"; exhaustion of latency effect of no-fault divorce laws; and a growing fear of the consequences of divorce. (p. 507)

One may conclude from all these data that the trend is still upward but the rate is leveling off.

While divorce is on the upswing, so is remarriage. Three out of four divorced people eventually remarry, with about half doing so within three years of their divorce. Men, particularly those with small children, remarry at the fastest rate. Most experts conclude from these statistics that people do not reject marriage itself but rather a particular marriage partner. While the trend toward remarriage seems likely to continue its upward swing, the time span between a divorce and

In this wedding, both the bride and groom have children from previous marriages. A woman minister performs the ceremony.

a remarriage is likely to lengthen. One reason is that many people who form new partnerships after divorce are living together, at least for a while, before remarrying. About 20 percent of people in their thirties today can expect to experience a redivorce at some time. About 5 percent can expect to go through a third divorce (Glick, 1984).

> One woman to another: "We aren't going out much anymore. All our friends are either multiplying or dividing."
> —HENRY E. LEABO

> Perhaps it's called "grounds for divorce" because of the dirt.

> Wife to husband: "I don't know what I'd do without you, but I'd rather."

> When you receive a reward for making a mistake, it's probably called alimony.

LIFE-CYCLE CHANGES

The changes in marriage and childbearing patterns have also caused changes in the overall life cycle of Americans. Generally speaking, people are marrying later, having fewer children, and spacing their children closer together than they did in the past. In addition, they are living longer than ever before. Therefore, their life-cycle pattern is different from that of their parents and grandparents. People have more time as single adults before they marry; they have more time as a couple before they start their family; they have more time as a couple after their children leave home.

THE ELDERLY

Similarly, the length of time that people can expect to spend as senior citizens, or in their years after retirement, is increasing steadily. This trend is expected to continue well into the twenty-first century. The percentage of people in the United States over 65 years of age in 1940 was less than 7 percent. In 1980, it was over 11 percent, and it is expected to increase to over 21 percent by the year 2040 (McMillen & Pugh, 1986). What is even more staggering is the prediction that the ratio of workers to retired people is expected to decline drastically. In 1980 there were nearly six workers for every retiree; by 2040 there will be fewer than three workers per retiree (McMillen & Pugh, 1986).

Those who reach retirement age today are in better shape than their predecessors were in past generations. Most live on their own, not as dependents of children or other family members. They are better educated than ever before and are in better health. Most are quite capable of continuing to take on challenging mental tasks, and they want to do so.

Some retirees are not really retiring from work fully but are merely shifting their activities from the workplace to other areas. For some, this means a general retirement from work—that is, putting in a shorter day for a few years before retiring completely. For others, it means serving as mentors for young people or working in volunteer positions rather than being paid. Many count such activities as crucial to their life satisfaction (Kouri, 1984).

The overall increase in people over age 65 may have consequences for the economy. For one thing, marketers are shifting their focus from adolescents to the elderly. Manufacturers and retailers will have to change the types of products they offer to meet the demands of this growing market.

The economic climate may show pulls in opposite directions. On the one hand, there has been a trend to keep older workers on the job for longer periods of time. The mandatory retirement age has been raised or eliminated in many organizations. On the other hand, with the tighter economy of the late 1980s, many companies have been offering their older employees the chance to retire early with reduced benefits.

Many people are concerned about the stability of the social security system because of the greater drain on the funds as more and more people reach retirement age. How public policy is set up and how businesses respond to the older worker will have effects on the financial well-being of people over 65.

Never resent growing old—many people are denied that privilege.

A neighbor who retired recently was heard to complain, "I wake up in the morning with nothing to do and go to bed with it only half done." —LYELL R. BROWN

SUMMARY

- Being able to predict the future is a valued skill but a difficult feat to accomplish, especially in personal areas.

- Projecting statistical trends is the safest method of prediction, although sudden changes in the economy, attitudes, technology, or some other factor can rapidly upset certain trends.

- Understanding the past and the present is important to determining what the future may hold.

- While changes in marriage and family life have occurred gradually throughout history, several events in the recent past have altered the pattern.

- The 1950s brought a period of familism and the 1960s and 1970s brought more liberal attitudes and behaviors. The 1980s have shown a leveling off from the previous decades of radical change.

- The women's movement has been said to be one of the biggest influences on attitudes toward changes in marriage and the family.

- Currently, intimate relationships, marriage, and the family have three major characteristics—continuity, diversity, and legitimation of choice.

- Although the trend has been toward more liberal attitudes and behavior in premarital sex, sexual permissiveness seems to be leveling off.

- Cohabitation may take an upward or downward swing if research reaches any conclusions about the good or ill effects of cohabitation.

- More people than ever before are delaying marriage or remaining single.

- Today, intimate relationships are not limited to traditional marriage patterns.

- Life-styles within marriage vary too, and while no alternative style has become widespread, many have been and will continue to be tried.

- Serial monogamy is apt to be the most prevalent marriage pattern.

- Changing husband and wife roles within a marriage have received widespread publicity; however, little change has actually taken place.

- Attitudes and technology have changed trends in reproduction rates and methods, which have led to moral and ethical issues that are far from being resolved.

- The biggest changes in parenting during the past decades have been an increase in the number of children in day care and an increase in single-parent households.

- People today often turn to other families and volunteers rather than to relatives and professionals for help with their personal problems.

- The upward trend in divorce and remarriage is likely to continue into the future.

- The elderly population in the United States is growing rapidly. This change alters people's life-cycle patterns as well as the country's economy.

PERSPECTIVE: THE IDEAL AMERICAN MARRIAGE AND FAMILY SYSTEM

Suppose your class is asked to design the ideal marriage and family system for our society. You are told that you may change our country's laws, folkways, mores, beliefs, attitudes, and practices. No doubt there are some things that you don't like about the way things are. Here is your chance to change them to the way you would prefer them to be.

Probably the biggest problem you will encounter in this assignment is the same one that legislators and policymakers already have to deal with—the fact that people are not ideal individuals. In fact, if they were, even thinking about the ideal marriage and family system would be not only easy but also unnecessary. These ideal people would handle their own problems. However, what you are dealing with are real people—people with faults, prejudices, and selfish natures. The need to contend with these factors makes your task infinitely more difficult.

The second problem is the sheer magnitude of the system. Let's say that you write down a couple of changes that you think would improve some area of marriage or family life. Most likely these few changes would also require changing many other areas of the system. Third, once you show your proposed changes to the other members of your class, you may quickly find that at least some of your ideas are not acceptable to others. No doubt you'll reject some of theirs. As a group you will have to make adjustments and work out compromises until you arrive at a document acceptable to the entire group. This process of give and take will give you a valuable lesson not only in policymaking and politics but also in negotiating within your own marriage and family, since all this involves change, adjustment and compromise.

Here are some excerpts from what one marriage-and-family class arrived at after a semester's work:

Establishment and Dissolution of Marriage

- There will be nonparental unions with minimal legal ties and no sexual restrictions.
- There will be parental unions with the following requirements:
  1. Partners must live together at least two consecutive years prior to having children.
  2. Partners must be at least twenty years old prior to having children.
  3. The unions must be formally registered in order to fix responsibility for children.
- There will be mandatory counseling for couples wishing to dissolve a parental union and voluntary counseling for those wishing to establish one.

Parenthood and Fertility Control

- It is essential to the concept of responsible parenthood that each child be a wanted and planned child.
- Educational programs on contraception, abortion, and parenthood will be widely available in the community and required in schools.
- When a woman has her third living child, she and the father of the child will be sterilized.

- For those couples who want to have more than two children, there is adoption.
- Parenthood will come to be seen as a privilege rather than a right.

Family Interaction and Regulation of Sexual Behavior

- The partners have responsibility to each other.
- The parents have responsibility for their children; the children have responsibility for their parents.
- There will be no restrictions on the sexual behavior of consenting partners over the age of 16 with the exception of incest.

The students in this particular group said they disliked the idea of telling others how they should behave and defining acceptable or unacceptable behavior. However, they were quite definite about some of the issues they were for or against. As in all things, these were ideas supported by most but not all of the students. As they concluded:

- Experimentation with alternative models will not be discouraged, but the above will remain the ideal model.

QUESTIONS FOR THOUGHT AND DISCUSSION

1. What is the value of being able to predict future events? What are some drawbacks? Which do you feel are more important, the costs or the benefits? Would you want to be able to predict the future? Why or why not?

2. What are the four "change agents" listed by Bernard? Describe each and then explain how they can affect predictions and future events.

3. How did the emergence of the women's movement affect society? Support or refute this statement: "Perhaps the most influential event to shape personal relationships and family life that occurred during the 1960s and 1970s was the women's movement."

4. What types of changes have taken place in people's views of marriage and the family from the 1950s through the 1980s? What are some reasons for these changes?

5. According to the chapter discussion, which of the current trends are likely to continue and which are not?

6. Why has cohabitation increased? Who is most likely to cohabit? What two trends are accompanying the increase in cohabitation? Would you consider cohabitation? Why or why not?

7. What are some of the alternatives to traditional marriage? Would you consider any of these for your life?

8. What types of changes have taken place in husband and wife roles? How has parenting changed?

9. How has the increasing divorce rate affected family relationships? Remarriage? How has parenting changed as a result of these changes in family structure?

10. How would you change the American idea of the "ideal" marriage and family?

Glossary

abortion Expulsion of an embryo or fetus from the uterus either spontaneously or via medical procedures.

abstinence Refraining from sexual intercourse.

abuse Behavior intended to hurt another person verbally, physically, or psychologically.

achieved status A position in a social organization attained through personal effort.

active listening Listening that involves careful attention to the other's verbal and nonverbal messages.

adultery Sexual intercourse between a married person and someone other than his or her spouse.

adversary divorce system A system in which divorce is granted on the theory that one party is wronged or innocent of any wrong doing.

afterbirth The placenta, amniotic sac, and remainder of the umbilical cord, all of which are expelled during delivery after the actual birth of the baby.

AIDS (acquired immunodeficiency syndrome) An incurable disease that attacks the immune system.

alcoholism An illness characterized by loss of control over drinking.

alimony The money paid, usually to a woman, by the spouse or former spouse after a legal separation or divorce.

androgyny The quality of having characteristics of both masculine and feminine roles.

ascribed status Social position based on such factors as age, race, and family over which the individual has no control.

attenuated family A nuclear family that loses a father or mother through death or divorce.

augmented family A family structure that includes both relatives and nonrelatives in the same household.

bachelor A man who has not married.

bestiality Sexual contact with animals.

bigamy The marriage of one person to two or more spouses at the same time.

bilineal (bilateral) Family descent traced along both wife/mother and husband/father lineage.

birthing room A room in a hospital for giving birth is changed to look like a home bedroom.

blended family A family consisting of two single parents who marry.

body language The message communicated by a person's expression, gesture, posture, dress, and so on.

bonding The emotional link created partly by cuddling, cooing, and physical and eye contact by the parent early in an infant's life.

caste system A closed form of social stratification in which status is determined at birth and is virtually lifelong.

celibate A person who abstains from sexual activity.

chastity Abstention from overt sexual activities, especially sexual intercourse.

child custody Legal award of responsibility for residence, control, and care of a child.

child support Income paid to a divorced spouse for the support of the dependent children.

child-free Without children.

chivalry Courtesy or gallantry to women.

climax An orgasm.

cohabitation Living together and having a sexual relationship without being married.

coitus Sexual intercourse.

commune A group of people who live together and hold collective ownership and use of property.

community property Property and debts acquired during a marriage by either or both spouses and which belongs equally to both.

commuter marriage Spouses who live apart because their jobs require that they live in different cities.

companionate love A love that is based on companionship more than on passion.

conception The moment at which an ovum (egg) joins with a sperm and an embryo begins to develop.

concubinage Cohabitation without legal sanction.

condom (prophylactic or rubber) A thin sheath that is rolled over the erect penis as a form of birth control or to help in the prevention of sexually transmitted diseases (STDs).

contraceptives Devices, techniques, or drugs used to prevent conception.

courtly love An intense romantic longing for someone other than one's marital partner.

courtship The association of an unmarried man and woman with a view to marriage.

cunnilingus Oral stimulation of the woman's vulva by her partner.

dating A prearranged couple activity for the purposes of socialization, recreation, and possible identification of a marriage partner.

defense mechanism An unconscious technique by which a person protects himself or herself from confronting painful or emotionally unacceptable thoughts and feelings.

dilation and curettage (D&C) An abortion technique in which the cervix is dilated and the embryo is removed from the uterus with an instrument.

dilation and evacuation (D&E) An abortion technique in which suction and forceps are used to remove the embryo or fetus.

divorce (marital dissolution) The legal termination of marriage.

divorce mediation A nonadversarial means of dispute resolution by which the couple, with the assistance of a mediator(s), negotiate the terms of their settlement of custody, support, property, and visitation issues.

dry orgasm Sexual climax in the male without any apparent ejaculation of semen.

dual-career marriage A marriage in which both husband and wife have careers.

ectopic pregnancy A fertilized egg that implants outside the uterus.

egalitarian family A family in which husband and wife enjoy equal power.

embryo The developing human organism from the time of implantation to the end of the eighth week after conception.

empathy Intellectual or emotional identification with another.

empty-nest syndrome The depression experienced by some parents when their children have left home.

endogamy A social requirement to marry within a certain group or groups.

engagement A formal commitment to marry.

erection The aroused state of the penis.

erogenous zone Areas of the body most sensitive to sexual arousal through touch.

erotic dream A dream that is high in sexual content.

exogamy A social requirement to marry outside one's own group of close relatives.

extended (consanguine) family A family consisting of a mother, a father, children, and other relatives.

extramarital relations Sexual relations outside or in addition to the marital relationship.

family A marriage with a child or children in any one of a variety of structures such as nuclear family, extended family, augmented family, attenuated family, and blended family.

fecundity The ability to have children.

fellatio Oral stimulation of the male's genitals by his partner.

feminist A person who advocates economic, political, and social rights for women.

fertility The actual number of births to women of childbearing age.

fetus A developing human organism from eight weeks after conception to birth.

fornication Heterosexual intercourse between two unmarried persons.

gay (slang) Homosexual.

genitalia The external reproductive parts of women and men.

Grafenberg spot (G-spot) An area about 1 to 2 centimeters from the vaginal entrance along the roof of the vagina that is believed to be erotically sensitive.

group marriage The marriage of two or more women to two or more men.

gunnysacking An alienating fight tactic in which a person saves up, or "gunnysacks," grievances until the sack gets too heavy, bursts, and lets ancient hostilities pour out.

gynecologist A physician who specializes in diseases affecting the female sex organs and in female reproductive physiology.

heterogamous marriage A marriage in which the husband and wife come from different backgrounds.

heterosexuality A sexual preference for members of the opposite sex.

homogamous marriage A marriage in which the husband and wife come from similar backgrounds.

homogeneity The quality characteristic of a population when the individuals within it show marked likeness of biologic and/or cultural traits.

homophobia Fear and hatred of homosexuals.

homosexuality A sexual preference for members of the same sex.

hymen In the female, a ring of tissue that partly covers the vaginal opening.

hypergamy Marrying upward in social class.

hypogamy Marrying downward in social class.

illegitimacy The birth of a child to an unmarried women.

implantation The burrowing of the fertilized egg into the lining of the uterus.

impotence The inability of a male to achieve and/or maintain an erection of the penis as a means to copulation.

incest The sexual activity, including but not limited to coitus, between individuals who are too closely related to ever contract legal marriage.

infanticide The killing of a newly or recently born child.

infatuation An unrealistic idealization of the loved one.

intercourse, sexual The insertion of the penis into the vagina.

joint custody A situation in which both divorced parents continue to take equal responsibility for important decisions regarding their child's general upbringing.

Lamaze method A method of preparing parents for childbirth to minimize the need for anesthesia and other medical intervention.

laparoscopy A medical procedure for the sterilization of females in which the fallopian tubes are either cauterized or clipped and tied off.

lesbian A homosexual female.

love Feelings that may involve emotional tension, sexual attraction, companionship, caring, and confirmation.

marriage   A socially sanctioned union of one man and one woman who are expected to play the roles of husband and wife.

marriage contract   A written agreement between married partners outlining the responsibilities and obligations of each.

masturbation   Stimulating one's own body in order to experience pleasurable sexual sensations.

maternity leave   The time women take off from work to care for their small children.

matriarchy   A family with a dominant wife/mother.

matrilineal   Family descent traced along wife/mother lineage.

matrilocal marriage   Marriage in which the couple resides with the parents of the wife.

menopause   The time in a woman's life, usually between ages 45 and 55, when the menstrual cycle ceases due to the cessation of ovulation and accompanying hormonal changes.

midlife crisis   The psychological difficulties of the role transition that takes place around age 40 when growing recognition of one's career limitations and of the unrealistic expectation of one's youth causes questioning and a renewed search for meaning to life.

misalliance   Marriage between people of different social classes.

modified extended family   A family that is nuclear in structure but extended in sentiment and communication.

monogamy   The marriage of one man to one woman.

multiparous woman   A woman who has experienced more than one childbirth.

neolocal   Marriage in which the couple resides at a new or independent address.

nidation   The implantation of the fertilized ovum in the lining of the uterus in pregnancy.

nocturnal orgasm   Involuntary orgasm that occurs during sleep in both men and women.

no-fault divorce   The dissolution of marriage based on irreconcilable differences, where neither party is "at fault."

norms   Guidelines to expected behavior.

nuclear (conjugal, immediate) family   A family consisting of a mother, a father, and children.

nulliparous woman   A woman who has never given birth.

oral-genital sex   Sexual activity in which the mouth is used to stimulate the genitals.

orgasm   The release of peak sexual tensions: it is characterized by involuntary, rhythmic, muscular contractions; a loss of self-awareness; and varying degrees of intense sensory pleasure.

ovaries   Two almond-sized organs in the female that store and release the egg cells (ova) and the female sex hormones estrogen and progesterone.

ovulation   The process in the fertile female whereby the ovary releases a mature egg (ovum) at regular intervals, usually once every 28 days.

ovum (pl. ova) Egg; female reproductive cell.

passionate love An intensely felt, typically short-term love that can be ignited by painful as well as pleasurable experiences.

paternity leave The time a man takes off from work to care for his newborn child.

patriarchy A family with a dominant husband/father.

patrilineal Family descent traced along husband/father lineage.

patrilocal marriage Marriage in which the couple resides with the parents of the husband.

penis The male sex organ.

phallus The penis, usually the erect penis.

philos The Greek concept of love, which includes one's feelings toward humanity in general.

"pill, the" Oral contraceptive.

placenta A mass of soft tissue formed during pregnancy and attached to the inner surface of the uterus.

polyandry The marriage of one woman to two or more men.

polygamy The marriage of one man or one woman to more than one wife or more than one husband at the same time.

polygyny The marriage of one man to two or more women.

posing Making a pretense of being what one is not, frequently part of courtship.

preejaculatory fluid A fluid containing some live sperm that sometimes appears at the tip of the penis during sexual arousal but before ejaculation.

pregnancy The condition of having a developing embryo or fetus in the body.

premarital sex Sex before marriage.

primogeniture A system of inheritance in which the oldest son gets all the land.

procreation The production of offspring.

pronatalism The strong positive value a society or group places on having children.

prostitution The exchange of sex acts for money or goods.

puberty The stage of life at which a child turns into a young man or young woman: the reproductive organs become functionally operative and secondary sex characteristics develop.

quickening The first fetal movements apparent to the pregnant woman.

random sample A selection made in such a way that each individual in a given population has an equal chance of being chosen.

rape Sexual intercourse with a person against his or her will or consent as defined by law.

remarriage The marriage of anyone who has previously been married.

role A set of behavioral expectations.

role conflict The situation in which incompatible expectations or behaviors accompany a given status or set of statuses.

role expectation   The generally expected social norms that prescribe how a role ought to be played.

role model   A person who serves as a source of learning and imitation.

romantic love   A love in which there is idealization of another, which may or may not be reciprocated.

Romeo and Juliet effect   The reaction that may occur when parents oppose their child's choice of date or decision to go steady. It leads to an increase in the child's romantic feelings for his or her partner.

scientific method   A systematic, organized series of steps that ensures maximum objectivity and consistency in researching a problem.

self-actualization   The development of one's own personal interests and talents.

self-concept   The sum of thoughts, feelings, and ideas that an individual has about oneself in reference to oneself as an object.

self-disclosure   The act of revealing personal information to others.

self-esteem   The positive or negative value we place on our self-concept.

seminal fluid   Semen.

serial monogamy   A succession of marriages such that one may have several spouses in the course of life but only one at a time.

sexism   The individual actions and institutional arrangements that discriminate against the opposite sex, usually women.

sex ratio   The number of males per hundred females in a given population.

sex roles   Prescriptions for masculine and feminine behavior.

sexual anarchy   The abolition of all controls over sexuality and notions of sexual immorality.

sexual double standard   Within a particular culture, the application of different standards of behavior to members of the two sexes.

sexual dysfunction   Any sexual inadequacy that inhibits a person's sexual functioning for the achievement of orgasm, either alone or with a partner.

sexual reproduction   Reproduction by fusion of a female ovum with a male sperm.

sexual revolution   An accelerated phase in a long-term evolutionary path of increased sexual permissiveness in America.

sexual scripts   Frameworks or contexts within which people interpret sexual events.

sexuality   All the human feelings, attitudes, and actions that people attach to their own and others' biological sex.

sexually transmitted diseases (STDs)   Bacterial or viral infections that attack the genital areas, with possibly severe complications in other parts of the body.

significant other   A person with whom one identifies and whose opinions one considers important.

singlehood   The state of being unmarried.

socioeconomic status (SES)   The measure of social status that takes into account several prestige factors, such as income, education, and occupation.

sperm   Male reproductive cells.

spermatozoa   The male's sperm cells, which must unite with a female's ovum for fertilization to occur.

spinster   An older unmarried woman.

spouse   One's husband or wife.

status   A socially defined position that may be ascribed or achieved.

stepchildren   The children of one's spouse by a former marriage.

stepfamily   A family comprising a man and a woman at least one of whom has been married before and one or more children from the previous marriage of either or both spouses.

stepparent   A person who occupies the parent role for the children by a former marriage of his or her spouse.

sterilization   Rendering a person sterile (unable to produce offspring) through medical procedures such as vasectomy in men or tubal ligation in women.

stroking   The process of complimenting another.

surrogate mother   A woman who agrees to be impregnated in order to carry another couple's baby to term and to deliver it.

swinging   A type of extramarital coitus in which the couple openly and willingly engages in sexual relationships with other married persons.

tender-years doctrine   In awarding child custody, the practice of giving more consideration to a mother than a father when the child is young.

term marriage   A marriage in which the couple agrees to live together for a set period of time with the option to renew their agreement.

two-step marriage   A marriage involving an agreement to remain child-free until, by mutual consent, the partners enter the second, more committed step and start having children.

unilineal (unilateral)   Family descent traced only in wife/mother or only in husband/father lineage.

uterus   The hollow, pear-shaped, muscular organ in the female that nurtures the fertilized egg until birth.

vacuum aspiration   Abortion method by which the blastocyst or embryo is sucked out of the uterus.

vagina   The tubular organ in the female into which the penis is inserted during intercourse and through which a baby passes during birth.

value judgment   A belief regarding what is desirable, right, or wrong.

vasectomy   A method of male sterilization in which a small piece of each vas deferens is removed and the ends tied off to prevent movement of the sperm into the seminal vesicles, so that the male ejaculate will be free of sperm.

venereal disease   Diseases transmitted by sexual contact.

viability   The capability of a baby to survive and function outside the mother's body.

virginity   The state of never having engaged in sexual intercourse.

vulva   The external female genitalia, including the labia majora, labia minora, clitoris, and vaginal opening.

widowhood   The loss of a spouse by death.

workaholic   A person whose work has become addictive; someone whose work has taken over such a major portion of his or her identity as to interfere with bodily health, personal happiness, interpersonal relationships, and often even effective work performance itself.

References

Abbott, D. A., & Brody, G. H. The relation of child age, gender, and number of children to the marital adjustment of wives. *Journal of Marriage and the Family*, 1985, *47*(1), 77–84.

Adam, J. H., & Adam, N. W. Should you get a divorce? Questions to ask yourself. *New Woman*, June 1982, pp. 74–80.

Adams, B. N. *The family* (3rd ed.). Chicago: Rand McNally, 1980.

————. The middle-class adult and his widowed or still-married mother. *Social Problems*, 1968, *16*(1), 50–59.

Adams, W. J. Honeymoon expectations of university students enrolled in marriage course: What do they reveal? *Canadian Home Economics Journal*, 1980, *30*(2), 101–105.

Ade-Ridder, L. Quality of marriage: A comparison between golden wedding couples and couples married less than fifty years. *Lifestyles: A Journal of Changing Patterns*, 1985, *7*(4), 224–237.

Ahrons, C. R. The continuing coparental relationship between divorced spouses. *American Journal of Orthopsychiatry*, 1981, *51*(3), 415–429.

Albrecht, S. L. Reactions and adjustments to divorce: Differences in the experience of males and females. *Family Relations*, 1980, *29*(1), 59–68.

————. Correlates of marital happiness among the remarried. *Journal of Marriage and the Family*, 1979, *41*(4), 857–868.

Aldous, J. New views on the family life of the elderly and the near-elderly. *Journal of Marriage and the Family*, 1987, *49*(2), 227–234.

————. *Family careers*. New York: Wiley, 1978.

Alexander, S. J. Protecting the child's rights in custody cases. *The Family Coordinator*, 1977, *26*(4), 377–382.

Alsofrom, J. The new sexual revolution: Human reproduction. *Self*, 1984, *6*(12), 64–68.

Alzate, H. Vaginal eroticism and female orgasm: A current appraisal. *Journal of Sex and Marital Therapy*, 1985, *11*(2), 271–284.

Amato, P. R., & Ochiltree, G. Family resources and the development of child competence. *Journal of Marriage and the Family,* 1986, *48*(1), 47–56.

Ambron, S. R. *Child development.* San Francisco: Rinehart, 1975.

Ammons, P., & Stinnett, N. The vital marriage: A closer look. *Family Relations,* 1980, *29*(1), 37–42.

Anderson, T. B. Widowhood as a life transition: Its impact on kinship ties. *Journal of Marriage and the Family,* 1984, *46*(1), 105–114.

Aneshensel, C. S., & Rosen, B. C. Domestic roles and sex differences in occupational expectations. *Journal of Marriage and the Family,* 1980, *42*(1), 121–131.

Anonymous. A crabbit old woman wrote this. *Transition,* 1981, *11*(2), 10.

Appleton, W. S. Why marriages become dull. *Medical Aspects of Human Sexuality,* 1980, *14*(3), 73–85.

Arafat, I. S., & Cotton, W. L. Masturbation practices of males and females. *Journal of Sex Research,* 1974, *10*(4), 293–307.

Armour, R. *Light armour.* New York: McGraw-Hill, 1954.

Ash, P. Pre-retirement counseling. *Gerontologist,* 1966, *6*(2), 97–99; 127–128.

Atchley, R. C. *The sociology of retirement.* Cambridge, MA: Schenkman, 1976.

———. The meaning of retirement. *Journal of Communication,* 1974, *24*(4), 97–100.

———. *The social forces in later life: An introduction to social gerontology.* Belmont, CA: Wadsworth, 1972.

———. Retirement and leisure participation: Continuity or crisis? *Gerontologist,* 1971, *11*(1), 13–17.

Atchley, R. C., & Miller, S. J. Older people and their families. In C. Eisdorfer (Ed.), *Annual Review of Gerontology and Geriatrics* (Vol. 1). New York: Springer, 1980.

Atwater, L. *The extramarital connection: Sex, intimacy, identity.* New York: Irvington, 1982.

Austrom, D. R. *The consequences of being single.* New York: Peter Lang, 1984.

Bach, G. R., & Deutsch, R. M. *Pairing.* New York: Wyden, 1970.

Bach, G. R., & Wyden, P. *The intimate enemy: How to fight fair in love and marriage.* New York: Avon, 1970.

Bagarozzi, J. I., & Bagarozzi, D. A. Financial counseling: A self control model for the family. *Family Relations,* 1980, *29*(3), 396–403.

Bahr, S. J. The effects of welfare on marital stability and remarriage. *Journal of Marriage and the Family,* 1979, *41*(3), 553–560.

Bahr, S. J., Chappell, C. B., & Leigh, G. K. Age at marriage, role enactment, role consensus, and marital satisfaction. *Journal of Marriage and the Family,* 1983, *45*(4), 795–803.

Bain, F. W. (Translator). *A digit of the moon: A Hindoo love story.* London: James Parker, 1899.

Bales, R. F., & Slater, P. E. Role differentiation in small decision-making groups. In T. Parsons & R. F. Bales (Eds.), *Family: Socialization and interaction process.* New York: Free Press, 1955.

Balswick, J. O., & Peek, C. W. The inexpressive male: A tragedy of American society. In R. H. Walsh & O. Pocs (Eds.), *Marriage and Family 81/82*. Guilford, CT: Dushkin, 1981.

Barkas, J. L. *Single in America*. New York: Atheneum, 1980.

Barranti, C. C. R. The grandparent/grandchild relationship: Family resource in an era of voluntary bonds. *Family Relations*, 1985, *34*(3), 343–352.

Barron, M. L., Streib, G. F., & Suchman, E. A. Research on the social disorganization of retirement. *American Sociological Review*, 1952, *17*(4), 479–482.

Bartell, G. D. Group sex among the mid-Americans. *Journal of Sex Research*, 1970, *6*(2), 113–130.

Beach, S. R. H., Jouriles, E. N., & O'Leary, K. D. Extramarital sex: Impact on depression and commitment in couples seeking marital therapy. *Journal of Sex and Marital Therapy*, 1985, *11*(2), 99–112.

Bean, F. D., Clark, M. P., Swicegood, G., & Williams, D. Husband-wife communication, wife's employment, and the decision for male or female sterilization. *Journal of Marriage and the Family*, 1983, *45*(2), 395–403.

Beck, S. H. Adjustment to and satisfaction with retirement. *Journal of Gerontology*, 1982, *37*(5), 616–624.

Beckman, L. J., & Houser, B. B. The more you have, the more you do: The relationship between wife's employment, sex-role attitudes, and household behavior. *Psychology of Women Quarterly*, 1979, *4*(2), 160–174.

Belkin, G. S., & Goodman, N. *Marriage, family, and intimate relationships*. Chicago: Rand McNally, 1980.

Bell, A. P., Weinberg, M. S., & Hammersmith, S. K. *Sexual preference: Its development in men and women*. Bloomington: University of Indiana Press, 1981.

Bell, J. E., & Eisenberg, N. Life satisfaction in midlife childless and empty-nest men and women. *Lifestyles: A Journal of Changing Patterns*, 1985, *7*(3), 146–155.

Bell, R. R., & Balter, S. Premarital sexual experiences of married women. *Medical Aspects of Human Sexuality*, 1975, *7*(11), 111–123.

Bell, R. R., & Coughey, K. Premarital sexual experience among college females, 1958, 1968, and 1978. *Family Relations*, 1980, *29*(3), 353–357.

Belskey, J., Lang, M. E., & Rovine, M. Stability and change in marriage across the transition to parenthood: A second study. *Journal of Marriage and the Family*, 1985, *47*,(4), 855–865.

Benassi, M. A. Effects of romantic love on perception of strangers' physical attractiveness. *Psychology Reports*, 1985, *56*(2), 355–358.

Benin, M. H., & Nienstedt, B. C. Happiness in single- and dual-earner career families: The effects of marital happiness, job satisfaction, and life cycle. *Journal of Marriage and the Family*, 1985, *47*(4), 975–984.

Benson, L. *The family bond: Marriage, love, and sex in America*. New York: Random House, 1971.

———. *Fatherhood: A sociological perspective*. New York: Random House, 1968.

Bentler, P. M., & Newcomb, M. D. Longitudinal study of marital success and failure. *Journal of Consulting and Clinical Psychology*, 1978, *46*(5), 1053–1070.

Berardo, D. H., Shehan, C. L., & Leslie, G. R. A residue of tradition: Jobs, careers, and spouses' time in housework. *Journal of Marriage and the Family*, 1987, *49*(2), 381–390.

Berger, C., Jacques, J., Brender, W., Gold, D., & Andres, D. Contraceptive knowledge and use of birth control as a function of sex guilt. *International Journal of Women's Studies*, 1985, *8*(1), 72.

Berger, D. G., & Wenger, M. G. The ideology of virginity. *Journal of Marriage and the Family*, 1973, *35*(4), 666–676.

Berger, R. M., & Kelly, J. J. Working with homosexuals of the older population. *Social Casework*, 1986, *67*(4), 203–210.

Berk, R. H., & Berk, S. F. A simultaneous equation model for the division of household labor. *Sociological Methods and Research*, 1978, *6*(4), 431–468.

Berman, W. H. Continued attachment after legal divorce. *Journal of Family Issues*, 1985, *6*(3), 375–392.

Bernard, J. *The future of marriage.* New Haven, CT: Yale University Press, 1982.

———. *The future of motherhood.* New York: Penguin, 1974.

———. *The sex game: Communication between the sexes.* New York: Atheneum, 1972.

———. Jealousy in marriage. *Medical Aspects of Human Sexuality*, 1971, *5*(4), 200–215.

Bernard, J., Buchanan, H. E., & Smith, W. M., Jr. *Dating, mating and marriage today: A documentary-case approach.* New York: Arco, 1959.

Bernard, J. L., & Bernard, M. L. The abusive male seeking treatment: Jekyll and Hyde. *Family Relations*, 1984, *33*(4), 543–547.

Bernard, J. L., Bernard, S. L., & Bernard, M. L. Courtship violence and sex-typing. *Family Relations*, 1985, *34*(4), 573–576.

Bersoff, D., & Crosby, F. Job satisfaction and family status. *Personality and Social Psychology Bulletin*, 1984, *10*(1), 79–83.

Berstein, B. E., & Collins, S. K. Remarriage counseling: Lawyer and therapists help with the second time around. *Family Relations*, 1985, *34*(3), 387–391.

The Bible. Ecclesiastes 3:1–8.

The Bible. Genesis 1:28.

Bienvenu, M. J. Measurement of marital communication. *The Family Coordinator*, 1970, *19*(4), 26–31.

Bird, G. W., Bird, G. A., & Scruggs, M. Determinants of family task sharing: A study of husbands and wives. *Journal of Marriage and the Family*, 1984, *46*(2), 345–355.

Black, H. C. *Black's law dictionary* (5th ed.). St. Paul, MN: West, 1979.

Black, K. N., & Stevenson, M. R. The relationship of self-reported sex-role characteristics and attitudes toward homosexuality. *Journal of Homosexuality*, 1984, *10*(1/2), 83–93.

Blank, R. H. Making babies: The state of the art. *The Futurist*, 1985, *19*(1), 11–17.

Blechman, E. A. Are children with one parent at psychological risk? A methodological review. *Journal of Marriage and the Family*, 1982, *44*(1), 179–195.

Blieszner, R. Trends in family gerontology research. *Family Relations,* 1986, *35*(4), 555–562.

Blieszner, R., & Mancini, J. A. Enduring ties: Older adults' parental role and responsibilities. *Family Relations,* 1987, *36*(2), 176–180.

Blitchington, W. P. Traditional sex roles result in healthier sexual relationships and healthier, more stable family life. In H. Feldman and A. Parrot (Eds.), *Human sexuality.* Beverly Hills, CA: Sage, 1984.

Block, J. D. *Friendship: How to give it and how to get it.* New York: Macmillan, 1980.

Blood, R. O., & Blood, M. *Marriage* (3rd ed.). New York: Free Press, 1978.

Blood, R. O., & Wolfe, D. M. *Husbands and wives: The dynamics of married living.* Glencoe, IL: Free Press, 1960.

Bloom, B. L., Asher, S. J., & White, S. W. Marital disruption as a stressor: A review and analysis. *Psychological Bulletin,* 1978, *85*(4), 867–894.

Bloom, B. L., & Kindle, K. R. Demographic factors in the continuing relationship between former spouses. *Family Relations,* 1985, *34*(3), 375–381.

Bloom, D. E. Putting off children. In O. Pocs and R. H. Walsh (Eds.), *Marriage and Family 86/87.* Guilford, CT: Dushkin, 1986.

Blumstein, P., & Schwartz, P. *American couples.* New York: Morrow, 1983.

Bohannan, P. *Divorce and after.* Garden City, NY: Doubleday, 1971.

Borland, D. C. A cohort analysis approach to the empty-nest syndrome among three ethnic groups of women: A theoretical position. *Journal of Marriage and the Family,* 1982, *44,*(1), 117–129.

Boss, P. G. Normative family stress: Family boundary changes across the life span. *Family Relations,* 1980, *29*(4), 445–450.

Bowman, H. A., & Spanier, G. B. *Modern marriage* (8th ed.). New York: McGraw-Hill, 1978.

Brecher, E. M. Love, sex, and aging. In O. Pocs (Ed.), *Human Sexuality 88/89.* Guilford, CT: Dushkin, 1988.

Breckenridge, J. N., Gallagher, D., Thompson, L. W., & Peterson, J. Characteristic depressive symptoms of bereaved elders. *Journal of Gerontology,* 1986, *41*(2), 163–168.

Brehm, S. S. *Intimate relationships.* New York: Random House, 1985.

Brewer, G. K. Promoting healthful aging through strengthening family ties. *Topics in Clinical Nursing,* April 3, 1981, pp. 45–50.

Brock, G. W., & Joanning, H. A comparison of the relationship enhancement program and the Minnesota couple communication program. *Journal of Marital and Family Therapy,* 1983, *9*(4), 413–421.

Brody, E. M., Johnsen, P. T., Fulcomer, M. C., & Lang, A. M. Women's changing roles and help to elderly parents: Attitudes of three generations of women. *Journal of Gerontology,* 1983, *38*(5), 597–607.

Brown, G. H. Bulletin: Divorce rate jumps from one percent to two percent in ten years. In R. H. Walsh & O. Pocs (Eds.), *Marriage and Family 82/83.* Guilford, CT: Dushkin, 1982.

Brown, P., & Manela, R. Changing family roles; Women and divorce. *Journal of Divorce*, 1978, *1*(4), 315–328.

Brubaker, T. H. *Later life families.* Beverly Hills, CA: Sage, 1985.

Bryson, J. B., & Bryson, R. *Salary and job performance differences in dual-career couples.* Beverly Hills, CA: Sage, 1980.

Bulcroft, K., & O'Conner-Roden, M. Never too late. *Psychology Today*, 1986, *20*(6), 66–69.

————. The importance of dating relationships on quality of life for older persons. *Family Relations*, 1986, *35*(3) 397–401.

Bullough, V. L. Weighing the shift from sexual identity to sexual relationships. *Journal of Homosexuality*, 1984, *10*(3/4), 3–5.

————. *The subordinate sex: A history of attitudes toward women.* New York: Penguin, 1974.

Bumpass, L. L., & Sweet, J. A. Differentials in marital instability: 1970. *American Sociological Review*, 1972, *37*(6), 754–766.

Burgess, E. W., Locke, H. J., & Thomes, M. M. *The family* (3rd ed.). New York: American, 1963.

Burgess, E. W., & Wallin, P. *Engagement and marriage.* Chicago: Lippincott, 1953.

Burstein, B. *Life history and current values as predictors of sexual behaviors and satisfaction in college women.* Paper presented at the meeting of the Western Psychological Association, Sacramento, CA, 1975.

Buss, D. M., & Barnes, M. Preferences in human mate selection. *Journal of Personality and Social Psychology*, 1986, *50*(3), 559–570.

Bytheway, W. R. The variation with age of age differences in marriage. *Journal of Marriage and the Family*, 1981, *43*(4), 923–927.

Cadwallader, M. Marriage as a wretched institution. *Atlantic Monthly*, 1966, *218*(5), 62–66.

Calhoun, A. W. *A social history of the American family: From Colonial times to the present* (Vol. 1). New York: Barnes & Noble, 1945.

Callan, V. J. The impact of the first birth: Married and single women preferring childlessness, one child, or two children. *Journal of Marriage and the Family*, 1986, *48*(2), 261–269.

————. Comparisons of mothers of one child by choice with mothers wanting a second birth. *Journal of Marriage and the Family*, 1985, *47*(1), 155–164.

Camp, S. L., Speidel, J. J., & Barberis, M. What's new in contraception? *USA Today*, May 1986, pp. 88–92.

Campbell, A. *The sense of well-being in America.* New York: McGraw-Hill, 1981.

Cannon, S. R. *Social functioning patterns in families of offspring receiving treatment for drug abuse.* Roslyn Heights, NY: Libra, 1976.

Cargan, L., & Melko, M. *Singles: Myths and realities.* Beverly Hills, CA: Sage, 1982.

Carlson, E., & Stinson, K. Motherhood, marriage timing, and marital stability: A research note. *Social Forces*, 1982, *61*(1), 258–267.

Carson, G. *The polite Americans.* New York: Morrow, 1966.

Carter, D., & Welch, D. Parenting styles and children's behavior. *Family Relations,* 1981, *30*(2), 191–195.

Carter, S. Still a woman's hardest decision: I don't want children. In O. Pocs and R. H. Walsh (Eds.), *Marriage and Family 84/85.* Guilford, CT: Dushkin, 1984.

Cass, V. C. Homosexual identity formation: Testing a theoretical model. *Journal of Sex Research,* 1984, *20*(2), 143–167.

Cavan, R. S. *Personal adjustment in old age.* Chicago: Science Research Associates, 1949.

Chafetz, J. S. Marital intimacy and conflict: The irony of spousal equality. *Free Inquiry in Creative Sociology,* 1985, *13*(2), 191–195.

Chappell, N. L., & Havens, B. Who helps the elderly person? A discussion of informal and formal care. In W. A. Peterson & J. S. Quadagno (Eds.), *Social bonds in later life.* Beverly Hills, CA: Sage, 1985.

Chassin, L., Zeiss, A., Cooper, K., & Reaven, J. Role perceptions, self-role congruence and marital satisfaction in dual-worker couples with preschool children. *Social Psychology Quarterly,* 1985, *48*(4), 301–311.

Cherlin, A. Work life and marital dissolution. In G. Levinger and O. C. Moles (Eds.), *Divorce and separation: Context causes and consequences.* New York: Basic Books, 1979.

Cherlin, A., & Furstenberg, F. F., Jr. The American family in the year 2000. *The Futurist,* 1983, *17*(3), 7–14.

Christopher, F. S., & Cate, R. M. Anticipated influences on sexual decision-making for first intercourse. *Family Relations,* 1985, *34*(2), 265–270.

———. Factors involved in premarital sexual decision-making. *Journal of Sex Research,* 1984, *20*(4), 363–376.

Cicirelli, V. G. Adult children's helping behavior to elderly parents. *Journal of Family Issues,* 1984, *5*(3), 419–440.

Ciernia, J. R. Myths about male midlife crises. *Psychological Reports,* 1985, *56*(3), 1003–1007.

Clanton, G. Social forces and the changing family. In L. A. Kirkendall and A. E. Gravett (Eds.), *Marriage and the family in the year 2020.* Buffalo, NY: Prometheus, 1984.

———. The contemporary experience of adultery: Bob and Carol and Updike and Rimmer. In R. W. Libby and R. N. Whitehurst (Eds.), *Marriage and alternatives: Exploring intimate relationships.* Glenview, IL: Scott, Foresman, 1977.

Clanton, G., & Smith, L. *Jealousy.* Englewood Cliffs, NJ: Prentice-Hall, 1977.

Clark, M., & Anderson, B. G. *Culture and aging: An anthropological study of older Americans.* Springfield, IL: Charles C. Thomas, 1967.

Clark, P. G., Siviski, R. W., & Weiner, R. Coping strategies of widowers in the first year. *Family Relations,* 1986, *35*(3), 425–430.

Clark, R. L. How women's magazines cover living alone. *Journalism Quarterly,* 1981, *58*(2), 291–294.

Clatworthy, N. M. Morals and the everchanging college student: 1968–1982. *Free Inquiry in Creative Sociology*, 1985, *13*(1), 83–86.

Clayton, R. R., & Bokemier, J. L. Premarital sex in the seventies. *Journal of Marriage and the Family*, 1980, *42*(4), 759–775.

Clemons, P. W., & Rust, J. O. Factors in adolescent rebellious feelings. *Adolescence*, 1979, *4*(53), 159–173.

Cleveland, M. Divorce in the middle years: The sexual dimension. *Journal of Divorce*, 1979, *2*(3), 255–262.

Clifford, C. The perfect contraceptive. *Self*, 1986, *8*(4), 136–139.

Clinch, T. A. Margaret Sanger: Rebel in the midst of Victorian moralism. In O. Pocs (Ed.), *Human Sexuality 81/82*. Guilford, CT: Dushkin, 1981.

Clingempeel, W. G., & Brand, E. Quasi-kin relationships, structural complexity, and marital quality in stepfamilies: A replication, extension, and clinical implications. *Family Relations*, 1985, *34*(3), 401–409.

Clingempeel, W. G., & Reppucci, N. D. Joint custody after divorce. In D. H. Olson & B. C. Miller (Eds.), *Family Studies Review Yearbook* (Vol. 2). Beverly Hills, CA: Sage, 1984.

Cockrum, J., and White, P. Influences on the life satisfaction of never-married men and women. *Family Relations*, 1985, *34*(4), 551–556.

Cole, C. L. Development tasks affecting the marital relationship in later life. *American Behavioral Scientist*, 1986, *29*(4), 389–403.

Coleman, E. M., Hoon, P. W., and Hoon, E. F. Arousability and sexual satisfaction in lesbian and heterosexual women. *Journal of Sex Research*, 1983, *19*(1), 58–73.

Coleman, J. C., and Glaros, A. C. *Contemporary psychology and effective behavior* (5th ed.). Glenview, IL: Scott, Foresman, 1983.

Colletta, N. D. Support systems after divorce: Incidence and impact. *Journal of Marriage and the Family*, 1979, *41*(4), 837–846.

Condran, J. G., & Bode, J. G. Rashomon, working wives, and family division of labor: Middletown, 1980. *Journal of Marriage and the Family*, 1982, *44*(2), 421–426.

Conley, J. A., & O'Rourke, T. W. Attitudes of college students toward selected issues in human sexuality. *The Journal of School Health*, 1973, *43*(5), 286–292.

Cook, A. S., West, J. B., & Hamner, T. J. Changes in attitudes toward parenting among college women: 1972 and 1979 samples. *Family Relations*, 1982, *31*(1), 109–113.

Cook, D. R., & Frantz-Cook, A. A systematic treatment approach to wife battering. *Journal of Marital and Family Therapy*, 1984, *10*(1), 83–93.

Cooley, C. H. *Human nature and the social order.* New York: Scribner, 1902.

Coombs, L. C., & Zumeta, Z. Correlates of marital dissolution in a prospective fertility study: A research note. *Social Problems*, 1970, *18*(1), 92–117.

Cordell, A. S., Parke, R. D., & Sawin, D. B. Father's views on fatherhood with special reference to infancy. *Family Relations*, 1980, *29*(3), 331–338.

Cornfield, N. The success of urban communes. *Journal of Marriage and the Family*, 1983, *45*(1), 115–126.

Cottle, T. The moment of truth. *Working Mother,* November 1981, pp. 69–97.

Cowan, C. P., Cowan, P. A., Heming, G., Garrett, E., Coysh, W. S., Curtis-Boles, H., & Boles, A. J., III. Transitions to parenthood: His, hers, and theirs. *Journal of Family Issues,* 1985, *6*(4), 451–481.

Crain, I. J. Afterplay. *Medical Aspects of Human Sexuality,* 1978, *12*(2), 72–85.

Creecy, R. F., Berg, W. E., & Wright, R. Loneliness among the elderly: A casual approach. *Journal of Gerontology,* 1985, *40*(4), 487–493.

Crooks, R., & Baur, K. *Our sexuality* (3rd ed.) Menlo Park, CA: Benjamin Cummings, 1987.

Crosby, J. F. *Illusion and disillusion: The self in love and marriage* (3rd ed.). Belmont, CA: Wadsworth, 1985.

Cuber, J. F., & Harroff, P. *The significant Americans.* Baltimore: Penguin, 1965.

Cudaback, D., Darden, C., Nelson, P., O'Brien, S., Pinsky, D., & Wiggins, E. Becoming successful parents: Can age-paced newsletters help? *Family Relations,* 1985, *34*(2), 271–275.

Dail, P. W., & Way, W. L. What do parents observe about parenting from prime time television? *Family Relations,* 1985, *34*(4), 491–499.

Daniels-Mohring, D., & Berger, M. Social network changes and the adjustment to divorce. *Journal of Divorce,* 1984, *8*(1), 17–32.

Darling, C. A., Kallen, D. J., & Van Dusen, J. E. Sex in transition, 1900–1980. *Journal of Youth and Adolescence,* 1984, *13*(5), 385–397.

D'Augelli, J. F., & Cross, H. J. Relationship of sex guilt and moral reasoning to premarital sex in college women and in couples. *Journal of Consulting and Clinical Psychology,* 1975, *43*(1), 40–47.

Davidson, J. K. Sexual fantasies among married males: An analysis of sexual satisfaction, situational contexts, and functions. *Sociological Spectrum,* 1985, *5*(1–2), 139–153.

Davis, C. A., & Dawson, B. G. Women, work, and life transitions. *Employment Counseling,* 1985, *22*(3), 117–123.

Davis, E. C., Hovestadt, A. J., Piercy, F. P., & Cochran, S. W. Effects of weekend and weekly marriage enrichment program formats. *Family Relations,* 1982, *31*(1), 85–90.

Davis, K. E. Near and dear: Friendship and love compared. *Psychology Today,* 1985, *19*(2), 22–28; 30.

Deaux, K., & Hanna, R. Courtship in the personals column: The influence of gender and sexual orientation. *Sex Roles,* 1984, *11*(5/6), 363–375.

DeBurger, J. E. *Marriage today.* New York: Wiley, 1977.

DeJong-Gierveld, J., & Aalberts, M. Singlehood: A creative or a lonely experience? *Alternative Lifestyles,* 1980, *3*(3), 350–368.

DeLamater, J., & MacCorquodale, P. *Premarital sexuality.* Madison: University of Wisconsin Press, 1979.

DeLora, J. S., Warren, C. A., & Ellison, C. R. *Understanding sexual interaction* (2nd ed.). Boston: Houghton Mifflin, 1981.

DeMaris, A., & Leslie, G. R. Cohabitation with the future spouse: Its influence upon marital satisfaction and communication. *Journal of Marriage and the Family,* 1984, *46*(1), 77–84.

Demos, J. *A little commonwealth: Family life in Plymouth.* New York: Oxford University Press, 1970.

Denney, N. W., Field, J. K., & Quadagno, D. Sex differences in sexual needs and desires. *Archives of Sexual Behavior,* 1984, *13*(3), 233–245.

Depner, C., & Ingersoll, B. Employment status and social support: The experience of the mature woman. In M. Szinovacz (Ed.), *Women's retirement: Policy implications of recent research.* Beverly Hills, CA: Sage, 1982.

DeRougemont, D. *The crisis of the modern couple* (Rev. ed.). New York: Harper and Brothers, 1959.

Deutsch, C. *Broken bottles, broken dreams: Understanding and helping the children of alcoholics.* New York: Teachers College Press, 1982.

DeVries, R. G. Birth and death: Social construction at the poles of existence. *Social Forces,* 1981, *59*(4), 1074–1093.

Diamond, M., and Karlen, A. *Sexual decisions.* Boston: Little, Brown, 1980.

Dixon, J. K. The commencement of bisexual activity in swinging married women over age thirty. *Journal of Sex Research,* 1984, *20*(1), 71–90.

Dixon, R. B., & Weitzman, L. J. When husbands file for divorce. *Journal of Marriage and the Family,* 1982, *44*(2), 103–114.

Dizard, J. E. The price of success. In L. K. Howe (Ed.), *The future of the family.* New York: Touchstone, 1972.

Dorfman, L. T., & Hill, E. A. Rural housewives and retirement: Joint decision-making matters. *Family Relations,* 1986, *35*(4), 507–514.

Dornbusch, S. M., Carlsmith, J. M., Gross, R. T., Martin, J. A., Jennings, D., Rosenberg, A., & Duke, P. Sexual development, age, and dating: A comparison of biological and social influences upon one set of behaviors. *Child Development,* 1981, *52*(1), 179–185.

Douvan, E. A., & Adelson, J. *The adolescent experience.* New York: Wiley, 1966.

Downs, W. R. Alcoholism as a developing family crisis. *Family Relations,* 1982, *31*(1), 5–12.

Doyle, J. A. *Sex and gender: The human experience.* Dubuque, IA: Wm. C. Brown, 1985.

Draper, T. W. On the relationship between welfare and marital stability: A research note. *Journal of Marriage and the Family,* 1981, *43*(2), 293–297.

Dryfoos, J. What the United States can learn about prevention of teenage pregnancy from other developed countries. *SIECUS Report,* 1985, *14*(2), 1–7.

Duberman, L. Step-kin relationships. *Journal of Marriage and the Family,* 1973, *35*(2), 283–292.

Duncan, D. F. Attitudes toward parents and delinquency in suburban adolescent males. *Adolescence,* 1978, *13*(50), 365–369.

Dutton, D. G., & Aron, A. P. Some evidence for heightened sexual attraction under conditions of high anxiety. *Journal of Personality and Social Psychology,* 1974, *30*(4), 510–517.

Duvall, E. M. *In-laws: Pro and con.* New York: Association Press, 1954.

Ebersole, P. Geriatric crisis intervention in the family context. In J. E. Hall & B. R. Weaver (Eds.), *Nursing of families in crisis*. Philadelphia: Lippincott, 1974.

Edleson, J. L., Miller, D. M., Stone, G. W., & Chapman, D. G. Group treatment for men who batter. *Social Work Research and Abstracts*, 1985, *21*(3), 18–21.

Edmiston, S. How to write your own marriage contract. In R. H. Walsh & O. Pocs (Eds.), *Marriage and Family 80/81*. Guilford, CT: Dushkin, 1980.

Edmondson, D. Birth control: What you need to know. *Parents*, 1986, *61*(10), 156–162.

Edwards, J. N., & Booth, A. Sexual behavior in and out of marriage: An assessment of correlates. *Journal of Marriage and the Family*, 1976, *38*(1), 73–81.

Eggebeen, D., & Uhlenberg, P. Changes in the organization of men's lives: 1960–1980. *Family Relations*, 1985, *34*(2), 251–257.

Eldridge, W. D. Therapist's use of information and dynamics from extramarital relationships to stimulate growth in married couples. *Family Therapy*, 1983, *10*(1), 1–11.

Elias, J. E. Adolescents and sex. In J. R. Barbour (Ed.), *Human Sexuality 80/81*. Guilford, CT: Dushkin, 1980.

Elkin, M. The missing links in divorce law: A redefinition of process and practice. *Journal of Divorce*, 1982, *6*(1/2), 37–63.

Ellis, A. *The American sexual tragedy* (2nd ed.). New York: Lyle Stuart, 1962.

England, P. The sex gap in work and wages. *Society*, 1985, *22*(5), 68–74.

Epstein, N. B., Bishop, D. S., & Baldwin, L. M. McMaster model of family functioning. In D. H. Olson & B. C. Miller (Eds.), *Family Studies Review Yearbook* (Vol. 2). Beverly Hills, CA: Sage, 1984.

Eshleman, J. R., & Clarke, J. N. Theoretical orientations and marital/family studies. In J. R. Eshleman and J. N. Clarke (Eds.), *Intimacy, commitments and marriage: Development of relationships*. Boston: Allyn & Bacon, 1978.

Ewer, P. A., Crimmins, E., & Oliver, R. An analysis of the relationship between husband's income, family size, and wife's employment in the early stages of marriage. *Journal of Marriage and the Family*, 1979, *41*(4), 727–738.

Exter, T. G., & Barber, F. Demographic forecasts: Women on their own. *American Demographics*, August 1987, pp. 35–37; 61–63.

Falbo, T., & Peplau, L. A. Power strategies in intimate relationships. *Journal of Personality and Social Psychology*, 1980, *38*(4), 618–628.

Farber, B. *Family organization and interaction*. San Francisco: Chandler, 1964.

Farson, R. Why good marriages fail. In J. DeBurger (Ed.), *Marriage today—Problems, issues and alternatives*. New York: Wiley, 1977.

Fengler, A. P. Romantic love in courtship: Divergent paths of male and female students. *Journal of Comparative Family Studies*, 1974, *5*(1), 134–139.

Ferber, M. A. Labor market participation of young married women: Causes and effects. *Journal of Marriage and the Family*, 1982, *44*(2), 457–468.

Ferber, M. A., & Huber, J. Husbands, wives, and careers. *Journal of Marriage and the Family*, 1979, *41*(2), 315–325.

Ferraro, K. F., & Wan, T. T. H. Marital contributions to well-being in later life: An examination of Bernard's thesis. *American Behavioral Scientist,* 1986, *29*(4), 423–437.

Ficher, I. V. Value of extended foreplay. *Medical Aspects of Human Sexuality,* 1979, *13*(12), 13–23.

Finger, F. W. Changes in sex practices and beliefs of male college students: Over 30 years. *Journal of Sex Research,* 1975, *11*(4), 304–317.

Firth, R., Hubert, J., & Forge, A. *Families and their relatives: Kinship in a middle-class sector of London.* New York: Humanities Press, 1970.

Fischer, L. R. Elderly parents and the caregiving role: An asymmetrical transition. In W. A. Peterson & J. S. Quadagno (Eds.), *Social bonds in later life: Aging and interdependence.* Beverly Hills, CA: Sage, 1985.

Fisher, B. L., Giblin, P. R., & Hoopes, M. H. Healthy family functioning: What therapists say and what families want. In D. H. Olson & B. C. Miller (Eds.), *Family Studies Review Yearbook* (Vol. 2). Beverly Hills, CA: Sage, 1984.

Fisher, C., Cohen, H. D., Schiavi, R. C., Davis, D., Furman, B., Ward, K., Edwards, A., & Cunningham, J. Patterns of female sexual arousal during sleep and waking: Vaginal thermoconductance studies. *Archives of Sexual Behavior,* 1983, *12*(2), 97–122.

Foote, N. Love. *Psychiatry, Journal for the Study of Interpersonal Processes,* 1953, *16*(3) 245–251.

Ford, D. A. Wife battery and criminal justice: A study of victim decision-making. *Family Relations,* 1983, *32*(4), 463–475.

Ford, J. D., Bashford, M. B., & DeWitt, K. N. Three approaches to marital enrichment: Toward optimal matching of participants and interventions. *Journal of Sex and Marital Therapy,* 1984, *10*(1), 41–48.

Forisha, B. L. *Sex roles and personal awareness.* Morristown, NJ: General Learning Press, 1978.

Francke, L. B. The sons of divorce. *The New York Times Magazine,* May 22, 1983, pp. 40–41.

Francoeur, R. T. The sexual revolution: Will hard times turn back the clock? *The Futurist,* 1980, *14*(2), 3–12.

French, J. R. P., & Raven, B. H. The bases of social power. In D. Cartwright (Ed.), *Studies in social power.* Ann Arbor: University of Michigan Press, 1959.

Friedman, E. A., & Orbach, H. L. Adjustment to retirement. In S. Arieti (Ed.), *American handbook of psychiatry* (2nd ed.). New York: Basic Books, 1974.

Fromm, E. *The art of loving.* New York: Bantam Books, 1963.

Furstenberg, F. F. Industrialization and the American family: A look backward. *American Sociological Review,* 1966, *31*(3), 326–337.

Futuyma, D. J., & Risch, S. J. Sexual orientation, sociobiology, and evolution. *Journal of Homosexuality,* 1983/1984, *9*(2/3), 157–168.

Gagnon, J. H. *Human sexualities.* Glenview, IL: Scott, Foresman, 1977.

Galloway, J. L., & Avery, P. A. America's forgotten resource: Grandparents. In O.

Pocs & R. H. Walsh (Eds.), *Marriage and Family 85/86.* Guilford, CT: Dushkin, 1985.

Gallup, G., Jr. What Americans think about their lives and families. *Families,* 1982, *2*(6), 40–41.

Gecas, V., & Schwalbe, M. L. Parental behavior and adolescent self-esteem. *Journal of Marriage and the Family,* 1986, *48*(1), 37–46.

Geer, J., Heiman, J., & Leitenberg, H. *Human sexuality.* Englewood Cliffs, NJ: Prentice-Hall, 1984.

Gelles, R. J. The myth of battered husbands and new facts about family violence. In O. Pocs & R. H. Walsh (Eds.), *Marriage and Family 83/84.* Guilford, CT: Dushkin, 1983.

George, L. K., & Weiler, S. J. Sexuality in middle and late life. *Archives of General Psychiatry,* 1981, *38*(8), 919–923.

Giele, J. Z. Changing sex roles and family structure. *Social Policy,* 1979, *9*(4), 32–43.

Giles-Sims, J. A longitudinal study of battered children of battered wives. *Family Relations,* 1985, *34*(2), 205–210.

Gilford, R. Contrasts in marital satisfaction throughout old age: An exchange theory analysis. *Journal of Gerontology,* 1984, *39*(3), 325–333.

Gilliam, K. Parents' ambivalence toward their newborn baby: A problem in community and professional denial. *Child Welfare,* 1981, *60*(7), 483–489.

Gilmartin, B. G. That swinging couple down the block. *Psychology Today,* 1975, *8*(9), 54–61.

Glass, S. P., & Wright, T. L. Sex differences in type of extramarital involvement and marital dissatisfaction. *Sex Roles,* 1985, *12*(9/10), 1101–1118.

Glasser, P. H., & Glasser, L. N. (Eds.). *Families in crises.* New York: Harper & Row, 1970.

Glenn, N. D. Interreligious marriage in the United States: Patterns and recent trends. *Journal of Marriage and the Family,* 1982, *44*(3), 555–566.

Glenn, N. D., & Shelton, B. A. Pre-adult background variables and divorce: A note of caution about overreliance on explained variance. *Journal of Marriage and the Family,* 1983, *45*(2), 405–410.

Glenn, N. D., & Weaver, C. N. The marital happiness of remarried divorced persons. *Journal of Marriage and the Family,* 1977, *39*(2), 331–337.

Glick, P. C. How American families are changing. *American Demographics,* 1984, *6*(1), 21–25.

———. Marriage, divorce, and living arrangements. *Journal of Family Issues,* 1984, *5*(1), 7–26.

Glick, P. C., & Norton, A. J. Marrying, divorcing, and living together in the United States today. *Population Bulletin,* 1977, *32*(5), 3–39.

Goldberg, S. Is homosexuality normal? *Policy Review,* Summer 1982, pp. 119–138.

Goldscheider, F. K., & Waite, L. J. Nest-leaving patterns and the transition to marriage for young men and women. *Journal of Marriage and the Family*, 1987, *49*(3), 507–516.

Goldstein, D., & Rosenbaum, A. An evaluation of the self-esteem of maritally violent men. *Family Relations*, 1985, *34*(3), 425–428.

Goldstein, M. The future of male birth control. *Planned Parenthood Review*, 1986, *6*(3), 11–12.

Goode, W. J. *World revolution and family patterns.* New York: Free Press, 1970.

Gordon, H. A., & Kammeyer, C. W. The gainful employment of women with small children. *Journal of Marriage and the Family*, 1980, *42*(2), 327–336.

Gordon, M. (Ed.). *The American family in social-historical perspective* (2nd ed.). New York: St. Martin's, 1978.

———. *The nuclear family in crisis: The search for an alternative.* New York: Harper & Row, 1972.

Gordon, S. Before we educate anyone else about sexuality, let's come to terms with our own. *Journal of Sex Education and Therapy*, 1985, *11*(1), 16–21.

Gordon, T. *Parent effectiveness training: The "no-lose" program for raising responsible children.* New York: Wyden, 1970.

Gottman, J. M. *Marital interaction.* New York: Academic Press, 1979.

Grando, R., & Ginsberg, B. G. Communication in the father-son relationship: The parent-adolescent relationship development program. *The Family Coordinator*, 1976, *25*(1), 465–473.

Granvold, D. K. Structured separation for marital treatment and decision-making. *Journal of Marital and Family Therapy*, 1983, *9*(4), 403–412.

Granvold, D. K., Pedler, L. M., & Schellie, S. G. A study of sex role expectancy and female post-divorce adjustment. *Journal of Divorce*, 1979, *2*(4), 383–393.

Green, M. *Fathering.* New York: McGraw-Hill, 1976.

Green, S. K., Buchanan, D. R., & Heuer, S. K. Winners, losers, and choosers: A field investigation of dating initiation. *Personality and Social Psychology Bulletin*, 1984, *10*(4), 502–511.

Greenberg, E. F., & Nay, W. R. The intergenerational transmission of marital instability reconsidered. *Journal of Marriage and the Family*, 1982, *44*(2), 335–347.

Greenblat, C. S. The salience of sexuality in the early years of marriage. *Journal of Marriage and the Family*, 1983, *45*(2), 289–299.

Greene, B., Lee, R., & Lustig, N. Conscious and unconscious factors in marital infidelity. *Medical Aspects of Human Sexuality*, 1974, *8*(8), 87–105.

Greer, S. Urbanism reconsidered: A comparative study of local areas in a metropolis. *American Sociological Review*, 1956, *21*(1), 19–25.

Greif, G. L. Children and housework in the single father family. *Family Relations*, 1985, *34*(3), 353–357.

Grieff, B. S., & Munter, P. K. Can a two-career family live happily ever after? In R. H. Walsh & O. Pocs (Eds.), *Marriage and Family 82/83.* Guilford, CT: Dushkin, 1982.

Grosskopf, D. *Sex and the married woman.* New York: Wallaby, 1983.

Grossman, A. S. More than half of all children have working mothers. *Monthly Labor Reviews*, 1982, *105*(2), 41–43.

Grossman, S. M., Shea, J. A., & Adams, G. R. Effects of parental divorce during early childhood on ego development and identity formation of college students. *Journal of Divorce,* 1980, *3*(3), 263–272.

Grotberg, E. H. Child and family programs and concerns in the 21st century. *Journal of Clinical and Child Psychology,* 1980, *9*(2), 148–151.

Grover, K. J., Russell, C. S., Schumm, W. R., & Paff-Bergen, L. A. Mate selection processes and marital satisfaction. *Family Relations,* 1985, *34*(3), 383–386.

Gurak, D. T., & Dean, G. The remarriage market: Factors influencing the selection of second husbands. *Journal of Divorce,* 1979, *3*(2), 161–173.

Gurel, L. Fertility related attitudes of minority mothers with large and small families. *Journal of Applied Social Psychology,* 1978, *8*(1), 1–14.

Haas, L. Role-sharing couples: A study of egalitarian marriages. *Family Relations,* 1980, *29*(3), 289–296.

Hale, L. C., & Knecht, J. A. *The legal divorce experience for families.* Normal: Illinois State University College of Continuing Education and Public Service, 1986.

Hansen, G. L. Dating jealousy among college students. *Sex Roles: A Journal of Research,* 1985, *12*(7/8), 713–720.

Hanson, S. L., Myers, D. E., & Ginsburg, A. L. The role of responsibility and knowledge in reducing teenage out-of-wedlock childbearing. *Journal of Marriage and the Family,* 1987, *49*(2), 241–256.

Harkins, E. B. Effects of empty-nest transition on self-report of psychological and physical well-being. *Journal of Marriage and the Family,* 1978, *40*(3), 549–556.

Harlow, M. K. Social deprivation in monkeys. *Scientific American,* 1962, *207*(5), 1–10.

Harman, D., & Brim, O. G. *Learning to be parents: Principles, programs, and methods.* Beverly Hills, CA: Sage, 1980.

Harmatz, M. G., & Novak, M. A. *Human sexuality.* New York: Harper & Row, 1983.

Harry, J. Decision making and age differences among gay male couples. *Journal of Homosexuality,* 1982, *8*(2), 9–21.

Hass, A. *Teenage sexuality.* New York: Macmillan, 1979.

Hatch, D., & Leighton, L. Comparison of men and women on self-disclosure. *Psychological Reports,* 1986, *58*(1), 175–178.

Hatcher, R. A., Guest, F., Stewart, F., Stewart, G. K., Trussell, J., Cerel, S., & Cates, W. *Contraceptive technology 1986–1987* (13th ed.). New York: Irvington, 1986.

Hatfield, E., Greenberger, D., Traupmann, J., & Lambert, P. Equity and sexual satisfaction in recently married couples. *Journal of Sex Research,* 1982, *18*(1), 18–32.

Hatfield, E., & Walster, G. W. *A new look at love.* Reading, MA: Addison-Wesley, 1981.

Heaton, T. B., Albrecht, S. L., & Martin, T. K. The timing of divorce. *Journal of Marriage and the Family,* 1985, *47*(3), 631–639.

Heer, D. M. The prevalence of black-white marriage in the United States, 1960 and 1970. *Journal of Marriage and the Family,* 1974, *36*(2), 246–258.

Hendrick, C., & Hendrick, S. A theory and method of love. *Journal of Personality and Social Psychology,* 1986, *50*(2), 392–402.

———. *Liking, loving and relating.* Monterey, CA: Brooks/Cole, 1983.

Hendrix, L., & Brown, F. D. Past, present, and future: A classroom exercise on family change. *Teaching Sociology,* 1980, *8*(1), 39–45.

Henshaw, S. K., & O'Reilly, K. Characteristics of abortion patients in the United States, 1970 and 1980. *Family Planning Perspectives,* 1983, *15*(1), 5–16.

Henslin, J. M. Dating and mate selection. In J. M. Henslin (Ed.), *Marriage and family in a changing society.* New York: Free Press, 1980.

Hewitt, J. P. *Self and society: A symbolic interactionist social psychology* (3rd ed.). Boston: Allyn & Bacon, 1984.

Hight, E. S. A contractual, working separation: A step between resumption and/or divorce. *Journal of Divorce,* 1977, *1*(1), 21–30.

Hill, C. T., Rubin, Z., & Peplau, L. A. Breakups before marriage: The end of 103 affairs. *Journal of Social Issues,* 1976, *32*(1), 147–168.

Hill, E. A., & Dorfman, L. T. Reaction of housewives to the retirement of their husbands. *Family Relations,* 1982, *31*(2), 195–200.

Hill, R. *Families under stress: Adjustment to the crises of war separation and reunion.* New York: Harper, 1949.

Hiller, D. V., & Philliber, W. W. Necessity, compatibility and status attainment as factors in the labor-force participation of married women. *Journal of Marriage and the Family,* 1980, *42*(2), 347–354.

Hiltz, S. R. Widowhood: A roleless role. *Marriage and Family Review,* 1978, *1*(6), 1; 3–10.

Hite, S. *The Hite report on male sexuality.* New York: Knopf, 1981.

Hoffman, S. R., & Levant, R. F. A comparison of childfree and child-anticipated married couples. *Family Relations,* 1985, *34*(2), 197–203.

Holahan, C. K. Marital attitudes over 40 years: A longitudinal and cohort analysis. *Journal of Gerontology,* 1984, *39*(1), 49–57.

Hollingshead, A. B. *Elmtown's youth and Elmtown revisited.* New York: Wiley, 1975.

Holman, T. B., & Burr, W. R. Beyond the beyond: The growth of family theories in the 1970's. In D. H. Olson and B. C. Miller (Eds.), *Family studies review yearbook* (Vol. 2). Beverly Hills, CA: Sage, 1984.

Holmes, T. H., & Rahe, R. H. The social readjustment rating scale. *Journal of Psychosomatic Research,* 1967, *11*(2), 213–218.

Hooker, K., & Ventis, D. G. Work ethic, daily activities, and retirement satisfaction. *Journal of Gerontology,* 1984, *39*(4), 478–484.

Horton, P. B., & Hunt, C. L. *Sociology.* New York: McGraw-Hill, 1964.

Hott, L. R., & Hott, J. R. Sexual misunderstandings. *Medical Aspects of Human Sexuality,* 1980, *14*(1), 13–31.

Hoult, T. F., Henze, L. F., & Hudson, J. W. *Courtship and marriage in America.* Boston: Little, Brown, 1978.

Houseknecht, S. K., Vaughan, S., & Macke, A. S. Marital disruption among professional women: The timing of career and family events. *Social Problems,* 1984, *31*(2), 273–284.

How optimistic are American women? *Ms.*, July/August 1987, pp. 172–176.

Huber, J., & Spitze, G. Wives' employment, household behaviors, and sex-role attitudes. *Social Forces*, 1981, *60*(1), 150–169.

———. Considering divorce: An expansion of Becker's theory of marital instability. *American Journal of Sociology*, 1980, *86*(1), 75–89.

Hudson, J. W., & Hoyt, L. L. *Campus values in mate selection: Forty years later.* Dittoed manuscript, 1978.

Hughes, J. Helplessness and frustration: The relatives' dilemma. *Nursing Times*, June 9, 1982, pp. 960–961.

Hunt, M. *Sexual behavior in the 1970's.* Chicago: Playboy Press, 1974.

———. Sexual behavior in the 1970's: Premarital sex. *Playboy*, 1973, *20*(12), 90–91; 256.

———. *The natural history of love.* New York: Knopf, 1959.

Hyde, J. S. *Understanding human sexuality* (3rd ed.). New York: McGraw-Hill, 1986.

Information please almanac 1986 (39th ed.). Boston: Houghton Mifflin, 1986.

Isaacson, W. The battle over abortion: Crusades and contests between those who advocate choice and life. *Time*, 1981, *117*(14), 20–28.

Jacoby, S. Forty-nine million singles can't be all right. *The New York Times Magazine*, 1974, *123*(42), 13; 41; 43; 46; 48–49.

Jahoda, M. Work, employment, and unemployment: Values, theories, and approaches in social research. *American Psychologist*, 1981, *36*(2), 184–191.

James, W. H. The honeymoon effect on marital coitus. *Journal of Sex Research*, 1981, *17*(2), 114–123.

Janda, L. H., O'Grady, K. E., & Barnhart, S. A. Effects of sexual attitudes and physical attractiveness on person perception of men and women. *Sex Roles*, 1981, *7*(2), 189–199.

Jesser, C. J. Male responses to direct verbal sexual initiatives of females. *Journal of Sex Research*, 1978, *14*(2), 118–128.

Jessor, S. L., & Jessor, R. Transition from virginity to nonvirginity among youth: A social-psychological study over time. *Developmental Psychology*, 1975, *11*(4), 473–484.

Jeter, K., & Sussman, M. B. Each couple should develop a marriage contract suitable to themselves. In H. Feldman & M. Feldman (Eds.), *Current controversies in marriage and family.* Beverly Hills, CA: Sage, 1985.

Jewson, R. H. After retirement: An exploratory study of the professional woman. In M. Szinovacz (Ed.), *Women's retirement: Policy implications of recent research.* Beverly Hills, CA: Sage, 1982.

Jimenez, S. L. M. Pregnancy: A time for marital stress? In O. Pocs and R. H. Walsh (Eds.), *Marriage and Family 84/85.* Guilford, CT: Dushkin, 1984.

Johnson, E. S., & Vinick, B. H. Support of the parent when an adult son or daughter divorces. *Journal of Divorce*, 1981, *5*(1/2), 69–76.

Johnson, R. E. Some correlates of extramarital coitus. *Journal of Marriage and the Family,* 1970, *32*(1), 449–456.

Jones, K. L., Shainberg, L. W., & Byer, C. O. *Dimensions of human sexuality.* Dubuque, IA: Wm. C. Brown, 1985.

Jorgensen, S. R. *Marriage and the family: Development and change.* New York: Macmillan, 1986.

Jourard, S. M. *The transparent self* (Rev. ed.). New York: Van Nostrand, 1971.

———. *Personal adjustment and approach through the study of healthy personality.* New York: Macmillan, 1958.

Jourard, S. M., & Rubin, J. E. Self-disclosure and touching: A study of two modes of interpersonal encounter and their inter-relation. *Journal of Humanistic Psychology,* 1968, *8*(1), 39–48.

Juhasz, A. M. Measuring self-esteem in early adolescents. *Adolescence,* 1985, *20*(79), 877–887.

Jurich, A. P., & Jurich, J. A. Effects of cognitive moral development upon the selection of premarital sexual standards. *Journal of Marriage and the Family,* 1974, *36*(4), 736–741.

Kalmuss, D. The intergenerational transmission of marital aggression. *Journal of Marriage and the Family,* 1984, *46*(1), 11–19.

Kando, T. M. *Sexual behavior and family life in transition.* New York: Elsevier, 1978.

Kanin, E., Davidson, K., & Scheck, S. A research note on male-female differentials in the experience of heterosexual love. *Journal of Sex Research,* 1970, *6*(1), 64–72.

Kaplan, H. *The evaluation of sexual disorders.* New York: Brunner/Mazel, 1983.

Kastenbaum, R. J. *Death, society, and human experience.* St. Louis: Mosby, 1981.

Katchadourian, H. A. *Fundamentals of human sexuality* (4th ed.). New York: Holt, Rinehart and Winston, 1985.

Kawash, G. F. A structural analysis of self-esteem from preadolescence through young adulthood: Anxiety and extraversion as agents on the development of self-esteem. *Journal of Clinical Psychology,* 1982, *38*(2), 301–311.

Keith, P. M. Isolation of the unmarried in later life. *Family Relations,* 1986, *35*(3), 389–395.

Kelley, H. H. *Personal relationships: Their structures and processes.* Hillsdale, NJ: Erlbaum, 1979.

Kelly, C., Huston, T. L., & Cate, R. M. Premarital relationship correlates of the erosion of satisfaction in marriage. *Journal of Social and Personal Relationships,* 1985, *2*(2), 167–178.

Kemper, T. D. Predicting the divorce rate: Down? *Journal of Family Issues,* 1983, *4*(1), 507–524.

Kent, M. M. *The American family: Changes and challenges.* Washington, DC: Population Reference Bureau, 1984.

Kephart, W. M. *Extraordinary groups.* New York: St. Martin's, 1982.

———. *The family, society and the individual* (5th ed.). Boston: Houghton Mifflin, 1981.

Kerckhoff, A. C., & Davis, K. E. Value consensus and need complementarity in mate selection. *American Sociological Review,* 1962, *27*(3), 295–303.

Kierkegaard, S. A. *The sickness unto death.* Princeton, NJ: Princeton University Press, 1941.

Kilmann, P. R. *Human sexuality in contemporary life.* Boston: Allyn & Bacon, 1984.

Kilpatrick, A. C. Job change in dual-career families: Danger or opportunity? *Family Relations,* 1982, *31*(3), 363–368.

Kinard, E. M., & Reinherz, H. Marital disruption: Effects on behavioral and emotional functioning in children. *Journal of Family Issues,* 1984, *5*(1), 90–115.

King, C. E., & Christensen, A. The relationship events scale: A Guttman scaling of progress in courtship. *Journal of Marriage and the Family,* 1983, *45*(3), 671–678.

King, S. H. *Perceptions of illness and medical practice.* New York: Russell Sage Foundation, 1962.

Kinsey, A. C., Pomeroy, W. B., & Martin, C. E. *Sexual behavior in the human male.* Philadelphia: Saunders, 1948.

Kinsey, A. C., Pomeroy, W. B., Martin, C. E., & Gebhard, P. H. *Sexual behavior in the human female.* Philadelphia: Saunders, 1953.

Kinsley, P. Scholars jolt old ideals of life and love: Doom of family and religion seen. *Chicago Tribune,* 1927, *86*(10), 1.

Kinsley, S. Women's dependency and federal programs. In J. R. Chapman and M. Gates (Eds.), *Women into wives: The legal and economic impact of marriage.* Beverly Hills, CA: Sage, 1977.

Kinzel, R. K. *Retirement: Creating promise out of threat.* New York: AMACOM, 1979.

Kirkendall, L. A. *Premarital intercourse and interpersonal relationships.* New York: Julian Press, 1961.

Kitson, G. Marital discord and marital separation: A county survey. *Journal of Marriage and the Family,* 1985, *47*(3), 693–700.

Kitson, G. C. Attachment to the spouse in divorce: A scale and its application. *Journal of Marriage and the Family,* 1982, *44*(2), 379–391.

Kitson, G. C., & Raschke, H. J. Divorce research: What we know; what we need to know. *Journal of Divorce,* 1981, *4*(3), 1–38.

Kitson, G. C., & Sussman, M. B. Marital complaints, demographic characteristics, and symptoms of mental distress in divorce. *Journal of Marriage and the Family,* 1982, *44*(1), 87–101.

Kivett, V. R. Grandfathers and grandchildren: Patterns of association, helping, and psychological closeness. *Family Relations,* 1985, *34*(4), 565–571.

Kivnick, H. Q. *The meaning of grandparenthood.* Ann Arbor: University of Michigan Research Press, 1982.

Klein, D. Adolescent driving as deviant behavior. In R. E. Grinder (Ed.), *Studies in adolescence: A book of readings in adolescent development.* New York: Macmillan, 1975.

Kliman, D. S., & Vukelich, C. Mothers and fathers: Expectations for infants. *Family Relations,* 1985, *34*(3), 305–313.

Knapp, M. L. *Interpersonal communication and human relationships.* Boston: Allyn & Bacon, 1984.

Knox, D. Breaking up: The cover story versus the real story. *Free Inquiry in Creative Sociology,* 1985, *13*(2), 131–132.

———. *Human sexuality: The search for understanding.* St. Paul, MN: West, 1984.

———. Conceptions of love at three developmental levels. *The Family Coordinator,* 1970, *19*(2), 151–157.

Knox, D., & Sporakowski, M. J. Attitudes of college students toward love. *Journal of Marriage and the Family,* 1968, *30*(4), 638–642.

Komarovsky, M. *Blue-collar marriage.* New York: Vintage, 1967.

———. Cultural contradictions and sex roles. *The American Journal of Sociology,* 1946, *52*(2), 184–189.

Korman, S. K. Nontraditional dating behavior: Date-initiation and date expense-sharing among feminists and nonfeminists. *Family Relations,* 1983, *32*(4), 575–581.

Kornhaber, A., & Woodward, K. L. *Grandparents/grandchildren: The vital connection.* Garden City, NY: Anchor Press/Doubleday, 1981.

Kotarba, J. A., & Fontana, A. *The existential self in society.* Chicago: University of Chicago Press, 1984.

Kotkin, M. To marry or live together? *Lifestyles: A Journal of Changing Patterns,* 1985, *7*(3), 156–169.

Kouri, M. K. From retirement to re-engagement: Young elders forge new futures. *The Futurist,* 1984, *18*(3), 35–42.

Kroeger, N. Preretirement preparation: Sex differences in access, sources, and use. In M. Szinovacz (Ed.), *Women's retirement: Policy implications of recent research.* Beverly Hills, CA: Sage, 1982.

Kübler-Ross, E. *On death and dying.* New York: Macmillan, 1969.

Kuhn, M. H., & McPartland, T. S. An empirical investigation of self-attitudes. *American Sociology Review,* 1954, *19*(1), 68–76.

Lake, A. The abortion repeaters. In O. Pocs (Ed.), *Human Sexuality: 81/82.* Guilford, CT: Dushkin, 1981.

Landis, J. T. Religiousness, family relationships, and family values in Protestant, Catholic, and Jewish families. *Marriage and Family Living,* 1960, *22*(4), 341–347.

Langston, E. J. The role and value of natural support systems in retirement. In E. P. Stanford (Ed.), *Retirement: Concepts and realities.* San Diego: Campanile Press, 1978.

Larsen, J. J., & Juhasz, A. M. The effects of knowledge of child development and social-emotional maturity on adolescent attitudes toward parenting. *Adolescence,* 1985, *20*(80), 823–839.

Laswell, T., & Lobsenz, N. *No-fault marriage.* New York: Ballantine, 1976.

LaTorre, R. A., & Kear, K. Attitudes toward sex in the aged. *Archives of Sexual Behavior,* 1977, *6*(1), 203–213.

Lauer, J., & Lauer, R. Marriages made to last. *Psychology Today,* 1985, *19*(6), 22–26.

Laury, G. V. Sensual activities of the aging couple. *Medical Aspects of Human Sexuality,* 1980, *14*(1), 32–36.

———. Sex in men over forty. *Medical Aspects of Human Sexuality,* 1980, *14*(2), 65–67.

Lavee, Y., McCubbin, H. I., & Patterson, J. M. The double ABCX model of family stress and adaptation: An empirical test by analysis of structural equations with latent variables. *Journal of Marriage and the Family,* 1985, *47*(4), 811–825.

Lavori, N. *Living together married or single: Your legal rights.* New York: Harper & Row, 1976.

Lawrance, L., Rubinson, L., & O'Rourke, T. Sexual attitudes and behaviors: Trends for a ten-year period 1972–1982. *Journal of Sex Education and Therapy,* 1984, *10*(2), 22–29.

Lazarus, R. S. *Psychological stress and the coping process.* New York: McGraw-Hill, 1966.

Lederer, W. J., & Jackson, D. D. Eight myths of marriage. In R. H. Walsh & O. Pocs (Eds.), *Marriage and Family 81/82.* Guilford, CT: Dushkin, 1981.

Lee, G. R., & Ellithorpe, E. Intergenerational exchange and subjective well-being among the elderly. *Journal of Marriage and the Family,* 1982, *44*(1), 217–224.

Lee, J. A. *The colors of love.* New York: Bantam, 1977.

Lehfeldt, H. Psychology of contraceptive failures. *Medical Aspects of Human Sexuality,* 1971, *68*(5), 73–77.

Leikin, C. Identifying and treating the alcoholic client. *Social Casework,* 1986, *67*(2), 67–73.

Lein, L. Male participation in home life: Impact of social supports and breadwinner responsibility on the allocation of tasks. *The Family Coordinator,* 1979, *28*(4), 489–495.

LeMasters, E. E. *Modern courtship and marriage.* New York: Macmillan, 1957.

LeMasters, E. E., & DeFrain, J. *Parents in contemporary America: A sympathetic view.* Homewood, IL: Dorsey, 1983.

Leonard, G. The end of sex. *The Futurist,* 1983, *17*(2), 22–28.

Leslie, G. R., & Leslie, E. M. *Marriage in a changing world.* New York: Wiley, 1980.

Leslie, L. A., & Grady, K. Changes in mother's social networks and social support following divorce. *Journal of Marriage and the Family,* 1985, *47*(3), 663–673.

Leupnitz, D. A. Which aspects of divorce affect children? *The Family Coordinator,* 1979, *28*(1), 79–85.

Levin, R. J. The Redbook report on premarital and extramarital sex: The end of the double standard? *Redbook,* 1975, *145*(6), 38–44; 190–192.

Levin, R. J., & Levin, A. Sexual pleasure: The surprising preferences of 100,000 women. *Redbook,* 1975, *145*(5), 51–58.

Levine, E. M. Middle-class family decline. *Society,* 1981, *18*(2), 72–78.

Levine, M. *Introduction to clinical nursing.* Philadelphia: F. A. Davis, 1969.

Levinger, G. A social psychological perspective on marital dissolution. In G. Levinger and O. C. Moles (Eds.), *Divorce and separation.* New York: Basic Books, 1979.

Lewis, H., & Liston, J. Stillbirth: Reaction and effect. In P. F. Pegg & E. Metze (Eds.), *Death and dying: A quality of life.* London: Pittman, 1981.

Libby, R. W., & Carlson, J. E. A theoretical framework for premarital sexual decisions in the dyad. In J. R. Eshlemen & J. N. Clarke (Eds.), *Intimacy, commitments and marriage development of relationships.* Boston: Allyn & Bacon, 1978.

Loewenstein, S. F., Bloch, N. E., Campion, J., Epstein, J. S., Gale, P., & Salvatore, M. A study of satisfactions and stresses of single women in midlife. *Sex Roles,* 1981, *7*(11), 1127–1141.

Lopata, H. Z. The absence of community resources in support systems of urban widows. *The Family Coordinator,* 1978, *27,*(4), 383–388.

————. *Women as widows: Support systems.* New York: Elsevier, 1979.

Lopata, H. Z., Barnervolt, D., & Norr, K. Spouse's contributions to each other's roles. In F. Pepitone-Rockwell (Ed.), *Dual-career couples.* Beverly Hills, CA: Sage, 1980.

Lopata, H. Z., Heinemann, G. D., & Baum, J. Loneliness: Antecedents and coping strategies in the lives of widows. In L. A. Peplau & D. Perlman (Eds.), *Loneliness: A sourcebook of current theory, research, and therapy.* New York: Wiley, 1982.

Luker, K. *Taking chances: Abortion and the decision not to contracept.* Berkeley: University of California Press, 1975.

Luria, Z., Friedman, S., & Rose, M. *Human sexuality.* New York: Wiley, 1987.

Lynch, C., & Blinder, M. The romantic relationship: Why and how people fall in love, the way couples connect, and why they break apart. *Family Therapy,* 1983, *10*(2), 91–104.

Lynn, M., & Shurgot, B. A. Responses to lonely hearts advertisements: Effect of reported physical attractiveness, physique, and coloration. *Personality and Social Psychology Bulletin,* 1984, *10*(3), 349–357.

McCabe, M. P., & Collins, J. K. Measurement of depth of desired and experienced sexual involvement at different stages of dating. *Journal of Sex Research,* 1984, *20*(4), 377–390.

McCall, M. M. Courtship as social exchange: Some historical comparisons. In B. Farber (Ed.), *Kinship and family organization.* New York: Wiley, 1966.

McCary, J. L. *Freedom and growth in marriage* (2nd ed.). New York: Wiley, 1980.

McCary, J. L., & McCary, S. P. *McCary's human sexuality* (4th ed.). Belmont, CA: Wadsworth, 1982.

McCluskey, N. G. Preparing for the transfer point. In N. G. McCluskey and E. F. Borgatta (Eds.), *Aging and retirement: Prospects, planning and policy.* Beverly Hills, CA: Sage, 1981.

McCoy, E. Kids and divorce. *Parents,* 1984, *59*(11), 112–116; 192.

McKim, M. K. Transition to what? New parents' problems in the first year. *Family Relations,* 1987, *36*(1), 22–25.

Macklin, E. D. Nonmarital heterosexual cohabitation. In A. S. Skolnick and J. H. Skolnick (Eds.), *Family in transition* (4th ed.). Boston: Little, Brown, 1983.

————. Nontraditional family forms: A decade of research. *Journal of Marriage and the Family,* 1980, *42*(4), 905–922.

McLaughlin, S. D. Differential patterns of female labor-force participation surrounding the first birth. *Journal of Marriage and the Family,* 1982, *44*(2), 407–420.

McMillen, M., and Pugh, R. E. Financing social security retirement of an aging population. *Research on Aging,* 1986, *8*(1), 3–21.

McMordie, W. R. Religiosity and fear of death: Strength of belief system. *Psychological Reports,* 1981, *49*(3), 921–922.

McNamara, M. L., & Bahr, H. M. The dimensionality of marital role satisfaction. *Journal of Marriage and the Family,* 1980, *42*(1), 45–55.

Macovsky, S. J. Coping with cohabitation. In O. Pocs and R. H. Walsh (Eds.), *Marriage and Family 83/84.* Guilford, CT: Dushkin, 1983.

McPhee, J. J. *Ambiguity and role transition in the post-divorce family: A symbolic interactional approach to role adjustment.* Paper presented at NCFR Pre-Conference Workshop, Washington, DC, October 12–13, 1982.

Madaras, L., & Patterson, J. *Womancare: A gynecological guide to your body.* New York: Avon Books, 1981.

Mahoney, E. R. *Human sexuality.* New York: McGraw-Hill, 1983.

Makarenko, A. S. *The collective family; A handbook for Russian parents* (R. Daglish, translator). New York: Doubleday, 1967. (Originally published 1937.)

Makepeace, J. M. Social factor and victim-offender differences in courtship violence. *Family Relations,* 1987, *36*(1), 87–91.

———. Courtship violence among college students. *Family Relations,* 1981, *30*(1), 97–102.

Makinson, C. The health consequences of teenage fertility. *Family Planning Perspectives,* 1985, *17*(3), 132–139.

Malinowski, B. *The sexual life of savages.* New York: Harcourt, Brace, 1929.

Malthus, T. R. *Essay on the principle of population* (7th ed.). London: J. M. Dent and Sons, Ltd., 1816.

Marecek, J., Finn, S. E., & Cardell, M. Gender roles in the relationships of lesbians and gay men. *Journal of Homosexuality,* 1982, *8*(2), 45–49.

Marotz-Baden, R., & Colvin, P. L. Coping strategies: A rural-urban comparison. *Family Relations,* 1986, *35*(2), 281–288.

Marshall, D. S. Sexual behavior in Mangaria. In D. S. Marshall & R. C. Suggs (Eds.), *Human sexual behavior.* Englewood Cliffs, NJ: Prentice-Hall, 1971.

Maslow, A. *Motivation and personality* (2nd ed.). New York: Harper & Row, 1970.

Masters, W. H., & Johnson, V. E. *Human sexual inadequacy.* Boston: Little, Brown, 1970.

Masters, W. H., Johnson, V. E., & Kolodny, R. C. *Human sexuality* (2nd ed.). Boston: Little, Brown, 1985.

———. *Human Sexuality* (3rd ed.). Glenview, IL: Scott, Foresman, 1988.

Masuda, M., & Holmes, T. H. Magnitude estimations of social readjustments. *Journal of Psychosomatic Research,* 1967, *11*(1) 219–225.

Mathes, E. W., & Moore, C. L. Reik's complementarity theory of romantic love. *The Journal of Social Psychology,* 1985, *125*(3), 321–327.

Matthaei, J. A. *An economic history of women in America.* New York: Schocken, 1982.

Mazur, R. *The new intimacy.* Boston: Beacon, 1973.

Mead, G. H. *Mind, self, and society: From the standpoint of a social behaviorist.* Chicago: University of Chicago Press, 1934.

Mead, M. Marriage in two steps. *Redbook,* 1966, *127*(3), 48–49; 84; 86.

——. *Sex and temperament in three primitive societies.* New York: Mentor, 1950.

Meer, J. Loneliness: Whether being lonely is a sometime thing or a sad way of life; understanding its causes can help. *Psychology Today,* 1985, *19*(6), 28–33.

Melichar, J., & Chiriboga, D. A. Timetables in the divorce process. *Journal of Marriage and the Family,* 1985, *47*(3), 701–708.

Menaghan, E. G., & Lieberman, M. A. Changes in depression following divorce: A panel study. *Journal of Marriage and the Family,* 1986, *48*(2), 319–328.

Messinger, L. Remarriage between divorced people with children from previous marriages: A proposal for preparation for remarriage. *Journal of Marriage and Family Counseling,* 1976, *2*(2), 193–200.

Meyners, J. R. Some serious thought about play. *MJI Newsletter,* 1980, *1*(3), 4–8.

Michener, H. A., DeLamater, J. D., & Schwartz, S. H. *Social psychology.* San Diego: Harcourt Brace Jovanovich, 1986.

Miller, B. A multivariate developmental model of marital satisfaction. *Journal of Marriage and the Family,* 1976, *38*(4), 643–658.

Miller, B. C., & Sollie, D. L. Normal stresses during the transition to parenthood. *Family Relations,* 1980, *29*(4), 459–465.

Miller, B. D., McCoy, J. K., Olson, T. D., & Wallace, C. M. Parental discipline and control attempts in relation to adolescent sexual attitudes and behavior. *Journal of Marriage and the Family,* 1986, *48*(3), 503–512.

Miller, W. B. Psychological vulnerability to pregnancy. *Family Planning Perspectives,* 1973, *5*(4), 199–201.

Moen, P. Unemployment, public policy, and families: Forecasts for the 1980's. *Journal of Marriage and the Family,* 1983, *45*(4), 751–760.

——. Family impacts of the 1975 recession: Duration of unemployment. *Journal of Marriage and the Family,* 1979, *41*(3), 561–572.

Moos, R. H., & Tsu, V. D. The crisis of physical illness: An overview. In R. H. Moos (Ed.), *Coping with physical illness.* New York: Plenum, 1977.

Morgan, L. A. Intergenerational economic assistance to children: The case of widows and widowers. *Journal of Gerontology,* 1983, *38*(6), 725–731.

——. Economic changes at midlife widowhood: A longitudinal analysis. *Journal of Marriage and the Family,* 1981, *43*(4), 899–912.

Moss, A. M. Men's mid-life crisis and the marital-sexual relationship. *Medical Aspects of Human Sexuality,* 1979, *13*(2), 109–110.

Mueller, C. W., & Pope, H. Marital instability: A study of its transmission between generations. *Journal of Marriage and the Family,* 1977, *39*(1), 83–93.

Muenchow, S. The truth about quality time. *Parents,* 1983, *58*(5), 59–64.

Mullins, J. B. The relationship between child abuse and handicapping conditions. *Journal of School Health,* 1986, *56*(4), 134–136.

Mumford, S. D. The vasectomy decision-making process. *Studies in Family Planning,* 1983, *14*(3), 83–88.

Mundis, H. Not now, honey, the baby's crying. In O. Pocs and R. H. Walsh (Eds.), *Marriage and Family 83/84.* Guilford, CT: Dushkin, 1983.

Murdock, G. P. *Social structure.* New York: Macmillan, 1949.

Murray, J., & Parks, B. *The Alan Guttmacher Institute News,* March 13, 1985.

Murstein, B. Stimulus-value-role: A theory of marital choice. *Journal of Marriage and the Family,* 1970, *32*(3), 465–481.

Murstein, B. I., & Brust, R. G. Humor and interpersonal attraction. *Journal of Personality Assessment,* 1985, *49*(6), 637–640.

Nadelson, C. C., & Nadelson, T. Dual-career marriages: Benefits and costs. In F. Pepitone-Rockwell (Ed.), *Dual-career couples.* Beverly Hills, CA: Sage, 1980.

Nass, G. D., & McDonald, G. W. *Marriage and the family* (2nd ed.). Reading, MA: Addison-Wesley, 1982.

Nathanson, C. A., & Becker, M. H. Family and peer influence on obtaining a method of contraception. *Journal of Marriage and the Family,* 1986, *48*(3), 513–525.

National Center for Health Statistics. Advance report of final marriage statistics, 1981. *Monthly Vital Statistics Report, 32*(11), Supp. DHHS Pub. No. (PHS) 84-1120. Hyattsville, MD: U.S. Public Health Service, February 29, 1984.

Neugarten, B. L. *Middle age and aging.* Chicago: University of Chicago Press, 1968.

Nevid, J. S. Sex differences in factors of romantic attraction. *Sex Roles,* 1984, *11*(5/6), 401–411.

The new morality. *Time,* 1977, *110*(21), 111–118.

Newman, J. Adolescents: Why they can be so obnoxious. *Adolescence,* 1985, *20*(79), 635–646.

Nishi-Strattner, M., & Meyers, J. E. Attitudes toward the elderly: An intergenerational examination. *Educational Gerontology,* 1983, *9*(5/6), 389–404.

Norton, A. J., & Glick, P. C. Marital instability in America: Past, present, and future. In A. Levinger and O. C. Moles (Eds.), *Divorce and separation: Context, causes, and consequences.* New York: Basic Books, 1979.

Norton, A. J., & Moorman, J. E. Current trends in marriage and divorce among American women. *Journal of Marriage and the Family,* 1987, *49*(1), 3–14.

Nye, F. I. Family mini theories as special instances of choice and exchange theory. *Journal of Marriage and the Family,* 1980, *42*(3), 479–489.

Oakley, D. Premarital childbearing decision-making. *Family Relations,* 1985, *34*(4), 561–563.

Offer, D., Ostrov, E., & Howard, K. *The adolescent: A psychological self portrait.* New York: Basic Books, 1981.

Olds, S. W. Is divorce contagious? In R. H. Walsh & O. Pocs (Eds.), *Marriage and Family 81/82.* Guilford, CT: Dushkin, 1981.

O'Neill, J. Role differentiation and the gender gap in wage rates. In L. Larwood, A. H. Stromberg, & B. A. Gutek (Eds.), *Women and work: An annual review*. Beverly Hills, CA: Sage, 1985.

O'Neill, N. *The marriage premise*. New York: Evans, 1977.

O'Neill, N., & O'Neill, G. *Open marriage*. New York: Avon, 1973.

————. *Open marriage: A new life style for couples*. New York: Evans, 1972.

Ory, M. G. The decision to parent or not: Normative and structural components. *Dissertation Abstracts International*, 1977, *37A*(8), 5388A (University Microfilms No. DCJ77-01755).

Palisi, B. J. Symptoms of readiness for divorce. *Journal of Family Issues*, 1984, *5*(1), 70–89.

Palmore, E. *Social patterns in normal aging: Findings from the Duke longitudinal study*. Durham, NC: Duke University Press, 1981.

Palson, C., & Palson, R. Swinging in wedlock. *Society*, 1972, *9*(4), 28–37.

Parsons, T. Illness and the role of the physicians: A sociological perspective. In C. Kluckhohn & H. A. Murray (Eds.), *Personality in nature, society, and culture* (2nd ed.). New York: Knopf, 1953.

Pearson, J., & Thoennes, N. Mediation and divorce: The benefits outweigh the cost. *Family Advocate*, 1982, *4*(3), 26; 28–32.

Pearson, W., & Hendrix, L. Divorce and the status of women. *Journal of Marriage and the Family*, 1979, *41*(2), 375–385.

Peck, E., & Senderowitz, J. Introduction. In E. Peck & J. Senderowitz (Eds.), *Pronatalism: The myth of mom and apple pie*. New York: Crowell, 1974.

Pedrick-Cornell, C., & Gelles, R. J. Elder abuse: The status of current knowledge. *Family Relations*, 1982, *31*(3), 457–465.

Penney, A. Great sex. *Ms.*, July 1985, pp. 38–39.

Peplau, L. A. What homosexuals want in relationships. *Psychology Today*, 1981, *15*(3), 28–38.

Perutz, K. *Marriage is hell*. New York: Morrow, 1972.

Peters, J. F. Adolescents as socialization agents to parents. *Adolescence*, 1985, *20*(80), 921–933.

Petersen, J. R. The Playboy readers' sex survey (Part 1). *Playboy*, 1983, *30*(1), 108; 241–250.

————. Sex on campus. *Playboy*, 1982, *29*(10), 144–149; 182–189.

Petersen, J. R., Kretchmer, A., Nellis, B., Lever, J., & Hertz, R. The Playboy readers' sex survey (Part 2). *Playboy*, 1983, *30*(3), 90–92; 178–184.

Phillips, D. The federal model child care standards act of 1985: Step in the right direction or hollow gesture? *American Journal of Orthopsychiatry*, 1986, 56(1), 56–64.

Piaget, J. *The child's conception of number*. London: Routledge & Kegan Paul, 1952.

Pietropinto, A., & Simenauer, J. *Husbands and wives*. New York: Time Books, 1979.

Pincus, L. The process of mourning and grief. In E. S. Schneidman (Ed.), *Death: Current perspectives*. Palo Alto, CA: Mayfield, 1984.

Pines, A., & Aronson, E. Antecedents, correlates, and consequences of sexual jealousy. *Journal of Personality*, 1983, *51*(1), 108–136.

Pink, J. E. T., & Wampler, K. S. Problem areas in stepfamilies: Cohesion, adaptability, and the stepfather-adolescent relationship. *Family Relations*, 1985, *34*(3), 327–335.

Pittman, J. F., Jr., Price-Bonham, S., & McKenry, P. C. Marital cohesion: A path model. *Journal of Marriage and the Family*, 1983, *45*(3), 521–531.

Pocs, O., & Godow, A. G. Can students view parents as sexual beings? *The Family Coordinator*, 1977, *26*(1), 31–36.

Pocs, O., Godow, A. G., Tolone, W. L., & Walsh, R. H. Is there sex after forty? In O. Pocs (Ed.), *Human Sexuality 83/84*. Guilford, CT: Dushkin, 1983.

Polit, D. F. Stereotypes relating to family-size status. *Journal of Marriage and the Family*, 1978, *40*(1), 105–114.

Pomeroy, W. B. Infidelity and extramarital relations are not the same thing. In O. Pocs (Ed.), *Human sexuality 81/82*. Guilford, CT: Dushkin, 1982.

———. Normal vs. abnormal sex. *Sexology*, 1966, *32*, 436–439.

Powell, D. H., & Driscoll, P. F. Middle-class professionals face unemployment. *Society*, 1973, *10*(2), 18–26.

Powell, J. *Why am I afraid to tell you who I am?* Niles, IL: Argus, 1969.

Price-Bonham, S., & Balswick, J. The non-institutions: Divorce, desertion, and remarriage. *Journal of Marriage and the Family*, 1980, *42*(4), 959–972.

Price-Bonham, S., & Johnson, C. K. Attitudes toward retirement: A comparison of professional and nonprofessional married women. In M. Szinovacz (Ed.), *Women's retirement: Policy implications of recent research*. Beverly Hills, CA: Sage, 1982.

Prochaska, J., & Coyle, J. R. Choosing parenthood: A needed family life education group. *Social Casework: The Journal of Contemporary Social Work*, 1979, *60*(5), 289–295.

Queen, S. A., Habenstein, R. W., & Quadagno, J. S. *The family in various cultures* (5th ed.). New York: Harper & Row, 1985.

Queijo, J. The paradox of intimacy. In O. Pocs and R. H. Walsh (Eds.), *Marriage and Family 86/87*. Guilford, CT: Dushkin, 1986.

Ramey, J. W. Emerging patterns of innovative behavior in marriage. *The Family Coordinator*, 1972, *21*(4), 435–456.

Ramy, G. N., & Tavuchis, N. The valuation of children and parenthood among the voluntarily childless and parental couples in Canada. *Journal of Comparative Family Studies*, 1986, *17*(1), 99–116.

Rao, V. V. P., & Rao, V. N. Correlates of marital happiness: A longitudinal analysis. *Free Inquiry in Creative Sociology*, 1986, *14*(1), 3–8.

Rapoport, R., & Rapoport, R. N. The dual career family: A variant pattern and social change. *Human Relations*, 1969, *22*(1), 3–30.

Rathbone-McCuan, E. Elderly victims of family violence and neglect. *Social Casework*, 1980, *61*(5), 296–304.

Rawlings, S. Perspectives on American husbands and wives. *U.S. Bureau of the Census, Special Studies Series P-23*, 1978, No. 77, p. 33.

Reed, J. *From private vice to public virtue: The birth control movement and American society since 1830.* New York: Basic Books, 1978.

Reiss, D., & Oliveri, M. E. Family paradigm and family coping. In D. H. Olson & B. C. Miller (Eds.), *Family Studies Review Yearbook* (Vol. 1). Beverly Hills, CA: Sage, 1983.

Reiss, I. L. *Journey into sexuality: An exploratory voyage.* Englewood Cliffs, NJ: Prentice-Hall, 1986.

————. *Family systems in America* (3rd ed.). New York: Holt, Rinehart and Winston, 1980.

————. *The social context of premarital sexual permissiveness.* New York: Holt, Rinehart and Winston, 1967.

————. *Premarital sexual standards in America.* New York: Free Press, 1960.

Reiss, I. L., Anderson, R. E., & Sponaugle, G. C. A multivariate model of the determinants of extramarital sexual permissiveness. *Journal of Marriage and the Family*, 1980, *42*(2), 395–411.

Rempel, J. Childless elderly: What are they missing? *Journal of Marriage and the Family*, 1985, *47*(2), 343–348.

Ricks, S. S. Father-infant interactions: A review of empirical research. *Family Relations*, 1985, *34*(4), 505–511.

Riddick, C. C. Life satisfaction among aging women: A causal model. In M. Szinovacz (Ed.), *Women's retirement: Policy implications of recent research.* Beverly Hills, CA: Sage, 1982.

Risman, B. J., Hill, C. T., Rubin, Z., & Peplau, L. A. Living together in college: Implications for courtship. *Journal of Marriage and the Family*, 1981, *43*(1), 77–83.

Roberts, W. L. Significant elements in the relationship of long-married couples. *International Journal of Aging and Human Development*, 1979, *10*(3), 265–271.

Robinson, I. E., & Jedlicka, D. Change in sexual attitudes and behavior of college students from 1965 to 1980: A research note. *Journal of Marriage and the Family*, 1982, *44*(1), 237–240.

Rogers, C. R. *Becoming partners: Marriage and its alternatives.* New York: Delacorte, 1972.

Rollins, B. C., & Cannon, K. L. Marital satisfaction over the family life cycle: A reevaluation. *Journal of Marriage and the Family*, 1974, *35*(5), 271–284.

Roman, M., & Haddad, W. The case for joint custody. In O. Pocs & R. H. Walsh (Eds.), *Marriage and Family 82/83.* Guilford, CT: Dushkin, 1983.

Roscoe, B., & Benaske, N. Courtship violence experienced by abused wives: Similarities in patterns of abuse. *Family Relations*, 1985, *34*(3), 419–424.

Rosen, R. Some crucial issues concerning children of divorce. *Journal of Divorce*, 1979, *3*(1), 19–25.

Rosenfeld, R. A. Women's intergenerational occupational mobility. *American Sociological Review*, 1978, *43*(1), 36–46.

Rossman, P. The network family: Support systems for times of crisis. *The Futurist,* 1985, 19(6), 19–21.

Roy, R., & Roy D. Is monogamy outdated? In J. R. Delora & J. S. Delora (Eds.), *Intimate lifestyles* (2nd ed.). Pacific Palisades, CA: Goodyear, 1975.

Rubenstein, C. Real men don't earn less than their wives. *Psychology Today,* November 1982, pp. 36–41.

Rubin, A. M. Sexually open versus sexually exclusive marriage: A comparison of dyadic adjustment. *Alternative Lifestyles,* 1982, 5(2), 101–108.

Rubin, I. Transition in sex values—Implications for the education of adolescents. *Journal of Marriage and the Family,* 1965, 27(2), 185–189.

Rubin, T. I. How can you measure the health of your relationship? In O. Pocs & R. H. Walsh (Eds.), *Marriage and Family 86/87.* Guilford, CT: Dushkin, 1986.

Rubin, Z. The love research. In R. H. Walsh & O. Pocs (Eds.), *Marriage and Family 82/83.* Guilford, CT: Dushkin, 1982.

———. *Liking and loving.* New York: Holt, Rinehart and Winston, 1973.

Rubin, Z., & McNeil, E. B. *The psychology of being human* (3rd ed.). New York: Harper & Row, 1981.

Rubinson, L., Ory, J. C., & Marmata, J. N. Differentiation between actual and perceived sexual behavior amongst male and female college students. *Journal of Sex Education and Therapy,* 1981, 7(1), 33–36.

Ruesch, H. *Top of the world.* New York: Harper, 1950.

Sabatelli, R. M., Buck, R., & Dreyer, A. Nonverbal communication accuracy in married couples: Relationship with marital complaints. *Journal of Personality and Social Psychology,* 1982, 43(5), 1088–1097.

Sack, A. R., Keller, J. F., & Hinkle, D. E. Premarital sexual intercourse: A test of the effects of peer group, religiosity, and sexual guilt. *Journal of Sex Research,* 1984, 20(2), 168–185.

Safran, C. Troubles that pull couples apart: A Redbook report. *Redbook,* 1979, 154(1), 83; 138–141.

Salovey, P., & Rodin, J. The heart of jealousy. *Psychology Today,* September 1985, pp. 22–29.

Sandberg, E. C., & Jacobs, R. I. Psychology of the misuse and rejection of contraception. *Medical Aspects of Human Sexuality,* 1972, 6(6), 34–64.

Sanders, G. F., & Walters, J. Life satisfaction and family strengths of older couples. *Lifestyles: A Journal of Changing Patterns,* 1985, 7(4), 194–195.

Sandler, J., Meyerson, M., & Kinder, B. N. *Human sexuality: Current perspectives.* Tampa, FL: Mariner, 1980.

Sarrel, P., & Sarrel, L. The Redbook report: Sexual relationships. *Redbook,* 1980, 155(6), 73–80.

Savells, J. Workaholism and modern matrimony: A do-it-yourself victimization kit. In J. Savells and L. J. Cross (Eds.), *The changing family: Making way for tomorrow.* New York: Holt, Rinehart and Winston, 1978.

Scales, P. C. How we can prevent teenage pregnancy (and why it's not the real problem). *Journal of Sex Education and Therapy*, 1987, *13*(1), 12–15.

Scanzoni, J. H. *Sexual bargaining: Power politics in the American marriage* (2nd ed.). Chicago: University of Chicago Press, 1982.

———. *Sex roles, lifestyles, and child bearing.* New York: Free Press, 1975.

———. *Sexual bargaining: Power politics in the American marriage.* Englewood Cliffs, NJ: Prentice-Hall, 1972.

Schenk, J., Pfrang, H., & Rausche, A. Personality traits versus the quality of the marital relationship as the determinant of marital sexuality. *Archives of Sexual Behavior*, 1983, *12*(1), 31–42.

Schimel, J. L. Interview: Do we overestimate sex? *Medical Aspects of Human Sexuality*, 1978, *12*(6), 8–17.

Schneidman, E. S. *Death: Current perspectives* (3rd ed.). Palo Alto, CA: Mayfield, 1984.

Schouler, J. *A treatise on the law of husband and wife.* Boston: Little, Brown, 1882.

Schulz, D. A., & Rodgers, S. F. *Marriage, the family, and personal fulfillment* (3rd ed.). Englewood Cliffs, NJ: Prentice-Hall, 1985.

Schuman, W. How to talk to your child. In O. Pocs and R. H. Walsh (Eds.), *Marriage and Family 83/84.* Guilford, CT: Dushkin, 1983.

———. The violent American way of life. In O. Pocs & R. H. Walsh (Eds.), *Marriage and Family 83/84.* Guilford, CT: Dushkin, 1983.

Schwanberg, S. L. Changes in labeling homosexuality in health sciences literature: A preliminary investigation. *Journal of Homosexuality*, 1986, *12*(1), 51–73.

Schwartz, T. (Ed.). Living together. *Newsweek*, 1977, *90*(5), 46–49.

Scott, D. M., & Wishy, B. (Eds.). *America's families: A documentary history.* New York: Harper & Row, 1982.

Seaborg, D. M. Sexual orientation, behavioral plasticity, and evolution. *Journal of Homosexuality*, 1984, *10*(3/4), 153–158.

Sebald, H. Adolescents' shifting orientation toward parents and peers: A curvilinear trend over recent decades. *Journal of Marriage and the Family*, 1986, *48*(1), 5–13.

Shah, F., & Zelnik, M. Parent and peer influence on sexual behavior, contraceptive use, and pregnancy experience of young women. *Journal of Marriage and the Family*, 1981, *43*(2), 339–348.

Shavelson, E., Biaggio, M. K., Cross, H. H., & Lehman, R. E. Lesbian women's perceptions of their parent-child relationships. *Journal of Homosexuality*, 1980, *5*(3), 205–215.

Sheehy, G. *Passages: Predictable crises of adult life.* New York: Dutton, 1976.

Simenauer, J., and Carroll, D. Do you wish you were single? *Family Weekly*, August 1, 1982.

Simkins, L., & Rinck, C. Male and female sexual vocabulary in different interpersonal contexts. *Journal of Sex Research*, 1982, *18*(2), 160–172.

Simon, W., Berger, A., & Gagnon, J. Beyond anxiety and fantasy: The coital experience of college youth. *Journal of Youth and Adolescence*, 1972, *1*(2), 203–221.

Simons, G. L. *Simon's book of world sexual records.* New York: Amjon, 1976.

Sinclair, K., & Ross, M. W. Consequences of decriminalization of homosexuality: A study of two Australian states. *Journal of Homosexuality*, 1986, *12*(1), 119–127.

Singer, B. Conceptualizing sexual arousal and attraction. *Journal of Sex Research*, 1984, *20*(3), 230–240.

Singer, D. G., & Singer, J. L. Television and the developing imagination of the child. *Journal of Broadcasting*, 1981, *25*(4), 373–388.

Sinnott, D. Older men, older women: Are their perceived sex roles similar? *Sex Roles*, 1984, *10*(11/12), 847–856.

Sirkin, M. I., & Mosher, D. L. Guided imagery of female sexual assertiveness: Turn on or turn off. *Journal of Sex and Marital Therapy*, 1985, *11*(1), 41–50.

Sitton, S., & Rippee, E. T. Women still want marriage: Sex differences in lonely hearts advertisements. *Psychological Reports*, 1986, *58*(1), 257–258.

Skinner, D. A. Dual-career family stress and coping: A literature review. *Family Relations*, 1980 *29*(4), 473–481.

Skipper, J. K., Jr., & Nass, G. Dating behavior: A framework for analysis and an illustration. *Journal of Marriage and the Family*, 1966, *28*(4), 412–420.

Skolnick, A. *The intimate environment: Exploring marriage and the family.* Boston: Little, Brown, 1978.

Smallwood, K. B., & Van Dyck, D. G. Menopause counseling: Coping with realities and myths. In O. Pocs (Ed.), *Human Sexuality 83/84.* Guilford, CT: Dushkin, 1983.

Smith, B. *A tree grows in Brooklyn.* New York: Harper & Row, 1943.

Smith, D. S. Parental power and marriage patterns: An analysis of historical trends in Hingham, Massachusetts. In M. Gordon (Ed.), *The American family in social-historical perspective* (2nd ed.). New York: St. Martin's, 1978.

Smith, K. R., & Zick, C. D. The incidence of poverty among the recently widowed: Mediating factors in the life course. *Journal of Marriage and the Family*, 1986, *48*(3), 619–630.

Smith, M. J. The social consequences of single parenthood: A longitudinal perspective. *Family Relations*, 1980, *29*(1), 75–81.

Smith, P., & Kolenda, K. The male role in teenage pregnancies. *USA Today*, May 1982, pp. 43–44.

Smith, R. E. (Ed.). *The subtle revolution: Women at work.* Washington DC: Urban Institute, 1979.

Smith, R. M., & Walters, J. Delinquent and non-delinquent males' perceptions of their fathers. *Adolescence*, 1978, *13*(49), 21–28.

Snyder, D. Multidimensional assessment of marital satisfaction. *Journal of Marriage and the Family*, 1979, *41*(4), 813–823.

Sorenson, R. C. *Adolescent sexuality in comtemporary America.* New York: World, 1973.

Sorokin, P. A. *Social and cultural dynamics: Fluctuation of systems of truth, ethics, and law* (4 vols.). New York: American Book Company, 1937–1941.

Spanier, G. B. Married and unmarried cohabitation in the United States: 1980. *Journal of Marriage and the Family*, 1983, *45*(2), 277–288.

———. Sexualization and premarital sexual behavior. *The Family Coordinator*, 1975, *24*(1), 33–41.

———. Romanticism and marital adjustment. *Journal of Marriage and the Family*, 1972, *34*(3), 481–487.

Spanier, G. B., & Casto, R. F. Adjustment to separation and divorce: An analysis of 50 case studies. *Journal of Divorce*, 1979, *2*(3), 241–253.

Spanier, G. B., & Lewis, R. A. Marital quality: A review of the seventies. *Journal of Marriage and the Family*, 1980, *42*(4), 825–839.

Spitze, G., & South, S. J. Women's employment, time expenditure, and divorce. *Journal of Family Issues*, 1985, *6*(3), 307–329.

Spitze, G. D., & Waite, L. J. Wives' employment: The role of husbands' perceived attitudes. *Journal of Marriage and the Family*, 1981, *43*(1), 117–124.

Spivey, P. B., & Scherman, A. The effects of time lapse on personality characteristics and stress on divorced women. *Journal of Divorce*, 1980, *4*(1), 49–59.

Spock, B. M. When you push a child too hard. In O. Pocs and R. H. Walsh (Eds.), *Marriage and Family 85/86*. Guilford, CT: Dushkin, 1985.

———. *The pocket book of baby and child care.* New York: Meredith, 1951.

Spreitzer, E., & Riley, L. E. Factors associated with singlehood. *Journal of Marriage and the Family*, 1974, *36*(3), 533–542.

Sprey, J. Conflict theory and the study of marriage and the family. In W. R. Burr, R. Hill, F. I. Nye, & I. L. Reiss (Eds.), *Contemporary theories about the family* (Vol. II). New York: Free Press, 1979.

Stack, S. The effects of marital dissolution on suicide. *Journal of Marriage and the Family*, 1980, *42*(1), 83–91.

Staines, G. L., Pottick, K. J., & Fudge, D. A. Wives' employment and husbands' attitudes toward work and life. *Journal of Applied Psychology*, 1986, *71*(1), 118–128.

Stammel, M. Why do men suddenly want to be fathers? In R. H. Walsh and O. Pocs (Eds.), *Marriage and Family 82/83*. Guilford, CT: Dushkin, 1982.

Stark, E. Young, innocent, and pregnant. *Psychology Today*, October 1986, pp. 26–30; 32–35.

Stayton, W. R. Lifestyle spectrum 1984. *SIECUS Report*, 1984, *12*(3), 1–4.

Steel, L., Abeles, R. P., & Card, J. J. Sex differences in the patterning of adult roles as a determinant of sex differences in occupational achievement. *Sex Roles*, 1982, *8*(9), 1009–1024.

Stein, P. J. (Ed.) *Single life: Unmarried adults in social context.* New York: St. Martin's, 1981.

Stein, P. J., & Fingrutd, M. The single life has more potential for happiness than marriage and parenthood for both men and women. In H. Feldman & M. Feldman (Eds.), *Current controversies in marriage and family*. Beverly Hills, CA: Sage, 1985.

Steinmetz, S. K. The use of force for resolving family conflict: The training ground for abuse. *The Family Coordinator*, 1977, *26*(1), 19–26.

Stephen, T. D., & Harrison, T. M. A longitudinal comparison of couples with sex-typical and non-sex-typical orientations in intimacy. *Sex Roles*, 1985, *12*(1/2), 195–205.

Stephens, W. N. *The family in cross-cultural perspective*. New York: Holt, Rinehart and Winston, 1963.

Stinnett, N., Carter, L. M., & Montgomery, J. E. Older persons' perceptions of their marriages. *Journal of Marriage and the Family*, 1972, *34*(4), 665–670.

Stoller, E. P. Exchange patterns in the informal support networks of the elderly: The impact of reciprocity on morale. *Journal of Marriage and the Family*, 1985, *47*(2), 335–342.

Storms, M. D. Theories of sexual orientation. *Journal of Personality and Social Psychology*, 1980, *38*(5), 783–792.

Stout, R. J. The case of the pregnant virgins. *Journal of Sex Education and Therapy*, 1977, *3*(1), 3–4.

Strauss, A. Personality needs and marital choice. *Social Forces*, 1947, *25*(3), 332–335.

Streib, G., & Schneider, C. *Retirement in American society*. Ithaca, NY: Cornell University Press, 1971.

Strong, B., Wilson, S., Robbins, M., & Johns, T. *Human sexuality essentials* (2nd ed.). St. Paul, MN: West, 1981.

Strube, M. J., & Barbour, L. S. The decision to leave an abusive relationship: Economic dependence and psychological commitment. *Journal of Marriage and the Family*, 1983, *45*(4), 785–794.

Sue, D. Erotic fantasies of college students during coitus. *Journal of Sex Research*, 1979, *15*(4), 299–305.

Sullivan, H. S. *The interpersonal theory of psychiatry*. New York: Norton, 1953.

Swensen, C. H., Eskew, R. W., & Kohlhepp, K. A. Five factors in long-term marriages. *Lifestyles: A Journal of Changing Patterns*, 1984, *7*(2), 94–106.

Symonds, P. M. Expressions of love. In R. S. Cavan (Ed.), *Marriage and family in the modern world* (4th ed.). New York: Crowell, 1974.

Szinovacz, M. E. *Women's retirement: Policy implications of recent research*. Beverly Hills, CA: Sage, 1982.

————. Relationships among marital power measures: A critical review and an empirical test. *Journal of Comparative Family Studies*, 1981, *12*(2), 151–169.

————. Female retirement, effects on spousal roles and marital adjustment. *Journal of Family Issues*, 1980, *1*(3), 423–440.

Tanfer, K. Patterns of premarital cohabitation among never married women in the United States. *Journal of Marriage and the Family*, 1987, *49*(3), 483–497.

Targ, D. B. *Ideology and utopia in family studies since World War II*. Paper presented at the meeting of the American Sociological Association, Boston, 1979.

Taublieb, A. B., & Lick, J. R. Female orgasm via penile stimulation: A criterion of adequate sexual functioning? *Journal of Sex and Marital Therapy*, 1986, *12*(1), 60–64.

Tavris, C., & Sadd, S. *The Redbook report on female sexuality.* New York: Delacorte, 1977.

Teachman, J. D., & Polonko, K. A. Timing of the transition to parenthood: A multidimensional birth-interval approach. *Journal of Marriage and the Family,* 1985, *47*(4), 867–879.

Thomas, S. P. After divorce: Personality factors related to the process of adjustment. *Journal of Divorce,* 1982, *5*(3), 19–36.

Thompson, A. P. Emotional and sexual components of extramarital relations. *Journal of Marriage and the Family,* 1984, *46*(1), 35–42.

Thompson, E. H., & Doll, W. The burden of families coping with the mentally ill: An invisible crisis. *Family Relations,* 1982, *31*(3), 379–388.

Thomson, E. The value of employment to mothers of young children. *Journal of Marriage and the Family,* 1980, *42*(3), 551–566.

Thornton, A., & Freedman, D. Changing attitudes toward marriage and single life. *Family Planning Perspectives,* 1982, *14*(6), 297–303.

Thwing, C. F., & Thwing, C. F. B. *The family: An historical and social study* (Rev. ed.). Boston: Lothrop, Lee, and Shepard, 1913.

Tierney, K. J. The battered woman movement and the creation of the wife-beating problem. *Social Problems,* 1982, *29*(3), 207–217.

Time. The new morality. 1977, *110*(21), 111–116.

Tognoli, J. The flight from domestic space: Men's role in the household. *The Family Coordinator,* 1979, *28*(4), 599–607.

Totenberg, N. How to write a marriage contract. In O. Pocs & R. H. Walsh (Eds.), *Marriage and Family 85/86.* Guilford, CT: Dushkin, 1985.

Townes, B. W., Beach, L. D., Campbell, F. L., & Martin, D. C. Birth planning values and decisions: The prediction of fertility. *Journal of Applied Social Psychology,* 1977, *7*(1), 73–88.

Trafford, A. New health hazard: Being out of work. *U.S. News & World Report,* 1982, *92*(23), 81–82.

Troiden, R. R. Becoming homosexual: A model of gay identity acquisition. *Psychiatry,* 1979, *42*(4), 362–373.

Troll, L. E. Grandparents: The family watchdogs. In T. Brubaker (Ed.), *Family relations in later life.* Beverly Hills, CA: Sage, 1983.

Trotter, R. J. Divorce: The first two years are the worst. In R. H. Walsh & O. Pocs (Eds.), *Marriage and Family 79/80.* Guilford, CT: Dushkin, 1979.

Trussell, J., & Westoff, C. F. Contraceptive practice and trends in coital frequency. *Family Planning Perspectives,* 1980, *12*(5), 246–249.

Turner, J. S. Our battered American families (Part 2). *Marriage and Family Living,* 1980, *62*(1), 19–21.

Udry, J. R. *The social context of marriage* (3rd ed.). Philadelphia: Lippincott, 1974.

———. Marital alternatives and marital disruption. *Journal of Marriage and the Family,* 1981, *43*(4), 889–897.

———. Changes in the frequency of marital intercourse from panel data. *Archives of Sexual Behavior,* 1980, *9*(4), 319–325.

U. S. Bureau of the Census. Current population reports (Series P-20, No. 410). *Marital status and living arrangements: March 1985*. Washington, DC: U.S. Government Printing Office, 1986.

———. *1980 census user's guide*. Washington, DC: U.S. Government Printing Office, 1980.

U.S. News & World Report. What the world's teenagers are saying. 1986, *100*(25), 68.

Vander Mey, B. J., & Neff, R. L. Adult-child incest: A sample of substantiated cases. *Family Relations*, 1984, *33*(4), 549–557.

Vander-Zanden, J. W. *Social psychology* (3rd ed.). New York: Random House, 1984.

Varni, C. A. An exploratory study of spouse-swapping. *Pacific Sociological Review*, 1972, *15*(4), 507–522.

Verbrugge, L. M. Marital status and health. *Journal of Marriage and the Family*, 1979, *41*(2), 267–285.

Vincent, C. E. *Sexual and marital health*. New York: McGraw-Hill, 1973.

Visher, E. B., & Visher, J. S. *Stepfamilies: A guide to working with stepparents and stepchildren*. New York: Brunner/Mazel, 1979.

Vreeland, R. S. Sex at Harvard. *Sexual Behavior*, 1972, *2*(2), 4–10.

Waite, L. J. U.S. women at work. *Population Bulletin*, 1981, *36*(2), 3–43.

Walker, M., Yoffe, B., & Gray, P. H. *The complete book of birth: From Grantly Dick-Read to Leboyer—A guide for expectant parents to all methods of birth*. New York: Simon & Schuster, 1979.

Wallach, L. In *Sexual latitude for and against*. New York: Hart, 1971.

Waller, W. *The family: A dynamic interpretation*. New York: Condon, 1938.

Waller, W., & Hill, R. *The family: A dynamic interpretation*. New York: Dryden, 1951.

Wallerstein, J. S., & Kelly, J. B. The effects of parental divorce: The adolescent experience. In E. J. Anthony & C. Koupernik (Eds.), *The child in his family: Children at psychiatric risk*. New York: Wiley, 1974.

Walsh, R. H. Sexual attitudes, standards, and behavior: A current assessment. In H. A. Otto (Ed.), *The new sex education: The sex educator's resource book*. Chicago: Follett, 1978.

Walsh, R. H., Ferrell, M., & Tolone, W. Selection of reference group, perceived reference group permissiveness, and personal permissiveness attitudes and behavior: A study of two consecutive panels (67–70: 71–74). *Journal of Marriage and the Family*, 1976, *38*(3), 495–508.

Walster, E. What causes love? In J. M. Henslin (Ed.), *Marriage and family in a changing society*. New York: Free Press, 1980.

———. Love and pairing. In A. Skolnick and J. H. Skolnick (Eds.), *Intimacy, family, and society*. Boston: Little, Brown, 1974.

Walster, E., Aronson, V., Abrahams, D., & Rottman, L. The importance of physical attractiveness in dating behavior. *Journal of Personality and Social Psychology*, 1966, *4*(5), 508–516.

Waterman, C. K., & Chiauzzi, E. J. The role of orgasm in male and female sexual enjoyment. *Journal of Sex Research*, 1982, *18*(2), 146–159.

Watson, J. B. *Chicago Tribune,* March 6, 1927.

Watson, M. A. Sexually open marriage: Three perspectives. *Alternative Lifestyles,* 1981, *4*(1), 3–21.

Weber, J. A., & Fournier, D. G. Family support and a child's adjustment to death. *Family Relations,* 1985, *34*(1), 43–49.

Weed, J. A. Divorce: Americans' style. *American Demographics,* 1982, *4*(3), 12–17.

Weinberg, G. Homophobia. *Forum,* November 1982, pp. 38; 40–44.

Weingarten, H. R. Marital status and well-being: A national study comparing first-married, currently divorced, and remarried adults. *Journal of Marriage and the Family,* 1985, *47*(3), 653–662.

Weiss, R. S. The study of loneliness. In P. J. Stein (Ed.), *Single life: Unmarried adults in social context.* New York: St. Martin's, 1981.

———. *Marital separation.* New York: Basic Books, 1975.

Weitzman, L. J. *The marriage contract.* New York: Free Press, 1981.

Welch, C. E., & Price-Bonham, S. A decade of no-fault divorce revisited: California, Georgia, and Washington. *Journal of Marriage and the Family,* 1983, *45*(2), 411–418.

Wells, C. G., Lucas, M. J., & Meyer, J. K. Unrealistic expectations of orgasm. *Medical Aspects of Human Sexuality,* 1980, *14*(4), 53; 56; 61; 64–65.

Werner, P. D., & LaRussa, G. W. Persistence and change in sex-role stereotypes. *Sex Roles,* 1985, *12*(9/10), 1089–1099.

What world's teenagers are saying. *U.S. News & World Report,* 1986, *100*(25), 68.

Wheeler, J., & Kilmann, P. R. Comarital sexual behavior: Individual and relationship variables. *Archives of Sexual Behavior,* 1983, *12*(4), 295–306.

White, J. M. Premarital cohabitation and marital stability in Canada. *Journal of Marriage and the Family,* 1987, *49*(3), 641–647.

———. Perceived similarity and understanding in married couples. *Journal of Social and Personal Relationships,* 1985, *2*(1), 45–57.

Whitehurst, R. N. Youth views marriage: Awareness of present and future potentials in relationships. In R. W. Libby and R. N. Whitehurst (Eds.), *Marriage and alternatives: Exploring intimate relationships.* Glenview, IL: Scott, Foresman, 1977.

Wilbur, A. E. The contraceptive crisis. *Science Digest,* 1986, *94*(9), 54–61; 84–85.

Wilcoxon, S. A., & Hovestadt, A. J. Perceived health and similarity of family of origin experiences as predictors of dyadic adjustment for married couples. *Journal of Marital and Family Therapy,* 1983, *9*(4), 431–434.

Wilkie, C. F., & Ames, E. The relationship of infant crying to parental stress in the transition to parenthood. *Journal of Marriage and the Family,* 1986, *48*(3), 545–550.

Wills, T. A., Weiss, R. L., & Patterson, G. R. A behavioral analysis of the determinants of marital satisfaction. *Journal of Consulting and Clinical Psychology,* 1974, *42*(6), 802–811.

Wilson, C. The family. In Camberwell Council on Alcoholism, *Women and alcohol.* New York: Tavistock, 1980.

Wilson, K. L., Zurcher, L. A., McAdams, D. C., & Curtis, R. L. Stepfathers and stepchildren: An exploratory analysis from two national surveys. *Journal of Marriage and the Family,* 1975, *37*(3), 526–536.

Winch, R. F. *The modern family.* New York: Holt, Rinehart and Winston, 1971.

Windemiller, D. *Sexuality, pairing, and family forms.* Cambridge, MA: Winthrop, 1976.

Winkelpleck, J. M., & Westfield, J. S. Counseling considerations with gay couples. *The Personnel and Guidance Journal,* 1982, *60*(5), 294–296.

Wolin, S. J., Bennett, L. A., Noonan, D. L., & Teitelbaum, M. A. Disrupted family rituals: A factor in the intergenerational transmission of alcoholism. *Journal of Studies on Alcohol,* 1980, *41*(3), 199–214.

The world almanac and book of facts 1984. New York: Newspaper Enterprise Association, 1984.

Wretmark, A. A. Prenatal death and the funeral. In P. F. Pegg & E. Metze (Eds.), *Death and dying: A quality of life.* London: Pittman, 1981.

Yankelovich, D. *The new morality: A profile of American youth in the 1970's.* New York: McGraw-Hill, 1974.

Yankelovich, Skelly & White, Inc. *The General Mills American family report.* Minneapolis: General Mills Corp., 1975.

Yllo, K. Sexual equality and violence against wives in American states. *Journal of Comparative Family Studies,* 1983, *14*(1), 67–86.

Yoger, S. Do professional women have egalitarian marital relationships? *Journal of Marriage and the Family,* 1981, *43*(4), 865–871.

Zelauskas, B. Siblings: The forgotten grievers. *Issues in Comprehensive Pediatric Nursing,* 1981, *5*(1), 45–52.

Zelditch, M., Jr. Role differentiation in the nuclear family: A comparative study. In T. Parsons and R. F. Bales (Eds.), *Family: Socialization and interaction process.* New York: Free Press, 1955.

Zelnik, M., Kantner, J. F., & Ford, K. *Sex and pregnancy in adolescence.* Beverly Hills, CA: Sage, 1981.

Zelnik, M., & Shah, F. K. First intercourse among young Americans. *Family Planning Perspectives,* 1983, *15*(2), 64–70.

Zigler, E., & Rubin, N. Why child abuse occurs. In O. Pocs & R. H. Walsh (Eds.), *Marriage and Family 86/87.* Guilford, CT: Dushkin, 1986.

Zube, M. Changing behavior and outlook of aging men and women: Implications for marriage in the middle and later years. *Family Relations,* 1982, *31*(1), 147–156.

Zuravin, S. J. Unplanned pregnancies, family planning problems and child maltreatment. *Family Relations,* 1987, *36*(2), 135–139.

Text and Illustration Credits

The use of the following quotations, illustrations, and photographs is gratefully acknowledged:*

Chapter 1 Photo, p. 2, reprinted from *The Saturday Evening Post,* © 1959 Curtis Publishing Co. Photo, p. 8, Mendoza, The Picture Cube. Photo, p. 9, Stone, Peter Arnold. Box 1.1, p. 10, Horton, P. B., & Hunt, C. L. *Sociology.* New York: McGraw-Hill, 1964. Reprinted by permission. Photo, p. 15, © 1982, Lapides, Design Conceptions. Photo, p. 17, Wallace Kirkland, LIFE Magazine. © TIME, Inc., 1948.

Chapter 2 Photo, p. 28, State Historical Society of Wisconsin. Photo, p. 40, © 1981, Joel Gordon. Photo, p. 46, Holland, Stock, Boston. Box 2.3, p. 48, Ruesch, H. *Top of the World.* New York: Harper & Row, 1950.

Chapter 3 Photo, p. 54, © Fusco, Magnum. Photo, p. 61, Franken, Stock, Boston. Photo, p. 63, Hartman, Magnum. Photo, p. 70, Gatewood/The Image Works. Box 3.1, p. 77, Gordon, T. *Parent Effectiveness Training.* Copyright © 1970 by David McKay Co., a division of Random House, Inc. Reprinted by permission.

Chapter 4 Photo, p. 82, © 1983, Joel Gordon. Photo, p. 86, Ken Karp. Photo, p. 92, © Hedman, Jeroboam. Photo, p. 97, © 1988, Joel Gordon. Photo, p. 99, © 1983, Joel Gordon.

Chapter 5 Photo, p. 108, © 1984, Kroll, Taurus. Photo, p. 117, Ballard, EKM-Nepenthe. Photo, p. 126, © Lejeune, Stock, Boston. Poem, p. 128, Armour, R. *Light Armour.* New York: McGraw-Hill, 1954. Reprinted by permission.

Chapter 6 Photo, p. 134, © 1978, Joel Gordon. Photo, p. 139, © 1981, Englebert, Photo Researchers. Table 6.1, p. 141, DeLamater, J., & MacCorquodale, P. *Premarital Sexuality.* Madison, WI: University of Wisconsin Press, 1979. Reprinted by permission. Photo, p. 144, Southwick, Stock, Boston. Photo, p. 149, Ritscher, Stock, Boston. Box 6.1, p. 156, from *A Tree Grows in Brooklyn* by Betty Smith. Copyright 1943, 1947 by Betty Smith. Reprinted by permission of Harper & Row, Publishers, Inc.

*An attempt has been made to obtain permission from all sources of illustrations and boxed material used in this edition. Some sources have not been located, but permission will be requested from them upon notification to us of their ownership of the material.

Name Index